International Macroeconomics *and* Finance

𝕁𝔹

To Shirley, Laurie, and Lesli

International Macroeconomics and Finance

Theory and Econometric Methods

Nelson C. Mark
Ohio State University

BLACKWELL
Publishers

First published 2001

2 4 6 8 10 9 7 5 3 1

Blackwell Publishers Inc.
350 Main Street
Malden, Massachusetts 02148
USA

Blackwell Publishers Ltd
108 Cowley Road
Oxford OX4 1JF
UK

Library of Congress Cataloging-in-Publication Data

Mark, Nelson C. (Nelson Chung), 1955–
    International macroeconomics and finance : theory and econometric
  methods / Nelson C. Mark.
      p. cm.
    Includes bibliographical references and index.
    ISBN 0-631-22287-1 (alk. paper) — ISBN 0-631-22288-X (pb. : alk. paper)
      1. International finance.   2. Macroeconomics.   3. Econometrics.   I. Title.

  HG3881 .M3334 2001
  339 — dc21   00-069791

British Library Cataloguing in Publication Data
A CIP catalogue record for this book is available from the British Library.

Typeset in 10 on 11½ Book Antiqua
by Newgen Imaging Systems (P) Ltd., Chennai, India
Printed in Great Britain by TJ International, Padstow, Cornwall

This book is printed on acid-free paper.

Contents

Preface

This book grew out of my lecture notes for a graduate course in international macroeconomics and finance that I teach at the Ohio State University. The book is targeted toward second-year graduate students in a Ph.D. program. The material is accessible to those who have completed core courses in statistics, econometrics, and macroeconomic theory, typically taken in the first year of graduate study.

These days, there is a high level of interaction between empirical and theoretical research. This book reflects this healthy development by integrating both theoretical and empirical issues. The theory is introduced by developing the canonical model in a topic area and then its predictions are evaluated quantitatively. Both the calibration method and standard econometric methods are covered. In many of the empirical applications, I have updated the data sets from the original studies and have re-done the calculations using the Gauss programming language. The data and Gauss programs will be available for downloading from my website: http://www.econ.ohio-state.edu/Mark.

There are several different "camps" in international macroeconomics and finance. One of the major divisions is between the use of *ad hoc* and optimizing models. The academic research frontier stresses the theoretical rigor and internal consistency of fully articulated general equilibrium models with optimizing agents. However, the *ad hoc* models that predate optimizing models are still used in policy analysis and evidently still have something useful to say. The book strikes a middle ground by providing coverage of both types of models.

Some of the other divisions in the field are flexible-price versus sticky-price models, rationality versus irrationality, and calibration versus statistical inference. The book gives consideration to each of these "mini debates." Each approach has its good points and its bad points. Although many people feel firmly about the particular way that research in the field should be done, I believe that beginning students should see a balanced treatment of the different views.

Here's a brief outline of what is to come. Chapter 1 derives some basic relations and gives some institutional background on international financial markets, national income and balance-of-payments accounts, and central bank operations.

Chapter 2 collects many of the time-series techniques that we draw upon. It is not necessary to work through this chapter carefully in the first reading. I would suggest that you skim the chapter and make note of the contents, then refer back to the relevant sections when the need arises. This chapter keeps the book reasonably self-contained and provides an efficient reference with uniform notation.

Many different time-series techniques have been implemented in the literature, and treatments of the various methods are scattered across different textbooks and journal articles. It would be really unkind to send you to multiple outside sources and require you to invest in new notation to acquire the background on these techniques. Such a strategy seems to me expensive in time and money. While this material is not central to international macroeconomics and finance, I was convinced not to place it in an appendix by feedback from my own students. They liked having this material early on for three reasons. First, they said that people often don't read appendices; second, they said that they liked seeing an econometric road map of what was to come; and, third, they said that in terms of reference, it is easier to flip pages toward the front of a book than it is to flip to the end.

Moving on, chapters 3–5 cover "flexible-price" models. We begin with the *ad hoc* monetary model and progress to dynamic equilibrium models with optimizing agents. These models offer limited scope for policy interventions, because they are set in a perfect world with no market imperfections and no nominal rigidities. However, they serve as a useful benchmark against which to measure refinements and progress.

The next two chapters are devoted to understanding two anomalies in international macroeconomics and finance. Chapters 6 covers deviations from uncovered interest parity (a.k.a. the forward-premium bias), and chapter 7 covers deviations from purchasing-power parity. Both topics have been the focus of a tremendous amount of empirical work.

Chapters 8 and 9 cover "sticky-price" models. Again, we begin with *ad hoc* versions, this time the Mundell–Fleming model, then progress to dynamic equilibrium models with optimizing agents. The models in these chapters do suggest positive roles for policy interventions, because they are set in imperfectly competitive environments with nominal rigidities.

Chapter 10 covers the analysis of exchange rates under target zones. We take the view that these are a class of fixed exchange rate models where the central bank is committed to keeping the exchange rate within a specified zone, although the framework is actually more general and works even when explicit targets are not announced. Chapter 11 continues in this direction with a treatment of the causes and timing of collapsing fixed exchange rate arrangements.

The field of international macroeconomics and finance is vast. Keeping the book sufficiently short to use in a one-quarter or one-semester course meant omitting coverage of some important topics. The book is not a literature survey and is pretty short on the history of thought in the area. Many excellent and influential papers are not included in the citation list. This simply could not be avoided. As my late colleague G. S. Maddala once said to me, "You can't learn anything from a fat book." Since I want you to learn from this book, I've aimed to keep it short, concrete, and to the point.

To avoid that "black-box" perception that beginning students sometimes have, almost all of the results that I present are derived step-by-step from first principles. This is annoying for a knowledgeable reader (i.e., the instructor), but hopefully it is a feature that new students will appreciate. My overall objective is to efficiently bring you up to the research frontier in international macroeconomics and finance. I hope that I have achieved this goal in some measure and that you find the book to be of some value.

Finally, I would like to express my appreciation to Chi-Young Choi, Roisin O'Sullivan, and Raphael Solomon, who gave me useful comments, and to Horag Choi and Young-Kyu Moh, who corrected innumerable mistakes in the manuscript. My very special thanks goes to Donggyu Sul, who read several drafts and who helped me to set up much of the data used in the book.

Nelson C. Mark
December 2000

1

Some Institutional Background

This chapter covers some institutional background and develops some basic relations that we rely on in international macroeconomics and finance. First, there is a basic description of some widely held international financial instruments and the markets in which they trade. This discussion allows us to quickly derive the fundamental parity relations implied by the absence of riskless arbitrage profits that relate to asset prices in international financial markets. These parity conditions are employed regularly in international macroeconomic theory and serve as jumping off points for more in-depth analyses of asset pricing in the international environment. Second, there is a brief overview of the national income accounts and their relation to the balance of payments. This discussion identifies some of the macroeconomic data that we want theory to explain and that are employed in empirical work. Third, you will see a discussion of the central bank's balance sheet – an understanding of which is necessary to appreciate the role of international (foreign exchange) reserves in the central bank's foreign exchange market intervention and the impact of intervention on the domestic money supply.

1.1 INTERNATIONAL FINANCIAL MARKETS

We begin with a description of some basic international financial instruments and the markets in which they trade. As a point of reference, we view the US as the *home country*.

FOREIGN EXCHANGE

Foreign exchange is traded *over the counter* through a spatially decentralized *dealer* network. Foreign currencies are mainly bought and sold by dealers housed in large money center banks located around the world. Dealers hold foreign exchange inventories and aim to earn trading profits by buying low and selling high. The foreign exchange market is highly liquid and the trading volume is quite large. The Federal Reserve Bank of New York [49] estimates that, on average, 405 billion dollars of foreign exchange was bought or sold in the US during April 1998. Assuming a 260 business day calendar, this implies an annual volume of 105.3 trillion dollars. The total volume of foreign exchange trading is much larger than this figure, because foreign exchange is also traded outside the US – in London, Tokyo, and Singapore, for example. Since 1998 US GDP was approximately 9 trillion dollars and the US is approximately one-seventh of the world economy, the volume of foreign exchange trading evidently exceeds, by a great amount, the quantity necessary to conduct international trade.

During most of the period after the Second World War, trading of convertible currencies took place with respect to the US dollar. This meant that converting yen to deutschemarks required two trades: first from yen to dollars then from dollars to deutschemarks. The dollar is said to be the *vehicle currency* for international transactions. In recent years cross-currency trading, that allows yen and deutschemarks to be exchanged directly, has become increasingly common.

The foreign currency price of a US dollar is the exchange rate quoted in *European terms*. The US dollar price of one unit of the foreign currency is the exchange rate quoted in *American terms*. In American terms, an *increase* in the exchange rate means that the dollar currency has *depreciated* in value relative to the foreign currency. In this book, we will always refer to the exchange rate in American terms.

The equilibrium condition in cross-rate markets is given by the absence of unexploited *triangular arbitrage* profits. To illustrate, assume that there are no transactions costs and consider three currencies – the dollar, the euro, and the pound. Let S_1 be the dollar price of the pound, S_2 be the dollar price of the euro, and S_3^x be the euro price of the pound. The cross-rate market is in equilibrium if the exchange rate quotations obey

$$S_1 = S_3^x S_2. \tag{1.1}$$

The opportunity to earn riskless arbitrage profits is available if (1.1) is violated. For example, suppose that you get price quotations of $S_1 = 1.60$ dollars per pound, $S_2 = 1.10$ dollars per euro, and $S_3^x = 1.55$ euros per pound. An arbitrage strategy is to put up 1.60 dollars to buy one pound, sell that pound for 1.55 euros, and then sell the euros for 1.1 dollars each. You begin with 1.6 dollars and end up with 1.705 dollars, which is quite a deal. But when you take money out of the foreign exchange market it comes at the expense of someone else. Very short-lived violations of the triangular arbitrage condition (1.1) may occasionally occur during episodes of high market volatility, but we do not think that foreign exchange dealers will allow this to happen on a regular basis.

Transaction Types

Foreign exchange transactions are divided into three categories. The first are *spot transactions* for immediate (actually, in two working days) delivery. Spot exchange rates are the prices at which foreign currencies trade in this spot market.

Second, *swap transactions* are agreements in which a currency sold (bought) today is to be repurchased (sold) at a future date. The price of both the current and future transaction is set today. For example, you might agree to buy 1 million euros at 0.98 million dollars today and sell the 1 million euros back in six months time for 0.95 million dollars. The *swap rate* is the difference between the repurchase (resale) price and the original sale (purchase) price. The swap rate and the spot rate together implicitly determine the *forward* exchange rate.

The third category of foreign exchange transactions is *outright forward transactions*. These are current agreements on the price, quantity, and maturity or future delivery date for a foreign currency. The agreed upon price is the forward exchange rate. Standard maturities for forward contracts are 1 and 2 weeks, and 1, 3, 6, and 12 months. We say that the forward foreign currency trades at a *premium* when the forward rate exceeds the spot rate in American terms. Conversely, if the spot rate exceeds the forward rate, we say that the forward foreign currency trades at *discount*.

Spot transactions form the majority of foreign exchange trading and most of that is inter-dealer trading. About one-third of the volume of foreign exchange trading consists of swap transactions. Outright forward transactions account for a relatively small portion of the total volume. Forward and swap transactions are arranged on an informal basis by money center banks for their corporate and institutional customers.

Short-Term Debt

A *Eurocurrency* is a foreign currency denominated deposit at a bank located outside the country where the currency is used as legal tender. Such an institution is called an offshore bank. Although they are called Eurocurrencies, the deposit does not have to be in Europe. A US dollar deposit at a London bank is a Eurodollar deposit, and a yen deposit at a San Francisco bank is a Euroyen deposit. Most Eurocurrency deposits are fixed-interest time-deposits with maturities that match those available for forward foreign exchange contracts. A small part of the Eurocurrency market is comprised of certificates of deposit, floating rate notes, and call money.

The *London Interbank Offer Rate (LIBOR)* is the rate at which banks are willing to lend to the most creditworthy banks participating in the London Interbank market. Loans to less creditworthy banks and/or companies outside the London Interbank market are often quoted as a premium to LIBOR.

COVERED INTEREST PARITY

Spot, forward, and Eurocurrency rates are mutually dependent through the *covered interest parity* condition. Let i_t be the date t interest rate on a one-period

Eurodollar deposit, let i_t^* be the interest rate on an Euroeuro deposit rate at the same bank, let S_t, be the spot exchange rate (dollars per euro), and let F_t be the one-period forward exchange rate. Because both Eurodollar and Euroeuro deposits are issued by the same bank, the two deposits have identical default and political risk. They differ only by the currency of their denomination.[1] Covered interest parity is the condition that the nominally risk-free dollar returns from the Eurodollar and the Euroeuro deposits are equal. That is,

$$1 + i_t = (1 + i_t^*)\frac{F_t}{S_t}. \qquad (1.2)$$

When (1.2) is violated, a riskless arbitrage profit opportunity is available and the market is not in equilibrium. For example, suppose that there are no transactions costs, and you get the following 12-month Eurocurrency, forward exchange rate, and spot exchange rate quotations:

$$i_t = 0.0678, \quad i_t^* = 0.0422, \quad F_t = 0.9961, \quad S_t = 1.0200.$$

You can easily verify that these quotes do not satisfy (1.2). These quotes allow you to borrow 0.9804 euros today, convert them to $1/S_t = 1$ dollar, and invest in the Eurodollar deposit with a future payoff of 1.0678, but you will need only $(1 + i_t^*)F_t/S_t = 1.0178$ dollars to repay the euro loan. Note that this arbitrage is a zero-net investment strategy, since it is financed with borrowed funds. Arbitrage profits that arise from such quotations come at the expense of other agents dealing in the international financial markets, such as the bank that quotes the rates. Since banks typically don't like losing money, swap or forward rates quoted by bank traders are routinely set according to quoted Eurocurrency rates and (1.2).

Using the logarithmic approximation, (1.2) can be expressed as

$$i_t \simeq i_t^* + f_t - s_t, \qquad (1.3)$$

where $f_t \equiv \ln(F_t)$ and $s_t \equiv \ln(S_t)$.

Testing Covered Interest Parity

Covered interest parity won't hold for assets that differ greatly in terms of default or political risk. If you look at prices for spot and forward foreign exchange and interest rates on assets that differ mainly in currency denomination, the question of whether covered interest parity holds depends on whether there there exist unexploited arbitrage profit opportunities after taking into account the relevant transactions costs, how large the profits are, and the length of the window during which the profits are available.

Foreign exchange dealers and bond dealers quote two prices. The low price is called the bid. If you want to sell an asset, you get the bid (low) price. The

[1] Political risk refers to the possibility that a government may impose restrictions that make it difficult for foreign investors to repatriate their investments. Covered interest arbitrage will not, in general, hold for other interest rates, such as T-bills or commercial bank prime lending rates.

high price is called the ask or offer price. If you want to buy the asset from the dealer, you pay the ask (high) price. In addition, there will be a brokerage fee associated with the transaction.

Frenkel and Levich [60] applied neutral-band analysis to test covered interest parity. The idea is that transaction costs create a neutral band within which prices of spot and forward foreign exchange and interest rates on domestic and foreign currency denominated assets can fluctuate, where there are no profit opportunities. The question is: How often are there observations that lie outside the bands?

Let the (proportional) transaction cost incurred from buying or selling a dollar debt instrument be τ, let the transaction cost from buying or selling a foreign currency debt instrument be τ^*, let the transaction cost from buying or selling foreign exchange in the spot market be τ_s, and let the transaction cost from buying or selling foreign exchange in the forward market be τ_f. A round-trip arbitrage conceptually involves four separate transactions. A strategy that *shorts* the dollar requires you to first sell a dollar-denominated asset (borrow a dollar at the gross rate $1 + i$). After paying the transaction cost, your net is $1 - \tau$ dollars. You then sell the dollars at $1/S$, which nets $(1 - \tau)(1 - \tau_s)$ foreign currency units. You invest the foreign money at the gross rate $1 + i^*$, incurring a transaction cost of τ^*. Finally, you cover the proceeds at the forward rate F, where you incur another cost of τ_f. Let

$$\bar{C} \equiv (1 - \tau)(1 - \tau_s)(1 - \tau^*)(1 - \tau_f),$$

and $f_p \equiv (F - S)/S$. The net dollar proceeds after paying the transaction costs are $\bar{C}(1 + i^*)(F/S)$. The arbitrage is *unprofitable* if $\bar{C}(1 + i^*)(F/S) \leq (1 + i)$ or, equivalently, if

$$f_p \leq \bar{f}_p \equiv \frac{(1 + i) - \bar{C}(1 + i^*)}{\bar{C}(1 + i^*)}. \tag{1.4}$$

By an analogous argument, it follows that an arbitrage that is *long* in the dollar remains unprofitable if

$$f_p \geq \underline{f}_p \equiv \frac{\bar{C}(1 + i) - (1 + i^*)}{(1 + i^*)}. \tag{1.5}$$

$[\underline{f}_p, \bar{f}_p]$ define a neutral band of activity within which f_p can fluctuate but still present no profitable covered interest arbitrage opportunities. Neutral-band analysis proceeds by estimating the transaction costs $\bar{C}$. These are then used to compute the bands $[\underline{f}_p, \bar{f}_p]$ at various points in time. Once the bands have been computed, an examination of the proportion of the actual f_p that lies *within* the bands can be conducted.

Frenkel and Levich estimate τ_s and τ_f to be the upper 95 percentile of the absolute deviation from spot and 90-day forward triangular arbitrage. τ is set to 1.25 times the ask-bid spread on 90-day Treasury bills and they set $\tau^* = \tau$. They examine covered interest parity for the dollar, the Canadian dollar, the pound, and the deutschemark. The sample is broken into three periods. The first period is the *tranquil peg* preceding British devaluation from January 1962 to November 1967. Their estimates of τ_s range from 0.051 percent to 0.058 percent, and their estimates of τ_f range from 0.068 percent to 0.076 percent. For securities, they estimate $\tau = \tau^*$ to be approximately 0.019 percent. The total cost of transactions falls in a range from 0.145 percent to 0.15 percent. Approximately 87 percent of the f_p observations lie within the neutral band.

The second period is the *turbulent peg* from January 1968 to December 1969, during which their estimate of $\bar{C}$ rises to approximately 0.24 percent. Now, violations of covered interest parity are more pervasive, with the proportion of f_p that lies within the neutral band ranging from 0.33 to 0.67.

The third period considered is the *managed float* from July 1973 to May 1975. Their estimate for $\bar{C}$ rises to about 1 percent, and the proportion of f_p within the neutral band also rises back to about 0.90. The conclusion is that covered interest parity holds during the managed float and the tranquil peg, but that there is something anomalous about the turbulent peg period.[2]

Taylor [123] examines data recorded by dealers at the Bank of England, and calculates the profit from covered interest arbitrage between dollar and pound assets predicted by quoted bid and ask prices that would be available to an individual. Let an "*a*" subscript denote an ask price (or ask yield), and a "*b*" subscript denote the bid price. If you buy pounds, you get the ask price S_a. Buying pounds is the same as selling dollars, so from the latter perspective, you can sell the dollars at the bid price $1/S_a$. Accordingly, we adopt the following notation:

S_a	Spot pound ask price.	F_a	Forward pound ask price.
$1/S_a$	Spot dollar bid price.	$1/F_a$	Forward dollar bid price.
S_b	Spot pound bid price.	F_b	Forward pound bid price.
$1/S_b$	Spot dollar ask price.	$1/F_b$	Forward dollar ask price.
i_a	Eurodollar ask interest rate.	i_a^*	Euro–pound ask interest rate.
i_b	Eurodollar bid interest rate.	i_b^*	Euro–pound bid interest rate.

It will be the case that $i_a > i_b$, $i_a^* > i_b^*$, $S_a > S_b$, and $F_a > F_b$. An arbitrage that shorts the dollar begins by borrowing a dollar at the gross rate $1 + i_a$ and selling the dollar for $1/S_a$ pounds, which are invested at the gross rate $1 + i_b^*$ and covered forward at the price F_b. The per-dollar profit is

$$(1 + i_b^*)\frac{F_b}{S_a} - (1 + i_a).$$

Using analogous reasoning, it follows that the per-pound profit that shorts the pound is

$$(1 + i_b)\frac{S_b}{F_a} - (1 + i_a^*).$$

Taylor finds virtually no evidence of unexploited covered interest arbitrage profits during normal or calm market conditions, but he is able to identify some

---

[2] Possibly, the period is characterized by a "peso problem," which is covered in chapter 6.

periods of high market volatility when economically significant violations may have occurred. The first of these is the 1967 British devaluation. Looking at an 11-day window spanning the event, an arbitrage that shorted 1 million pounds at a 1-month maturity could potentially have earned a 4,521 pound profit on Wednesday, November 24 at 7:30 a.m., but by 4:30 p.m. on Thursday, November 24 the profit opportunity had vanished. A second event that he looks at is the 1987 UK general election. Examining a window that spans from June 1 to June 19, profit opportunities were generally unavailable. Among the few opportunities to emerge was a quote at 7:30 a.m. on Wednesday, June 17, where a 1 million pound short position predicted 712 pounds of profit at a 1-month maturity. But by noon of the same day, the predicted profit fell to 133 pounds, and by 4:00 p.m. the opportunities had vanished.

To summarize, the empirical evidence suggests that covered interest parity works pretty well. Occasional violations occur after accounting for transaction costs, but they are short-lived and present themselves only during rare periods of high market volatility.

UNCOVERED INTEREST PARITY

Let $E_t(X_{t+1}) = E(X_{t+1}|I_t)$ denote the mathematical expectation of the random variable X_{t+1} conditioned on the date-t publicly available information set I_t. If foreign exchange participants are risk neutral, they care only about the mean value of asset returns and do not care at all about the variance of returns. Risk-neutral individuals are also willing to take unboundedly large positions on bets that have a positive expected value. Since $F_t - S_{t+1}$ is the profit from taking a position in forward foreign exchange, under risk-neutrality expected forward speculation profits are driven to zero and the forward exchange rate must, in equilibrium, be market participants' expected future spot exchange rate:

$$F_t = E_t(S_{t+1}). \qquad (1.6)$$

Substituting (1.6) into (1.2) gives the *uncovered interest parity* condition:

$$1 + i_t = (1 + i_t^*)\frac{E_t[S_{t+1}]}{S_t}. \qquad (1.7)$$

If (1.7) is violated, a zero net investment strategy of borrowing in one currency and simultaneously lending uncovered in the other currency has a positive payoff in expectation. We use the uncovered interest parity condition as a first approximation to characterize international asset market equilibrium, especially in conjunction with the monetary model (chapters 3, 10, and 11). However, as you will see in chapter 6, violations of uncovered interest parity are common, and they present an important empirical puzzle for international economists.

Risk premia. What reason can be given if uncovered interest parity does not hold? One possible explanation is that market participants are risk averse and require compensation to bear the currency risk involved in an uncovered foreign currency investment. To see the relation between risk aversion and uncovered interest parity, consider the following two-period partial equilibrium portfolio problem. Agents take interest rate and exchange rate dynamics as given and can invest a fraction α of their current wealth W_t in a nominally safe domestic bond with next-period payoff $(1 + i_t)\alpha W_t$. The remaining $1 - \alpha$ of wealth can be invested uncovered in the foreign bond with future home-currency payoff $(1 + i_t^*)(S_{t+1}/S_t)(1 - \alpha)W_t$. We assume that covered interest parity holds, so that a covered investment in the foreign bond is equivalent to the investment in the domestic bond. The next-period nominal wealth is the payoff from the bond portfolio:

$$W_{t+1} = \left[\alpha(1 + i_t) + (1 - \alpha)(1 + i_t^*)\frac{S_{t+1}}{S_t}\right]W_t. \tag{1.8}$$

Domestic market participants have constant absolute risk aversion utility defined over wealth: $U(W) = -e^{-\gamma W}$, where $\gamma \geq 0$ is the coefficient of absolute risk aversion. The domestic agent's problem is to choose the investment share α to maximize expected utility:

$$\mathrm{E}_t[U(W_{t+1})] = -\mathrm{E}_t\left(e^{-\gamma W_{t+1}}\right). \tag{1.9}$$

Notice that the right-hand side of (1.9) is the *moment generating function* of next-period wealth.[3]

If people believe that W_{t+1} is normally distributed conditional on currently available information, with a conditional mean and a conditional variance,

$$\mathrm{E}_t W_{t+1} = \left[\alpha(1 + i_t) + (1 - \alpha)(1 + i_t^*)\frac{\mathrm{E}_t S_{t+1}}{S_t}\right]W_t, \tag{1.10}$$

$$\mathrm{Var}_t(W_{t+1}) = \frac{(1 - \alpha)^2(1 + i_t^*)^2 \mathrm{Var}_t(S_{t+1})W_t^2}{S_t^2}, \tag{1.11}$$

it follows that maximizing (1.9) is equivalent to maximizing the simpler expression

$$\mathrm{E}_t W_{t+1} - \frac{\gamma}{2}\mathrm{Var}(W_{t+1}). \tag{1.12}$$

We say that traders are mean–variance optimizers. These individuals like high mean values of wealth, and dislike variance in wealth.

Differentiating (1.12) with respect to α and rearranging the first-order conditions for optimality yields

$$(1 + i_t) - (1 + i_t^*)\frac{\mathrm{E}_t[S_{t+1}]}{S_t} = \frac{-\gamma W_t(1 - \alpha)(1 + i_t^*)^2 \mathrm{Var}_t(S_{t+1})}{S_t^2}, \tag{1.13}$$

---

[3]   The moment generating function for the normally distributed random variable $X \sim \mathrm{N}(\mu, \sigma^2)$ is $\psi_X(z) = \mathrm{E}\left(e^{zX}\right) = \exp\left(\mu z + \sigma^2 z^2/2\right)$. Substituting W for X, $-\gamma$ for z, $\mathrm{E}_t W_{t+1}$ for μ, and $\mathrm{Var}(W_{t+1})$ for σ^2, and taking logs, results in (1.12).

which implicitly determines the optimal investment share α. Even if there is an expected uncovered profit available, risk aversion limits the size of the position that investors will take. If all market participants are risk neutral, then $\gamma = 0$ and it follows that uncovered interest parity will hold. If $\gamma > 0$, violations of uncovered interest parity can occur and the forward rate becomes a biased predictor of the future spot rate, the reason being that individuals need to be paid a premium to bear foreign currency risk. Uncovered interest parity will hold if $\alpha = 1$, regardless of whether $\gamma > 0$. However, the determination of α requires us to be specific about the dynamics that govern S_t, and that is information that we have not specified here. The point that we want to make here is that the forward foreign exchange market can be in equilibrium and there can be no unexploited risk-adjusted arbitrage profits even though the forward exchange rate is a biased predictor of the future spot rate. We will study deviations from uncovered interest parity in more detail in chapter 6.

 ## FUTURES CONTRACTS

Participation in the forward foreign exchange market is largely limited to institutions and large corporate customers, owing to the size of the contracts involved. The futures market is available to individuals and is a close substitute for the forward market. The futures market is an institutionalized form of forward contracting. Four main features distinguish futures contracts from forward contracts.

First, foreign exchange futures contracts are traded on organized exchanges. In the US, futures contracts are traded on the International Money Market (IMM) at the Chicago Mercantile Exchange. In Britain, futures are traded at the London International Financial Futures Exchange (LIFFE). Some of the currencies traded are the Australian dollar, the Brazilian real, the Canadian dollar, the euro, the Mexican peso, the New Zealand dollar, the pound, the South African rand, the Swiss franc, the Russian ruble and the yen.

Second, contracts mature at standardized dates throughout the year. The maturity date is called the last trading day. Delivery occurs on the third Wednesday of March, June, September, and December, provided that it is a business day. Otherwise, delivery takes place on the next business day. The last trading day is two business days prior to the delivery date. Contracts are written for fixed face values. For example, the face value of a euro contract is 125,000 euros.

Third, the exchange serves to match buyers to sellers and maintains a zero net position.[4] Settlement between sellers (who take *short* positions) and buyers (who take *long* positions) takes place daily. You purchase a futures contract by putting up an initial margin with your broker. If your contract decreases in value, the loss is debited from your margin account. This debit is then used to credit the account of the individual who sold you the futures contract. If your

---

[4] If you need foreign exchange before the maturity date, you are said to have short exposure in foreign exchange, which can be hedged by taking a long position in the futures market.

contract increases in value, the increment is credited to your margin account. This settlement takes place at the end of each trading day and is called "marking to market." Economically, the main difference between futures and forward contracts is the interest opportunity cost associated with the funds in the margin account. In the US, some part of the initial margin can be put up in the form of Treasury bills, which mitigates the loss of interest income.

Fourth, the futures exchange operates a clearing house, whose function is to guarantee marking to market and delivery of the currencies upon maturity. Technically, the clearing house takes the other side of any transaction, so your legal obligations are to the exchange. But, as mentioned above, the clearing house maintains a zero net position.

Most futures contracts are reversed prior to maturity and are not held to the last trading day. In these situations, futures contracts are simply bets between two parties regarding the direction of future exchange rate movements. If you are long in a foreign currency futures contract and I am short, you are betting that the price of the foreign currency will rise, while I expect the price to decline. Bets in the futures market are a zero-sum game, because your winnings are my losses.

How a Futures Contract Works

For a futures contract with k days to maturity, denote the date $T-k$ futures price by F_{T-k}, and the face value of the contract by V_T. The contract value at $T-k$ is $F_{T-k}V_T$.

Table 1.1 displays the closing spot rate and the price of an actual 12,500,000 yen contract that matured in June 1999 (multiplied by 100) and the evolution of the margin account. When the futures price increases, the long position gains value, as reflected by an increment in the margin account. This increment comes at the expense of the short position.

Suppose that you buy the yen futures contract on June 16, 1998 at 0.007346 dollars per yen. The initial margin is 2,835 dollars and the spot exchange rate is 0.006942 dollars per yen. The contract value is 91,825 dollars. If you held the contract to maturity, you would take delivery of the 12,500,000 yen on June 23, 1999 at a unit price of 0.007346 dollars. Suppose that you actually want the yen on December 17, 1998. You close out your futures contract and buy the yen in the spot market. The appreciation of the yen means that buying 12,500,000 yen costs 20,675 dollars more on December 17, 1998 than it did on June 16, 1998, but most of the higher cost is offset by the gain of $21,197.5 - 2,835 = 18,362.5$ dollars on the futures contract.

The hedge comes about because there is a covered interest parity-like relation that links the futures price to the spot exchange rate, with Eurocurrency rates as a reference point. Let i_{T-k} be the Eurodollar rate at $T-k$, which matures at T, let i^*_{T-k} be the analogous 1-year Euroeuro rate, assume a 360-day year, and let

$$\phi_{T-k} = \left(1 + \frac{ki_{T-k}}{360}\right) \bigg/ \left(1 + \frac{ki^*_{T-k}}{360}\right)$$

Table 1.1 Yen futures for June 1999 delivery

Date	F_{T-k}	S_{T-k}	ΔF_{T-k}	$\Delta(F_{T-k}V_T)$	Margin	ϕ_{T-k}
				Long yen position		
June 16, 1998	0.7346	0.6942	0.0000	0.0	2,835.0	1.0581
June 17, 1998	0.7720	0.7263	0.0374	4,675.0	7,510.0	1.0628
July 17, 1998	0.7507	0.7163	−0.0213	−2,662.5	4,847.5	1.0479
August 17, 1998	0.7147	0.6859	−0.0360	−4,500.0	347.5	1.0418
September 17, 1998	0.7860	0.7582	0.0713	8,912.5	9,260.0	1.0365
October 16, 1998	0.8948	0.8661	0.1088	13,600.0	22,860.0	1.0330
November 17, 1998	0.8498	0.8244	−0.0450	−5,625.0	17,235.0	1.0308
December 17, 1998	0.8815	0.8596	0.0317	3,962.5	21,197.5	1.0254
January 19, 1999	0.8976	0.8790	0.0161	2,012.5	23,210.0	1.0211
February 17, 1999	0.8524	0.8401	−0.0452	−5,650.0	17,560.0	1.0146
March 17, 1999	0.8575	0.8463	0.0051	637.5	18,197.5	1.0131

be the ratio of the domestic to foreign gross returns on a Eurocurrency deposit that matures in k days. The parity relation for futures prices is

$$F_{T-k} = \phi_{T-k}S_{T-k}. \tag{1.14}$$

Here, the futures price varies in proportion to the spot price, with ϕ_{T-k} being the factor of proportionality. As the contract approaches the last trading day, $k \to 0$. It follows that $\phi_{T-k} \to 1$ and $F_T = S_T$. This means that you can obtain the foreign exchange in two equivalent ways. You can buy a futures contract on the last trading day and take delivery, or you can buy the foreign currency in the inter-bank market, because arbitrage will equate the two prices near the maturity date.

Equation (1.14) also tells you the extent to which the futures contract hedges risk. If you have long exposure, an increase in S_{T-k} (a weakening of the home currency) makes you worse off, while an increase in the futures price makes you better off. The futures contract provides a perfect hedge if changes in F_{T-k} exactly offset changes in S_{T-k}, but this only happens if $\phi_{T-k} = 1$. To obtain a perfect hedge when $\phi_{T-k} \neq 1$, you need to take out a contract of size $1/\phi$, and because ϕ changes over time, the hedge will need to be rebalanced periodically.

1.2 NATIONAL ACCOUNTING RELATIONS

This section gives an overview of the national income accounts and their relation to the balance of payments. These accounts form some of the international time-series that we want our theories to explain. The national income accounts are a record of expenditures and receipts at various phases in the circular flow of income, while the balance of payments is a record of the economic transactions between domestic residents and residents in the rest of the world.

● NATIONAL INCOME ACCOUNTING

In real (constant dollar) terms, we will use the following notation:

Y	Gross domestic product (GDP).
Q	National income.
C	Consumption.
I	Investment.
G	Government final goods purchases.
A	$A = C + I + G$, aggregate expenditure (absorption).
IM	Imports.
EX	Exports.
R	Net foreign income receipts.
T	Tax revenues.
S	Private saving.
NFA	Net foreign asset holdings.

Closed-economy national income accounting. We'll begin with a quick review of the national income accounts for a closed economy. Abstracting from capital depreciation, which is that part of total final goods output devoted to replacing worn-out capital stock, the value of output is gross domestic product Y. When the goods and services are sold, the sales become income Q. If we ignore capital depreciation, then GDP is equal to national income:

$$Y = Q. \tag{1.15}$$

In the closed economy, there are only three classes of agents – households, businesses, and the government. Aggregate expenditure on goods and services is the sum of the component spending by these agents:

$$A = C + I + G. \tag{1.16}$$

The nation's output Y has to be purchased by some person A. If there is any excess supply, firms are assumed to buy the extra output in the form of inventory accumulation. We therefore have the accounting identity

$$Y = A = Q. \tag{1.17}$$

The open economy. To handle an economy that engages in foreign trade, we must account for net factor receipts from abroad, R, which includes items such as fees and royalties from direct investment, dividends and interest from portfolio investment, and income for labor services provided abroad by domestic residents. In the open economy, the national income is called the gross national product (GNP): $Q = \text{GNP}$. This is income paid to factors of production owned by domestic residents, regardless of where the factors are employed. GNP can differ from GDP, since some of this income may be earned from abroad. GDP can be sold either to domestic agents $(A - \text{IM})$ or to the foreign sector EX. This can be stated equivalently as the sum of domestic aggregate expenditures or *absorption* and net exports:

$$Y = A + (\text{EX} - \text{IM}). \tag{1.18}$$

National income (GNP) is the sum of gross domestic product and net factor receipts from abroad:

$$Q = Y + R. \tag{1.19}$$

Substituting (1.18) into (1.19) yields

$$Q = A + \underbrace{(\text{EX} - \text{IM}) + R}_{\text{Current account}} \tag{1.20}$$

A country uses the excess of national income over absorption to finance an accumulation of claims against the rest of the world. This is national saving, and is called the balance on current account. A country with a current account surplus is accumulating claims on the rest of the world. Thus, rearranging (1.20) gives

$$\begin{aligned}
Q - A &= \Delta(\text{NFA}) \\
&= (\text{EX} - \text{IM}) + R \\
&= Q - (C + I + G) \\
&= [(Q - T) - C] - I + (T - G) \\
&= (S - I) + (T - G),
\end{aligned}$$

which we summarize by

$$\Delta(\text{NFA}) = \text{EX} - \text{IM} + R = [S - I] + [T - G] = Q - A. \tag{1.21}$$

The change in the country's net foreign asset position, ΔNFA in (1.21), is the nation's accumulation of claims against the foreign sector and includes official (central bank) as well as private capital transactions. The distinction between private and official changes in net foreign assets is developed further below.

Although (1.21) is an accounting identity and *not* a theory, it can be used for "back of the envelope" analyses of current account problems. For example, if the home country experiences a current account surplus $(\text{EX} - \text{IM} + R > 0)$ and the government's budget is in balance $(T = G)$, you see from (1.21) that the current account surplus arises because there are insufficient investment opportunities at home. To satisfy domestic residents' desired saving, they accumulate foreign assets so that $\Delta\text{NFA} > 0$. If the inequality is reversed, domestic savings would seem to be insufficient to finance the desired amount of domestic investment.[5] On the other hand, the current account might also depend on net government saving. If net private saving is in balance ($S = I$), then the current account imbalance is determined by the imbalance in the government's budget. Some people believed that the US current account deficits of the 1980s were the result of government budget deficits.

Because current account imbalances reflect a nation's saving decision, the current account is largely a macroeconomic phenomenon as well as an intertemporal problem. The current account will depend on fluctuations in relative prices of goods, such as the real exchange rate or the terms of trade, only to the extent that these prices affect intertemporal saving decisions.

THE BALANCE OF PAYMENTS

The balance of payments is a summary record of the transactions between the residents of a country and the rest of the world. These include the exchange of goods and services, capital, unilateral transfer payments, and *official* (central bank) and private transactions. A *credit transaction* arises whenever payment is received from abroad. Credits contribute toward a surplus or *improvement* of the balance of payments. Examples of credit transactions include the export of goods, financial assets, and foreign direct investment in the home country. The latter two examples are sometimes referred to as *inflows* of capital. Credits are also generated from receipts of foreign aid and cash remittances from abroad and from income received for factor services rendered abroad – such as labor, interest from foreign bonds, and dividends from foreign equities. *Debit transactions* arise whenever payment is made to agents that reside abroad. Debits contribute toward a deficit, or *worsening*, of the balance of payments.[6]

Subaccounts

The precise format of balance-of-payments subaccount reporting differs across countries. For the US, the main subaccounts of the balance of payments that you need to know are the current account, which records transactions involving goods, services, and unilateral transfers, the capital account, which records transactions involving real or financial assets, and the official settlements balance, which records foreign exchange transactions undertaken by the central bank.

---

[5] This was a popular argument that was used to explain Japan's current account surpluses with the US.

[6] Note the unfortunate terminology: capital inflows reduce net foreign asset holdings, while capital outflows increase net foreign asset holdings.

Credit transactions generate a supply of foreign currency and also a demand for US dollars, because US residents involved in credit transactions require foreign currency payments to be converted into dollars. Similarly, debit transactions create a demand for foreign exchange and a supply of dollars. As a result, the combined deficits on the current account and the capital account can be thought of as the excess demand for foreign exchange by the private (non central bank) sector. This combined current and capital account balance is commonly called the *balance of payments*.

Under a system of pure floating exchange rates, the exchange rate is determined by equilibrium in the foreign exchange market. Excess demand for foreign exchange in this case is necessarily zero. It follows that it is not possible for a country to have a balance-of-payments problem under a regime of pure floating exchange rates, because the balance of payments is always zero and the current account deficit always is equal to the capital account surplus.

When central banks intervene in the foreign exchange market either by buying or selling foreign currency, their actions, which are designed to prevent exchange rate adjustment, allow the balance of payments to be nonzero. To prevent a depreciation of the home currency, a privately determined excess demand for foreign exchange can be satisfied by sales of the central bank's foreign exchange reserves. Alternatively, if the home country spends less abroad than it receives, there will be a privately determined excess supply of foreign exchange. The central bank can absorb the excess supply by accumulating foreign exchange reserves. Changes in the central bank's foreign exchange reserves are recorded in the *official settlements balance*, which – as argued above – is the balance of payments. Central bank foreign exchange reserve losses are credits and their reserve gains are debits to the official settlements account.

1.3 THE CENTRAL BANK'S BALANCE SHEET

The monetary liabilities of the central bank are called the *monetary base, B*. They are comprised of currency and commercial bank reserves or deposits at the central bank. The central bank's assets can be classified into two main categories. The first is domestic credit, D. In the US, domestic credit is extended to the Treasury when the central bank engages in open market operations and purchases US Treasury debt, and to the commercial banking system through discount lending. The second asset category is the central bank's net holdings of foreign assets, NFA^{cb}. These are mainly foreign exchange reserves held by the central bank minus its domestic currency liabilities held by foreign central banks. Foreign exchange reserves include foreign currency, foreign government Treasury bills, and gold. We state the central bank's balance sheet identity as

$$B = D + \text{NFA}^{cb}. \tag{1.22}$$

Since the money supply varies in proportion to changes in the monetary base, you can see from (1.22) that in the open economy there are two determinants of the money supply. The central bank can alter the money supply through a change in discount lending, through open market operations, or via foreign exchange intervention. Under a regime of perfectly flexible exchange rates, $\Delta \text{NFA}^{cb} = 0$, which implies that the central bank controls the money supply just as it does in the closed economy case.

● THE MECHANICS OF INTERVENTION

Suppose that the central bank wants to the dollar to fall in value against the yen. To achieve this result, it must buy yen, which increases NFA^{cb}, B, and hence the money supply M. If the Fed buys the yen from Citibank (say), in New York, the Fed pays for the yen by crediting Citibank's reserve account. Citibank then transfers ownership of a yen deposit at a Japanese bank to the Fed.

If the intervention ends here, the US money supply increases but the Japanese money supply is unaffected. In Japan, all that happens is a swap of deposit liabilities in the Japanese commercial bank. The Fed could go a step further and convert the deposit into Japanese T-bills. It might do so by buying T-bills from a Japanese resident, which it pays for by writing a check drawn on the Japanese bank. The Japanese resident deposits that check in a bank, and still, there is no net effect on the Japanese monetary base.

If, on the other hand, the Fed converts the deposit into currency, the Japanese monetary base does decline. The reason for this is that the Japanese monetary base is reduced when the Fed withdraws currency from circulation. The Fed would never do this, however, because currency pays no interest. The intervention described above is referred to as an unsterilized intervention, because the central bank's foreign exchange transactions have been allowed to affect the domestic money supply. A sterilized intervention, on the other hand, occurs when the central bank offsets its foreign exchange operations with transactions in domestic credit so that no net change in the money supply occurs. To sterilize the yen purchase described above, the Fed would simultaneously undertake an open market sale, so that D would decrease by exactly the amount by which NFA^{cb} increases from the foreign exchange intervention. It is an open question whether sterilized interventions can have a permanent effect on the exchange rate.

2

Some Useful
Time-Series Methods

International macroeconomic and finance theory is typically aimed at explaining the evolution of the open economy over time. The natural way to empirically evaluate these theories is with time-series methods. This chapter summarizes some of the time-series tools that are used in later chapters to estimate and to test predictions of the theory. The material is written assuming that you have had a first course in econometrics covering linear regression theory and is presented without proofs of the underlying statistical theory. There are now several accessible textbooks that contain careful treatments of the associated econometric theory.[1] If you like, you may skip this chapter for now and use it as reference when the relevant material is encountered.

You will encounter the following notation and terminology. Underlined variables will denote vectors and bold-faced variables will denote matrices. $a = \text{plim}(X_T)$ indicates that the sequence of random variables $\{X_T\}$ *converges in probability* to the number a as $T \to \infty$. This means that, for sufficiently large T, X_T can be treated as a constant. $\text{N}(\mu, \sigma^2)$ stands for the normal distribution with mean μ and variance σ^2, $U[a, b]$ stands for the uniform distribution over the interval $[a, b]$, $X_t \overset{iid}{\sim} \text{N}(\mu, \sigma^2)$ means that the random variable X_t is independently and identically distributed as $\text{N}(\mu, \sigma^2)$, $X_t \overset{iid}{\sim} (\mu, \sigma^2)$ means that X_t is independently and identically distributed according to some unspecified distribution with mean μ and variance σ^2, and $Y_T \overset{D}{\to} \text{N}(\mu, \sigma^2)$ indicates that, as $T \to \infty$, the sequence of random variables Y_T *converges in distribution* to the normal with mean μ and variance σ^2 and is called the *asymptotic distribution* of Y_T. This means that, for sufficiently large T, the random variable $\{Y_T\}$ has the normal distribution with mean μ and variance σ^2. We will say that a time-series $\{x_t\}$ is *covariance stationary* if its first and second moments are finite and are time-invariant; for example, if $\text{E}(x_t) = \mu$ and $\text{E}(x_t x_{t-j}) = \gamma_j$. AR($p$) stands for *autoregression* of order p, MA(n) stands for a *moving average* of order n, ARIMA

---

[1] See Hamilton [63], Hatanaka [71], and Johansen [79].

stands for "autoregressive integrated moving average," VAR stands for *vector autoregression*, and VECM stands for *vector error correction model*.

2.1 UNRESTRICTED VECTOR AUTOREGRESSIONS

Consider a zero-mean covariance stationary bivariate vector time-series, $\underline{q}_t = (q_{1t}, q_{2t})'$ and assume that it has the pth-order autoregressive representation[2]

$$\underline{q}_t = \sum_{j=1}^{p} \mathbf{A}_j \underline{q}_{t-j} + \underline{\epsilon}_t, \tag{2.1}$$

where

$$\mathbf{A}_j = \begin{pmatrix} a_{11,j} & a_{12,j} \\ a_{21,j} & a_{22,j} \end{pmatrix}$$

and the error vector has mean $E(\underline{\epsilon}_t) = 0$ and covariance matrix $E(\underline{\epsilon}_t \underline{\epsilon}_t') = \Sigma$. The unrestricted vector autoregression VAR is a statistical model for the vector time-series $\underline{q}_t$. The same variables appear in each equation as the independent variables, so the VAR can be efficiently estimated by running least squares (OLS) individually on each equation.

To estimate a pth-order VAR for this two-equation system, let $\underline{z}_t' = (q_{1t-1}, \ldots, q_{1t-p}, q_{2t-1}, \ldots, q_{2t-p})$ and write (2.1) out as

$$q_{1t} = \underline{z}_t' \underline{\beta}_1 + \epsilon_{1t},$$

$$q_{2t} = \underline{z}_t' \underline{\beta}_2 + \epsilon_{2t}.$$

Let the grand coefficient vector be $\underline{\beta} = (\underline{\beta}_1', \underline{\beta}_2')'$, and let $\mathbf{Q} = \text{plim}[(1/T) \sum_{t=1}^{T} \underline{q}_t \underline{q}_t']$ be a positive definite matrix of constants which exists by the law of large numbers and the covariance stationarity assumption. Then, as $T \to \infty$,

$$\sqrt{T}(\hat{\beta} - \beta) \overset{D}{\to} N(0, \mathbf{\Omega}), \tag{2.2}$$

where $\mathbf{\Omega} = \Sigma \otimes \mathbf{Q}^{-1}$. The asymptotic distribution can be used to test hypotheses about the $\underline{\beta}$ vector.

⬤ LAG-LENGTH DETERMINATION

Unless you have a good reason to do otherwise, you should let the data determine the lag length p. If the $\underline{q}_t$ are drawn from a normal distribution, the log

---

[2] $\underline{q}_t$ will be covariance stationary if $E(\underline{q}_t) = \underline{\mu}$, $E(\underline{q}_t - \underline{\mu})(\underline{q}_{t-j} - \underline{\mu})' = \Sigma_j$.

likelihood function for (2.1) is $-2 \ln |\mathbf{\Sigma}| + c$, where c is a constant.[3] If you choose the lag-length to *maximize* the normal likelihood, you just choose p to *minimize* $\ln |\hat{\mathbf{\Sigma}}_p|$, where $\hat{\mathbf{\Sigma}}_p = [1/(T-p)] \sum_{t=p+1}^{T} \hat{\epsilon}_t \hat{\epsilon}'_t$ is the estimated error covariance matrix of the VAR(p). In applications with sample sizes typically available to international macroeconomists – 100 or so quarterly observations – using the likelihood criterion typically results in choosing p values that are too large. To correct for the upward small-sample bias, two popular information criteria are frequently used for data-based lag-length determination. They are AIC, suggested by Akaike [1], and BIC, suggested by Schwarz [118]. Both AIC and BIC modify the likelihood by attaching a penalty for adding additional lags.

Let k be the total number of regression coefficients (the $a_{ij,r}$ coefficients in (2.1)) in the system. In our bivariate case, $k = 4p$.[4] The log-likelihood cannot decrease when additional regressors are included. Akaike [1] proposed attaching a penalty to the likelihood for adding lags and to choose p to minimize

$$\text{AIC} = 2 \ln |\hat{\mathbf{\Sigma}}_p| + \frac{2k}{T}.$$

Even with the penalty, AIC often suggests values of p that are too large. An alternative criterion, suggested by Schwarz [118], imposes an even greater penalty for additional parameters:

$$\text{BIC} = 2 \ln |\hat{\mathbf{\Sigma}}_p| + \frac{k \ln T}{T}. \tag{2.3}$$

GRANGER CAUSALITY, ECONOMETRIC EXOGENIETY, AND CAUSAL PRIORITY

In VAR analysis, we say that q_{1t} does not *Granger cause* q_{2t} if lagged q_{1t} do not appear in the equation for q_{2t}. That is, conditional upon current and lagged q_{2t}, current and lagged q_{1t} do not help to predict future q_{2t}. You can test the null hypothesis that q_{1t} does not Granger cause q_{2t} by regressing q_{2t} on lagged q_{1t} and lagged q_{2t} and doing an F-test for the joint significance of the coefficients on lagged q_{1t}.

If q_{1t} does not Granger cause q_{2t}, we say that q_{2t} is *econometrically exogenous* with respect to q_{1t}. If it is also true that q_{2t} *does* Granger cause q_{1t}, we say that q_{2t} is *causally prior* to q_{1t}.

---

[3] $|\mathbf{\Sigma}|$ denotes the determinant of the matrix $\mathbf{\Sigma}$.
[4] This is without constants in the regressions. If constants are included in the VAR, then $k = 4p + 2$.

THE VECTOR MOVING-AVERAGE REPRESENTATION

Given the lag length p, you can estimate the $\mathbf{A}_j$ coefficients by OLS and invert the VAR(p) to get the *Wold vector moving-average representation*

$$\underline{q}_t = \left(\mathbf{I} - \sum_{j=1}^{p} \mathbf{A}_j L^j\right)^{-1} \underline{\epsilon}_t$$

$$= \sum_{j=0}^{\infty} \mathbf{C}_j L^j \underline{\epsilon}_t, \tag{2.4}$$

where L is the lag operator such that $L^j x_t = x_{t-j}$ for any variable x_t. To solve for the $\mathbf{C}_j$ matrices, you equate coefficients on powers of the lag operator. From (2.4), you know that $(\sum_{j=0}^{\infty} \mathbf{C}_j L^j)(\mathbf{I} - \sum_{j=1}^{p} \mathbf{A}_j L^j) = \mathbf{I}$. Write it out as

$$\mathbf{I} = \mathbf{C}_0 + (\mathbf{C}_1 - \mathbf{C}_0\mathbf{A}_1)L + (\mathbf{C}_2 - \mathbf{C}_1\mathbf{A}_1 - \mathbf{C}_0\mathbf{A}_2)L^2$$
$$+ (\mathbf{C}_3 - \mathbf{C}_2\mathbf{A}_1 - \mathbf{C}_1\mathbf{A}_2 - \mathbf{C}_0\mathbf{A}_3)L^3$$
$$+ (\mathbf{C}_4 - \mathbf{C}_3\mathbf{A}_1 - \mathbf{C}_2\mathbf{A}_2 - \mathbf{C}_1\mathbf{A}_3 - \mathbf{C}_0\mathbf{A}_4)L^4 + \cdots$$
$$= \sum_{j=0}^{\infty} \left(\mathbf{C}_j - \sum_{k=1}^{j} \mathbf{C}_{j-k}\mathbf{A}_k\right) L^j.$$

Now, to equate coefficients on powers of L, first note that $\mathbf{C}_0 = \mathbf{I}$ and the rest of the $\mathbf{C}_j$ follow recursively:

$$\mathbf{C}_1 = \mathbf{A}_1,$$
$$\mathbf{C}_2 = \mathbf{C}_1\mathbf{A}_1 + \mathbf{A}_2,$$
$$\mathbf{C}_3 = \mathbf{C}_2\mathbf{A}_1 + \mathbf{C}_1\mathbf{A}_2 + \mathbf{A}_3,$$
$$\mathbf{C}_4 = \mathbf{C}_3\mathbf{A}_1 + \mathbf{C}_2\mathbf{A}_2 + \mathbf{C}_1\mathbf{A}_3 + \mathbf{A}_4,$$
$$\vdots$$
$$\mathbf{C}_k = \sum_{j=1}^{k} \mathbf{C}_{k-j}\mathbf{A}_j.$$

For example, if $p = 2$, set $\mathbf{A}_j = 0$ for $j \geq 3$. Then $\mathbf{C}_1 = \mathbf{A}_1$, $\mathbf{C}_2 = \mathbf{C}_1\mathbf{A}_1 + \mathbf{A}_2$, $\mathbf{C}_3 = \mathbf{C}_2\mathbf{A}_1 + \mathbf{C}_1\mathbf{A}_2$, $\mathbf{C}_4 = \mathbf{C}_3\mathbf{A}_1 + \mathbf{C}_2\mathbf{A}_2$, and so on.

IMPULSE–RESPONSE ANALYSIS

Once you get the moving-average representation, you will want employ impulse–response analysis to evaluate the dynamic effect of innovations in each of the variables on (q_{1t}, q_{2t}). When you go to simulate the dynamic response of q_{1t} and q_{2t} to a shock to ϵ_{1t}, you are immediately confronted with two problems. The first one is how big should the shock be? This becomes an issue because you will want to compare the response of q_{1t} across different shocks. You'll have to make a normalization for the size of the shocks, and a popular choice is to consider shocks one standard deviation in size. The second problem is to get shocks that can be unambiguously attributed to q_{1t} and to q_{2t}. If ϵ_{1t} and ϵ_{2t} are contemporaneously correlated, however, you can't just shock ϵ_{1t} and hold ϵ_{2t} constant.

To deal with these problems, first standardize the innovations. Since the correlation matrix is given by

$$\mathbf{R} = \mathbf{\Lambda}\mathbf{\Sigma}\mathbf{\Lambda} = \begin{pmatrix} 1 & \rho \\ \rho & 1 \end{pmatrix},$$

where

$$\mathbf{\Lambda} = \begin{pmatrix} \dfrac{1}{\sqrt{\sigma_{11}}} & 0 \\ 0 & \dfrac{1}{\sqrt{\sigma_{22}}} \end{pmatrix}$$

is a matrix with the inverse of the standard deviations on the diagonal and zeros elsewhere, the error covariance matrix can be decomposed as $\mathbf{\Sigma} = \mathbf{\Lambda}^{-1}\mathbf{R}\mathbf{\Lambda}^{-1}$. This means that the Wold vector moving-average representation (2.4) can be rewritten as

$$\underline{q}_t = \left(\sum_{j=0}^{\infty} \mathbf{C}_j L^j \right) \mathbf{\Lambda}^{-1}(\mathbf{\Lambda}\underline{\epsilon}_t)$$

$$= \left(\sum_{j=0}^{\infty} \mathbf{D}_j L^j \right) \underline{v}_t. \tag{2.5}$$

where $\mathbf{D}_j \equiv \mathbf{C}_j \mathbf{\Lambda}^{-1}$, $\underline{v}_t \equiv \mathbf{\Lambda}\underline{\epsilon}_t$, and $\mathrm{E}(\underline{v}_t\underline{v}_t') = \mathbf{R}$. The newly defined innovations v_{1t} and v_{2t} both have a variance of 1.

Now, to unambiguously attribute an innovation to q_{1t}, you must orthogonalize the innovations by taking the unique upper triangular Choleski matrix decomposition of the correlation matrix $\mathbf{R} = \mathbf{S}'\mathbf{S}$, where

$$\mathbf{S} = \begin{pmatrix} s_{11} & s_{12} \\ 0 & s_{22} \end{pmatrix}.$$

Now insert $\mathbf{S}\mathbf{S}^{-1}$ into the normalized moving average (2.5), to give

$$\underline{q}_t = \left(\sum_{j=0}^{\infty} \mathbf{D}_j L^j \right) \mathbf{S} \left(\mathbf{S}^{-1}\underline{v}_t \right) = \sum_{j=0}^{\infty} \mathbf{B}_j L^j \underline{\eta}_t, \tag{2.6}$$

where $\mathbf{B_j} \equiv \mathbf{D}_j\mathbf{S} = \mathbf{C}_j\mathbf{\Lambda}^{-1}\mathbf{S}$, and $\underline{\eta_t} \equiv \mathbf{S}^{-1}\underline{v_t}$ is the 2×1 vector of zero-mean orthogonalized innovations with covariance matrix $\mathrm{E}(\underline{\eta_t}\underline{\eta}_t' = \mathbf{I})$. Note that $\mathbf{S}^{-1}$ is also upper triangular.

Now write out the individual equations in (2.6), to give

$$q_{1t} = \sum_{j=0}^{\infty} b_{11,j}\eta_{1,t-j} + \sum_{j=0}^{\infty} b_{12,j}\eta_{2,t-j}, \tag{2.7}$$

$$q_{2t} = \sum_{j=0}^{\infty} b_{21,j}\eta_{1,t-j} + \sum_{j=0}^{\infty} b_{22,j}\eta_{2,t-j}. \tag{2.8}$$

The effect on q_{1t} at time k of a one standard deviation orthogonalized innovation in η_1 at time 0 is $b_{11,k}$. Similarly, the effect on q_{2k} is $b_{21,k}$. Graphing the transformed moving-average coefficients is an efficient method for examining the impulse responses.

You may also want to calculate standard error bands for the impulse responses. You can do this using the following parametric bootstrap procedure.[5] Let T be the number of time-series observations that you have and let a "tilde" denote pseudo-values generated by the computer. Then:

1. Take $T + M$ independent draws from the $\mathrm{N}(0, \hat{\mathbf{\Sigma}})$ to form the vector series $\{\tilde{\underline{\varepsilon}}_t\}$.
2. Set startup values of $\underline{q}_t$ at their mean values of 0, and then recursively generate the sequence $\{\tilde{\underline{q}}_t\}$ of length $T + M$ according to (2.1) using the estimated $\mathbf{A}_j$ matrices.
3. Drop the first M observations to eliminate the dependence on starting values. Estimate the simulated VAR. Call the estimated coefficients $\tilde{\mathbf{A}}_j$.
4. Form the matrices $\tilde{\mathbf{B}}_j = \tilde{\mathbf{C}}_j\tilde{\mathbf{\Lambda}}^{-1}\tilde{\mathbf{S}}$. You now have one realization of the parametric bootstrap distribution of the impulse response function.
5. Repeat the process, say, 5,000 times. The collection of observations on the $\tilde{\mathbf{B}}_j$ forms the bootstrap distribution. Take the standard deviation of the bootstrap distribution as an estimate of the standard error.

FORECAST-ERROR VARIANCE DECOMPOSITION

In (2.7), you have decomposed q_{1t} into orthogonal components. The innovation η_{1t} is attributed to q_{1t} and the innovation η_{2t} is attributed to q_{2t}. You may be interested in estimating how much of the underlying variability in q_{1t} is due to q_{1t} innovations and how much is due to q_{2t} innovations. For example, if q_{1t} is a real variable such as the log real exchange rate and q_{2t} is a nominal quantity such as money, you might want to know what fraction of log real exchange rate variability is attributable to innovations in money. In the VAR framework, you

---

[5]   The bootstrap is a resampling scheme done by computer to estimate the underlying probability distribution of a random variable. In a parametric bootstrap the observations are drawn from a particular probability distribution such as the normal. In the nonparametric bootstrap, the observations are resampled from the data.

can ask this question by decomposing the variance of the k-step-ahead forecast error into contributions from the separate orthogonal components. At $t + k$, the orthogonalized and standardized moving-average representation is

$$\underline{q}_{t+k} = \mathbf{B}_0 \underline{\eta}_{t+k} + \cdots + \mathbf{B}_k \underline{\eta}_t + \cdots \qquad (2.9)$$

Take expectations of both sides of (2.9), conditional on information available at time t, to get

$$\mathrm{E}_t \underline{q}_{t+k} = \mathbf{B}_k \underline{\eta}_t + \mathbf{B}_{k+1} \underline{\eta}_{t-1} + \cdots \qquad (2.10)$$

Now subtract (2.10) from (2.9) to obtain the k-period-ahead forecast error vector

$$\underline{q}_{t+k} - \mathrm{E}_t \underline{q}_{t+k} = \mathbf{B}_0 \underline{\eta}_{t+k} + \cdots + \mathbf{B}_{k-1} \underline{\eta}_{t+1}. \qquad (2.11)$$

Because the $\underline{\eta}_t$ are serially uncorrelated and have covariance matrix $\mathbf{I}$, the covariance matrix of these forecast errors is

$$\mathrm{E}[\underline{q}_{t+k} - \mathrm{E}_t \underline{q}_{t+k}][\underline{q}_{t+k} - \mathrm{E}_t \underline{q}_{t+k}]' = \mathbf{B}_0 \mathbf{B}_0' + \mathbf{B}_1 \mathbf{B}_1' + \cdots + \mathbf{B}_{k-1} \mathbf{B}_{k-1}'$$

$$= \sum_{j=0}^{k} \mathbf{B}_j \mathbf{B}_j' = \sum_{j=0}^{k} \left(\underline{b}_{1,j}, \underline{b}_{2,j} \right) \left(\begin{array}{c} \underline{b}_{1,j}' \\ \underline{b}_{2,j}' \end{array} \right)$$

$$= \underbrace{\sum_{j=0}^{k} \underline{b}_{1,j} \underline{b}_{1,j}'}_{(a)} + \underbrace{\sum_{j=0}^{k} \underline{b}_{2,j} \underline{b}_{2,j}'}_{(b)}, \qquad (2.12)$$

where $\underline{b}_{1,j}$ is the first column of $\mathbf{B}_j$ and $\underline{b}_{2,j}$ is the second column of $\mathbf{B}_j$. As $k \to \infty$, the k-period-ahead forecast error covariance matrix tends toward the unconditional covariance matrix of $\underline{q}_t$.

The forecast-error variance of q_{1t} attributable to the orthogonalized innovations in q_{1t} is the first diagonal element in the first summation, which is labeled (a) in (2.12). The forecast error variance in q_{1t} attributable to innovations in q_{2t} is given by the first diagonal element in the second summation (labeled (b)). Similarly, the second diagonal element of a is the forecast error variance in q_{2t} attributable to innovations in q_{1t}, and the second diagonal element in (b) is the forecast error variance in q_{2t} attributable to innovations in itself.

A problem that you may encounter in practice is that the forecast error decomposition and impulse–responses may be sensitive to the ordering of the variables in the orthogonalizing process, so it may be a good idea to experiment with which variable is q_{1t} and which one is q_{2t}. A second problem is that the procedures outlined above are purely of a statistical nature and have little or no economic content. In section 8.4.2 we will cover a popular method for using economic theory to identify the shocks.

POTENTIAL PITFALLS OF UNRESTRICTED VARS

Cooley and LeRoy [31] criticize unrestricted VAR accounting because the statistical concepts of Granger causality and econometric exogeneity are very different from standard notions of economic exogeneity. Their point is that the unrestricted VAR is the *reduced form* of some structural model from which it is not possible to discover the true relations of cause and effect. Impulse–response analyses from unrestricted VARs do not necessarily tell us anything about the effect of policy interventions on the economy. In order to deduce cause and effect, you need to make explicit assumptions about the underlying economic environment.

We present the Cooley–LeRoy critique in terms of the two-equation model consisting of the money supply and the nominal exchange rate:

$$m = \epsilon_1, \tag{2.13}$$

$$s = \gamma m + \epsilon_2, \tag{2.14}$$

where the error terms are related by $\epsilon_2 = \lambda \epsilon_1 + \epsilon_3$, with $\epsilon_1 \overset{iid}{\sim} N(0, \sigma_1^2)$, $\epsilon_3 \overset{iid}{\sim} N(0, \sigma_3^2)$, and $E(\epsilon_1 \epsilon_3) = 0$. Then you can rewrite (2.13) and (2.14) as

$$m = \epsilon_1, \tag{2.15}$$

$$s = \gamma m + \lambda \epsilon_1 + \epsilon_3. \tag{2.16}$$

m is exogenous in the economic sense and $m = \epsilon_1$ determines part of ϵ_2. The effect of a change of money on the exchange rate, $ds = (\lambda + \gamma) \, dm$, is well defined.

A reversal of the causal link gets you into trouble because you will not be able to unambiguously determine the effect of an m shock on s. Suppose that instead of (2.13), the money supply is governed by two components, $\epsilon_1 = \delta \epsilon_2 + \epsilon_4$, with $\epsilon_2 \overset{iid}{\sim} N(0, \sigma_2^2)$, $\epsilon_4 \overset{iid}{\sim} N(0, \sigma_4^2)$, and $E(\epsilon_4 \epsilon_2) = 0$. Then

$$m = \delta \epsilon_2 + \epsilon_4, \tag{2.17}$$

$$s = \gamma m + \epsilon_2. \tag{2.18}$$

If the shock to m originates with ϵ_4, the effect on the exchange rate is $ds = \gamma \, d\epsilon_4$. If the m shock originates with ϵ_2, then the effect is $ds = (1 + \gamma \delta) \, d\epsilon_2$.

Things get really confusing if the monetary authorities follow a feedback rule that depends on the exchange rate:

$$m = \theta s + \epsilon_1, \tag{2.19}$$

$$s = \gamma m + \epsilon_2, \tag{2.20}$$

where $E(\epsilon_1 \epsilon_2) = 0$. The reduced form is

$$m = \frac{\epsilon_1 + \theta \epsilon_2}{1 - \gamma \theta}, \tag{2.21}$$

$$s = \frac{\gamma \epsilon_1 + \epsilon_2}{1 - \gamma \theta}. \tag{2.22}$$

Again, you cannot use the reduced form to unambiguously determine the effect of m on s, because the m shock may have originated with ϵ_1, ϵ_2, or some combination of the two. The best you can do in this case is to run the regression $s = \beta m + \eta$, and get $\beta = \text{Cov}(s, m)/\text{Var}(m)$, which is a function of the population moments of the joint probability distribution for m and s. If the observations are normally distributed, then $E(s|m) = \beta m$, so you learn something about the conditional expectation of s given m. But you have not learned anything about the effects of policy intervention.

To relate these ideas to unrestricted VARs, consider the dynamic model

$$m_t = \theta s_t + \beta_{11} m_{t-1} + \beta_{12} s_{t-1} + \epsilon_{1t}, \tag{2.23}$$

$$s_t = \gamma m_t + \beta_{21} m_{t-1} + \beta_{22} s_{t-1} + \epsilon_{2t}, \tag{2.24}$$

where $\epsilon_{1t} \overset{iid}{\sim} N(0, \sigma_1^2)$, $\epsilon_{2t} \overset{iid}{\sim} N(0, \sigma_2^2)$, and $E(\epsilon_{1t}\epsilon_{2s}) = 0$ for all t, s. Without additional restrictions, ϵ_{1t} and ϵ_{2t} are exogenous but both m_t and s_t are endogenous. Notice also that m_{t-1} and s_{t-1} are exogenous with respect to the current values m_t and s_t.

If $\theta = 0$, then m_t is said to be econometrically exogenous with respect to s_t. m_t, m_{t-1}, and s_{t-1} would be predetermined in the sense that an intervention due to a shock to m_t can unambiguously be attributed to ϵ_{1t} and the effect on the current exchange rate is $ds_t = \gamma \, dm_t$. If $\beta_{12} = \theta = 0$, then m_t is strictly exogenous to s_t.

Eliminate the current value observations from the right-hand side of (2.23) and (2.24) to get the reduced form

$$m_t = \pi_{11} m_{t-1} + \pi_{12} s_{t-1} + u_{mt}, \tag{2.25}$$

$$s_t = \pi_{21} m_{t-1} + \pi_{22} s_{t-1} + u_{st}, \tag{2.26}$$

where

$$\pi_{11} = \frac{(\beta_{11} + \theta\beta_{21})}{(1 - \gamma\theta)}, \qquad \pi_{12} = \frac{(\beta_{12} + \theta\beta_{22})}{(1 - \gamma\theta)},$$

$$\pi_{21} = \frac{(\beta_{21} + \gamma\beta_{11})}{(1 - \gamma\theta)}, \qquad \pi_{22} = \frac{(\beta_{22} + \gamma\beta_{12})}{(1 - \gamma\theta)},$$

$$u_{mt} = \frac{(\epsilon_{1t} + \theta\epsilon_{2t})}{(1 - \gamma\theta)}, \qquad u_{st} = \frac{(\epsilon_{2t} + \gamma\epsilon_{1t})}{(1 - \gamma\theta)},$$

$$\text{Var}(u_{mt}) = \frac{(\sigma_1^2 + \theta^2\sigma_2^2)}{(1 - \gamma\theta)^2}, \qquad \text{Var}(u_{st}) = \frac{(\gamma^2\sigma_1^2 + \sigma_2^2)}{(1 - \gamma\theta)^2},$$

$$\text{Cov}(u_{mt}, u_{st}) = \frac{(\gamma\sigma_1^2 + \theta\sigma_2^2)}{(1 - \gamma\theta)^2}.$$

If you were to apply the VAR methodology to this system, you would estimate the π coefficients. If you determined that $\pi_{12} = 0$, you would say that s does not Granger cause m (and therefore m is econometrically exogenous to s). But when you look at (2.23) and (2.24), m is exogenous in the structural or economic sense when $\theta = 0$, but this is not implied by $\pi_{12} = 0$. The failure of s to Granger cause m need not tell us anything about structural exogeneity.

Suppose that you orthogonalize the error terms in the VAR. Let $\delta = \text{Cov}(u_{mt}, u_{st})/\text{Var}(u_{mt})$ be the slope coefficient from the linear projection of u_{st} onto u_{mt}. Then $u_{st} - \delta u_{mt}$ is orthogonal to u_{mt} by construction. An orthogonalized system is obtained by multiplying (2.25) by δ and subtracting this result from (2.26):

$$m_t = \pi_{11} m_{t-1} + \pi_{12} s_{t-1} + u_{mt}, \tag{2.27}$$

$$s_t = \delta m_t + (\pi_{21} - \delta \pi_{11}) m_{t-1} + (\pi_{22} - \delta \pi_{12}) s_{t-1} + u_{st} - \delta u_{mt}. \tag{2.28}$$

The orthogonalized system includes a current value of m_t in the s_t equation, but it does not recover the structure of (2.23) and (2.24). The orthogonalized innovations are

$$u_{mt} = \frac{\epsilon_{1t} + \theta \epsilon_{2t}}{1 - \gamma \theta}, \tag{2.29}$$

$$u_{st} - \delta u_{mt} = \left[(\gamma \epsilon_{1t} + \epsilon_{2t}) - \left(\frac{\gamma \sigma_1^2 + \theta \sigma_2^2}{\sigma_1^2 + \theta^2 \sigma_2^2} \right) (\epsilon_{1t} + \theta \epsilon_{2t}) \right] \Big/ (1 - \gamma \theta), \tag{2.30}$$

which allows you to look at shocks that are unambiguously attributable to u_{mt} in an impulse–response analysis, but the shock is not unambiguously attributable to the structural innovation, ϵ_{1t}.

To summarize, impulse–response analyses of unrestricted VARs provide summaries of dynamic correlations between variables, but correlations do not imply causality. In order to make structural interpretations, you need to make assumptions about the economic environment and build them into the econometric model.[6]

2.2 THE GENERALIZED METHOD OF MOMENTS

OLS can be viewed as a special case of the generalized method of moments (GMM) estimator studied by Hansen [67]. Since you are presumably familiar with OLS, you can build your intuition about GMM by first thinking about using it to estimate a linear regression. After getting that under your belt, thinking about GMM estimation in more complicated and possibly nonlinear environments is straightforward.

---

[6] You've no doubt heard the phrase made famous by Milton Friedman, "There's no such thing as a free lunch." Michael Mussa's paraphrasing of that principle in doing economics is "If you don't make assumptions, you don't get conclusions."

OLS and GMM. Suppose that you want to estimate the coefficients in the regression

$$q_t = \underline{z}_t' \underline{\beta} + \epsilon_t, \tag{2.31}$$

where $\underline{\beta}$ is the k-dimensional vector of coefficients, $\underline{z}_t$ is a k-dimensional vector of regressors, $\epsilon_t \overset{iid}{\sim} (0, \sigma^2)$, and $(q_t, \underline{z}_t)$ are jointly covariance stationary. The OLS estimator of $\underline{\beta}$ is chosen to minimize

$$\frac{1}{T} \sum_{t=1}^{T} \epsilon_t^2 = \frac{1}{T} \sum_{t=1}^{T} (q_t - \underline{\beta}' \underline{z}_t)(q_t - \underline{z}_t' \underline{\beta})$$

$$= \frac{1}{T} \sum_{t=1}^{T} q_t^2 - 2\underline{\beta} \frac{1}{T} \sum_{t=1}^{T} \underline{z}_t q_t + \underline{\beta}' \frac{1}{T} \sum_{t=1}^{T} (\underline{z}_t \underline{z}_t') \underline{\beta}. \tag{2.32}$$

When you differentiate (2.32) with respect to $\underline{\beta}$ and set the result to zero, you obtain the first-order conditions,

$$\underbrace{-\frac{2}{T} \sum_{t=1}^{T} \underline{z}_t \epsilon_t}_{(a)} = \underbrace{-2 \frac{1}{T} \sum_{t=1}^{T} (\underline{z}_t q_t) + 2\underline{\beta} \frac{1}{T} \sum_{t=1}^{T} (\underline{z}_t \underline{z}_t')}_{(b)} = 0. \tag{2.33}$$

If the regression is correctly specified, the first-order conditions form a set of k orthogonality or "zero" conditions that you used to estimate $\underline{\beta}$. These orthogonality conditions are labeled (a) in (2.33). OLS estimation is straightforward, because the first-order conditions are the set of k linear equations in k unknowns labeled (b) in (2.33), which are solved by matrix inversion.[7] Solving (2.33) for the minimizer $\hat{\underline{\beta}}$, you obtain

$$\underline{\beta} = \left(\frac{1}{T} \sum_{t=1}^{T} \underline{z}_t \underline{z}_t' \right)^{-1} \left(\frac{1}{T} \sum_{t=1}^{T} (\underline{z}_t q_t) \right). \tag{2.34}$$

Let $\mathbf{Q} = \text{plim}(1/T) \sum \underline{z}_t \underline{z}_t'$ and let $\mathbf{W} = \sigma^2 \mathbf{Q}$. Because $\{\epsilon_t\}$ is an *iid* sequence, $\{\underline{z}_t \epsilon_t\}$ is also *iid*. It follows from the Lindeberg–Levy central limit theorem that $(1/\sqrt{T}) \sum_{t=1}^{T} \underline{z}_t \epsilon_t \overset{D}{\to} \mathrm{N}(0, \mathbf{W})$. Let the residuals be $\hat{\epsilon}_t = q_t - \underline{z}_t' \hat{\underline{\beta}}$, let the estimated error variance be $\hat{\sigma}^2 = (1/T) \sum_{t=1}^{T} \hat{\epsilon}_t^2$, and let $\hat{\mathbf{W}} = (\hat{\sigma}^2/T) \sum_{t=1}^{T} \underline{z}_t \underline{z}_t'$. While it may seem like a silly thing to do, you can set up a quadratic form using the orthogonality conditions and get the OLS estimator by minimizing

$$\left(\frac{1}{T} \sum_{t=1}^{T} (\underline{z}_t \epsilon_t) \right)' \hat{\mathbf{W}}^{-1} \left(\frac{1}{T} \sum_{t=1}^{T} (\underline{z}_t \epsilon_t) \right), \tag{2.35}$$

---

[7] In matrix notation, we usually write the regression as $\underline{q} = \mathbf{Z}\underline{\beta} + \underline{\epsilon}$, where $\underline{q}$ is the T-dimensional vector of observations on q_t, $\mathbf{Z}$ is the $(T \times k)$-dimensional matrix of observations on the independent variables, whose tth row is $\underline{z}_t'$, $\underline{\beta}$ is the k-dimensional vector of parameters that we want to estimate, $\underline{\epsilon}$ is the T-dimensional vector of regression errors, and $\hat{\underline{\beta}} = (\mathbf{Z}'\mathbf{Z})^{-1}\mathbf{Z}'\underline{q}$.

with respect to β. This is the GMM estimator for the linear regression (2.31). The first-order conditions for this problem are

$$\hat{\mathbf{W}}^{-1} \frac{1}{T} \sum \underline{z}_t \epsilon_t = \frac{1}{T} \sum \underline{z}_t \epsilon_t = 0,$$

which are identical to the OLS first-order conditions (2.33). You also know that the asymptotic distribution of the OLS estimator of $\underline{\beta}$ is

$$\sqrt{T}(\hat{\underline{\beta}} - \underline{\beta}) \xrightarrow{D} N(0, \mathbf{V}), \tag{2.36}$$

where $\mathbf{V} = \sigma^2 \mathbf{Q}^{-1}$. If you let $\mathbf{D} = E(\partial(\underline{z}_t \epsilon_t)/\partial \beta') = \mathbf{Q}$, the GMM covariance matrix $\mathbf{V}$ can be expressed as $\mathbf{V} = \sigma^2 \mathbf{Q}^{-1} = [\mathbf{D}' \mathbf{W}^{-1} \mathbf{D}]^{-1}$. The first equality is the standard OLS calculation for the covariance matrix and the second equality follows from the properties of (2.35).

You would never do OLS by minimizing (2.35), since to get the weighting matrix $\hat{\mathbf{W}}^{-1}$ you need an estimate of β, which is what you want in the first place. But this is what you do in the generalized environment.

Generalized environment. Suppose that you have an economic theory that relates q_t to a vector $\underline{x}_t$. The theory predicts the set of orthogonality conditions

$$E[\underline{z}_t \epsilon_t (q_t, \underline{x}_t, \underline{\beta})] = 0,$$

where $\underline{z}_t$ is a vector of instrumental variables, which may be different from $\underline{x}_t$, and $\epsilon_t(q_t, \underline{x}_t, \beta)$ may be a nonlinear function of the underlying k-dimensional parameter vector β and observations on q_t and $\underline{x}_t$.[8] To estimate β by GMM, let $\underline{w}_t \equiv \underline{z}_t \epsilon_t (q_t, \underline{x}_t, \beta)$, where we now write the vector of orthogonality conditions as $E(\underline{w}_t) = 0$. Mimicking the steps above for GMM estimation of the linear regression coefficients, you'll want to choose the parameter vector $\underline{\beta}$ to minimize

$$\left(\frac{1}{T} \sum_{t=1}^{T} \underline{w}_t \right)' \hat{\mathbf{W}}^{-1} \left(\frac{1}{T} \sum_{t=1}^{T} \underline{w}_t \right), \tag{2.37}$$

where $\hat{\mathbf{W}}$ is a consistent estimator of the asymptotic covariance matrix of $(1/\sqrt{T}) \sum \underline{w}_t$. It is sometimes called the long-run covariance matrix. You cannot guarantee that $\underline{w}_t$ is *iid* in the generalized environment. It may be serially correlated and conditionally heteroskedastic. To allow for these possibilities, the formula for the weighting matrix is

$$\mathbf{W} = \mathbf{\Omega}_0 + \sum_{j=1}^{\infty} (\mathbf{\Omega}_j + \mathbf{\Omega}_j'), \tag{2.38}$$

---

[8] Alternatively, you may be interested in a multiple equation system in which the theory imposes parameter restrictions across equations, so that not only may the model be nonlinear, but ϵ_t could be a vector of error terms.

where $\mathbf{\Omega}_0 = \mathrm{E}(\underline{w}_t \underline{w}_t')$ and $\mathbf{\Omega}_j = \mathrm{E}(\underline{w}_t \underline{w}_{t-j}')$. A popular choice for estimating $\hat{\mathbf{W}}$ is the method of Newey and West [109]:

$$\hat{\mathbf{W}} = \hat{\mathbf{\Omega}}_0 + \frac{1}{T} \sum_{j=1}^{m} \left(1 - \frac{j+1}{T}\right) \left(\hat{\mathbf{\Omega}}_j + \hat{\mathbf{\Omega}}_j'\right), \tag{2.39}$$

where $\hat{\mathbf{\Omega}}_0 = (1/T) \sum_{t=1}^{T} \underline{w}_t \underline{w}_t'$ and $\hat{\mathbf{\Omega}}_j = (1/T) \sum_{t=j+1}^{T} \underline{w}_t \underline{w}_{t-j}'$. The weighting function $1 - (j+1)/T$ is called the *Bartlett window*. When $\hat{\mathbf{W}}$ is constructed by Newey and West, it is guaranteed to be positive definite, which is a good thing since you need to invert it to do GMM. To guarantee consistency, the Newey–West lag length (m) needs go to infinity, but at a slower rate than T.[9] You might try values such as $m = T^{1/4}$. To test hypotheses, use the fact that

$$\sqrt{T}(\hat{\underline{\beta}} - \underline{\beta}) \xrightarrow{D} \mathrm{N}(\mathbf{0}, \mathbf{V}), \tag{2.40}$$

where $\mathbf{V} = (\mathbf{D}'\mathbf{W}^{-1}\mathbf{D})^{-1}$ and $\mathbf{D} = \mathrm{E}(\partial \underline{w}_t / \partial \underline{\beta}')$. To estimate $\mathbf{D}$, you can use $\hat{\mathbf{D}} = (1/T) \sum_{t=1}^{T} (\partial \hat{w}_t / \partial \underline{\beta}')$.

Let $\mathbf{R}$ be a $k \times q$ restriction matrix and let $\underline{r}$ be a q-dimensional vector of constants. Consider the q linear restrictions $\mathbf{R}\underline{\beta} = \underline{r}$ on the coefficient vector. The Wald statistic has an asymptotic chi-square distribution under the null hypothesis that the restrictions are true:

$$W_T = T(\mathbf{R}\hat{\underline{\beta}} - \underline{r})'[\mathbf{R}\mathbf{V}\mathbf{R}']^{-1}(\mathbf{R}\hat{\underline{\beta}} - \underline{r}) \xrightarrow{D} \chi_q^2. \tag{2.41}$$

It follows that the linear restrictions can be tested by comparing the Wald statistic against the chi-square distribution with q degrees of freedom.

GMM also allows you to conduct a generic test of a set of overidentifying restrictions. The theory predicts that there are as many orthogonality conditions, n, as is the dimensionality of $\underline{w}_t$. The parameter vector $\underline{\beta}$ is of dimension $k < n$, so actually only k linear combinations of the orthogonality conditions are set to zero in estimation. If the theoretical restrictions are true, however, the remaining $n-k$ orthogonality conditions should differ from zero only by chance. The minimized value of the GMM objective function, obtained by evaluating the objective function at $\hat{\underline{\beta}}$, turns out to be asymptotically χ_{n-k}^2 under the null hypothesis that the model is correctly specified.

2.3 THE SIMULATED METHOD OF MOMENTS

Under GMM, you chose $\underline{\beta}$ to match the theoretical moments to sample moments computed from the data. In applications where it is difficult or impossible to

---

[9] Andrews [2] and Newey and West [110] offer recommendations for letting the data determine m.

obtain analytic expressions for the moment conditions $E(\underline{w}_t)$ they can be generated by numerical simulation. This is the simulated method of moments (SMM), proposed by Lee and Ingram [90] and Duffie and Singleton [39].

In SMM, we match computer-simulated moments to the sample moments. We use the following notation:

β is the vector of parameters to be estimated.

$\{q_t\}_{t=1}^T$ is the actual time-series data of length T. Let $\underline{q}' = (q_1, q_2, \ldots, q_T)$ denote the collection of the observations.

$\{\tilde{q}_i(\underline{\beta})\}_{i=1}^M$ is a computer-simulated time-series of length M, which is generated according to the underlying economic theory. Let $\underline{\tilde{q}}'(\underline{\beta}) = (\tilde{q}_1(\underline{\beta}), \tilde{q}_2(\underline{\beta}), \ldots, \tilde{q}_M(\underline{\beta}))$ denote the collection of these M observations.

$\underline{h}(q_t)$ is some vector function of the data from which to simulate the moments. For example, setting $\underline{h}(q_t) = (q_t, q_t^2, q_t^3)'$ will pick off the first three moments of q_t.

$\underline{H}_T(\underline{q}) = (1/T) \sum_{t=1}^T \underline{h}(q_t)$ is the vector of sample moments of q_t.

$\underline{H}_M(\underline{\tilde{q}}(\underline{\beta})) = (1/M) \sum_{i=1}^M \underline{h}(\tilde{q}_i(\underline{\beta}))]$ is the corresponding vector of simulated moments, where the length of the simulated series is M.

$\underline{u}_t = \underline{h}(q_t) - \underline{H}_T(\underline{q})$ is $\underline{h}$ in deviation from the mean form.

$\hat{\mathbf{\Omega}}_0 = (1/T) \sum_{t=1}^T \underline{u}_t \underline{u}_t'$ is the sample short-run variance of $\underline{u}_t$.

$\hat{\mathbf{\Omega}}_j = (1/T) \sum_{t=1}^T \underline{u}_t \underline{u}_{t-j}'$ is the sample cross-covariance matrix of $\underline{u}_t$.

$\hat{\mathbf{W}}_T = \hat{\mathbf{\Omega}}_0 + (1/T) \sum_{j=1}^m [1 - (j+1)/T(\hat{\mathbf{\Omega}}_j + \hat{\mathbf{\Omega}}_j')]$ is the Newey–West estimate of the long-run covariance matrix of $\underline{u}_t$.

$\underline{g}_{T,M}(\underline{\beta}) = \underline{H}_T(\underline{q}) - \underline{H}_M(\underline{\tilde{q}}(\underline{\beta}))$ is the deviation of the sample moments from the simulated moments.

The SMM estimator is that value of β that minimizes the quadratic distance between the simulated moments and the sample moments:

$$g_{T,M}(\underline{\beta})' \left[\mathbf{W}_{T,M}^{-1} \right] g_{T,M}(\underline{\beta}), \qquad (2.42)$$

where $\mathbf{W}_{T,M} = [(1 + T/M)\mathbf{W}_T]$. Let $\hat{\underline{\beta}}_S$ be the SMM estimator. It is asymptotically normally distributed, with

$$\sqrt{T}(\hat{\underline{\beta}}_S - \underline{\beta}) \xrightarrow{D} N(0, \mathbf{V}_S),$$

as T and $M \to \infty$, where $\mathbf{V}_S = [\mathbf{B}'[(1 + T/M)\mathbf{W}]\mathbf{B}]^{-1}$ and $\mathbf{B} = E\partial \underline{h}[\tilde{q}_j(\beta)]/\partial \underline{\beta}$. You can estimate the theoretical value of $\mathbf{B}$ using its sample counterparts.

When you do SMM, there are three points to keep in mind. First, you should choose M to be much larger than T. SMM is less efficient than GMM, because the simulated moments are only estimates of the true moments. This part of the sampling variability is decreasing in M and will be lessened by choosing M sufficiently large.[10] Second, the SMM estimator is the minimizer of the objective function for a *fixed* sequence of random errors. The random errors must be held

---

[10]   Lee and Ingram [90] suggest $M = 10T$, but with computing costs now so low it might be a good idea to experiment with different values to ensure that your estimates are robust to M.

fixed in the simulations, so that each time the underlying random sequence is generated it must have the same seed. This is important because the minimization algorithm may never converge if the error sequence is redrawn at each iteration. Third, when working with covariance-stationary observations, it is a good idea to purge the effects of initial conditions. This can be done by initially generating a sequence of length $2M$, discarding the first M observations, and computing the moments from the remaining M observations.

2.4 UNIT ROOTS

Unit-root analysis figures prominently in exchange rate studies. A unit-root process is *not* covariance stationary. To fix ideas, consider the AR(1) process:

$$(1 - \rho L)q_t = \alpha(1 - \rho) + \epsilon_t, \tag{2.43}$$

where $\epsilon_t \overset{iid}{\sim} N(0, \sigma_\epsilon^2)$ and L is the lag operator.[11] Most economic time-series display persistence, so for concreteness we assume that $0 \leq \rho \leq 1$.[12] $\{q_t\}$ is covariance stationary if the autoregressive polynomial $(1 - \rho z)$ is invertible. In order for that to be true, we need $\rho < 1$, which is the same as saying that the root z in the autoregressive polynomial $(1 - \rho z) = 0$ lies outside the unit circle, which in turn is equivalent to saying that the root is greater than 1.[13]

The stationary case. To appreciate some of the features of a unit-root time-series, we first review some properties of stationary observations. If $0 \leq \rho < 1$ in (2.43), then $\{q_t\}$ is covariance stationary. It is straightforward to show that $E(q_t) = \alpha$ and $Var(q_t) = \sigma_\epsilon^2/(1 - \rho^2)$, which are finite and time-invariant. By repeated substitution of lagged values of q_t into (2.43), you get the moving-average representation with initial condition q_0:

$$q_t = \alpha(1 - \rho) \left(\sum_{j=0}^{t-1} \rho^j \right) + \rho^t q_0 + \sum_{j=0}^{t-1} \rho^j \epsilon_{t-j}. \tag{2.44}$$

The effect of an ϵ_{t-j} shock on q_t is ρ^j. More recent ϵ_t shocks have a larger effect on q_t than those from the more distant past. The effects of an ϵ_t shock are *transitory*, because they eventually die out.

To estimate ρ, we can simplify the algebra by setting $\alpha = 0$, so that $\{q_t\}$ from (2.43) evolves according to

$$q_{t+1} = \rho q_t + \epsilon_{t+1},$$

---

[11]   For any variable X_t, $L^k X_t = X_{t-k}$.
[12]   If we admit negative values of ρ, we require $-1 \leq \rho \leq 1$.
[13]   Most economic time-series are better characterized with positive values of ρ, but the requirement for stationarity is actually $|\rho| < 1$. We assume $0 \leq \rho \leq 1$ to keep the presentation concrete.

where $0 \leq \rho < 1$. The OLS estimator is $\hat{\rho} = \rho + [(\sum_{t=1}^{T-1} q_t \epsilon_{t+1})/(\sum_{t=1}^{T-1} q_t^2)]$. Multiplying both sides by $\sqrt{T}$ and rearranging gives

$$\sqrt{T}(\hat{\rho} - \rho) = \left(\frac{1}{\sqrt{T}} \sum_{t=1}^{T-1} q_t \epsilon_{t+1} \right) \bigg/ \left(\frac{1}{T} \sum_{t=1}^{T-1} q_t^2 \right). \tag{2.45}$$

The reason why you multiply by $\sqrt{T}$ is because that is the correct normalizing factor to get both the numerator and the denominator on the right-hand side of (2.45) to remain well behaved as $T \to \infty$. By the law of large numbers, plim $1/T \sum_{t=1}^{T-1} q_t^2 = \text{Var}(q_t) = \sigma_\epsilon^2/(1 - \rho^2)$, so that for sufficiently large T, the denominator can be treated like $\sigma_\epsilon^2/(1 - \rho^2)$, which is constant. Since $\epsilon_t \overset{iid}{\sim} N(0, \sigma_\epsilon^2)$ and $q_t \sim N(0, \sigma_\epsilon^2/(1 - \rho^2))$, the product sequence $\{q_t \epsilon_{t+1}\}$ is *iid* with mean $E(q_t \epsilon_{t+1}) = 0$ and variance $\text{Var}(q_t \epsilon_{t+1}) = E(\epsilon_{t+1}^2) E(q_t^2) = \sigma_\epsilon^4/(1 - \rho^2) < \infty$. By the Lindeberg–Levy central limit theorem, you have $(1/\sqrt{T}) \sum_{t=1}^{T-1} q_t \epsilon_{t+1} \overset{D}{\to} N(0, \sigma_\epsilon^4/(1 - \rho^2))$ as $T \to \infty$. For sufficiently large T, the numerator is a normally distributed random variable and the denominator is a constant, so it follows that

$$\sqrt{T}(\hat{\rho} - \rho) \overset{D}{\to} N(0, 1 - \rho^2). \tag{2.46}$$

You can test hypotheses about ρ by doing the usual t-test.

ESTIMATING THE HALF-LIFE TO CONVERGENCE

If the sequence $\{q_t\}$ follows the stationary AR(1) process, $q_t = \rho q_{t-1} + \epsilon_t$, its unconditional mean is zero, and the expected time, t^*, for it to adjust halfway back to zero following a one-time shock (its half-life) can be calculated as follows. Initialize by setting $q_0 = 0$. Then $q_1 = \epsilon_1$ and $E_1(q_t) = \rho^t q_1 = \rho^t \epsilon_1$. The half-life is that t such that the expected value of q_t has reverted to half its initial post-shock size – the t that sets $E_1(q_t) = \epsilon_1/2$. So we look for the t^* that sets $\rho^{t^*} \epsilon_1 = \epsilon_1/2$:

$$t^* = \frac{-\ln(2)}{\ln(\rho)}. \tag{2.47}$$

If the process follows higher-order serial correlation, the formula in (2.47) only gives the approximate half-life, although empirical researchers continue to use it anyway. To see how to get the exact half-life, consider the AR(2) process, $q_t = \rho_1 q_{t-1} + \rho_2 q_{t-2} + \epsilon_t$, and let

$$\underline{y}_t = \begin{bmatrix} q_t \\ q_{t-1} \end{bmatrix}; \quad \mathbf{A} = \begin{bmatrix} \rho_1 & \rho_2 \\ 1 & 0 \end{bmatrix}, \quad \underline{u}_t = \begin{bmatrix} \epsilon_t \\ 0 \end{bmatrix}.$$

Now rewrite the process in the *companion* form,

$$\underline{y}_t = \mathbf{A} \mathbf{y}_{t-1} + \underline{u}_t, \tag{2.48}$$

and let $\underline{e}_1 = (1,0)$ be a 2×1 row *selection vector*. Now $q_t = \underline{e}_1 \underline{y}_t$, $E_1(q_t) = \underline{e}_1 \mathbf{A}^t \underline{y}_1$, where $\mathbf{A}^2 = \mathbf{A}\mathbf{A}$, $\mathbf{A}^3 = \mathbf{A}\mathbf{A}\mathbf{A}$, and so forth. The half-life is the value t^* such that

$$\underline{e}_1 \mathbf{A}^{t^*} \mathbf{y}_1 = \tfrac{1}{2} \underline{e}_1 \underline{y}_1 = \tfrac{1}{2} \epsilon_1.$$

The extension to higher-ordered processes is straightforward.

The nonstationary case. If $\rho = 1$, q_t has the driftless random walk process[14]

$$q_t = q_{t-1} + \epsilon_t.$$

Setting $\rho = 1$ in (2.44) gives the analogous moving-average representation:

$$q_t = q_0 + \sum_{j=0}^{t-1} \epsilon_{t-j}.$$

The effect on q_t from an ϵ_{t-j} shock is 1, regardless of how far in the past it occurred. The ϵ_t shocks therefore exert a *permanent* effect on q_t.

The statistical theory developed for estimating ρ for stationary time-series doesn't work for unit-root processes, because we have terms such as $1 - \rho$ in denominators and the variance of q_t won't exist. To see why that is the case, initialize the process by setting $q_0 = 0$. Then $q_t = (\epsilon_t + \epsilon_{t-1} + \cdots + \epsilon_1) \sim N(0, t\sigma_\epsilon^2)$. You can see that the variance of q_t grows linearly with t. Now a typical term in the numerator of (2.45) is $\{q_t \epsilon_{t+1}\}$, which is an independent sequence with mean $E(q_t \epsilon_{t+1}) = E(q_t)E(\epsilon_{t+1}) = 0$, but the variance is $\mathrm{Var}(q_t \epsilon_{t+1}) = E(q_t^2)E(\epsilon_{t+1}^2) = t\sigma_\epsilon^4$, which goes to infinity over time. Since an infinite variance violates the regularity conditions of the usual central limit theorem, a different asymptotic distribution theory is required to deal with nonstationary data. Likewise, the denominator in (2.45) does not have a fixed mean. In fact, $E[(1/T) \sum q_t^2] = \sigma^2 \sum t = T/2$ doesn't converge to a finite number either.

The essential point is that the asymptotic distribution of the OLS estimator of ρ is different when $\{q_t\}$ has a unit root than when the observations are stationary, and the source of this difference is that the variance of the observations grows "too fast." It turns out that a different scaling factor is needed on the left-hand side of (2.45). In the stationary case, we scaled by $\sqrt{T}$, but in the unit-root case, we scale by T. It turns out that

$$T(\hat{\rho} - \rho) = \frac{1/T \sum_{t=1}^{T-1} q_t \epsilon_{t+1}}{1/T^2 \sum_{t=1}^{T-1} q_t^2} \tag{2.49}$$

converges asymptotically to a random variable with a well-behaved distribution, and we say that $\hat{\rho}$ converges at rate T; whereas in the stationary case we say that convergence takes place at rate $\sqrt{T}$. The distribution for $T(\hat{\rho} - \rho)$ is not normal, however; nor does it have a closed form, so that its computation must be done

---

14 When $\rho = 1$, we need to set $\alpha = 0$ to prevent q_t from trending. This will become clear when we see the Bhargava [12] formulation below.

by computer simulation. Similarly, the *Studentized coefficient* or the "*t*-statistic" for $\hat{\rho}$ reported by regression packages, $\tau = T\hat{\rho}(\sum_{t=1}^{T} q_t^2)/(\sum_{t=1}^{T} \epsilon_t^2)$, also behaves according to a well-behaved but nonnormal asymptotic distribution.[15]

● TEST PROCEDURES

The discussion above did not include a constant, but in practice one is almost always required, and sometimes it is a good idea also to include a time trend. Bhargava's [12] framework is useful for thinking about including constants and trends in the analysis. Let ξ_t be the deviation of q_t from a linear trend:

$$q_t = \gamma_0 + \gamma_1 t + \xi_t. \tag{2.50}$$

If $\gamma_1 \neq 0$, the question is whether the deviation from the trend is stationary or whether it is a driftless unit-root process. If $\gamma_1 = 0$ and $\gamma_0 \neq 0$, the question is whether the deviation of q_t from a constant is stationary. Let's ask the first question – whether the deviation from the trend is stationary. Let

$$\xi_t = \rho\xi_{t-1} + \epsilon_t, \tag{2.51}$$

where $0 < \rho \leq 1$ and $\epsilon_t \overset{iid}{\sim} N(0, \sigma_\epsilon^2)$. You want to test the null hypothesis $H_0 :$ $\rho = 1$ against the alternative $H_a : \rho < 1$. Under the null hypothesis,

$$\Delta q_t = \gamma_1 + \epsilon_t,$$

and q_t is a random walk with drift γ_1. Add the increments, to give

$$q_t = \sum_{j=1}^{t} \Delta q_j = \gamma_1 t + (\epsilon_0 + \epsilon_1 + \cdots + \epsilon_t) = \gamma_0 + \gamma_1 t + \xi_t, \tag{2.52}$$

where $\gamma_0 = \epsilon_0$ and $\xi_t = (\epsilon_1 + \epsilon_2 + \cdots + \epsilon_t)$. You can initialize by assuming $\epsilon_0 = 0$, which is the unconditional mean of ϵ_t. Now substitute (2.51) into (2.50). Use the fact that $\xi_{t-1} = q_{t-1} - \gamma_0 - \gamma_1(t-1)$ and subtract q_{t-1} from both sides to get

$$\Delta q_t = [(1-\rho)\gamma_0 + \rho\gamma_1] + (1-\rho)\gamma_1 t + (\rho - 1)q_{t-1} + \epsilon_t. \tag{2.53}$$

Equation (2.53) says that you should run the regression

$$\Delta q_t = \alpha_0 + \alpha_1 t + \beta q_{t-1} + \epsilon_t, \tag{2.54}$$

where $\alpha_0 = (1-\rho)\gamma_0 + \rho\gamma_1$, $\alpha_1 = (1-\rho)\gamma_1$, and $\beta = \rho - 1$. The null hypothesis, $\rho = 1$, can be tested by doing the joint test of the restriction $\beta = \alpha_1 = 0$. To test if the deviation from a constant is stationary, do a joint test of the restriction

---

[15] In fact, these distributions look like chi-square distributions, so the least-squares estimator is biased downward under the null that $\rho = 1$.

$\beta = \alpha_1 = \alpha_0 = 0$. If the random walk with drift is a reasonable null hypothesis, evidence of trending behavior will probably be obvious upon visual inspection. If this is the case, including a trend in the test equation would make sense.

In most empirical studies, researchers do the Dickey–Fuller test of the hypothesis $\beta = 0$ instead of the joint tests recommended by Bhargava. Nevertheless, the Bhargava formulation is useful for deciding whether to include a trend or just a constant. To complicate matters further, the asymptotic distributions of ρ and τ depend on whether a constant or a trend is included in the test equation, so a different set of critical values need to be computed for each specification of the test equation. Tables of critical values can be found in textbooks on time-series econometrics, such as Davidson and MacKinnon [34] or Hamilton [63].

PARAMETRIC ADJUSTMENTS FOR HIGHER-ORDERED SERIAL CORRELATION

You will need to make additional adjustments if ξ_t in (2.51) exhibits higher-order serial correlation. The augmented Dickey–Fuller test is a procedure that employs a parametric correction for such a time dependence. To illustrate, suppose that ξ_t follows the AR(2) process

$$\xi_t = \rho_1 \xi_{t-1} + \rho_2 \xi_{t-2} + \epsilon_t, \tag{2.55}$$

where $\epsilon_t \overset{iid}{\sim} N(0, \sigma_\epsilon^2)$. Then, by (2.50), $\xi_{t-1} = q_{t-1} - \gamma_0 - \gamma_1(t-1)$ and $\xi_{t-2} = q_{t-2} - \gamma_0 - \gamma_1(t-2)$. Substitute these expressions into (2.55) and then substitute this result into (2.50), to get $q_t = \alpha_0 + \alpha_1 t + \rho_1 q_{t-1} + \rho_2 q_{t-2} + \epsilon_t$, where $\alpha_0 = \gamma_0[1 - \rho_1 - \rho_2] + \gamma_1[\rho_1 + 2\rho_2]$ and $\alpha_1 = \gamma_1[1 - \rho_1 - \rho_2]$. Now subtract q_{t-1} from both sides of this result, add and subtract ρq_{t-1} to the right-hand side, and you end up with

$$\Delta q_t = \alpha_0 + \alpha_1 t + \beta q_{t-1} + \delta_1 \Delta q_{t-1} + \epsilon_t, \tag{2.56}$$

where $\beta = (\rho_1 + \rho_2 - 1)$ and $\delta_1 = -\rho_2$. (2.56) is called the augmented Dickey–Fuller (ADF) regression. Under the null hypothesis that q_t has a unit root, $\beta = 0$.

As before, a test of the unit-root null hypothesis can be conducted by estimating the regression (2.56) by OLS and comparing the Studentized coefficient, τ on β (the t-ratio reported by standard regression routines) to the appropriate table of critical values. The distribution of τ, while dependent on the specification of the deterministic factors, is fortunately invariant to the number of lagged dependent variables in the augmented Dickey–Fuller regression.[16]

---

[16] An alternative strategy for dealing with higher-order serial correlation is the Phillips and Perron [116] method. They suggest a test that employs a nonparametric correction of the OLS Studentized coefficient for $\hat{\beta}$, so that its asymptotic distribution is the same as that when there is no higher-ordered serial correlation. We will not cover their method.

PERMANENT-AND-TRANSITORY-COMPONENTS REPRESENTATION

It is often useful to model a unit-root process as the sum of different sub-processes. In section 2.2.7 we will model the time-series as being the sum of "trend" and "cyclical" components. Here, we will think of a unit-root process $\{q_t\}$ as the sum of a random walk $\{\xi_t\}$ and an orthogonal stationary process $\{z_t\}$:

$$q_t = \xi_t + z_t. \tag{2.57}$$

To fix ideas, let $\xi_t = \xi_{t-1} + \epsilon_t$ be a driftless random walk with $\epsilon_t \overset{iid}{\sim} N(0, \sigma_\epsilon^2)$ and let $z_t = \rho z_{t-1} + v_t$ be a stationary AR(1) process with $0 \leq \rho < 1$ and $v_t \overset{iid}{\sim} N(0, \sigma_v^2)$.[17] Because the effect of the ϵ_t shocks on q_t lasts for ever, the random walk $\{\xi_t\}$ is called the *permanent component*. The stationary AR(1) part of the process, $\{z_t\}$, is called the *transitory component*, because the effect of v_t shocks on z_t, and therefore on q_t, eventually dies out. This random walk–AR(1) model has an ARIMA(1,1,1) representation.[18] To deduce the ARIMA formulation, take first differences of (2.57), to get

$$
\begin{aligned}
\Delta q_t &= \epsilon_t + \Delta z_t \\
&= \epsilon_t + (\rho \Delta z_{t-1} + \Delta v_t) + (\rho \epsilon_{t-1} - \rho \epsilon_{t-1}) \\
&= \rho[\Delta z_{t-1} + \epsilon_{t-1}] + (\epsilon_t - \rho \epsilon_{t-1} + v_t - v_{t-1}) \\
&= \rho \Delta q_{t-1} + \underbrace{(\epsilon_t - \rho \epsilon_{t-1} + v_t - v_{t-1})}_{(a)},
\end{aligned}
\tag{2.58}
$$

where $\rho \Delta q_{t-1}$ is the autoregressive part. The term labeled (a) in the last line of (2.58) is the moving-average part. To see the connection, write this term out, as

$$\epsilon_t + v_t - (\rho \epsilon_{t-1} + v_{t-1}) = u_t + \theta u_{t-1}, \tag{2.59}$$

where u_t is an *iid* process with $E(u_t) = 0$ and $E(u_t^2) = \sigma_u^2$. Now you want to choose θ and σ_u^2 such that $u_t + \theta u_{t-1}$ is observationally equivalent to $\epsilon_t + v_t - (\rho \epsilon_{t-1} + v_{t-1})$, which you can do by matching corresponding moments. Let $\zeta_t = \epsilon_t + v_t - (\rho \epsilon_{t-1} + v_{t-1})$ and $\eta_t = u_t + \theta u_{t-1}$. Then, you have

$$E(\zeta_t^2) = \sigma_\epsilon^2 (1 + \rho^2) + 2\sigma_v^2,$$

$$E(\eta_t^2) = \sigma_u^2 (1 + \theta^2),$$

$$E(\zeta_t \zeta_{t-1}) = -(\sigma_v^2 + \rho \sigma_\epsilon^2),$$

$$E(\eta_t \eta_{t-1}) = \theta \sigma_u^2.$$

---

[17] Not all unit-root processes can be built up in this way. Beveridge and Nelson [11] show that any unit-root process can be decomposed into the sum of a permanent component and a transitory component, but the two components will in general be correlated.

[18] ARIMA(p, d, q) is shorthand for a pth-order autoregressive, qth-order moving-average process that is integrated of order d.

Set $E(\zeta_t^2) = E(\eta_t^2)$ and $E(\zeta_t\zeta_{t-1}) = E(\eta_t\eta_{t-1})$, to give

$$\sigma_u^2(1 + \theta^2) = \sigma_\epsilon^2(1 + \rho^2) + 2\sigma_v^2, \tag{2.60}$$

$$\theta\sigma_u^2 = -(\sigma_v^2 + \rho\sigma_\epsilon^2). \tag{2.61}$$

These are two equations in the unknowns σ_u^2 and θ, which can be solved. The equations are nonlinear in σ_u^2 and getting the exact solution is pretty messy. To sketch out what to do, first obtain $\theta^2 = [\sigma_v^2 + \rho\sigma_\epsilon^2]^2/(\sigma_u^2)^2$ from (2.61). Substitute it into (2.60) to get $x^2 + bx + c = 0$, where $x = \sigma_u^2$, $b = -[\sigma_\epsilon^2(1 + \rho^2) + 2\sigma_v^2]$, and $c = [\sigma_v^2 + \rho\sigma_\epsilon^2]^2$. The solution for σ_u^2 can then be obtained by the quadratic formula.

Variance Ratios

The variance ratio statistic at horizon k is the variance of the k-period change of a variable divided by k times the one-period change:

$$VR_k = \frac{\text{Var}(q_t - q_{t-k})}{k\text{Var}(\Delta q_t)} = \frac{\text{Var}(\Delta q_t + \cdots + \Delta q_{t-k+1})}{k\text{Var}(\Delta q_t)}. \tag{2.62}$$

The use of these statistics was popularized by Cochrane [28], who used them to conduct nonparametric tests of the unit-root hypothesis in GNP and to measure the relative size of the random walk component in a time-series.

Denote the kth autocovariance of the stationary time-series $\{x_t\}$ by $\gamma_k^x = \text{Cov}(x_t, x_{t-k})$. The denominator of (2.62) is $k\gamma_0^{\Delta q}$ and the numerator is $\text{Var}(q_t - q_{t-k+1}) = k[\gamma_0^{\Delta q} + \sum_{j=1}^{k-1}(1 - j/k)(\gamma_j^{\Delta q} + \gamma_{-j}^{\Delta q})]$, so the variance ratio statistic can be written as

$$VR_k = \frac{\gamma_0^{\Delta q} + \sum_{j=1}^{k-1}(1 - j/k)(\gamma_j^{\Delta q} + \gamma_{-j}^{\Delta q})}{\gamma_0^{\Delta q}}$$

$$= 1 + \frac{2\sum_{j=1}^{k-1}(1 - j/k)\gamma_j^{\Delta q}}{\gamma_0^{\Delta q}}$$

$$= 1 + 2\sum_{j=1}^{k-1}(1 - j/k)\rho_j^{\Delta q}, \tag{2.63}$$

where $\rho_j^{\Delta q} = \gamma_j^{\Delta q}/\gamma_0^{\Delta q}$ is the jth autocorrelation coefficient of Δq_t.

Measuring the size of the random walk. Suppose that q_t evolves according to the permanent–transitory components model of (2.57). If $\rho = 1$, the increments Δq_t are independent and the numerator of VR_k is $\text{Var}(q_t - q_{t-k}) = \text{Var}(\Delta q_t + \Delta q_{t-1} + \cdots \Delta q_{t-k+1}) = k\text{Var}(\Delta q_t)$, where $\text{Var}(\Delta q_t) = \sigma_\epsilon^2 + \sigma_v^2$. In the absence of transitory component dynamics, $VR_k = 1$ for all $k \geq 1$.

If $0 < \rho < 1$, $\{q_t\}$ is still a unit-root process, but its dynamics are driven in part by the transitory part, $\{z_t\}$. To evaluate VR_k, first note that $\gamma_0^z = \sigma_v^2/(1-\rho^2)$. The kth autocovariance of the transitory component is $\gamma_k^z = E(z_t z_{t-k}) = \rho^k \gamma_0^z$, $\gamma_0^{\Delta z} = E[\Delta z_t][\Delta z_t] = 2(1-\rho)\gamma_0^z$ and the kth autocovariance of Δz_t is

$$\gamma_k^{\Delta z} = E[\Delta z_t][\Delta z_{t-k}] = -(1-\rho)^2 \rho^{k-1} \gamma_0^z < 0. \tag{2.64}$$

By (2.64), Δz_t is negatively correlated with its past values and therefore exhibits *mean reverting* behavior, because a positive change today is expected to be reversed in the future. You also see that $\gamma_0^{\Delta q} = \sigma_\epsilon^2 + \gamma_0^{\Delta z}$ and, for $k > 1$,

$$\gamma_k^{\Delta q} = \gamma_k^{\Delta z} < 0. \tag{2.65}$$

By (2.65), the serial correlation in $\{\Delta q_t\}$ is seen to be determined by the dynamics in the transitory component $\{z_t\}$. Interactions between *changes* are referred to as the *short-run* dynamics of the process. Thus, working on (2.63), the variance ratio statistic for the random walk–AR(1) model can be written as

$$VR_k = 1 - \frac{2(1-\rho)^2 \gamma_0^z \sum_{j=1}^{k-1}\left(1 - j/k\right)\rho^{j-1}}{\gamma_0^{\Delta q}}$$

$$\rightarrow 1 - \frac{2(1-\rho)\gamma_0^z}{\gamma_0^{\Delta q}} \quad \text{as } k \rightarrow \infty$$

$$= 1 - \frac{\gamma_0^{\Delta z}}{\sigma_\epsilon^2 + \gamma_0^{\Delta z}}. \tag{2.66}$$

$1 - VR_\infty$ is the fraction of the short-run variance of Δq_t generated by changes in transitory component. VR_∞ is therefore increasing in the relative size of the random walk component $\sigma_\epsilon^2/\gamma_0^{\Delta z}$.

Near Observational Equivalence

Blough [15], Faust [48], and Cochrane [29] point out that, for a sample with fixed T, any unit-root process is observationally equivalent to a very persistent stationary process. As a result, the power of unit-root tests whose null hypothesis is that there is a unit root can be no larger than the size of the test.[19]

To see how the problem comes up, consider again the permanent–transitory representation of (2.57). Assume that $\sigma_\epsilon^2 = 0$ in (2.57), so that $\{q_t\}$ is truly an AR(1) process. Now, for any fixed sample size $T < \infty$, it would be possible to add to this AR(1) process a random walk with an infinitesimal σ_ϵ^2 which leaves the essential properties of $\{q_t\}$ unaltered, even though when we drive $T \rightarrow \infty$, the random walk will dominate the behavior of q_t. The practical implication is

---

[19] Power is the probability of rejecting the null when it is false. The size of a test is the probability of rejecting the null when it is true.

that it may be difficult or even impossible to distinguish between a persistent but stationary process and a unit-root process with *any* finite sample. So, even though the AR(1) plus the very small random walk process is in fact a unit-root process, σ_ϵ^2 can always be chosen sufficiently small – regardless of how large we make T, so long as it is finite – that its behavior is observationally equivalent to a stationary AR(1) process.

Turning the argument around, suppose that we begin with a true unit-root process but the random walk component, σ_ϵ^2, is infinitesimally small. For any finite T, this process can be arbitrarily well approximated by an AR(1) process with a judicious choice of ρ and σ_u^2.

2.5 PANEL UNIT-ROOT TESTS

Univariate/single-equation econometric methods for testing unit roots can have low power and can give imprecise point estimates when working with small sample sizes. Consider the popular Dickey–Fuller test for a unit root in a time-series $\{q_t\}$ and assume that the time-series is generated by

$$\Delta q_t = \alpha_0 + \alpha_1 t + (\rho - 1)q_{t-1} + \epsilon_t, \qquad (2.67)$$

where $\epsilon_t \overset{iid}{\sim} N(0, \sigma^2)$. If $\rho = 1$ and $\alpha_1 = \alpha_0 = 0$, q_t follows a driftless unit-root process. If $\rho = 1, \alpha_1 = 0$, and $\alpha_0 \neq 0$, q_t follows a unit-root process with drift. If $|\rho| < 1$, y_t is stationary. It is mean reverting if $\alpha_1 = 0$, and is stationary around a trend if $\alpha_1 \neq 0$.

To do the Dickey–Fuller test for a unit root in q_t, run the regression (2.67) and compare the Studentized coefficient for the slope to the Dickey–Fuller distribution critical values. Table 2.1 shows the power of the Dickey–Fuller test when the truth is $\rho = 0.96$. With 100 observations, the test with 5 percent size rejects the unit root only 9.6 percent of the time when the truth is a mean reverting process.

One hundred quarterly observations is about what is available for exchange rate studies over the post Bretton Woods floating period, so low power is a potential pitfall in unit-root tests for international economists. But again, from table 2.1, if you have 1,000 observations, you are almost guaranteed to reject the unit root when the truth is that q_t is stationary with $\rho = 0.96$. How do you get 1,000 observations without having to wait 250 years? How about combining the 100 time-series observations from ten roughly similar countries?[20] This is the motivation for recently proposed panel unit-root tests by Levin and Lin [89], Im, Pesaran and Shin [76], and Maddala and Wu [97]. We begin with the popular Levin–Lin test.

---

[20] It turns out that the 1,000 cross-section–time-series observations contain less information than 1,000 observations from a single time-series. In the time-series, $\hat\rho$ converges at rate T, but in the panel, $\hat\rho$ converges at rate $T\sqrt{N}$, where N is the number of cross-section units, so in terms of convergence toward the asymptotic distribution, it's better to get more time-series observations.

Table 2.1 The finite sample power of the Dickey–Fuller test, $\rho = 0.96$

	T	5 percent	10 percent
Test equation includes constant	25	5.885	11.895
	50	6.330	12.975
	75	7.300	14.460
	100	9.570	18.715
	1,000	99.995	100.000
Test equation includes trend	25	5.715	10.720
	50	5.420	10.455
	75	5.690	11.405
	100	7.650	14.665
	1,000	99.960	100.000

The table reports the percentage of rejections at a 5 percent or a 10 percent critical value when the alternative hypothesis is true with $\rho = 0.96$. 20,000 replications. Critical values are from Hamilton [63], Table B.6.

THE LEVIN–LIN TEST

Let $\{q_{it}\}$ be a balanced panel[21] of N time-series with T observations, which are generated by

$$\Delta q_{it} = \delta_i t + \beta_i q_{it-1} + u_{it}, \tag{2.68}$$

where $-2 < \beta_i \leq 0$, and u_{it} has the error-components representation

$$u_{it} = \alpha_i + \theta_t + \epsilon_{it}. \tag{2.69}$$

α_i is an individual–specific effect, θ_t is a single-factor common time effect, and ϵ_{it} is a stationary but possibly serially correlated idiosyncratic effect that is independent across individuals. For each individual i, ϵ_{it} has the Wold moving-average representation

$$\epsilon_{it} = \sum_{j=0}^{\infty} \theta_{ij}\epsilon_{it-j} + u_{it}. \tag{2.70}$$

q_{it} is a unit-root process if $\beta_i = 0$ and $\delta_i = 0$. If there is no drift in the unit-root process, then $\alpha_i = 0$. The common time effect θ_t is a crude model of cross-sectional dependence.

Levin–Lin propose to test the null hypothesis that all individuals have a unit root,

$$H_0: \beta_1 = \cdots = \beta_N = \beta = 0,$$

against the alternative hypothesis that all individuals are stationary,

$$H_a: \beta_1 = \cdots = \beta_N = \beta < 0.$$

---

[21] A panel is balanced if every individual has the same number of observations T.

The test imposes the homogeneity restrictions that β_i are identical across individuals under both the null and the alternative hypotheses.

The test proceeds as follows. First, you need to decide if you want to control for the common time effect θ_t. If you do, you subtract off the cross-sectional mean and the basic unit of analysis is

$$\tilde{q}_{it} = q_{it} - \frac{1}{N} \sum_{j=1}^{N} q_{jt}. \tag{2.71}$$

Potential pitfalls of including a common-time effect. However, doing so involves a potential pitfall. θ_t, as part of the error-components model, is assumed to be *iid*. The problem is that there is no way to impose independence. Specifically, if it is the case that each q_{it} is driven in part by a *common* unit-root factor, θ_t is a unit-root process. Then $\tilde{q}_{it} = q_{it} - (1/N) \sum_{j=1}^{N} q_{jt}$ will be stationary. The transformation renders all the deviations from the cross-sectional mean stationary. This might cause you to reject the unit-root hypothesis when it is true. Subtracting off the cross-sectional average is not necessarily a fatal flaw in the procedure, however, because you are subtracting off only one potential unit root from each of the N time-series. It is possible that the N individuals are driven by N distinct and independent unit roots. The adjustment will cause all originally nonstationary observations to be stationary only if all N individuals are driven by the *same* unit root. An alternative strategy for modeling cross-sectional dependence is to do a bootstrap, which is discussed below. For now, we will proceed with the transformed observations. The resulting test equations are

$$\Delta \tilde{q}_{it} = \alpha_i + \delta_i t + \beta_i \tilde{q}_{it-1} + \sum_{j=1}^{k_i} \phi_{ij} \Delta \tilde{q}_{it-j} + \epsilon_{it}. \tag{2.72}$$

The slope coefficient on $\tilde{q}_{it-1}$ is constrained to be equal across individuals, but no such homogeneity is imposed on the coefficients on the lagged differences, nor on the number of lags k_i. To allow for this specification in estimation, regress $\Delta \tilde{q}_{it}$ and $\tilde{q}_{it-1}$ on a constant (and possibly a trend) and k_i lags of $\Delta \tilde{q}_{it}$:[22]

$$\Delta \tilde{q}_{it} = a_i + b_i t + \sum_{j=1}^{k_i} c_{ij} \Delta \tilde{q}_{it-j} + \hat{e}_{it}, \tag{2.73}$$

$$\tilde{q}_{it-1} = a_i' + b_i' t + \sum_{j=1}^{k_i} c_{ij}' \Delta \tilde{q}_{it-j} + \hat{v}_{it}, \tag{2.74}$$

---

[22] To choose k_i, one option is to use AIC or BIC. Another option is to use Hall's [66] general-to-specific method, recommended by Campbell and Perron [18]. Start with some maximal lag order l and estimate the regression. If the absolute value of the t-ratio for $\hat{c}_{il}$ is less than some appropriate critical value, c^*, reset k_i to $l-1$ and repeat the process until the t-ratio of the estimated coefficient with the longest lag exceeds the critical value c^*.

where $\hat{e}_{it}$ and $\hat{v}_{it}$ are OLS residuals. Now run the regression

$$\hat{e}_{it} = \delta_i \hat{v}_{it-1} + \hat{u}_{it}, \tag{2.75}$$

set $\hat{\sigma}_{ei}^2 = [1/(T - k_i - 1)] \sum_{t=k_i+2}^{T} \hat{u}_{it}^2$, and form the normalized observations

$$\tilde{e}_{it} = \frac{\hat{e}_{it}}{\hat{\sigma}_{ei}}, \quad \tilde{v}_{it} = \frac{\hat{v}_{it}}{\hat{\sigma}_{ei}}. \tag{2.76}$$

Denote the long-run variance of Δq_{it} by $\sigma_{qi}^2 = \gamma_0^i + 2 \sum_{j=0}^{\infty} \gamma_j^i$, where $\gamma_0^i = \mathrm{E}(\Delta q_{it}^2)$ and $\gamma_j^i = \mathrm{E}(\Delta q_{it} \Delta q_{it-j})$. Let $\bar{k} = (1/N) \sum_{i=1}^{N} k_i$ and estimate σ_{qi}^2 by Newey and West [109]:

$$\hat{\sigma}_{qi}^2 = \hat{\gamma}_0^i + 2 \sum_{j=1}^{\bar{k}} \left(1 - \frac{j}{\bar{k}+1}\right) \hat{\gamma}_j^i, \tag{2.77}$$

where $\hat{\gamma}_j^i = [1/(T-1)] \sum_{t=2+j}^{T} \Delta \tilde{q}_{it} \Delta \tilde{q}_{it-j}$. Let $s_i = \hat{\sigma}_{qi}/\hat{\sigma}_{ei}$, $S_N = (1/N) \sum_{i=1}^{N} s_i$, and run the pooled cross-section time-series regression

$$\tilde{e}_{it} = \beta \tilde{v}_{it-1} + \tilde{\epsilon}_{it}. \tag{2.78}$$

The *Studentized coefficient* is $\tau = \hat{\beta} \sum_{i=1}^{N} \sum_{t=1}^{T} \tilde{v}_{it-1}/\hat{\sigma}_{\tilde{\epsilon}}$, where $\hat{\sigma}_{\tilde{\epsilon}} = (1/NT) \sum_{i=1}^{N} \sum_{t=1}^{T} \tilde{\epsilon}_{it}$. As in the univariate case, τ is not asymptotically standard normally distributed. In fact, τ diverges as the number of observations NT gets large, but Levin and Lin show that the adjusted statistic

$$\tau^* = \frac{\tau - N\tilde{T}S_N \tau \mu_{\tilde{T}}^* \hat{\sigma}_\epsilon^{-2} \hat{\beta}^{-1}}{\sigma_{\tilde{T}}^*} \xrightarrow{D} \mathrm{N}(0, 1), \tag{2.79}$$

as $\tilde{T} \to \infty, N \to \infty$, where $\tilde{T} = T - \bar{k} - 1$, and $\mu_{\tilde{T}}^*$ and $\sigma_{\tilde{T}}^*$ are adjustment factors, reproduced from Levin and Lin's paper in table 2.2.

The performance of Levin and Lin's adjustment factors in a controlled environment.
Suppose that the data-generating process (the truth) is that each individual is the unit-root process

$$\Delta q_{it} = \alpha_i + \sum_{j=1}^{2} \phi_{ij} \Delta q_{it-j} + \epsilon_{it}, \tag{2.80}$$

where $\epsilon_{it} \overset{iid}{\sim} \mathrm{N}(0, \sigma_i)$, and each of the σ_i is drawn from a uniform distribution over the range 0.1–1.1. That is, $\sigma_i \sim U[0.1, 1.1]$. Also, $\phi_{ij} \sim U[-0.3, 0.3]$, and $\alpha_i \sim \mathrm{N}(0, 1)$ if a drift is included (otherwise, $\alpha = 0$).[23] Table 2.3 shows the Monte Carlo distribution of Levin and Lin's τ and τ^* generated from this process. Here

---

[23]   Instead of arbitrarily choosing values of these parameters for each of the individual units, I let the computer pick out some numbers at random.

Table 2.2 Mean and standard deviation adjustments for the Levin–Lin τ statistic, reproduced from Levin and Lin [89]

$\tilde{T}$	$\overline{K}$	τ^*_{NC}		τ^*_{C}		τ^*_{CT}	
		$\mu^*_{\tilde{T}}$	$\sigma^*_{\tilde{T}}$	$\mu^*_{\tilde{T}}$	$\sigma^*_{\tilde{T}}$	$\mu^*_{\tilde{T}}$	$\sigma^*_{\tilde{T}}$
25	9	0.004	1.049	−0.554	0.919	−0.703	1.003
30	10	0.003	1.035	−0.546	0.889	−0.674	0.949
35	11	0.002	1.027	−0.541	0.867	−0.653	0.906
40	11	0.002	1.021	−0.537	0.850	−0.637	0.871
45	11	0.001	1.017	−0.533	0.837	−0.624	0.842
50	12	0.001	1.014	−0.531	0.826	−0.614	0.818
60	13	0.001	1.011	−0.527	0.810	−0.598	0.780
70	13	0.000	1.008	−0.524	0.798	−0.587	0.751
80	14	0.000	1.007	−0.521	0.789	−0.578	0.728
90	14	0.000	1.006	−0.520	0.782	−0.571	0.710
100	15	0.000	1.005	−0.518	0.776	−0.566	0.695
250	20	0.000	1.001	−0.509	0.742	−0.533	0.603
∞	−	0.000	1.000	−0.500	0.707	−0.500	0.500

Table 2.3 How well do Levin–Lin adjustments work? Percentiles from a Monte Carlo experiment

Statistic	N	T	Trend	2.5%	5%	50%	95%	97.5%
τ	20	100	No	−7.282	−6.995	−5.474	−3.862	−3.543
	20	500	No	−7.202	−6.924	−5.405	−3.869	−3.560
τ^*	20	100	No	−2.029	−1.732	−0.092	1.613	1.965
	20	500	No	−1.879	−1.557	0.012	1.595	1.894
τ	20	100	Yes	−10.337	−10.038	−8.642	−7.160	−6.896
	20	500	Yes	−10.126	−9.864	−8.480	−7.030	−6.752
τ^*	20	100	Yes	−1.171	−0.825	0.906	2.997	3.503
	20	500	Yes	−1.028	−0.746	0.702	2.236	2.571

are some things to note from the table. First, the median value of τ is very far from zero. It would get bigger (in absolute value) if we let N get bigger. Second, τ^* looks like a standard normal variate when there is no drift in the data-generating process (DGP) (and no trend in the test equation). Third, the Monte Carlo distribution for τ^* looks quite different from the asymptotic distribution when there is drift in the DGP and a trend is included in the test equation. This is what we call finite sample size distortion of the test. When there is known size distortion, you might want to control for it by doing a bootstrap, which is covered below.

Another option is to try to correct for the size distortion. The question here is: If you correct for size distortion, does the Levin–Lin test have good power? That is, will it reject the null hypothesis when it is false with high probability?

Table 2.4 The size-adjusted power of the Levin–Lin test with $T = 100$ and $N = 20$

	Constant		Trend	
Proportion stationary[a]	5%	10%	5%	10%
0.2	0.141	0.275	0.124	0.218
0.4	0.329	0.439	0.272	0.397
0.6	0.678	0.761	0.577	0.687
0.8	0.942	0.967	0.906	0.944
1.0	1.000	1.000	1.000	1.000

[a]The proportion of individuals in the panel that are stationary.
Stationary components have a root equal to 0.96.
Source: Choi [25]

The answer suggested in table 2.4 is yes. It should be noted that even though the Levin–Lin test is motivated in terms of a homogeneous panel, it has moderate ability to reject the null when the truth is a mixed panel in which some of the individuals are unit-root process and others are stationary.

Bias Adjustment

The OLS estimator $\hat{\rho}$ is biased downward in small samples. Kendall [83] showed that the bias of the least-squares estimator is $E(\hat{\rho}) - \rho \simeq -(1 + 3\rho)/T$. A bias-adjusted estimate of ρ is

$$\hat{\rho}^* = \frac{T\hat{\rho} + 1}{T - 3}. \tag{2.81}$$

The panel estimator of the serial correlation coefficient is also biased downward in small samples. A first-order bias adjustment of the panel estimate of ρ can be done using a result by Nickell [111], who showed that

$$(\hat{\rho} - \rho) \rightarrow \frac{A_T B_T}{C_T}, \tag{2.82}$$

as $T \rightarrow \infty, N \rightarrow \infty$, where

$$A_T = \frac{-(1 + \rho)}{T - 1}, \qquad B_T = 1 - \frac{1}{T}\frac{(1 - \rho^T)}{(1 - \rho)}, \qquad \text{and} \qquad C_T = 1 - \frac{2\rho(1 - B_T)}{[(1 - \rho)(T - 1)]}.$$

Bootstrapping τ^*

The fact that τ diverges can be distressing. Rather than relying on the asymptotic adjustment factors, that may not work well in some regions of the parameter space, researchers often choose to test the unit-root hypothesis using a bootstrap distribution of τ.[24] Furthermore, the bootstrap provides an alternative way to model cross-sectional dependence in the error terms, as discussed above. The method discussed here is called the *residual* bootstrap, because we will be resampling from the residuals.

To build a bootstrap distribution under the null hypothesis that all individuals follow a unit-root process, begin with the DGP:

$$\Delta q_{it} = \mu_i + \sum_{j=1}^{k_i} \phi_{ij} \Delta q_{i,t-j} + \epsilon_{it}. \tag{2.83}$$

Since each q_{it} is a unit-root process, its first difference follows an autoregression. While you may prefer to specify the DGP as an unrestricted vector autoregression for all N individuals, the estimation for such a system turns out not to be feasible for even moderately sized N.

The individual equations of the DGP can be fitted by least squares. If a linear trend is included in the test equation, a constant must be included in (2.83). To account for dependence across cross-sectional units, estimate the joint error covariance matrix $\Sigma = E(\underline{\epsilon}_t \underline{\epsilon}_t')$ by $\hat{\Sigma} = (1/T) \sum_{t=1}^{T} \underline{\hat{\epsilon}}_t \underline{\hat{\epsilon}}_t'$, where $\underline{\hat{\epsilon}}_t = (\hat{\epsilon}_{1t}, \dots, \hat{\epsilon}_{Nt})$ is the vector of OLS residuals.

The parametric bootstrap distribution for τ is built as follows:

1. Draw a sequence of length $T + R$ innovation vectors from $\underline{\tilde{\epsilon}}_t \sim N(0, \hat{\Sigma})$.
2. Recursively build up pseudo–observations $\{\hat{q}_{it}\}, i = 1, \dots, N, t = 1, \dots, T + R$, according to (2.83) with the $\underline{\tilde{\epsilon}}_t$ and estimated values of the coefficients $\hat{\mu}_i$ and $\hat{\phi}_{ij}$.
3. Drop the first R pseudo-observations, then run the Levin–Lin test on the pseudo-data. *Do not* transform the data by subtracting off the cross-sectional mean and do not make the τ^* adjustments. This yields a realization of τ generated in the presence of cross-sectional dependent errors.
4. Repeat a large number (2,000 or 5,000) of times and the collection of τ and $\bar{t}$ statistics form the bootstrap distribution of these statistics under the null hypothesis.

This is called a parametric bootstrap, because the error terms are drawn from the parametric normal distribution. An alternative is to do a nonparametric bootstrap. Here, you resample the estimated residuals, which are, in a sense, the data. To do a nonparametric bootstrap, do the following. Estimate (2.83) using the data. Denote the OLS residuals by

$$(\hat{\epsilon}_{11}, \hat{\epsilon}_{21}, \dots, \hat{\epsilon}_{N1}) \quad \leftarrow \text{obs. 1}$$
$$(\hat{\epsilon}_{12}, \hat{\epsilon}_{22}, \dots, \hat{\epsilon}_{N2}) \quad \leftarrow \text{obs. 2}$$
$$\vdots \qquad\qquad \vdots$$
$$(\hat{\epsilon}_{1T}, \hat{\epsilon}_{2T}, \dots, \hat{\epsilon}_{NT}) \quad \leftarrow \text{obs.} T$$

---

[24] For example, Wu [127] and Papell [113].

Now resample the residual *vectors* with replacement. For each observation $t = 1, \ldots, T$, draw one of the T possible residual vectors with probability $1/T$. Because the entire vector is being resampled, the cross-sectional correlation observed in the data is preserved. Let the resampled vectors be

$$
\begin{aligned}
(\epsilon_{11}^*, \epsilon_{21}^*, \ldots, \epsilon_{N1}^*) &\quad \leftarrow \text{obs. 1} \\
(\epsilon_{12}^*, \epsilon_{22}^*, \ldots, \epsilon_{N2}^*) &\quad \leftarrow \text{obs. 2} \\
\vdots &\qquad \vdots \\
(\epsilon_{1T}^*, \epsilon_{2T}^*, \ldots, \epsilon_{NT}^*) &\quad \leftarrow \text{obs.} T,
\end{aligned}
$$

use these resampled residuals to build up values of Δq_{it} recursively using (2.83) with $\hat{\mu}_i$ and $\hat{\phi}_{ij}$, and run the Levin–Lin test on these observations but do not subtract off the cross-sectional mean, and do not make the τ^* adjustments. This gives a realization of τ. Now repeat a large number of times to get the nonparametric bootstrap distribution of τ.

● THE IM, PESARAN, AND SHIN TEST

Im, Pesaran, and Shin (IPS [76]) suggest a very simple panel unit-root test. They begin with the ADF representation (2.72) for individual i (reproduced here for convenience):

$$
\Delta \tilde{q}_{it} = \alpha_i + \delta_i t + \beta_i \tilde{q}_{it-1} + \sum_{j=1}^{k_i} \phi_{ij} \Delta \tilde{q}_{it-j} + \epsilon_{it}, \tag{2.84}
$$

where $E(\epsilon_{it}\epsilon_{js}) = 0, i \neq j$, for all t, s. A common time effect may be removed, in which case $\tilde{q}_{it} = q_{it} - (1/N) \sum_{j=1}^{N} q_{jt}$ is the deviation from the cross-sectional average as the basic unit of analysis.

Let τ_i be the Studentized coefficient from the ith ADF regression. Since the ϵ_{it} are assumed to be independent across individuals, the τ_i are also independent and, by the central limit theorem, $\bar{\tau}_{NT} = (1/N) \sum_{i=1}^{N} \tau_i$ converges to the standard normal distribution first as $T \to \infty$ and then as $N \to \infty$. That is,

$$
\frac{\sqrt{N}[\bar{\tau}_{NT} - E(\tau_{it}|\beta_i = 0)]}{\sqrt{\text{Var}(\tau_{it}|\beta = 0)}} \xrightarrow{D} N(0, 1), \tag{2.85}
$$

as $T \to \infty, N \to \infty$. IPS report selected critical values for $\bar{\tau}_{NT}$ with the conditional mean and variance adjustments of the distribution. A selected set of these critical values is reproduced in table 2.5. An alternative to relying on the asymptotic distribution is to do a residual bootstrap of the $\bar{\tau}_{NT}$ statistic. As before, when doing the bootstrap, do not subtract off the cross-sectional mean.

The Im, Pesaran, and Shin test as well as the Maddala–Wu test (discussed below) relax the homogeneity restrictions under the alternative hypothesis.

Table 2.5 Selected exact critical values for the IPS $\bar{t}_{NT}$ statistic

		Constant			Trend		
T		20	40	100	20	40	100
A. 5 percent							
N	5	−2.19	−2.16	−2.15	−2.82	−2.77	−2.75
	10	−1.99	−1.98	−1.97	−2.63	−2.60	−2.58
N	15	−1.91	−1.90	−1.89	−2.55	−2.52	−2.51
	20	−1.86	−1.85	−1.84	−2.49	−2.48	−2.46
	25	−1.82	−1.81	−1.81	−2.46	−2.44	−2.43
B. 10 percent							
N	5	−2.04	−2.02	−2.01	−2.67	−2.63	−2.62
	10	−1.89	−1.88	−1.88	−2.52	−2.50	−2.49
N	15	−1.82	−1.81	−1.81	−2.46	−2.44	−2.44
	20	−1.78	−1.78	−1.77	−2.42	−2.41	−2.40
	25	−1.75	−1.75	−1.75	−2.39	−2.38	−2.38

Source: Im, Pesaran, and Shin [76]

Here, the null hypothesis,

$$H_0: \beta_1 = \cdots = \beta_N = \beta = 0,$$

is tested against the alternative,

$$H_a: \beta_1 < 0 \cup \beta_2 < 0 \cdots \cup \beta_N < 0.$$

The alternative hypothesis is *not* H_0, which is less restrictive than the Levin–Lin alternative hypothesis.

 ## THE MADDALA AND WU TEST

Maddala and Wu [97] point out that the IPS strategy of combining independent tests to construct a joint test is an idea suggested by R. A. Fisher [51]. Maddala and Wu follow Fisher's suggestion and propose the following test. Let the *p*-value of τ_i from the augmented Dickey–Fuller test for a unit root be $p_i = \text{Prob}(\tau < \tau_i) = \int_{-\infty}^{\tau_i} f(x)\,dx$, where $f(\tau)$ is the probability density function of τ. Solve for $g(p)$, the density of p_i, by the method of transformations, $g(p_i) = f(\tau_i)|J|$, where $J = d\tau_i/dp_i$ is the Jacobian of the transformation and $|J|$ is its absolute value. Since $dp_i/d\tau_i = f(\tau_i)$, the Jacobian is $1/f(\tau_i)$ and $g(p_i) = 1$ for $0 \le p_i \le 1$. That is, p_i is uniformly distributed on the interval $[0, 1]$ ($p_i \sim U[0, 1]$).

Next, let $y_i = -2 \ln(p_i)$. Again, using the method of transformations, the probability density function of y_i is $h(y_i) = g(p_i)|dp_i/dy_i|$. But $g(p_i) = 1$ and

$|dp_i/dy_i| = p_i/2 = (1/2)e^{-y_i/2}$, so it follows that $h(y_i) = (1/2)e^{-y_i/2}$, which is the chi-square distribution with two degrees of freedom. Under cross-sectional independence of the error terms ϵ_{it}, the joint test statistic also has a chi-square distribution:

$$\lambda = -2 \sum_{i=1}^{N} \ln(p_i) \sim \chi^2_{2N}. \tag{2.86}$$

The asymptotic distribution of the IPS test statistic was established by sequential $T \to \infty, N \to \infty$ asymptotics, which some econometricians view as being too restrictive.[25] Levin and Lin derive the asymptotic distribution of their test statistic by allowing both N and T simultaneously to go to infinity. A remarkable feature of the Maddala–Wu–Fisher test is that it avoids issues of sequential or joint N, T asymptotics. Equation (2.86) gives the exact distribution of the test statistic.

The IPS test is based on the sum of τ_i, whereas the Maddala–Wu test is based on the sum of the log p-values of τ_i. Asymptotically, the two tests should be equivalent, but can differ in finite samples. Another advantage of Maddala–Wu is that the test statistic distribution does not depend on nuisance parameters, as does IPS and LL. The disadvantage is that p-values need to be calculated numerically.

⬤ POTENTIAL PITFALLS OF PANEL UNIT-ROOT TESTS

Panel unit-root tests need to be applied with care. One potential pitfall with panel tests is that the rejection of the null hypothesis does not mean that all series are stationary. It is possible that out of N time-series, only one is stationary and $(N-1)$ are unit-root processes. This is an example of a mixed panel. Whether or not we want the rejection of the unit-root process to be driven by a single outlier depends on the purpose for which the researcher uses the test.[26]

A second potential pitfall is that cross-sectional independence is a regularity condition for these tests. Transforming the observations by subtracting off the cross-sectional means will leave some residual dependence across individuals if common time effects are generated by a multi-factor process. This residual cross-sectional dependence can potentially generate errors in inference.

A third pitfall concerns the potential small sample size distortion of the tests. While most of the attention has been aimed at improving the power of unit-root tests, Schwert [119] shows that there are regions of the parameter space under which the size of the augmented Dickey–Fuller test is wrong in small samples.

---

[25]   That is, they deduce the limiting behavior of the test statistic first by letting $T \to \infty$, holding N fixed, then letting $N \to \infty$ and invoking the central limit theorem.

[26]   Bowman [16] shows that both the LL and IPS tests have low power against outlier driven alternatives. He proposes a test that has maximal power. Taylor and Sarno [124] propose a test based on Johansen's [78] maximum likelihood approach that can test for the number of unit-root series in the panel. Computational considerations, however, generally limit the number of time-series that can be analyzed to five or less.

Since the panel tests are based on the augmented Dickey–Fuller test in some way or another, it is probably the case that this size distortion will get impounded into the panel test. To the extent that size distortion is an issue, however, it is not a problem that is specific to the panel tests.

2.6 COINTEGRATION

The unit-root processes $\{q_t\}$ and $\{f_t\}$ will be *cointegrated* if there exists a linear combination of the two time-series that is stationary. To understand the implications of cointegration, let's first look at what happens when the observations are not cointegrated.

No cointegration.   Let $\xi_{qt} = \xi_{qt-1} + u_{qt}$ and $\xi_{ft} = \xi_{ft-1} + u_{ft}$ be two independent random walk processes, where $u_{qt} \overset{iid}{\sim} N(0, \sigma_q^2)$ and $u_{ft} \overset{iid}{\sim} N(0, \sigma_f^2)$. Let $\underline{z}_t = (z_{qt}, z_{ft})'$ follow a stationary bivariate process such as a VAR. The exact process for $\underline{z}_t$ doesn't need to be explicitly modeled at this point. Now consider the two unit-root series built up from these components:

$$q_t = \xi_{qt} + z_{qt},$$
$$f_t = \xi_{ft} + z_{ft}. \tag{2.87}$$

Since q_t and f_t are driven by *independent* random walks, they will drift arbitrarily far apart from each other over time. If you try to find a value of β to form a stationary linear combination of q_t and f_t, you will fail, because

$$q_t - \beta f_t = (\xi_{qt} - \beta \xi_{ft}) + (z_{qt} - \beta z_{ft}). \tag{2.88}$$

For any value of β, $\xi_{qt} - \beta \xi_{ft} = (\tilde{u}_1 + \tilde{u}_2 + \cdots + \tilde{u}_t)$, where $\tilde{u}_t \equiv u_{qt} - \beta u_{ft}$, so the linear combination is itself a random walk. q_t and f_t clearly do not share a long-run relationship. There may, however, be short-run interactions between their first differences:

$$\begin{pmatrix} \Delta q_t \\ \Delta f_t \end{pmatrix} = \begin{pmatrix} \Delta z_{qt} \\ \Delta z_{ft} \end{pmatrix} + \begin{pmatrix} \epsilon_{qt} \\ \epsilon_{ft} \end{pmatrix}. \tag{2.89}$$

By analogy with the derivation of (2.58), if $\underline{z}_t$ follows a first-order VAR, you can show that (2.89) follows a vector ARMA process. Thus, when both $\{q_t\}$ and $\{f_t\}$ are unit-root processes but are driven by independent random walks, they can be first differenced to induce stationarity and then their first differences modeled as a stationary vector process.

Cointegration. $\{q_t\}$ and $\{f_t\}$ will be cointegrated if they are driven by the *same* random walk, $\xi_t = \xi_{t-1} + \epsilon_t$, where $\epsilon_t \overset{iid}{\sim} N(0, \sigma^2)$. For example, if

$$q_t = \xi_t + z_{qt},$$
$$f_t = \phi(\xi_t + z_{ft}), \tag{2.90}$$

and you look for a value of β that renders

$$q_t - \beta f_t = (1 - \beta\phi)\xi_t + z_{qt} - \beta\phi z_{ft} \qquad (2.91)$$

stationary, you will succeed by choosing $\beta = 1/\phi$ since $q_t - f_t/\phi = z_{qt} - z_{ft}$ is the difference between two stationary processes, so it will itself be stationary. $\{q_t\}$ and $\{f_t\}$ share a long-run relationship. We say that they are cointegrated, with cointegrating vector $(1, -1/\phi)$. Since random walks are sometimes referred to as stochastic trend processes, when two series are cointegrated we sometimes say that they share a common trend.[27]

● THE VECTOR ERROR-CORRECTION REPRESENTATION

Recall that, for the univariate AR(2) process, you can rewrite $q_t = \rho_1 q_{t-1} + \rho_2 q_{t-2} + u_t$ in augmented Dickey–Fuller test equation form as

$$\Delta q_t = (\rho_1 + \rho_2 - 1)q_{t-1} - \rho_2 \Delta q_{t-1} + u_t, \qquad (2.92)$$

where $u_t \overset{iid}{\sim} N(0, \sigma_u^2)$. If q_t is a unit-root process, then $(\rho_1 + \rho_2 - 1) = 0$, and $(\rho_1 + \rho_2 - 1)^{-1}$ clearly doesn't exist. There is, in a sense, a singularity in q_{t-1}, because Δq_t is stationary and this can be true only if q_{t-1} drops out from the right-hand side of (2.92).

By analogy, suppose that in the bivariate case the vector (q_t, f_t) is generated according to

$$\begin{bmatrix} q_t \\ f_t \end{bmatrix} = \begin{bmatrix} a_{11} & a_{12} \\ a_{21} & a_{22} \end{bmatrix} \begin{bmatrix} q_{t-1} \\ f_{t-1} \end{bmatrix} + \begin{bmatrix} b_{11} & b_{12} \\ b_{21} & b_{22} \end{bmatrix} \begin{bmatrix} q_{t-2} \\ f_{t-2} \end{bmatrix} + \begin{bmatrix} u_{qt} \\ u_{ft} \end{bmatrix}, \qquad (2.93)$$

where $(u_{qt}, u_{ft})' \overset{iid}{\sim} N(0, \boldsymbol{\Sigma}_u)$. Rewrite (2.93) as the vector analog of the augmented Dickey–Fuller test equation,

$$\begin{bmatrix} \Delta q_t \\ \Delta f_t \end{bmatrix} = \begin{bmatrix} r_{11} & r_{12} \\ r_{21} & r_{22} \end{bmatrix} \begin{bmatrix} q_{t-1} \\ f_{t-1} \end{bmatrix} - \begin{bmatrix} b_{11} & b_{12} \\ b_{21} & b_{22} \end{bmatrix} \begin{bmatrix} \Delta q_{t-1} \\ \Delta f_{t-1} \end{bmatrix} + \begin{bmatrix} u_{qt} \\ u_{ft} \end{bmatrix},$$

$$\qquad (2.94)$$

where

$$\begin{bmatrix} r_{11} & r_{12} \\ r_{21} & r_{22} \end{bmatrix} = \begin{bmatrix} a_{11} + b_{11} - 1 & a_{12} + b_{12} \\ a_{21} + b_{21} & a_{22} + b_{22} - 1 \end{bmatrix} \equiv \mathbf{R}.$$

If $\{q_t\}$ and $\{f_t\}$ are unit-root processes, their first differences are stationary. This means that the terms on the right-hand side of (2.94) are stationary. Linear combinations of levels of the variables appear in the system. $r_{11}q_{t-1} + r_{12}f_{t-1}$ appears in the equation for Δq_t and $r_{21}q_{t-1} + r_{22}f_{t-1}$ appears in the equation for Δf_t.

---

[27] Suppose that you are analyzing three variables (q_{1t}, q_{2t}, q_{3t}). If they are cointegrated, there can be at most two independent random walks driving the series. If there are two random walks, there can be only one cointegrating vector. If there is only one random walk, there can be as many as two cointegrating vectors.

If $\{q_t\}$ and $\{f_t\}$ do not cointegrate, there are no values of the r_{ij} coefficients that can be found to form stationary linear combinations of q_t and f_t. The level terms must drop out. $\mathbf{R}$ is the null matrix, and $(\Delta q_t, \Delta f_t)$ follows a vector autoregression.

If $\{q_t\}$ and $\{f_t\}$ *do* cointegrate, then there is a unique combination of the two variables that is stationary. The levels enter on the right-hand side, but do so in the same combination in both equations. This means that the columns of $\mathbf{R}$ are linearly dependent and the $\mathbf{R}$, which is singular, can be written as

$$\mathbf{R} = \begin{bmatrix} r_{11} & -\beta r_{11} \\ r_{21} & -\beta r_{21} \end{bmatrix}.$$

Equation (2.94) can now be written as

$$\begin{bmatrix} \Delta q_t \\ \Delta f_t \end{bmatrix} = \begin{bmatrix} r_{11} \\ r_{21} \end{bmatrix} (q_{t-1} - \beta f_{t-1}) - \begin{bmatrix} b_{11} & b_{12} \\ b_{21} & b_{22} \end{bmatrix} \begin{bmatrix} \Delta q_{t-1} \\ \Delta f_{t-1} \end{bmatrix} + \begin{bmatrix} u_{qt} \\ u_{ft} \end{bmatrix}$$

$$= \begin{bmatrix} r_{11} \\ r_{21} \end{bmatrix} z_{t-1} - \begin{bmatrix} b_{11} & b_{12} \\ b_{21} & b_{22} \end{bmatrix} \begin{bmatrix} \Delta q_{t-1} \\ \Delta f_{t-1} \end{bmatrix} + \begin{bmatrix} u_{qt} \\ u_{ft} \end{bmatrix}, \qquad (2.95)$$

where $z_{t-1} \equiv q_{t-1} - \beta f_{t-1}$ is called the *error-correction term*, and (2.95) is the *vector error-correction representation* (VECM). A VAR in first differences would be misspecified, because it omits the error-correction term.

To express the dynamics governing z_t, multiply the equation for Δf_t by β and subtract the result from the equation for Δq_t, to give

$$z_t = (1 + r_{11} - \beta r_{21})z_{t-1} - (b_{11} - \beta b_{21})\Delta q_{t-1}$$
$$- (b_{12} + \beta b_{22})\Delta f_{t-1} + u_{qt} - \beta u_{ft}. \qquad (2.96)$$

The entire system is then given by

$$\begin{bmatrix} \Delta q_t \\ \Delta f_t \\ z_t \end{bmatrix} = \begin{bmatrix} b_{11} & b_{12} & r_{11} \\ b_{21} & b_{22} & r_{12} \\ -(b_{11} + \beta b_{21}) & -(b_{12} + \beta b_{22}) & 1 + r_{11} - \beta r_{21} \end{bmatrix} \begin{bmatrix} \Delta q_{t-1} \\ \Delta f_{t-1} \\ z_{t-1} \end{bmatrix}$$
$$+ \begin{bmatrix} u_{qt} \\ u_{ft} \\ u_{qt} - \beta u_{ft} \end{bmatrix}. \qquad (2.97)$$

$(\Delta q_t, \Delta f_t, z_t)'$ is a stationary vector, and (2.97) looks like a VAR(1) in these three variables, except that the columns of the coefficient matrix are linearly dependent. In many applications, the cointegration vector $(1, -\beta)$ is given *a priori* by economic theory and does not need to be estimated. In these situations, the linear dependence of the VAR (2.97) tells you that all of the information contained in the VECM is preserved in a bivariate VAR formed with z_t and *either* Δq_t or Δf_t.

Suppose that you follow this strategy. To obtain the VAR for $(\Delta q_t, z_t)$, substitute $f_{t-1} = (q_{t-1} - z_{t-1})/\beta$ into the equation for Δq_t, to get

$$\Delta q_t = b_{11}\Delta q_{t-1} + b_{12}\Delta f_{t-1} + r_{11}z_{t-1} + u_{qt}$$
$$= a_{11}\Delta q_{t-1} + a_{12}z_{t-1} + a_{13}z_{t-2} + u_{qt},$$

where $a_{11} = b_{11} + b_{12}/\beta$, $a_{12} = r_{11} - b_{12}/\beta$, and $a_{13} = b_{12}/\beta$. Similarly, substitute f_{t-1} out of the equation for z_t, to give

$$z_t = a_{21} \Delta q_{t-1} + a_{22} z_{t-1} + a_{23} z_{t-2} + (u_{qt} - \beta u_{ft}),$$

where $a_{21} = -(b_{11} + \beta b_{21} + b_{12}/\beta + b_{22})$, $a_{22} = 1 + r_{11} - \beta r_{21} + b_{22} + b_{12}/\beta$, and $a_{23} = -(b_{22} + b_{12}/\beta)$. Together, you have the VAR(2)

$$\begin{bmatrix} \Delta q_t \\ z_t \end{bmatrix} = \begin{bmatrix} a_{11} & a_{12} \\ a_{21} & a_{22} \end{bmatrix} \begin{bmatrix} \Delta q_{t-1} \\ z_{t-1} \end{bmatrix} + \begin{bmatrix} 0 & a_{13} \\ 0 & a_{23} \end{bmatrix} \begin{bmatrix} \Delta q_{t-2} \\ z_{t-2} \end{bmatrix}$$
$$+ \begin{bmatrix} u_{qt} \\ u_{qt} - \beta u_{ft} \end{bmatrix}. \tag{2.98}$$

Equation (2.98) is easier to estimate than the VECM and the standard forecasting formulae for VARs can be employed without modification.

2.7 FILTERING

Many international macroeconomic time-series contain a trend. The trend may be deterministic or stochastic (i.e., a unit-root process). Real business cycle (RBC) theories are designed to study the cyclical features of the data, not the trends. So, in RBC research, the data that is being studied is usually passed through a linear filter to remove the low-frequency or trend component of the data. To understand what filtering does to the data, you need to have some understanding of the *frequency* or *spectral* representation of time-series, where we think of the observations as being built up from individual sub-processes that exhibit cycles over different frequencies.

Linear filters take a possibly two-sided moving average of an original set of observations q_t to create a new series $\tilde{q}_t$:

$$\tilde{q}_t = \sum_{j=-\infty}^{\infty} a_j q_{t-j}, \tag{2.99}$$

where the weights are summable, $\sum_{j=-\infty}^{\infty} |a_j| < \infty$. One way to assess how the filter transforms the properties of the original data is to see which frequency components from the original data are allowed to pass through and how these frequency components are weighted. That is, are the particular frequency components that are allowed through relatively more or less important than they were in the original data?

THE SPECTRAL REPRESENTATION OF A TIME-SERIES

In section 2.4.4, a unit-root time-series was decomposed into the sum of a random walk and a stationary AR(1) component. Here, we want to think of

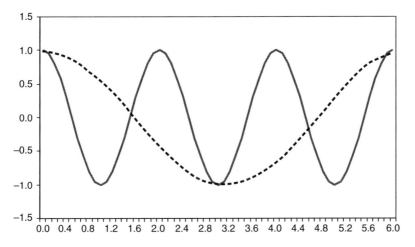

Figure 2.1 Deterministic cycles: $q_{1t} = \cos(t)$ (dashed line) cycles every $2\pi = 6.28$ years and $q_{2t} = \cos(\pi t)$ (solid line) cycles every 2 years.

the time-series observations as being built up of underlying cyclical (cosine) functions, each with different amplitudes and exhibiting cycles of different frequencies. A key question in spectral analysis is: Which of these frequency components are relatively important in determining the behavior of the observed time-series?

To fix ideas, begin with the deterministic time-series, $q_t = a\cos(\omega t)$, where time is measured in years. This function exhibits a cycle every $t = 2\pi/\omega$ years. By choosing values of ω between 0 and π, you can get the process to exhibit cycles at any length that you desire. This is illustrated in figure 2.1, where $q_{1t} = a\cos(t)$ exhibits a cycle every $2\pi = 6.28$ years and $q_{2t} = a\cos(\pi t)$ displays a cycle every 2 years.

Something is clearly missing at this point – it is randomness. We introduce uncertainty with a random *phase shift*. If you compare $q_{1t} = a\cos(t)$ to $q_{3t} = a\cos(t + \pi/2)$, q_{3t} is just q_{1t} with a phase shift (horizontal movement) of $\pi/2$. This phase shift is illustrated in figure 2.2. Now let $\tilde{\lambda} \sim U[0, \pi]$.[28] Imagine that we take a draw from this distribution. Let the realization be λ, and form the time-series

$$q_t = a\cos(\omega t + \lambda). \tag{2.100}$$

Once λ is realized, q_t is a deterministic function with periodicity $2\pi/\omega$ and phase shift λ, but q_t is a random function *ex ante*. We will need the following two basic trigonometric relations.

[28] You only need to worry about the interval $[0, \pi]$, because the cosine function is symmetric about zero: $\cos(x) = \cos(-x)$ for $0 \leq x \leq \pi$.

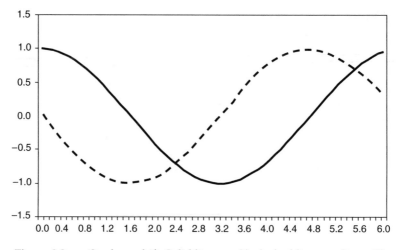

Figure 2.2 $\pi/2$ sphase shift. Solid line, $\cos(t)$; dashed line, $\cos(t + \pi/2)$.

Two useful trigonometric relations.   Let b and c be constants, and let i be the imaginary number, where $i^2 = -1$. Then

$$\cos(b + c) = \cos(b)\cos(c) - \sin(b)\sin(c), \qquad (2.101)$$

$$e^{ib} = \cos(b) + i\sin(b). \qquad (2.102)$$

Equation (2.102) is known as de Moivre's theorem. You can rearrange it to give

$$\cos(b) = \frac{(e^{ib} + e^{-ib})}{2} \quad \text{and} \quad \sin(b) = \frac{(e^{ib} - e^{-ib})}{2i}. \qquad (2.103)$$

Now let $b = \omega t$ and $c = \lambda$, and use (2.101) to represent (2.100) as

$$\begin{aligned} q_t &= a\cos(\omega t + \lambda) \\ &= \cos(\omega t)[a\cos(\lambda)] - \sin(\omega t)[a\sin(\lambda)]. \end{aligned}$$

Next, build the time-series $q_t = q_{1t} + q_{2t}$ from the two sub-series q_{1t} and q_{2t}, where, for $j = 1, 2$,

$$q_{jt} = \cos(\omega_j t)[a_j \cos(\lambda_j)] - \sin(\omega_j t)[a_j \sin(\lambda_j)].$$

and $\omega_1 < \omega_2$. The result is a periodic function which is displayed on the left-hand side of figure 2.3.

The composite process with $N = 2$ is clearly deterministic, but if you build up the analogous series with $N = 100$ of these components, as shown in figure 2.3(b), the series begins to look like a random process. It turns out that any stationary random process can be arbitrarily well approximated in this fashion, letting $N \to \infty$.

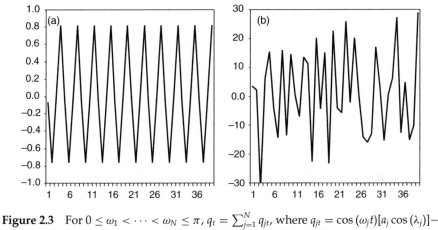

Figure 2.3 For $0 \leq \omega_1 < \cdots < \omega_N \leq \pi$, $q_t = \sum_{j=1}^{N} q_{jt}$, where $q_{jt} = \cos(\omega_j t)[a_j \cos(\lambda_j)] - \sin(\omega_j t)[a_j \sin(\lambda_j)]$. (a) $N = 2$; (b) $N = 1{,}000$.

To summarize at this point, for a sufficiently large number N of these underlying periodic components, we can represent a time-series q_t as

$$q_t = \sum_{j=1}^{N} \cos(\omega_j t) u_j - \sin(\omega_j t) v_j, \tag{2.104}$$

where $u_j = a_j \cos(\lambda_j)$ and $v_j = a_j \sin(\lambda_j)$, $E(u_i^2) = \sigma_i^2$, $E(u_i u_j) = 0$, $i \neq j$, $E(v_i^2) = \sigma_i^2$, and $E(v_i v_j) = 0$, $i \neq j$.

Now suppose that $E(u_i v_j) = 0$ for all i, j and let $N \to \infty$.[29] You are carving the interval into successively more subintervals and you are cramming more ω_j into the interval $[0, \pi]$. Since each u_j and v_j is associated with an ω_j, in the limit, write $u(\omega)$ and $v(\omega)$ as functions of ω. For future reference, notice that because $\cos(-a) = \cos(a)$, you have $u(-\omega) = u(\omega)$, whereas because $\sin(-a) = -\sin(a)$, you have $v(-\omega) = -v(\omega)$. The limit of sums of the areas in these intervals is the integral

$$q_t = \int_0^{\pi} \cos(\omega t)\, du(\omega) - \sin(\omega t)\, dv(\omega). \tag{2.105}$$

Using (2.103), (2.105) can be represented as

$$q_t = \int_0^{\pi} \frac{e^{i\omega t} + e^{-i\omega t}}{2}\, du(\omega) - \underbrace{\int_0^{\pi} \frac{e^{i\omega t} - e^{-i\omega t}}{2i}\, dv(\omega)}_{(a)}. \tag{2.106}$$

---

[29] In fact, this is not true because $E(u_i v_i) \neq 0$, but as we let $N \to \infty$, the importance of these terms becomes negligible.

Let $dz(\omega) = \frac{1}{2}[du(\omega) + idv(\omega)]$. The second integral labeled (a) can be simplified as

$$\int_0^\pi \frac{e^{i\omega t} - e^{-i\omega t}}{2i} dv(\omega) = \int_0^\pi \frac{e^{i\omega t} - e^{-i\omega t}}{2i} \left(\frac{2 dz(\omega) - du(\omega)}{i} \right)$$

$$= \int_0^\pi \frac{e^{-i\omega t} - e^{i\omega t}}{2} (2 dz(\omega) - du(\omega))$$

$$= \int_0^\pi (e^{-i\omega t} - e^{i\omega t}) dz(\omega) + \int_0^\pi \frac{e^{i\omega t} - e^{-i\omega t}}{2} du(\omega).$$

Substitute this last result back into (2.106) and cancel terms, to give

$$q_t = \underbrace{\int_0^\pi e^{-i\omega t} du(\omega)}_{(a)} + \underbrace{\int_0^\pi e^{i\omega t} dz(\omega)}_{(b)} - \underbrace{\int_0^\pi e^{-i\omega t} dz(\omega)}_{(c)}. \qquad (2.107)$$

Since $u(-\omega) = u(\omega)$, the term labeled (a) in (2.107) can be written as $\int_0^\pi e^{-i\omega t} du(\omega) = \int_{-\pi}^0 e^{i\omega t} du(\omega)$. The term labeled (c) in (2.107) is $\int_0^\pi e^{-i\omega t} dz(\omega)$ $= \frac{1}{2} \int_0^\pi e^{-i\omega t} du(\omega) + \frac{1}{2} \int_0^\pi ie^{-i\omega t} dv(\omega) = \frac{1}{2} \int_{-\pi}^0 e^{i\omega t} du(\omega) - \frac{1}{2} \int_{-\pi}^0 ie^{i\omega t} dv(\omega)$. Substituting these results back into (2.107) and canceling terms, you get $q_t =$ $\frac{1}{2} \int_{-\pi}^0 e^{i\omega t}[du(\omega) + idv(\omega)] + \int_0^\pi e^{i\omega t} dz(\omega) = \int_{-\pi}^\pi e^{i\omega t} dz(\omega)$. This is known as the *Cramer representation* of q_t, which we restate as

$$q_t = \lim_{N \to \infty} \sum_{j=1}^N a_j \cos(\omega_j t + \lambda_j) = \int_{-\pi}^\pi e^{i\omega t} dz(\omega). \qquad (2.108)$$

The point of all this is that any time-series can be thought of as being built up from a set of underlying sub-processes whose individual frequency components exhibit cycles of varying frequency. The other side of this argument is that you can, in principle, take any time-series q_t and figure out what fraction of its variance is generated from those sub-processes that cycle within a given frequency range. The business cycle frequency, which lies between 6 and 32 quarters, is of key interest to, of all people, business cycle researchers.

Notice that the process $dz(\omega)$ is built up from independent increments. For coincident increments, you can define the function $s(\omega) d\omega$ to be

$$E[dz(\omega) \overline{dz(\lambda)}] = \begin{cases} s(\omega) d\omega & \lambda = \omega, \\ 0 & \text{otherwise}, \end{cases} \qquad (2.109)$$

where an overbar denotes the complex conjugate.[30] Since $e^{i\omega t}\overline{e^{i\omega t}} = \cos^2(\omega t) + \sin^2(\omega t) = 1$ at frequency ω, it follows that $E[e^{i\omega t}\overline{e^{i\omega t}} dz(\omega) \overline{dz(\omega)}] = s(\omega) d\omega$.

---

[30]   If a and b are real numbers and $z = a + bi$ is a complex number, the complex conjugate of z is $\bar{z} = a - bi$. The product $z\bar{z} = a^2 + b^2$ is real.

That is, $s(\omega)\,d\omega$ is the variance of the ω-frequency component of q_t, and is called the *spectral density function* of q_t. Since, by (2.108), q_t is built up from frequency components in the range $[-\pi,\pi]$, the total variance of q_t must be the integral of $s(\omega)$. That is,[31]

$$
\begin{aligned}
E(q_t^2) &= E\left[\int_{-\pi}^{\pi} e^{i\omega t}\,dz(\omega) \int_{-\pi}^{\pi} e^{i\lambda t}\,dz(\lambda)\right] \\
&= E\left[\int_{-\pi}^{\pi}\int_{-\pi}^{\pi} e^{i\omega t}\overline{e^{i\lambda t}}\,dz(\omega)\,\overline{dz(\lambda)}\right] \\
&= \int_{-\pi}^{\pi} E[dz(\omega)\,\overline{dz(\omega)}] \\
&= \int_{-\pi}^{\pi} s(\omega)\,d\omega.
\end{aligned}
\tag{2.110}
$$

The spectral density and autocovariance generating functions. The autocovariance generating function for a time-series q_t is defined to be

$$
g(z) = \sum_{j=-\infty}^{\infty} \gamma_j z^j,
$$

where $\gamma_j = E(q_t q_{t-j})$ is the jth autocovariance of q_t. If we let $z = e^{-i\omega}$, then

$$
\frac{1}{2\pi}\int_{-\pi}^{\pi} g(e^{-i\omega})e^{i\omega k}\,d\omega = \frac{1}{2\pi}\sum_{j=-\infty}^{\infty}\gamma_j \int_{-\pi}^{\pi} e^{i\omega(k-j)}\,d\omega.
$$

Let $a = k - j$. Then $e^{i\omega a} = \cos(\omega a) + i\sin(\omega a)$ and the integral becomes $\int_{-\pi}^{\pi}\cos(\omega a)\,d\omega + i\int_{-\pi}^{\pi}\sin(\omega a)\,d\omega = (1/a)\sin(a\omega)|_{-\pi}^{\pi} - (i/a)\cos(a\omega)|_{-\pi}^{\pi}$. The second term is zero, because $\cos(-a\pi) = \cos(a\pi)$. The first term is zero too, because the sine of any nonzero integer multiple of π is zero and a is an integer. Therefore, the only value of a that matters is $a = k - j = 0$, which implies that $\gamma_k = (1/2\pi)\int_{-\pi}^{\pi} g(e^{-i\omega})e^{i\omega k}\,d\omega$. Setting $k = 0$, you have $\gamma_0 = \text{Var}(q_t) = (1/2\pi)\int_{-\pi}^{\pi} g(e^{i\omega})\,d\omega$, but you know that $\text{Var}(q_t) = \int_{-\pi}^{\pi} s(\omega)\,d\omega$, so the spectral density function is proportional to the autocovariance generating function with $z = e^{-i\omega}$. Notice also that when you set $\omega = 0$, then $s(0) = \sum_{j=-\infty}^{\infty}\gamma_j$. The spectral density function of q_t at frequency zero is the same thing as the long-run variance of q_t. It follows that

$$
\text{Var}(q_t) = \int_{-\pi}^{\pi} s(\omega)\,d\omega = \frac{1}{2\pi}\int_{-\pi}^{\pi} g(e^{-i\omega})\,d\omega,
\tag{2.111}
$$

where $g(z) = \sum_{j=-\infty}^{\infty}\gamma_j z^j$.

---

[31] We obtain the last equality because $dz(\omega)$ is a process with independent increments, so unless $\lambda = \omega$, $E\,dz(\omega)\,dz(\lambda) = 0$.

 **LINEAR FILTERS**

You can see how a filter changes the character of a time-series by comparing the spectral density function of the original observations with that of the filtered data.

Let the original data q_t have the Wold moving-average representation $q_t = b(L)\epsilon_t$, where $b(L) = \sum_{j=0}^{\infty} b_j L^j$ and $\epsilon_t \sim iid$, with $E(\epsilon_t) = 0$ and $Var(\epsilon_t) = \sigma_{\epsilon}^2$. The kth autocovariance is

$$\gamma_k = E(q_t q_{t-k}) = E[b(L)\epsilon_t b(L)\epsilon_{t-k}]$$

$$= E\left(\sum_{j=0}^{\infty} b_j \epsilon_{t-j} \sum_{s=0}^{\infty} b_s \epsilon_{t-s-k}\right) = \sigma_{\epsilon}^2 \left(\sum_{j=0}^{\infty} b_j b_{j-k}\right),$$

and the autocovariance generating function for q_t is

$$g(z) = \sum_{k=-\infty}^{\infty} \gamma_k z^k = \sum_{k=-\infty}^{\infty} \sigma_{\epsilon}^2 \left(\sum_{j=0}^{\infty} b_j b_{j-k}\right) z^k$$

$$= \sum_{k=-\infty}^{\infty} \left(\sigma_{\epsilon}^2 \sum_{j=0}^{\infty} b_j b_{j-k}\right) z^k z^j z^{-j} = \sigma_{\epsilon}^2 \sum_{k=-\infty}^{\infty} \sum_{j=0}^{\infty} b_j z^j b_{j-k} z^{-(j-k)}$$

$$= \sigma_{\epsilon}^2 \left(\sum_{j=0}^{\infty} b_j z^j \sum_{k=j}^{\infty} b_{j-k} z^{-(j-k)}\right) = \sigma_{\epsilon}^2 b(z) b(z^{-1}).$$

But, from (2.111), you know that $s(\omega) = g(e^{i\omega})/2\pi$. To summarize these results, the *spectral density* of q_t can be represented as

$$s(\omega) = \frac{1}{2\pi} g(e^{-i\omega}) = \frac{1}{2\pi} \sigma_{\epsilon}^2 b(e^{-i\omega}) b(e^{i\omega}). \tag{2.112}$$

Let the transformed (filtered) data be given by $\tilde{q}_t = a(L)q_t$, where $a(L) = \sum_{j=-\infty}^{\infty} a_j L^j$. Then $\tilde{q}_t = a(L)q_t = a(L)b(L)\epsilon_t = \tilde{b}(L)\epsilon_t$, where $\tilde{b}(L) = a(L)b(L)$. Clearly, the autocovariance generating function of the filtered data is $\tilde{g}(z) = \sigma_{\epsilon}^2 \tilde{b}(z)\tilde{b}(z^{-1})$ $= \sigma_{\epsilon}^2 a(z)b(z)b(z^{-1})a(z^{-1}) = a(z)a(z^{-1})g(z)$ and, letting $z = e^{-i\omega}$, the spectral density function of the filtered data is

$$\tilde{s}(\omega) = a(e^{-i\omega})a(e^{i\omega})s(\omega). \tag{2.113}$$

The filter has the effect of scaling the spectral density of the original observations by $a(e^{-i\omega})a(e^{i\omega})$. Depending on the properties of the filter, some frequencies will be magnified while others are downweighted.

One way to classify filters is according to the frequencies that are allowed to pass through and those that are blocked. A high-pass filter lets through only the high-frequency components. A low-pass filter allows through the trend or growth frequencies. A business cycle pass filter allows through frequencies ranging from 6 to 32 quarters. The most popular filter used in RBC research is the Hodrick–Prescott filter, which we discuss next.

● THE HODRICK–PRESCOTT FILTER

Hodrick and Prescott [74] assume that the original series q_t is generated by the sum of a trend component (τ_t) and a cyclical (c_t) component, $q_t = \tau_t + c_t$. The trend is a slow-moving low-frequency component and is in general *not* deterministic. The objective is to construct a filter to get rid of τ_t from the data. This leaves c_t, which is the part of the data to be studied. The problem is that, for each observation q_t, there are two unknowns (τ_t and c_t). The question is how to identify the separate components.

The cyclical part is just the deviation of the original series from the long-run trend, $c_t = q_t - \tau_t$. Suppose that your identification scheme is to minimize the variance of the cyclical part. You would end up setting its variance to zero, which means setting $\tau_t = q_t$. This doesn't help at all – the trend is just as volatile as the original observations. It therefore makes sense to attach a penalty for making τ_t too volatile. Do this by minimizing the variance of c_t subject to a given amount of prespecified "smoothness" in τ_t. Since $\Delta \tau_t$ is like the first derivative of the trend and $\Delta^2 \tau_t$ is like the second derivative of the trend, one way to get a smoothly evolving trend is to force the first derivative of the trend to evolve smoothly over time by limiting the size of the second derivative. This is what Hodrick and Prescott suggest. Choose a sequence of points $\{\tau_t\}$ to minimize

$$\sum_{t=1}^{T} (q_t - \tau_t)^2 + \lambda \sum_{t=1}^{T-1} (\Delta^2 \tau_{t+1})^2, \tag{2.114}$$

where λ is the penalty attached to the volatility of the trend component. For quarterly data, researchers typically set $\lambda = 1,600$.[32] Noting that $\Delta^2 \tau_{t+1} = \tau_{t+1} - 2\tau_t + \tau_{t-1}$, differentiate (2.114) with respect to τ_t and rearrange the first-order

---

[32] The following derivation of the filter follows Pederson [115].

conditions to give the Euler equations

$$q_1 - \tau_1 = \lambda[\tau_3 - 2\tau_2 + \tau_1],$$

$$q_2 - \tau_2 = \lambda[\tau_4 - 4\tau_3 + 5\tau_2 - 2\tau_1],$$

$$\vdots \qquad \vdots$$

$$q_t - \tau_t = \lambda[\tau_{t+2} - 4\tau_{t+1} + 6\tau_t - 4\tau_{t-1} + \tau_{t-2}], \quad t = 3, \ldots, T-2,$$

$$\vdots \qquad \vdots$$

$$q_{T-1} - \tau_{T-1} = \lambda[-2\tau_T + 5\tau_{T-1} - 4\tau_{T-2} + \tau_{T-3}],$$

$$q_T - \tau_T = \lambda[\tau_T - 2\tau_{T-1} + \tau_{T-2}].$$

Let $\underline{c} = (c_1, \ldots, c_T)'$, $\underline{q} = (q_1, \ldots, q_T)'$, and $\underline{\tau} = (\tau_1, \ldots, \tau_T)'$, and write the Euler equations in matrix form:

$$\underline{q} = (\lambda \mathbf{G} + \mathbf{I}_T)\underline{\tau}, \tag{2.115}$$

where the $T \times T$ matrix $\mathbf{G}$ is given by

$$\mathbf{G} = \begin{bmatrix}
1 & -2 & 1 & 0 & \cdots & & & & & \cdots & 0 \\
-2 & 5 & -4 & 1 & 0 & \cdots & & & & \cdots & 0 \\
1 & -4 & 6 & -4 & 1 & 0 & \cdots & & & \cdots & 0 \\
0 & 1 & -4 & 6 & -4 & 1 & 0 & & & & \\
\vdots & & \ddots & & & & & \ddots & & & \vdots \\
0 & & & & & & 0 & 1 & -4 & 6 & -4 & 1 & 0 \\
& & & & & & & 0 & 1 & -4 & 6 & -4 & 1 \\
& & & & & & & & 0 & 1 & -4 & 5 & -2 \\
0 & \cdots & & & & & & & \cdots & 0 & 1 & -2 & 1
\end{bmatrix}.$$

Get the trend component from $\underline{\tau} = (\lambda\mathbf{G} + \mathbf{I}_T)^{-1}\underline{q}$. The cyclical component follows by subtracting the trend from the original observations:

$$\underline{c} = \underline{q} - \underline{\tau} = [\mathbf{I}_T - (\lambda\mathbf{G} + \mathbf{I}_T)^{-1}]\underline{q}.$$

The properties of the Hodrick–Prescott Filter

For $t = 3, \ldots, T-2$, the Euler equations can be written $q_t - \tau_t = \lambda u(L)\tau_t$, where $u(L) = (1-L)^2(1-L^{-1})^2 = \sum_{j=-2}^{2} u_j L^j$, with $u_{-2} = u_2 = 1$, $u_{-1} = u_1 = -4$, and $u_0 = 6$. We note for future reference that $c_t = q_t - \tau_t$ implies that $c_t = \lambda u(L)\tau_t$.

You've already determined that $q_t = (\lambda u(L) + 1)\tau_t = v(L)\tau_t$, where $v(L) = 1 + \lambda u(L) = 1 + \lambda(1-L)^2(1-L^{-1})^2$, so it follows that

$$\tau_t = v(L)^{-1}q_t = \frac{q_t}{1 + \lambda(1-L)^2(1-L^{-1})^2}.$$

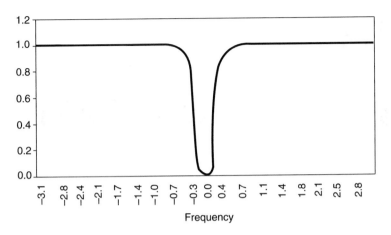

Figure 2.4 The scale factor $|\delta(\omega)|^2$ for the cyclical component in the Hodrick–Prescott filter.

$v^{-1}(L)$ is the trend filter. Once you have computed τ_t, subtract the result from the data, q_t, to get c_t. This is equivalent to forming $c_t = \delta(L)q_t$, where

$$\delta(L) = 1 - v^{-1}(L) = \frac{\lambda(1 - L)^2(1 - L^{-1})^2}{1 + \lambda(1 - L)^2(1 - L^{-1})^2}.$$

Since $(1 - L)^2(1 - L^{-1}) = L^{-2}(1 - L)^4$, the filter is equivalent to first applying $(1 - L)^4$ on q_t, and then applying $\lambda L^{-2}v^{-1}(L)$ on the result.[33] This means that the Hodrick–Prescott filter can induce stationary into the cyclical component from a process that is $I(4)$.

The spectral density function of the cyclical component is $s_c(\omega) = \delta(e^{-i\omega})\delta(e^{i\omega})s_q(\omega)$, where

$$\delta(e^{-i\omega}) = \frac{\lambda[(1 - e^{-i\omega})(1 - e^{i\omega})]^2}{\lambda[(1 - e^{-i\omega})(1 - e^{i\omega})]^2 + 1}.$$

From our trigonometric identities, $(1 - e^{-i\omega})(1 - e^{i\omega}) = 2(1 - \cos(\omega))$, it follows that

$$\delta(\omega) = \frac{4\lambda[1 - \cos(\omega)]^2}{4\lambda[1 - \cos(\omega)]^2 + 1}. \tag{2.116}$$

Each frequency of the original series is therefore scaled by

$$|\delta(\omega)|^2 = \left[\frac{4\lambda(1 - \cos(\omega))^2}{4\lambda(1 - \cos(\omega))^2 + 1}\right]^2. \tag{2.117}$$

This scaling factor is plotted in figure 2.4.

---

[33] This is shown in King and Rebelo [82].

3

The Monetary Model

The monetary model is central to international macroeconomic analysis and is a recurrent theme in this book. The model identifies a set of underlying economic fundamentals that determine the nominal exchange rate in the long run. The monetary model was originally developed as a framework to analyze balance-of-payments adjustments under fixed exchange rates. After the breakdown of the Bretton Woods system, the model was modified into a theory of nominal exchange rate determination.

The monetary approach assumes that all prices are perfectly flexible and centers on conditions for stock equilibrium in the money market. Although it is an *ad hoc* model, we will see in chapters 4 and 9 that many predictions of the monetary model are implied by optimizing models both in flexible-price and in sticky-price environments. The monetary model also forms the basis for work on target zones (chapter 10) and in the analysis of balance-of-payments crises (chapter 11).

A Note on Notation. Throughout this chapter, the level of a variable will be denoted in upper case letters and the natural logarithm in lower case. The only exception to this rule is that the level of the interest rate is always denoted in lower case. Thus i_t is the nominal interest rate and in logs, s_t is the nominal exchange rate in American terms, p_t is the price level, and y_t is real income. Stars are used to denote foreign-country variables.

3.1 PURCHASING-POWER PARITY

A key building block of the monetary model is purchasing-power parity (PPP), which can be motivated according to the Casselian approach or by the commodity-arbitrage view.

CASSEL'S APPROACH

The intellectual origins of PPP began in the early 1800s, with the writings of Wheatly and Ricardo. These ideas were subsequently revived by Cassel [21]. The Casselian approach begins with the observation that the exchange rate S is the relative price of two currencies. Since the purchasing power of the home currency is $1/P$ and the purchasing power of the foreign currency is $1/P^*$, in equilibrium, the relative value of the two currencies should reflect their relative purchasing powers, $S = P/P^*$.

What is the appropriate definition of the price level? The Casselian view suggests using the general price level. Whether or not the general price level samples prices of nontradable goods is irrelevant. As a result, the consumer price index (CPI) is typically used in empirical implementations of this theory. The following passage from Cassel is used by Frenkel [58] to motivate the use of the CPI in PPP research:

> "Some people believe that Purchasing Power Parities should be calculated exclusively on price indices for such commodities as for the subject of trade between the two countries. This is a misinterpretation of the theory ... The whole theory of purchasing power parity essentially refers to the internal value of the currencies concerned, and variations in this value can be measured only by general index figures representing as far as possible the whole mass of commodities marketed in the country."

The theory implies that the log real exchange rate, $q \equiv s + p^* - p$, is constant over time. However, even casual observation rejects this prediction. Figure 3.1 displays foreign currency values of the US dollar and PPPs relative to four industrialized countries formed from CPIs, expressed in logarithms over the floating period. Figure 3.2 shows the analogous series for the US and UK over a long historical period which extends from 1871 to 1997. While there are protracted periods in which the nominal exchange rate deviates from the PPP, the two series tend to revert toward each other over time.

As a result, international macroeconomists view Casselian PPP as a theory of the long-run determination of the exchange rate, in which the PPP $(p - p^*)$ is a long-run attractor for the nominal exchange rate.

THE COMMODITY-ARBITRAGE APPROACH

The commodity-arbitrage view of PPP, articulated by Samuelson [117], simply says that the "law of one price" holds for all internationally tradable goods. Thus if the "law of one price" is true for the goods individually, it will also be true for the appropriate price index as well. Here, the appropriate price index should cover only those goods that are traded internationally. It can be argued that the producer price index (PPI) is a better choice for studying PPP, since it is more heavily weighted toward tradable goods than the CPI, which includes items

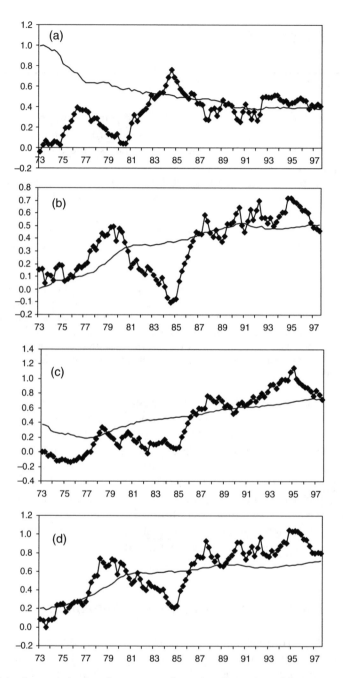

Figure 3.1 Log nominal exchange rates (boxes) and CPI-based PPPs (solid lines).
(a) US–UK; (b) US–Germany; (c) US–Japan; (d) US–Switzerland.

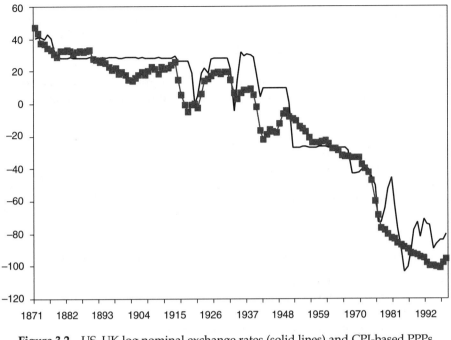

Figure 3.2   US–UK log nominal exchange rates (solid lines) and CPI-based PPPs (boxes) multiplied by 100: 1871–1997.

such as housing services which do not trade internationally. We will consider empirical analyses on PPP in chapter 7.

PPP is clearly violated in the short run. Casual observation of figures 3.1 and 3.2 suggests, however, that PPP may hold in the long run. There exists econometric evidence to support long-run PPP, but we will defer discussion of these issues until chapter 7.

In spite of the obvious short-run violations, PPP is one of the building blocks in the monetary model and, as we will see, in the Lucas model (chapter 4) and in the Redux model (chapter 9) as well. Why is that? One reason frequently given is that we don't have a good theory for why PPP doesn't hold, so there is no obvious alternative way to provide international price-level linkages. A second and perhaps more convincing reason is that all theories involve abstractions that are false at some level and, as Friedman [61] argues, we should judge a theory not by the realism of its assumptions but by the quality of its predictions.

3.2   THE MONETARY MODEL OF THE BALANCE OF PAYMENTS

The Frenkel and Johnson [59] collection develops the monetary approach to the balance of payments under fixed exchange rates. To illustrate the main idea, consider a small open economy that maintains a perfectly credible fixed exchange rate $\bar{s}$.[1] i_t is the domestic nominal interest rate, B_t is the monetary base, R_t is the stock of foreign exchange reserves held by the central bank, and D_t is domestic credit extended by the central bank. In logarithms, m_t is the money stock, y_t is national income, and p_t is the price level. The money supply is $M_t = \mu B_t = \mu(R_t + D_t)$, where μ is the money multiplier. A logarithmic expansion of the money supply and its components about their mean values allows us to write

$$m_t = \theta r_t + (1 - \theta)d_t, \tag{3.1}$$

where $\theta = E(R_t)/E(B_t)$, $r_t = \ln(R_t)$, and $d_t = \ln(D_t)$.[2]

A transactions motive gives rise to the demand for money, in which log real money demand, $m_t^d - p_t$, depends positively on y_t and negatively on the opportunity cost of holding money, i_t:

$$m_t^d - p_t = \phi y_t - \lambda i_t + \epsilon_t. \tag{3.2}$$

$0 < \phi < 1$ is the income elasticity of money demand, $0 < \lambda$ is the interest semi-elasticity of money demand, and $\epsilon_t \overset{iid}{\sim} (0, \sigma_\epsilon^2)$.

Assume that purchasing-power parity (PPP) and uncovered interest parity (UIP) hold. Since the exchange rate is fixed, PPP implies that the price level $p_t = \bar{s} + p_t^*$ is determined by the exogenous foreign price level. Because the fix is perfectly credible, market participants expect no change in the exchange rate and UIP implies that the interest rate $i_t = i_t^*$ is given by the exogenous foreign interest rate. Assume that the money market is continuously in equilibrium by equating m_t^d in (3.2) to m_t in (3.1) and rearrange, to give

$$\theta r_t = \bar{s} + p_t^* + \phi y_t - \lambda i_t^* - (1 - \theta)d_t + \epsilon_t. \tag{3.3}$$

Equation (3.3) embodies the central insights of the monetary approach to the balance of payments. If the home country experiences any one, or a combination, of a high rate of income growth, declining interest rates, or rising prices, the demand for nominal money balances will grow. If growth in the money demand is not satisfied by an accommodating increase in domestic credit, d_t, the public will obtain the additional money by running a balance-of-payments surplus and accumulating international reserves. If, on the other hand, the central bank engages in excessive domestic credit expansion that exceeds growth in the money demand, the public will eliminate the excess supply of money by running a balance-of-payments deficit.

We will meet this model again in chapters 10 and 11, in the study of target zones and balance-of-payments crises. In the remainder of this chapter, we develop

---

[1] A small open economy takes world prices and world interest rates as given.

[2] A first-order expansion about mean values gives $M_t - E(M_t) = \mu[R_t - E(R_t)] + \mu[D_t - E(D_t)]$. But $\mu = E(M_t)/E(B_t)$, where $B_t = R_t + D_t$ is the monetary base. Now divide both sides by $E(M_t)$, to get $[M_t - E(M_t)]/E(M_t) = \theta[R_t - E(R_t)]/E(R_t) + (1 - \theta)[D_t - E(D_t)]/E(D_t)$. Noting that, for a random variable X_t, $[X_t - E(X_t)]/E(X_t) \simeq \ln(X_t) - \ln(E(X_t))$, apart from an arbitrary constant, we obtain (3.1) in the text.

the model as a theory of exchange rate determination in a flexible exchange rate environment.

3.3 THE MONETARY MODEL UNDER FLEXIBLE EXCHANGE RATES

The monetary model of exchange rate determination consists of a pair of stable money demand functions, continuous stock equilibrium in the money market, uncovered interest parity, and purchasing-power parity. Under flexible exchange rates, the money stock is exogenous. Equilibrium in the domestic and foreign money markets is given by

$$m_t - p_t = \phi y_t - \lambda i_t, \tag{3.4}$$

$$m_t^* - p_t^* = \phi y_t^* - \lambda i_t^*, \tag{3.5}$$

where $0 < \phi < 1$ is the income elasticity of money demand and $\lambda > 0$ is the interest rate semi-elasticity of money demand. Money demand parameters are identical across countries.

International capital market equilibrium is given by uncovered interest parity:

$$i_t - i_t^* = E_t s_{t+1} - s_t, \tag{3.6}$$

where $E_t s_{t+1} \equiv E(s_{t+1}|I_t)$ is the expectation of the exchange rate at date $t + 1$, conditioned on all public information, I_t, available to economic agents at date t.

Price levels and the exchange rate are related through purchasing-power parity:

$$s_t = p_t - p_t^*. \tag{3.7}$$

To simplify the notation, call

$$f_t \equiv (m_t - m_t^*) - \phi (y_t - y_t^*)$$

the economic *fundamentals*. Now, substituting (3.4), (3.5), and (3.6) into (3.7), to get

$$s_t = f_t + \lambda(E_t s_{t+1} - s_t), \tag{3.8}$$

and solving for s_t gives

$$s_t = \gamma f_t + \psi E_t s_{t+1}, \tag{3.9}$$

where

$$\gamma \equiv 1/(1 + \lambda),$$

$$\psi \equiv \lambda \gamma = \lambda/(1 + \lambda).$$

Equation (3.9) is the basic first-order stochastic difference equation of the monetary model and serves the same function as an "Euler equation" in optimizing models. It says that expectations of future values of the exchange rate are embodied in the current exchange rate. High relative money growth at home leads to a weakening of the home currency, while high relative income growth leads to a strengthening of the home currency.

Next, advance time by one period in (3.9), to get $s_{t+1} = \gamma f_{t+1} + \psi E_{t+1} s_{t+2}$. Take expectations conditional on time t information, use the law of iterated expectations to get $E_t s_{t+1} = \gamma E_t f_{t+1} + \psi E_t s_{t+2}$, and substitute back into (3.9). Now do this again for $s_{t+2}, s_{t+3}, \ldots, s_{t+k}$, and you have

$$s_t = \gamma \sum_{j=0}^{k} (\psi)^j E_t f_{t+j} + (\psi)^{k+1} E_t s_{t+k+1}. \tag{3.10}$$

Eventually, you'll want to drive $k \to \infty$, but in doing so you need to specify the behavior of the term $(\psi)^k E_t s_{t+k}$.

The fundamentals (no-bubbles) solution. Since $\psi < 1$, you obtain the unique fundamentals (no-bubbles) solution by restricting the rate at which the exchange rate grows by imposing the transversality condition

$$\lim_{k \to \infty} (\psi)^k E_t s_{t+k} = 0, \tag{3.11}$$

which limits the rate at which the exchange rate can grow asymptotically. If the transversality condition holds, let $k \to \infty$ in (3.10), to give the present-value formula:

$$s_t = \gamma \sum_{j=0}^{\infty} (\psi)^j E_t f_{t+j}. \tag{3.12}$$

The exchange rate is the discounted present value of expected future values of the fundamentals. In finance, the present-value model is a popular theory of asset pricing. There, s is the stock price and f is the firm's dividends. Since the exchange rate is given by the same basic formula as stock prices, the monetary approach is sometimes referred to as the "asset" approach to the exchange rate. According to this approach, we should expect the exchange rate to behave just like the prices of other assets, such as stocks and bonds. From this perspective, it will come as no surprise that the exchange rate is more volatile than the fundamentals, just as stock prices are much more volatile than dividends. Before exploring further the relation between the exchange rate and the fundamentals, consider what happens if the transversality condition is violated.

Rational bubbles. If the transversality condition does not hold, it is possible for the exchange rate to be governed in part by an explosive bubble $\{b_t\}$, that will eventually dominate its behavior. To see why, let the bubble evolve according to

$$b_t = (1/\psi) b_{t-1} + \eta_t, \tag{3.13}$$

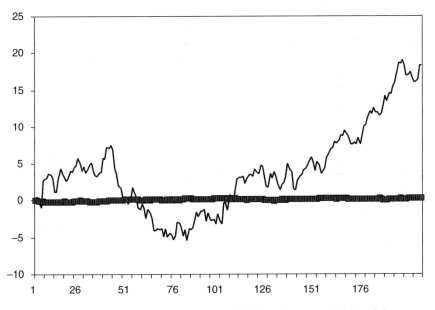

Figure 3.3 A realization of a rational bubble, where $\psi = 0.99$ and the fundamentals follow a random walk. The stable line is the realization of the fundamentals.

where $\eta_t \overset{iid}{\sim} N\left(0, \sigma_\eta^2\right)$. The coefficient $(1/\psi)$ exceeds 1, so the bubble process is explosive. Now add the bubble to the fundamental solution (3.12) and call the result

$$\hat{s}_t = s_t + b_t. \tag{3.14}$$

You can see that $\hat{s}_t$ violates the transversality condition by substituting (3.14) into (3.11), to give

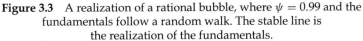

$$\psi^{t+k} E_t \hat{s}_{t+k} = \underbrace{\psi^{t+k} E_t s_{t+k}}_{0} + \psi^{t+k} E_t b_{t+k} = b_t.$$

However, $\hat{s}_t$ is a solution to the model, because it solves (3.9). You can check this out by substituting (3.14) into (3.9), to give

$$s_t + b_t = (\psi/\lambda)f_t + \psi[E_t S_{t+1} + (1/\psi)b_t].$$

The b_t terms on either side of the equality cancel out, so $\hat{s}_t$ is indeed another solution to (3.9), but the bubble will eventually dominate and will drive the exchange rate arbitrarily far away from the fundamentals f_t. The bubble arises in a model where people have rational expectations, so it is referred to as a rational bubble. What does a rational bubble look like? Figure 3.3 displays a realization of an $\hat{s}_t$ for 200 time periods, where $\psi = 0.99$ and the fundamentals follow a driftless random walk with innovation variance 0.035^2. Early on, the exchange rate seems to return to the fundamentals, but it diverges as time goes on.

Now it may be the case that the foreign exchange market is occasionally driven by bubbles, but real-world experience suggests that such bubbles eventually pop. It is unlikely that foreign exchange markets are characterized by rational bubbles which do not pop. As a result, we will focus on the no-bubbles solution from this point on.

3.4 FUNDAMENTALS AND EXCHANGE RATE VOLATILITY

A major challenge to international economic theory is to understand the volatility of the exchange rate in relation to the volatility of the economic fundamentals. Let's first take a look at the stylized facts concerning volatility. Then we'll examine how the monetary model is able to explain these facts.

STYLIZED FACTS ON VOLATILITY AND DYNAMICS

Some descriptive statistics for dollar quarterly returns on the pound, deutschemark, and yen are shown in the first panel of table 3.1. To underscore the similarity between the exchange rate and equity prices, the table also includes statistics for the Standard and Poors composite stock price index. The second panel displays descriptive statistics for the deviation of the respective asset prices from their fundamentals. For equities, this is the S&P log dividend yield. For currency values, it is the deviation of the exchange rate from the monetary fundamentals, $f_t - s_t$, that has been normalized to have zero mean. The volatility of a time-series is measured by its sample standard deviation.

The main points that can be drawn from the table are as follows:

1. The volatility of exchange rate returns, Δs_t, is virtually indistinguishable from stock return volatility.
2. Returns for both stocks and exchange rates have low first-order serial correlation.
3. From our discussion about the properties of the variance ratio statistic in section 2.4, the negative autocorrelations in exchange rate returns at 16 quarters suggest the possibility of mean reversion.
4. The deviation of the price from the fundamentals displays substantial persistence, and much less volatility than returns. The behavior of the dividend yield, while similar to the behavior of the exchange rate deviations from the monetary fundamentals, displays slightly more persistence and appears to be nonstationary over the sample period.

The data on returns and deviations from the fundamentals are shown in figure 3.4, where you clearly see how the exchange rate is *excessively volatile* in comparison to its fundamentals.

Table 3.1 Descriptive statistics for exchange rate and equity returns, and their fundamentals

| | Mean | Std. Dev. | Min. | Max. | Autocorrelations | | | |
					ρ_1	ρ_4	ρ_8	ρ_{16}
Returns								
S&P	2.75	5.92	−13.34	18.31	0.24	−0.10	0.15	0.09
UKP	0.41	5.50	−13.83	16.47	0.12	0.03	0.01	−0.29
DEM	0.46	6.35	−13.91	15.74	0.09	0.23	0.04	−0.07
YEN	0.73	6.08	−15.00	16.97	0.13	0.18	0.06	−0.29
Deviation from fundamentals								
Div.	1.31	0.30	0.49	1.82	1.01	1.03	1.05	0.94
UKP	0	0.18	−0.46	0.47	0.89	0.61	0.25	−0.12
DEM	0	0.31	−0.61	0.59	0.98	0.91	0.77	0.55
YEN	0	0.38	−0.85	0.50	0.98	0.88	0.76	0.68

Quarterly observations from 1973.1 to 1997.4. Percentage returns on the Standard and Poors composite index (S&P) and its log dividend yield (Div.) are from *Datastream*. Percentage exchange rate returns and deviation of exchange rate from fundamentals ($s_t - f_t$) with $f_t = (m_t - m_t^*) - (y_t - y_t^*)$ are from the *International Financial Statistics* CD-ROM. ($s_t - f_t$) are normalized to have zero mean. The US dollar is the numeraire currency. UKP is the UK pound, DEM is the deutschemark, and YEN is the Japanese yen.

EXCESS VOLATILITY AND THE MONETARY MODEL

The monetary model can be made consistent with the excess volatility in the exchange rate if the *growth* rate of the fundamentals is a persistent stationary process:

$$\Delta f_t = \rho \Delta f_{t-1} + \epsilon_t, \tag{3.15}$$

with $\epsilon_t \overset{iid}{\sim} N(0, \sigma_\epsilon^2)$. The implied k-step-ahead prediction formula is $E_t(\Delta f_{t+k}) = \rho^k \Delta f_t$. Converting to levels, you get $E_t(f_{t+k}) = f_t + \sum_{i=1}^k \rho^i \Delta f_t = f_t + [(1 - \rho^k)/(1 - \rho)]\rho \Delta f_t$. The use of these prediction formulae in (3.12) gives

$$s_t = \gamma \sum_{j=0}^\infty \psi^j f_t + \gamma \sum_{j=0}^\infty \frac{\psi^j}{1 - \rho}\rho \Delta f_t - \gamma \sum_{j=0}^\infty \frac{(\rho\psi)^j}{1 - \rho}\rho \Delta f_t$$

$$= f_t + \frac{\rho\psi}{1 - \rho\psi} \Delta f_t, \tag{3.16}$$

where we have used the fact that $\gamma = 1 - \psi$. Some additional algebra reveals that

$$Var(\Delta s_t) = \frac{(1 - \rho\psi)^2 + 2\rho\psi(1 - \rho)}{(1 - \rho\psi)^2} Var(\Delta f_t) > Var(\Delta f_t).$$

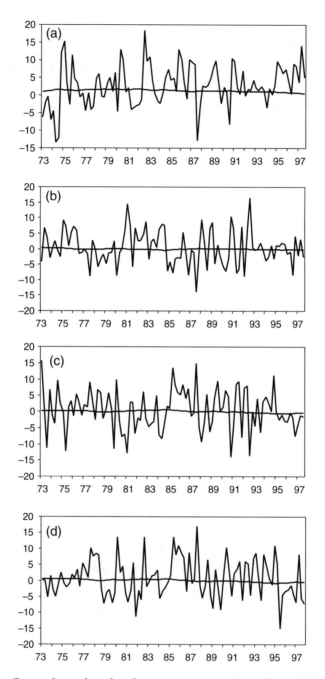

Figure 3.4 Quarterly stock and exchange rate returns (jagged line), 1973.1 through 1997.4, with price deviations from the fundamentals (smooth line). (a) Stock dividends and log dividend yield; (b) dollar/pound; (c) dollar/deutschemark; (d) dollar/yen.

This is not very encouraging, since the levels of the fundamentals are explosive. The end-of-chapter problems show that neither an AR(1) nor a permanent–transitory components representation (section 2.4) for the fundamentals allows the monetary model to explain why exchange rate returns are more volatile than the growth rate of the fundamentals.

3.5 TESTING MONETARY MODEL PREDICTIONS

This section looks at two empirical strategies for evaluating the monetary model of exchange rates.

⬤ MacDonald and Taylor's Test

The first strategy that we look at is based on MacDonald and Taylor's [96] adaptation of Campbell and Shiller's [19] tests of the present-value model.[3] This section draws on material on cointegration presented in section 2.6.

Let I_t be the time t information set available to market participants. Subtracting f_t from both sides of (3.8) gives

$$s_t - f_t = \lambda E(s_{t+1} - s_t | I_t) = \lambda(i_t - i_t^*). \qquad (3.17)$$

s_t is by all indications a unit-root process, whereas Δs_t and $E(\Delta s_{t+1}|I_t)$ are clearly stationary. It follows from the first equality in (3.17) that s_t and f_t must be cointegrated. Using (3.12) and noting that $\psi = \lambda\gamma$ gives

$$\lambda E_t(\Delta s_{t+1}) = \lambda \left(\gamma \sum_{j=0}^{\infty} \psi^j E_t f_{t+1+j} - \gamma \sum_{j=0}^{\infty} \psi^j E_t f_{t+j} \right)$$

$$= \sum_{j=1}^{\infty} \psi^j E_t \Delta f_{t+j}. \qquad (3.18)$$

Equations (3.17) and (3.18) allow you to represent the deviation of the exchange rate from the fundamental as the present value of future fundamentals growth:

$$\zeta_t = s_t - f_t = \sum_{j=1}^{\infty} \psi^j E_t \Delta f_{t+j}. \qquad (3.19)$$

Since s_t and f_t are cointegrated, they can be represented by a vector error correction model (VECM) that describes the evolution of $(\Delta s_t, \Delta f_t, \zeta_t)$, where $\zeta_t \equiv s_t - f_t$. As shown in section 2.6, the linear dependence among $(\Delta s_t, \Delta f_t, \zeta_t)$

---

[3] The seminal contributions to this literature are Leroy and Porter [88] and Shiller [120].

induced by cointegration implies that the information contained in the VECM is preserved in a bivariate vector autoregression (VAR) that consists of ζ_t and either Δs_t or Δf_t. Thus we will drop Δs_t and work with the pth-order VAR for $(\Delta f_t, \zeta_t)$:

$$\begin{pmatrix} \Delta f_t \\ \zeta_t \end{pmatrix} = \sum_{j=1}^{p} \begin{pmatrix} a_{11,j} & a_{12,j} \\ a_{21,j} & a_{22,j} \end{pmatrix} \begin{pmatrix} \Delta f_{t-j} \\ \zeta_{t-j} \end{pmatrix} + \begin{pmatrix} \epsilon_t \\ v_t \end{pmatrix}. \tag{3.20}$$

The information set available to the econometrician consists of current and lagged values of Δf_t and ζ_t. We will call this information $H_t = \{\Delta f_t, \Delta f_{t-1}, \dots, \zeta_t, \zeta_{t-1}, \dots\}$. Presumably, H_t is a subset of the economic agent's information set, I_t. Take expectations on both sides of (3.19) conditional on H_t and use the law of iterated expectations, to get[4]

$$\zeta_t = \sum_{j=1}^{\infty} \psi^j \mathrm{E}(\Delta f_{t+j}|H_t). \tag{3.21}$$

What is the point of deriving (3.21)? The point is to show that you can use the prediction formulae implied by the data-generating process (3.20) to compute the necessary expectations. Expectations of market participants, $\mathrm{E}(\Delta f_{t+j}|I_t)$, are unobservable, but you can still test the theory by substituting the true expectations with your estimate of these expectations, $\mathrm{E}(\Delta f_{t+j}|H_t)$.

To simplify computations of the conditional expectations of future fundamentals growth, reformulate the VAR in (3.20) in the VAR(1) *companion form*

$$\underline{Y}_t = \mathbf{B}\underline{Y}_{t-1} + \underline{u}_t, \tag{3.22}$$

where

$$\underline{Y}_t = \begin{pmatrix} \Delta f_t \\ \Delta f_{t-1} \\ \vdots \\ \Delta f_{t-p+1} \\ \zeta_t \\ \zeta_{t-1} \\ \vdots \\ \zeta_{t-p+1} \end{pmatrix}, \qquad \underline{u}_t = \begin{pmatrix} \epsilon_t \\ 0 \\ \vdots \\ 0 \\ v_t \\ 0 \\ \vdots \\ 0 \end{pmatrix},$$

---

[4]   Let X, Y, and Z be random variables. The law of iterated expectations says that $\mathrm{E}[\mathrm{E}(X|Y,Z)|Y] = \mathrm{E}(X|Y)$.

$$
\mathbf{B} = \begin{pmatrix}
a_{11,1} & a_{11,2} & \cdots & a_{11,p} & a_{12,1} & a_{12,2} & \cdots & a_{12,p} \\
1 & 0 & \cdots & 0 & 0 & 0 & \cdots & 0 \\
0 & 1 & 0\cdots & 0 & 0 & 0 & \cdots & 0 \\
\vdots & \cdots & \cdots & \vdots & \vdots & \vdots & \vdots & \vdots \\
0 & \cdots & \cdots 1 & 0 & 0 & \cdots & \cdots & 0 \\
a_{21,1} & a_{21,2} & \cdots & a_{21,p} & a_{22,1} & a_{22,2} & \cdots & a_{22,p} \\
0 & \cdots & \cdots & 0 & 1 & 0 & \cdots & 0 \\
0 & \cdots & \cdots & 0 & 0 & 1 & 0\cdots & 0 \\
\vdots & \cdots & \cdots & \vdots & \vdots & \vdots & \vdots & \vdots \\
0 & \cdots & \cdots & 0 & 0 & \cdots & \cdots 1 & 0
\end{pmatrix}.
$$

Now let $\underline{e}_1$ be a $(1 \times 2p)$ row vector with a 1 in the first element and zeros elsewhere, and let $\underline{e}_2$ be a $(1 \times 2p)$ row vector with a 1 as the $(p + 1)$th element and zeros elsewhere:

$$
\underline{e}_1 = (1, 0, \ldots, 0), \quad \underline{e}_2 = (0, \ldots, 0, 1, 0, \ldots, 0).
$$

These are selection vectors that give

$$
\underline{e}_1 \underline{Y}_t = \Delta f_t, \quad \underline{e}_2 \underline{Y}_t = \zeta_t.
$$

Now the j-step-ahead forecast of f_t is conveniently expressed as

$$
E(\Delta f_{t+j} | H_t) = \underline{e}_1 E(\underline{Y}_{t+j} | H_t) = e_1 \mathbf{B}^j \underline{Y}_t. \tag{3.23}
$$

Substitute (3.23) into (3.21), to give

$$
\zeta_t = \underline{e}_2 \underline{Y}_t = \sum_{j=1}^{\infty} \psi^j \underline{e}_1 \mathbf{B}^j \underline{Y}_t
$$

$$
= e_1 \left(\sum_{j=1}^{\infty} \psi^j \mathbf{B}^j \right) \underline{Y}_t
$$

$$
= e_1 \psi \mathbf{B} (\mathbf{I} - \psi \mathbf{B})^{-1} \underline{Y}_t. \tag{3.24}
$$

Equating coefficients on elements of $\underline{Y}_t$ yields a set of nontrivial restrictions predicted by the theory, which can be subjected to statistical hypothesis tests:

$$
\underline{e}_2 (\mathbf{I} - \psi \mathbf{B}) = \underline{e}_1 \psi \mathbf{B}. \tag{3.25}
$$

Estimating and Testing the Present-Value Model

We use quarterly US and German observations on the exchange rate, money supplies, and industrial production indices from the *International Financial Statistics* CD-ROM from 1973.1 to 1997.4, to re-estimate the MacDonald and Taylor formulation and test the restrictions (3.25). We view the US as the home country. The bivariate VAR is run on $(\Delta f_t, \zeta_t)$ with observations demeaned prior to estimation. The fundamentals are given by $f_t = (m_t - m_t^*) - (y_t - y_t^*)$, where the income elasticity of money demand is fixed at $\phi = 1$.

The BIC (section 2.1) tells us that a VAR(4) is appropriate. Estimation proceeds by letting $x_t' = (\Delta f_{t-1}, \ldots, \Delta f_{t-4}, \zeta_{t-1}, \ldots, \zeta_{t-4})$ and running least squares on

$$\Delta f_t = x_t' \underline{\beta} + \epsilon_t,$$

$$\zeta_t = x_t' \underline{\delta} + v_t.$$

Expanding (3.25) and making the correspondence between the coefficients in the matrix **B** and the regressions, we write out the testable restrictions explicitly as

$$\beta_1 + \delta_1 = 0, \qquad \beta_5 + \delta_5 = 1/\psi,$$
$$\beta_2 + \delta_2 = 0, \qquad \beta_6 + \delta_6 = 0,$$
$$\beta_3 + \delta_3 = 0, \qquad \beta_7 + \delta_7 = 0,$$
$$\beta_4 + \delta_4 = 0, \qquad \beta_8 + \delta_8 = 0.$$

These restrictions are tested for a given value of the interest semi-elasticity of money demand, $\lambda = \psi/(1 - \psi)$. To set up the Wald test, let $\underline{\pi}' = (\beta', \delta')$ be the grand coefficient vector from the OLS regressions, let $\mathbf{R} = (\mathbf{I}_8 : \mathbf{I}_8)$ be the restriction matrix, and let $\underline{r}' = (0, 0, 0, 0, (1/\psi), 0, 0, 0)$, and also let $\mathbf{\Omega}_T = \mathbf{\Sigma}_T \otimes Q_T^{-1}$, where $\mathbf{\Sigma}_T = (1/T) \sum \underline{\epsilon}_t \underline{\epsilon}_t'$ and $\mathbf{Q}_T = (1/T) \sum \underline{x}_t \underline{x}_t'$. Then, as $T \to \infty$, the Wald statistic

$$W = (\mathbf{R}\underline{\pi} - \underline{r})'[\mathbf{R}\mathbf{\Omega}_T\mathbf{R}']^{-1}(\mathbf{R}\underline{\pi} - \underline{r}) \overset{D}{\sim} \chi_8^2.$$

Here are the results. The Wald statistics and their associated values of λ are $W = 284,160$ ($\lambda = 0.02$), $W = 113,872$ ($\lambda = 0.10$), $W = 44,584$ ($\lambda = 0.16$), and $W = 18,291$ ($\lambda = 0.25$). The restrictions are strongly rejected for reasonable values of λ.

One reason why the model fares poorly can be seen by comparing the theoretically implied deviation of the spot rate from the fundamentals,

$$\tilde{\zeta}_t = \underline{e}_1 \psi \mathbf{B}(\mathbf{I} - \psi\mathbf{B})^{-1}\underline{Y}_t,$$

which is referred to as the "spread" with the actual deviation, $\zeta_t = s_t - f_t$. These are displayed in figure 3.5, where you can see that the implied spread is much too smooth.

● LONG-RUN EVIDENCE FOR THE MONETARY MODEL FROM PANEL DATA

The statistical evidence against the rational expectations monetary model is pretty strong. One of the potential weak points of the model is that PPP is

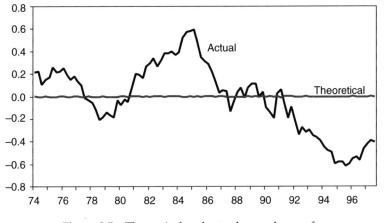

Figure 3.5   Theoretical and actual spreads, $s_t - f_t$.

assumed to hold as an exact relationship, whereas it is probably more realistic to think that it holds in the long run.

Mark and Sul [99] investigate the empirical link between the monetary model fundamentals and the exchange rate using quarterly observations for 19 industrialized countries from 1973.1 to 1997.4 and the *panel* exchange rate predictive regression

$$s_{it+k} - s_{it} = \beta \zeta_{it} + \eta_{it+k},\tag{3.26}$$

where $\eta_{it+k} = \gamma_i + \theta_t + u_{it+k}$ has an error-components representation with individual effect γ_i, common time effect θ_{t+1}, and idiosyncratic effect u_{it+k}. A panel combines the time-series observations of several cross-sectional units. The individuals in the cross-section are different countries, which are indexed by $i = 1, \ldots, N$.

Out-of-Sample Fit and Prediction

Mark and Sul's primary objective is to use the regression to generate out-of-sample forecasts of the depreciation. They base their methodology on the work of Meese and Rogoff [102], who sought to evaluate the empirical performance of alternative exchange rate models that were popular in the 1970s by conducting a monthly postsample fit analysis.

Suppose that there are $j = 1, \ldots, J$ models under consideration. Let $\underline{x}_t^j$ be a vector of exchange rate determinants implied by "model j", and let $s_t = \underline{x}_t'^j \beta^j + e_t^j$ be the regression representation of model j. What Meese and Rogoff did was to divide the complete size T (time-series) sample in two. Sample 1 consists of observations $t = 1, \ldots, t_1$ and sample 2 consists of observations $t = t_1 + 1, \ldots, T$, where $t_1 < T$. Using sample 1 to estimate $\underline{\beta}^j$, they then formed the out-of-estimation sample fit of the exchange rate predicted by model j, $\hat{s}_t^j = \underline{x}_t^{j\prime} \underline{\hat{\beta}}_j$, for $t = t_1 + 1, \ldots, T$.

The Meese–Rogoff regressions were contemporaneous relationships between the dependent variable and the vector of independent variables. To truly generate forecasts of future values of s_t they needed to forecast future values of the $\underline{x}_t^j$ vectors. Instead, Meese and Rogoff used realized values of the $\underline{x}_t^j$ vectors – hence the term out-of-sample fit. The various models were judged on the accuracy of their out-of estimation sample fit.

The models were compared to the predictions of the driftless random walk model for the exchange rate. This is an important benchmark for evaluation, because the random walk says that there is no information that helps to predict future change. You would think that an econometric model with any amount of economic content would dominate the "no-change" prediction of the random walk. Even though they biased the results in favor of the model-based regressions by using realized values of the independent variables, Meese and Rogoff found that that the out-of-sample fits from the theory-based regressions were uniformly less accurate than the random walk.

Their study showed that many models may fit well in sample but they have a tendency to fall apart out of sample. There are many possible explanations for the instability but, ultimately, the reason boils down to the failure to find a time-invariant relationship between the exchange rate and the fundamentals. Although their conclusions regarding the importance of macroeconomic fundamentals for the exchange rate were nihilistic, Meese and Rogoff established a rigorous tradition in international macroeconomics, of using out-of-sample fit or forecasting performance as model evaluation criteria.

Panel Long-Horizon Regression

Let's return to Mark and Sul's analysis. They evaluate the predictive content of the monetary model fundamentals by initially estimating the regression on observations through 1983.1. Note that the regressand in (3.26) is the past (not contemporaneous) deviation of the exchange rate from the fundamentals. It is a predictive regression that generates actual out-of-sample forecasts. The $k = 1$ regression is used to forecast one quarter ahead, and the $k = 16$ regression is used to forecast 16 quarters ahead. The sample is then updated by one observation and a new set of forecasts is generated. This recursive updating of the sample and forecast generation is repeated until the end of the data set is reached. If the monetary fundamentals contain no predictive content, or if the exchange rate and the fundamentals do not cointegrate, $\beta = 0$.

Let observations $T - T_0$ to T be samples reserved for forecast evaluation. If $\hat{s}_{it+k} - s_{it}$ is the k-step-ahead regression forecast formed at t, the root-mean-square

Table 3.2 Monetary fundamentals out-of-sample forecasts of US dollar returns with nonparametric bootstrapped *p*-values under cointegration

Country	One quarter ahead		16 quarters ahead	
	U-statistic	p-value	U-statistic	p-value
Australia	1.024	0.904	**0.864**	0.222
Austria	**0.984**	**0.013**	0.837	0.131
Belgium	**0.999**	0.424	0.405	**0.001**
Canada	0.985	**0.074**	0.552	**0.009**
Denmark	1.014	0.912	**0.858**	0.174
Finland	1.001	0.527	**0.859**	0.164
France	**0.994**	0.155	**0.583**	**0.004**
Germany	**0.986**	**0.056**	**0.518**	**0.003**
Greece	1.016	0.909	1.046	0.594
Italy	**0.997**	0.269	**0.745**	**0.016**
Japan	1.003	0.579	**0.996**	0.433
Korea	**0.912**	**0.002**	0.486	**0.012**
Netherlands	**0.986**	**0.041**	0.703	**0.032**
Norway	**0.998**	0.380	0.537	**0.002**
Spain	0.996	0.341	0.672	**0.028**
Sweden	**0.975**	**0.034**	0.372	**0.001**
Switzerland	**0.982**	**0.008**	0.751	**0.049**
UK	**0.983**	**0.077**	0.570	**0.012**
Mean	**0.991**	**0.010**	0.686	**0.001**
Median	**0.995**	0.163	**0.688**	**0.001**

Bold face indicates statistical significance at the 10 percent level.

prediction error (RMSPE) of the regression is

$$R_1 = \sqrt{\frac{1}{T_0} \sum_{t=T_0}^{T} (\hat{s}_{it} - s_{it-k})^2}.$$

The monetary fundamentals regression is compared to the random walk with drift, $s_{it+1} = \mu_i + s_{it} + \epsilon_{it}$, where $\epsilon_{it} \overset{iid}{\sim} (0, \sigma_i^2)$. The k-step-ahead forecasted change from the random walk is $\hat{s}_{it+k} - s_{it} = k\mu_i$. Let R_2 be the random walk model's RMSPE. Theil's [125] statistic, $U = R_1/R_2$, is the ratio of the RMSPEs of the two models. The regression outperforms the random walk in prediction accuracy when $U < 1$.

Table 3.2 shows the results of the prediction exercise. The nonparametric residual bootstrap (see section 2.5) is used to generate *p*-values for a test of the hypothesis that the regression and the random walk models give equally accurate predictions. There is a preponderance of statistically superior predictive performance by the monetary model exchange rate regression.

Chapter Summary

1. The monetary model builds on purchasing-power parity, uncovered interest parity, and stable transactions-based money demand functions.
2. Domestic and foreign money and real income levels are the fundamental determinants of the nominal exchange rate.
3. The exchange rate is viewed as the relative price of two monies, which are assets. Since asset prices are in general more volatile than their fundamentals, it comes as no surprise that exchange rates exhibit excess volatility. The present-value form of the solution underscores the concept that the exchange rate is an asset price.
4. The monetary model is a useful first approximation in fixing our intuition about exchange rate dynamics, even though it fails to explain the data on many dimensions. Because purchasing-power parity is assumed to hold as an exact relationship, the model cannot explain the dynamics of the real exchange rate. Indeed, the main reason to study nominal exchange rate behavior is if we think that nominal exchange rate movements are correlated with real exchange rate changes, so that they have real consequences.

Problems

Let the fundamentals have the permanent–transitory components representation

$$f_t = \bar{f}_t + z_t, \tag{3.27}$$

where $\bar{f}_t = \bar{f}_{t-1} + \epsilon_t$ is the permanent part with $\epsilon_t \overset{iid}{\sim} N\left(0, \sigma_\epsilon^2\right)$ and $z_t = \rho z_{t-1} + u_t$ is the transitory part with $u_t \overset{iid}{\sim} N\left(0, \sigma_u^2\right)$, and $0 < \rho < 1$. Note that the time-t expectation of a random walk k periods ahead is $E_t(\bar{f}_{t+k}) = \bar{f}_t$, and the time-$t$ expectation of the AR(1) part k periods ahead is $E_t z_{t+k} = \rho^k z_t$. Equation (3.27) implies the k-step-ahead prediction formula $E_t(f_{t+k}) = \bar{f}_t + \rho^k z_t$.

1. Show that

$$s_t = \bar{f}_t + \frac{1}{1 + \lambda(1 - \rho)} z_t. \tag{3.28}$$

2. Suppose that the fundamentals are stationary by setting $\sigma_\epsilon = 0$. Then the permanent part $\bar{f}_t$ drops out and the fundamentals are governed by a stationary AR(1) process. Show that

$$\text{Var}(s_t) = \left(\frac{1}{1 + \lambda(1 - \rho)}\right)^2 \text{Var}(f_t). \tag{3.29}$$

3. Let's restore the unit-root component in the fundamentals by setting $\sigma_\epsilon^2 > 0$, but turn off the transitory part by setting $\sigma_u^2 = 0$. Now the fundamentals follow a random walk and the exchange rate is given exactly by the fundamentals

$$s_t = f_t. \tag{3.30}$$

The exchange rate inherits the unit root from f_t. Since unit-root processes have infinite variances, we should take first differences to induce stationarity. Doing so and taking the variance, (3.30) predicts that the variance of the exchange rate is exactly equal to the variance of the fundamentals. Now re-introduce the transitory part, $\sigma_u^2 > 0$. Show that depreciation of the home currency is

$$\Delta s_t = \epsilon_t + \frac{(\rho - 1)z_{t-1} + u_t}{1 + \lambda(1 - \rho)}, \tag{3.31}$$

where

$$\text{Var}(\Delta s_t) = \sigma_\epsilon^2 + \frac{2(1 - \rho)}{[1 + \lambda(1 - \rho)]^2}\text{Var}(z_t).$$

Why does the variance of the depreciation still not exceed the variance of the fundamentals growth?

4

The Lucas Model

The present-value interpretation of the monetary model underscores the idea that we should expect the exchange rate to behave like the prices of other assets – such as stocks and bonds. This is one of that model's attractive features. One of its unattractive features is that the model is *ad hoc* in the sense that the money demand functions upon which it rests were not shown to arise explicitly from decisions of optimizing agents. Lucas's [93] neoclassical model of exchange rate determination gives a rigorous theoretical framework for pricing foreign exchange and other assets in a flexible-price environment and is not subject to this criticism. It is a dynamic general equilibrium model of an endowment economy, with complete markets, where the fundamental determinants of the exchange rate are the same as those in the monetary model.

The economic environment for dynamic general equilibrium analysis needs to be specified in some detail. To make this task manageable, we will begin by modeling the real part of the economy that operates under a barter system. We will obtain a solution for the real exchange rate and real stock-pricing formulae. This perfect-markets real general equilibrium model is sometimes referred to as an Arrow [3] – Debreu [33] model, because it can be mapped into their static general equilibrium framework. We know that the Arrow–Debreu competitive equilibrium yields a Pareto optimum. Why is this connection useful? Because it tells us that we can understand the behavior of the market economy by solving for the social optimum, and it is typically more straightforward to obtain the social optimum than to directly solve for the market equilibrium.

In order to study the exchange rate, we need to have a monetary economy. The problem is that there is no role for fiat money in the Arrow–Debreu environment. The way that Lucas gets around this problem is to require people to use money when they buy goods. This requirement is called a "cash-in-advance" constraint, and is a popular strategy for introducing money in general equilibrium along the lines of the transactions motive for holding money. A second popular strategy that puts money in the utility function will be developed in chapter 9.

The models that we will study in this chapter and in chapter 5 have no market imperfections and exhibit no nominal rigidities. Market participants have complete information and rational expectations. Why study such a perfect world? First, we have a better idea for solving frictionless and perfect-markets models, so it is a good idea to start in familiar territory. Naturally, these models of idealized economies will not fully explain the real world. So we want to view these models as providing a benchmark against which to measure progress. If and when the data "reject" these models, one should note the manner in which they are rejected to guide the appropriate extensions and refinements to the theory.

There is a good deal of notation for the model, which is summarized in table 4.1 (see page 97).

| 4.1 THE BARTER ECONOMY

Consider two countries, each inhabited by a large number of individuals who have identical utility functions and identical wealth. People may believe that they are individuals, but they respond in the same way to changes in incentives. Because people are so similar, you can normalize the constant populations of each country to 1 and model the people in each country by the actions of a single *representative agent (household) in the Lucas model*. This is the simplest way to aggregate across individuals so that we can model macroeconomic behavior.

"Firms" in each country are pure endowment streams that generate a homogeneous nonstorable country-specific good, using no labor or capital inputs. Some people like to think of these firms as fruit trees. You can also normalize the number of firms in each country to 1. x_t is the exogenous domestic output and y_t is the exogenous foreign output. The evolution of output is given by $x_t = g_t x_{t-1}$ at home and by $y_t = g_t^* y_{t-1}$ abroad, where g_t and g_t^* are *random* gross rates of change that evolve according to a stochastic process that is known by agents. Each firm issues one perfectly divisible share of common stock which is traded in a competitive stock market. The firms pay out all of their output as dividends to shareholders. Dividends form the sole source of support for individuals. We will let x_t be the *numeraire* good and q_t be the price of y_t in terms of x_t. e_t is the ex-dividend market value of the domestic firm and e_t^* is the ex-dividend market value of the foreign firm.

The domestic agent consumes c_{xt} units of the home good and c_{yt} units of the foreign good, and holds ω_{xt} shares of the domestic firm and ω_{yt} shares of the foreign firm. Similarly, the foreign agent consumes c_{xt}^* units of the home good and c_{yt}^* units of the foreign good, and holds ω_{xt}^* shares of the domestic firm and ω_{yt}^* shares of the foreign firm.

The domestic agent brings into period t wealth valued at

$$W_t = \omega_{xt-1}(x_t + e_t) + \omega_{yt-1}(q_t y_t + e_t^*), \tag{4.1}$$

where $x_t + e_t$ and $q_t y_t + e_t^*$ are the with-dividend values of the home and foreign firms. The individual then allocates current wealth toward new share purchases,

$e_t \omega_{xt} + e_t^* \omega_{yt}$, and consumption $c_{xt} + q_t c_{yt}$:

$$W_t = e_t \omega_{xt} + e_t^* \omega_{yt} + c_{xt} + q_t c_{yt}. \tag{4.2}$$

Equating (4.1) to (4.2) gives the consolidated budget constraint:

$$c_{xt} + q_t c_{yt} + e_t \omega_{xt} + e_t^* \omega_{yt} = \omega_{xt-1}(x_t + e_t) + \omega_{yt-1}(q_t y_t + e_t^*). \tag{4.3}$$

Let $u(c_{xt}, c_{yt})$ be current period utility and let $0 < \beta < 1$ be the subjective discount factor. The domestic agent's problem then is to choose sequences of consumption and stock purchases, $\{c_{xt+j}, c_{yt+j}, \omega_{xt+j}, \omega_{yt+j}\}_{j=0}^{\infty}$, to maximize the expected lifetime utility

$$E_t \left(\sum_{j=0}^{\infty} \beta^j u(c_{xt+j}, c_{yt+j}) \right), \tag{4.4}$$

subject to (4.3).

You can transform the constrained optimum problem into an unconstrained optimum problem by substituting c_{xt} from (4.3) into (4.4). The objective function becomes

$$u(\omega_{xt-1}(x_t + e_t) + \omega_{yt-1}(q_t y_t + e_t^*) - e_t \omega_{xt} - e_t^* \omega_{yt} - q_t c_{yt}, c_{yt})$$

$$+ E_t[\beta u(\omega_{xt}(x_{t+1} + e_{t+1}) + \omega_{yt}(q_{t+1} y_{t+1} + e_{t+1}^*)$$

$$- e_{t+1} \omega_{xt+1} - e_{t+1}^* \omega_{yt+1} - q_{t+1} c_{yt+1}, c_{yt+1})] + \cdots \tag{4.5}$$

Let $u_1(c_{xt}, c_{yt}) = \partial u(c_{xt}, c_{yt})/\partial c_{xt}$ be the marginal utility of x-consumption, and let $u_2(c_{xt}, c_{yt}) = \partial u(c_{xt}, c_{yt})/\partial c_{yt}$ be the marginal utility of y-consumption. Differentiating (4.5) with respect to c_{yt}, ω_{xt}, and ω_{yt}, setting the result to zero, and rearranging yields the Euler equations:

$$c_{yt}: \quad q_t u_1(c_{xt}, c_{yt}) = u_2(c_{xt}, c_{yt}), \tag{4.6}$$

$$\omega_{xt}: \quad e_t u_1(c_{xt}, c_{yt}) = \beta E_t[u_1(c_{xt+1}, c_{yt+1})(x_{t+1} + e_{t+1})], \tag{4.7}$$

$$\omega_{yt}: \quad e_t^* u_1(c_{xt}, c_{yt}) = \beta E_t[u_1(c_{xt+1}, c_{yt+1})(q_{t+1} y_{t+1} + e_{t+1}^*)]. \tag{4.8}$$

These equations must hold if the agent is behaving optimally. Equation (4.6) is the standard intratemporal optimality condition that equates the relative price between x and y to their marginal rate of substitution. Reallocating consumption by adding a unit of c_y increases utility by $u_2(\cdot)$. This is financed by giving up q_t units of c_x, each unit of which costs $u_1(\cdot)$ units of utility for a total utility cost of $q_t u_1(\cdot)$. If the individual is behaving optimally, no such reallocations of the consumption plan yield a net gain in utility.

Equation (4.7) is the intertemporal Euler equation for purchases of the domestic equity. The left-hand side is the utility cost of the marginal purchase of domestic equity. To buy incremental shares of the domestic firm costs the individual e_t units of c_x, each unit of which lowers utility by $u_1(c_{xt}, c_{yt})$. The right-hand side of (4.7) is the utility expected to be derived from the payoff of the marginal investment. If the individual is behaving optimally, no such reallocations between consumption and saving can yield a net increase in utility. An analogous interpretation holds for intertemporal reallocations of consumption and purchases of the foreign equity in (4.8).

The foreign agent has the same utility function and faces the analogous problem of maximizing

$$E_t\left(\sum_{j=0}^{\infty} \beta^j u\left(c^*_{xt+j}, c^*_{yt+j}\right)\right),\tag{4.9}$$

subject to

$$c^*_{xt} + q_t c^*_{yt} + e_t \omega^*_{xt} + e^*_t \omega^*_{yt} = \omega^*_{xt-1}(x_t + e_t) + \omega^*_{yt-1}(q_t y_t + e^*_t).\tag{4.10}$$

The analogous set of Euler equations for the foreign individual is

$$c^*_{yt}: \qquad q_t u_1(c^*_{xt}, c^*_{yt}) = u_2(c^*_{xt}, c^*_{yt}),\tag{4.11}$$

$$\omega^*_{xt}: \qquad e_t u_1(c^*_{xt}, c^*_{yt}) = \beta E_t[u_1(c^*_{xt+1}, c^*_{yt+1})(x_{t+1} + e_{t+1})],\tag{4.12}$$

$$\omega^*_{yt}: \qquad e^*_t u_1(c^*_{xt}, c^*_{yt}) = \beta E_t[u_1(c^*_{xt+1}, c^*_{yt+1})(q_{t+1}y_{t+1} + e^*_{t+1})].\tag{4.13}$$

A set of four adding up constraints on outstanding equity shares and the exhaustion of output in home and foreign consumption complete the specification of the barter model:

$$\omega_{xt} + \omega^*_{xt} = 1,\tag{4.14}$$

$$\omega_{yt} + \omega^*_{yt} = 1,\tag{4.15}$$

$$c_{xt} + c^*_{xt} = x_t,\tag{4.16}$$

$$c_{yt} + c^*_{yt} = y_t.\tag{4.17}$$

A digression on the social optimum.   You can solve the model by grinding out the equilibrium, but the complete markets and the competitive setting makes available a "backdoor" solution strategy of solving the problem that confronts a fictitious social planner. The stochastic dynamic barter economy can conceptually be reformulated in terms of a static competitive general equilibrium model – the properties of which are well known. The reformulation goes like this.

We want to narrow the definition of a "good" so that it is defined precisely by its characteristics (whether it is an x-good or a y-good), the date of its delivery (t), and the state of the world when it is delivered (x_t, y_t). Suppose that there are only two possible values for x_t (y_t) in each period – a high value x_h (y_h) and a low value x_ℓ (y_ℓ). Then there are four possible states of the world: (x_h, y_h), (x_h, y_ℓ), (x_ℓ, y_h), and (x_ℓ, y_ℓ). "Good 1" is x delivered at $t = 0$ in state 1. "Good 2" is x delivered at $t = 0$ in state 2, "good 8" is y delivered at $t = 1$ in state 4, and so on. In this way, all possible future outcomes are completely spelled out. The reformulation of what constitutes a good corresponds to a complete system of forward markets. Instead of waiting for nature to reveal itself over time, we can have people meet and contract for all future trades today. (Domestic agents agree to sell so many units of x to foreign agents at $t = 2$ if state 3 occurs in exchange for q_2 units of y, and so on.) After trades in future contingencies have been contracted, we allow time to evolve. People in the economy simply fulfill their contractual obligations and make no further decisions. The point is that the dynamic economy has been reformulated as a static general equilibrium model.

You know from static general equilibrium analysis that the solution to the social planner's problem is a Pareto optimal allocation, and you know by the fundamental theorems of welfare economics that the Pareto optimum supports a competitive equilibrium. It follows that the solution to the planner's problem will also describe the equilibrium for the market economy.[1]

We apply that concept here and let the social planner attach weights ϕ to the home individual and $1 - \phi$ to the foreign individual. The planner's problem is to allocate the x and y endowments optimally between the domestic and foreign individuals in each period, by maximizing

$$E_t \sum_{j=0}^{\infty} \beta^j \left[\phi u \left(c_{xt+j}, c_{yt+j} \right) + (1 - \phi) u \left(c^*_{xt+j}, c^*_{yt+j} \right) \right], \qquad (4.18)$$

subject to the resource constraints (4.16) and (4.17). Since the goods are not storable, the planner's problem reduces to the timeless problem of maximizing

$$\phi u(c_{xt}, c_{yt}) + (1 - \phi) u(c^*_{xt}, c^*_{yt}),$$

subject to (4.16) and (4.17). The Euler equations for this problem are

$$\phi u_1(c_{xt}, c_{yt}) = (1 - \phi) u_1(c^*_{xt}, c^*_{yt}), \qquad (4.19)$$

$$\phi u_2(c_{xt}, c_{yt}) = (1 - \phi) u_2(c^*_{xt}, c^*_{yt}). \qquad (4.20)$$

Equations (4.19) and (4.20) are the optimal or efficient risk-sharing conditions. Risk-sharing is efficient when consumption is allocated so that the marginal utility of the home individual is proportional, and therefore perfectly correlated, to the marginal utility of the foreign individual. Because individuals enjoy consuming both goods and the utility function is concave, it is optimal for the planner to split the available x and y between the home and foreign individuals according to the relative importance of the individuals to the planner.

The weight ϕ can be interpreted as a measure of the size of the home country in the market version of the world economy. Since we assumed at the outset that agents have equal wealth, we will let both agents be equally important to

---

[1]   Under certain regularity conditions that are satisfied in the relatively simple environments considered here, the results from welfare economics that we need are that (i) a competitive equilibrium yields a Pareto optimum, and (ii) any Pareto optimum can be replicated by a competitive equilibrium.

the planner and set $\phi = 1/2$. Then the Pareto optimal allocation is to split the available output of x and y equally:

$$c_{xt} = c_{xt}^* = \frac{x_t}{2} \quad \text{and} \quad c_{yt} = c_{yt}^* = \frac{y_t}{2}.$$

Having determined the optimal quantities, to get the market solution we look for the competitive equilibrium that supports this Pareto optimum. Models that can be solved like this are called Arrow–Debreu models.

The market equilibrium. If agents owned only their own country's firms, individuals would be exposed to idiosyncratic country-specific risk that they would prefer to avoid. The risk facing the home agent is that the home firm experiences a bad year with low output of x when the foreign firm experiences a good year with high output of y. One way to insure against this risk is to hold a diversified portfolio of assets.

A diversification plan that perfectly insures against country-specific risk and which replicates the social optimum is for each agent to hold stock in half of each country's output.[2] The stock portfolio that achieves complete insurance of idiosyncratic risk is for each individual to own half of the domestic firm and half of the foreign firm:[3]

$$\omega_{xt} = \omega_{xt}^* = \omega_{yt} = \omega_{yt}^* = \tfrac{1}{2}. \tag{4.21}$$

We call this a "pooling" equilibrium, because the implicit insurance scheme at work is that agents agree in advance that they will pool their risk by sharing the realized output equally.

The solution under constant relative risk-aversion utility. Let's adopt a particular functional form for the utility function to get explicit solutions. We'll let the period utility function be constant relative-risk aversion in $C_t = c_{xt}^\theta c_{yt}^{1-\theta}$, a Cobb–Douglas index of the two goods:

$$u(c_{xt}, c_{yt}) = \frac{C_t^{1-\gamma}}{1-\gamma}. \tag{4.22}$$

Then

$$u_1(c_{xt}, c_{yt}) = \frac{\theta C_t^{1-\gamma}}{c_{xt}},$$

$$u_2(c_{xt}, c_{yt}) = \frac{(1-\theta)C_t^{1-\gamma}}{c_{yt}},$$

---

[2] Agents cannot insure against world-wide macroeconomic risk (simultaneously low x_t and y_t).
[3] Actually, Cole and Obstfeld [30] showed that trade in goods alone is sufficient to achieve efficient risk-sharing in the present model. These issues are dealt with in the end-of-chapter problems.

and the Euler equations (4.6)–(4.13) become

$$q_t = \frac{1 - \theta}{\theta} \frac{x_t}{y_t}, \tag{4.23}$$

$$\frac{e_t}{x_t} = \beta E_t \left[\left(\frac{C_{t+1}}{C_t} \right)^{(1-\gamma)} \left(1 + \frac{e_{t+1}}{x_{t+1}} \right) \right], \tag{4.24}$$

$$\frac{e_t^*}{q_t y_t} = \beta E_t \left[\left(\frac{C_{t+1}}{C_t} \right)^{(1-\gamma)} \left(1 + \frac{e_{t+1}^*}{q_{t+1} y_{t+1}} \right) \right]. \tag{4.25}$$

From (4.23), the real exchange rate q_t is determined by relative output levels. Equations (4.24) and (4.25) are stochastic difference equations in the "dividend–price" ratios e_t/x_t and $e_t^*/(q_t y_t)$. If you iterate forward on them as you did in (3.9) for the monetary model, the equity price–dividend ratio can be expressed as the present-discounted value of future consumption growth raised to the power $1 - \gamma$. You can then get an explicit solution once you make an assumption about the stochastic process governing output. This will be covered in section 4.5 below.

An important point to note is that there is no actual asset trading in the Lucas model. Agents hold their investments for ever and never rebalance their portfolios. The asset prices produced by the model are *shadow prices* that must be respected in order for agents to willingly to hold the outstanding equity shares according to (4.21).

4.2 THE ONE-MONEY MONETARY ECONOMY

In this section, we introduce a single world currency. The economic environment can be thought of as a two-sector closed economy. The idea is to introduce money without changing the real equilibrium that we characterized above. One of the difficulties in getting money into the model is that the people in the barter economy get along just fine without it. An unbacked currency in the Arrow–Debreu world that does not generate consumption payoffs will not have any value in equilibrium. To get around this problem, Lucas prohibits barter in the monetary economy and imposes a "cash-in-advance" constraint that requires people to use money to buy goods. As we enter period t, the following specific cash-in-advance transactions technology must be adhered to:

1. x_t and y_t are revealed.
2. λ_t, the exogenous stochastic gross rate of change in money, is revealed. The total money supply, M_t, evolves according to $M_t = \lambda_t M_{t-1}$. The economy-wide increment $\Delta M_t = (\lambda_t - 1)M_{t-1}$, is distributed evenly to the home and foreign individuals, where each agent receives the lump-sum transfer $(\Delta M_t/2) = (\lambda_t - 1)(M_{t-1}/2)$.

3. A centralized securities market opens, where agents allocate their wealth toward stock purchases and the cash that they will need to purchase goods for consumption. To distinguish between the aggregate money stock M_t and the cash holdings selected by agents, we denote an individual's choice variables by lower case letters, m_t and m_t^*. The securities market closes.
4. Decentralized goods trading now takes place in the "shopping mall." Each household is split into "worker–shopper" pairs. The shopper takes the cash from security markets trading and buys x- and y-goods from *other* stores in the mall (shoppers are not allowed to buy from their own stores). The home-country worker collects the x-endowment and offers it for sale in an x-good store in the "mall." The y-goods come from the foreign-country "worker" in the foreign country, who collects and sells the y-endowment in the mall. The goods market closes.
5. The cash value of goods sales is distributed to stockholders as dividends. Stockholders carry these nominal dividend payments into the next period.

The state of the world is summarized by the gross growth rate of home output, foreign output, and money (g_t, g_t^*, λ_t), and is revealed *prior to* trading. Because the within-period uncertainty is revealed before any trading takes place, the household can determine the precise amount of money that it needs to finance the current-period consumption plan. As a result, it is not necessary to carry extra cash from one period to the next. If the (shadow) nominal interest rate is always positive, households will make sure that all the cash is spent each period.[4]

To formally derive the domestic agent's problem, let P_t be the *nominal* price of x_t. Current-period wealth is comprised of dividends from last period's goods sales, the market value of ex-dividend equity shares, and the lump-sum monetary transfer:

$$W_t = \underbrace{\frac{P_{t-1}(\omega_{xt-1}x_{t-1} + \omega_{yt-1}q_{t-1}y_{t-1})}{P_t}}_{\text{Dividends}}$$

$$+ \underbrace{\omega_{xt-1}e_t + \omega_{yt-1}e_t^*}_{\substack{\text{Ex-dividend} \\ \text{share values}}} + \underbrace{\frac{\Delta M_t}{2P_t}}_{\substack{\text{Money} \\ \text{transfer}}}. \qquad (4.26)$$

In the securities market, the domestic household allocates W_t toward cash m_t to finance shopping plans, and to equities:

$$W_t = \frac{m_t}{P_t} + \omega_{xt}e_t + \omega_{yt}e_t^*. \qquad (4.27)$$

[4] It may seem strange to talk about the interest rate and bonds, since individuals neither hold nor trade bonds. That is because bonds are redundant assets in the current environment and consequently are in zero net supply. But we can compute the shadow interest rate to keep the bonds in zero net supply. The equilibrium interest rate is such that individuals have no incentive either to issue or to buy nominal debt contracts. We will use the model to price nominal bonds at the end of this section.

The household knows that the amount of cash required to finance the current-period consumption plan is

$$m_t = P_t(c_{xt} + q_t c_{yt}). \tag{4.28}$$

The cash-in-advance constraint is said to bind. Substituting (4.28) into (4.27), and equating the result to (4.26), eliminates m_t and gives the simpler consolidated budget constraint

$$c_{xt} + q_t c_{yt} + \omega_{xt} e_t + \omega_{yt} e_t^* = \frac{P_{t-1}}{P_t} [\omega_{xt-1} x_{t-1} + \omega_{yt-1} q_{t-1} y_{t-1}]$$

$$+ \frac{\Delta M_t}{2P_t} + \omega_{xt-1} e_t + \omega_{yt-1} e_t^*. \tag{4.29}$$

The domestic household's problem is therefore to maximize

$$E_t \left(\sum_{j=0}^{\infty} \beta^j u(c_{xt+j}, c_{yt+j}) \right), \tag{4.30}$$

subject to (4.29). As before, the terms that matter at date t are

$$u(c_{xt}, c_{yt}) + \beta E_t u(c_{xt+1}, c_{yt+1}),$$

so you can substitute (4.29) into the utility function to eliminate c_{xt} and c_{xt+1}, and to transform the problem into one of unconstrained optimization. The Euler equations that characterize optimal household behavior are

$$c_{yt}: \qquad q_t u_1(c_{xt}, c_{yt}) = u_2(c_{xt}, c_{yt}), \tag{4.31}$$

$$\omega_{xt}: \qquad e_t u_1(c_{xt}, c_{yt}) = \beta E_t \left[u_1(c_{xt+1}, c_{yt+1}) \left(\frac{P_t}{P_{t+1}} x_t + e_{t+1} \right) \right], \tag{4.32}$$

$$\omega_{yt}: \qquad e_t^* u_1(c_{xt}, c_{yt}) = \beta E_t \left[u_1(c_{xt+1}, c_{yt+1}) \left(\frac{P_t}{P_{t+1}} q_t y_t + e_{t+1}^* \right) \right]. \tag{4.33}$$

The foreign household solves an analogous problem. Using the foreign cash-in-advance constraint,

$$m_t^* = P_t(c_t^* + q_t c_{yt}^*), \tag{4.34}$$

the consolidated budget constraint for the foreign household is

$$c_{xt}^* + q_t c_{yt}^* + \omega_{xt}^* e_t + \omega_{yt}^* e_t^* = \frac{P_{t-1}}{P_t} [\omega_{xt-1}^* x_{t-1} + \omega_{yt-1}^* q_{t-1} y_{t-1}]$$

$$+ \frac{\Delta M_t}{2P_t} + \omega_{xt-1}^* e_t + \omega_{yt-1}^* e_t^*. \tag{4.35}$$

The job is to maximize

$$E_t \left(\sum_{j=0}^{\infty} \beta^j u \left(c_{xt+j}^*, c_{yt+j}^* \right) \right), $$

subject to (4.35).

The foreign household's problem generates a symmetric set of Euler equations:

$$c_{yt}^*: \quad q_t u_1\left(c_{xt}^*, c_{yt}^*\right) = u_2(c_{xt}^*, c_{yt}^*),$$

$$\omega_{xt}^*: \quad e_t u_1\left(c_{xt}^*, c_{yt}^*\right) = \beta \mathrm{E}_t\left[u_1\left(c_{xt+1}^*, c_{yt+1}^*\right)\left(\frac{P_t}{P_{t+1}}x_t + e_{t+1}\right)\right],$$

$$\omega_{yt}^*: \quad e_t^* u_1\left(c_{xt}^*, c_{yt}^*\right) = \beta \mathrm{E}_t\left[u_1\left(c_{xt+1}^*, c_{yt+1}^*\right)\left(\frac{P_t}{P_{t+1}}q_t y_t + e_{t+1}^*\right)\right].$$

The adding-up constraints that complete the model are

$$1 = \omega_{xt} + \omega_{xt}^*,$$
$$1 = \omega_{yt} + \omega_{yt}^*,$$
$$M_t = m_t + m_t^*,$$
$$x_t = c_{xt} + c_{xt}^*,$$
$$y_t = c_{yt} + c_{yt}^*.$$

To solve the model, aggregate the cash-in-advance constraints over the home and foreign agents and use the adding-up constraints, to give

$$M_t = P_t(x_t + q_t y_t). \tag{4.36}$$

This is the quantity equation for the world economy, where velocity is always 1. The single money generates no new idiosyncratic country-specific risk. The equilibrium established for the barter economy (constant and equal portfolio shares) is still the perfect risk-pooling equilibrium:

$$\omega_{xt} = \omega_{xt}^* = \omega_{yt} = \omega_{yt}^* = \tfrac{1}{2},$$

$$c_{xt} = c_{xt}^* = \frac{x_t}{2},$$

$$c_{yt} = c_{yt}^* = \frac{y_t}{2}.$$

The only thing that has changed is the equity pricing formulae, which now incorporate an "inflation premium." The inflation premium arises because the nominal dividends of the current period, must be carried over into the next period, at which time their real value can potentially be eroded by an inflation shock.

The solution under constant relative risk-aversion utility. Under the utility function (4.22), the real exchange rate is $q_t = [(1-\theta)/\theta](x_t/y_t)$. Substituting this into (4.36), the inverse of the gross inflation rate is

$$\frac{P_t}{P_{t+1}} = \frac{M_t}{M_{t+1}}\frac{x_{t+1}}{x_t}.$$

Together, these expressions can be used to rewrite the equity pricing equations, as

$$\frac{e_t}{x_t} = \beta E_t \left[\left(\frac{C_{t+1}}{C_t} \right)^{(1-\gamma)} \left(\frac{M_t}{M_{t+1}} + \frac{e_{t+1}}{x_{t+1}} \right) \right], \tag{4.37}$$

$$\frac{e_t^*}{q_t y_t} = \beta E_t \left[\left(\frac{C_{t+1}}{C_t} \right)^{(1-\gamma)} \left(\frac{M_t}{M_{t+1}} + \frac{e_{t+1}^*}{q_{t+1} y_{t+1}} \right) \right]. \tag{4.38}$$

To price nominal bonds, you are looking for the shadow price of a hypothetical nominal bond such that the public willingly keeps it in zero net supply. Let b_t be the nominal price of a bond that pays one dollar at the end of the period. The utility cost of buying the bond is $u_1(c_{xt}, c_{yt}) b_t / P_t$. In equilibrium, this is offset by the discounted expected marginal utility of the one-dollar payoff, $\beta E_t[u_1(c_{xt+1}, c_{yt+1})/P_{t+1}]$. Under the constant relative risk-aversion utility function (4.22), we have

$$b_t = \beta E_t \left[\left(\frac{C_{t+1}}{C_t} \right)^{(1-\gamma)} \frac{M_t}{M_{t+1}} \right]. \tag{4.39}$$

If i_t is the nominal interest rate, then $b_t = (1 + i_t)^{-1}$. Nominal interest rates will be positive in all states of nature if $b_t < 1$, and this is likely to be true when the endowment growth rate and monetary growth rates are positive.

4.3 THE TWO-MONEY MONETARY ECONOMY

To address exchange rate issues, you need to introduce a second national currency. Let the home country money be the "dollar" and the foreign country money be the "euro." We now amend the transactions technology to require that the home country's x-goods can only be purchased with dollars and the foreign country's y-goods can only be purchased with euros. In addition, x-dividends are paid out in dollars and y-dividends are paid out in euros. Agents can acquire the foreign currency required to finance consumption plans during securities market trading.

Let P_t be the dollar price of x, let P_t^* be the euro price of y, and let S_t be the exchange rate expressed as the dollar price of euros. M_t is the outstanding stock of dollars, N_t is the outstanding stock of euros, and they evolve over time according to

$$M_t = \lambda_t M_{t-1} \quad \text{and} \quad N_t = \lambda_t^* N_{t-1},$$

where (λ_t, λ_t^*) are exogenous random gross rates of change in M and N.

If the domestic household received transfers only of M, it would face foreign purchasing-power risk, because it it also needs N to buy y-goods. Introducing the second currency creates a new country-specific risk that households will want to hedge. The complete-markets paradigm allows markets to develop whenever there is a demand for a product. The products that individuals desire are claims to future dollar and euro transfers.[5] So, to develop this idea, let r_t be the price of a claim to all future dollar transfers in terms of x, and let r_t^* be the price to all future euro transfers in terms of x. Let there be one perfectly divisible claim outstanding for each of these monetary transfer streams. Let the domestic agent hold ψ_{Mt} claims on the dollar streams and ψ_{Nt} claims on the euro streams, whereas the foreign agent holds ψ_{Mt}^* claims on the dollar stream and ψ_{Nt}^* claims on the euro stream. Initially, the home agent is endowed with $\psi_M = 1, \psi_N = 0$ and the foreign agent has $\psi_N^* = 1, \psi_M^* = 0$, which they are free to trade.

Now, to develop the problem that confronts the domestic household, note that current-period wealth consists of nominal dividends paid from equity ownership carried over from last period, current-period monetary transfers, the market value of equity, and monetary transfer claims:

$$W_t = \underbrace{\frac{P_{t-1}}{P_t}\omega_{xt-1}x_{t-1} + \frac{S_tP_{t-1}^*}{P_t}\omega_{yt-1}y_{t-1}}_{\text{Dividends}}$$

$$+ \underbrace{\frac{\psi_{Mt-1}\Delta M_t}{P_t} + \frac{\psi_{Nt-1}S_t\Delta N_t}{P_t}}_{\text{Monetary transfers}}$$

$$+ \underbrace{\omega_{xt-1}e_t + \omega_{yt-1}e_t^* + \psi_{Mt-1}r_t + \psi_{Nt-1}r_t^*}_{\text{Market value of securities}}. \tag{4.40}$$

In securities market trading, this wealth is allocated to stocks, claims to future monetary transfers, and dollars and euros for shopping according to

$$W_t = \omega_{xt}e_t + \omega_{yt}e_t^* + \psi_{Mt}r_t + \psi_{Nt}r_t^* + \frac{m_t}{P_t} + \frac{n_tS_t}{P_t}. \tag{4.41}$$

The current values of x_t, y_t, M_t, and N_t are revealed before trading occurs, so domestic households acquire the exact amount of dollars and euros required to finance current-period consumption plans. In equilibrium, we have the binding cash-in-advance constraints

$$m_t = P_t c_{xt}, \tag{4.42}$$

$$n_t = P_t^* c_{yt}, \tag{4.43}$$

which you can use to eliminate m_t and n_t from the allocation of current-period wealth, to rewrite (4.41) as

$$W_t = \underbrace{c_{xt} + \frac{S_tP_t^*}{P_t}c_{yt}}_{\text{Goods}} + \underbrace{\omega_{xt}e_t + \omega_{yt}e_t^*}_{\text{Equity}} + \underbrace{\psi_{Mt}r_t + \psi_{Nt}r_t^*}_{\text{Money transfers}}. \tag{4.44}$$

---

[5] In the real world, this type of hedge might be constructed by taking appropriate positions in futures contracts for foreign currencies.

The consolidated budget constraint of the home individual is therefore

$$c_{xt} + \frac{S_t P_t^*}{P_t} c_{yt} + \omega_{xt} e_t + \omega_{yt} e_t^* + \psi_{Mt} r_t + \psi_{Nt} r_t^*$$

$$= \frac{P_{t-1}}{P_t} \omega_{xt-1} x_{t-1} + \frac{S_t P_{t-1}^*}{P_t} \omega_{yt-1} y_{t-1} + \frac{\psi_{Mt-1} \Delta M_t}{P_t}$$

$$+ \frac{\psi_{Nt-1} S_t \Delta N_t}{P_t} + \omega_{xt-1} e_t + \omega_{yt-1} e_t^* + \psi_{xt-1} r_t + \psi_{yt-1} r_t^*. \qquad (4.45)$$

The domestic household's problem is to maximize

$$\mathrm{E}_t \left(\sum_{j=0}^{\infty} \beta^j u(c_{xt+j}, c_{yt+j}) \right) \qquad (4.46)$$

subject to (4.45). The associated Euler equations are

$$c_{yt}: \qquad \frac{S_t P_t^*}{P_t} u_1(c_{xt}, c_{yt}) = u_2(c_{xt}, c_{yt}), \qquad (4.47)$$

$$\omega_{xt}: \qquad e_t u_1(c_{xt}, c_{yt}) = \beta \mathrm{E}_t \left[u_1(c_{xt+1}, c_{yt+1}) \left(\frac{P_t}{P_{t+1}} x_t + e_{t+1} \right) \right], \qquad (4.48)$$

$$\omega_{yt}: \qquad e_t^* u_1(c_{xt}, c_{yt}) = \beta \mathrm{E}_t \left[u_1(c_{xt+1}, c_{yt+1}) \left(\frac{S_{t+1} P_t^*}{P_{t+1}} y_t + e_{t+1}^* \right) \right], \qquad (4.49)$$

$$\psi_{Mt}: \qquad r_t u_1(c_{xt}, c_{yt}) = \beta \mathrm{E}_t \left[u_1(c_{xt+1}, c_{yt+1}) \left(\frac{\Delta M_{t+1}}{P_{t+1}} + r_{t+1} \right) \right], \qquad (4.50)$$

$$\psi_{Nt}: \qquad r_t^* u_1(c_{xt}, c_{yt}) = \beta \mathrm{E}_t \left[u_1(c_{xt+1}, c_{yt+1}) \left(\frac{\Delta N_{t+1} S_{t+1}}{P_{t+1}} + r_{t+1}^* \right) \right]. \qquad (4.51)$$

The foreign agent solves the analogous problem, which generates a set of symmetric Euler equations that do not need to be stated here.

We know that, in equilibrium, the cash-in-advance constraints bind. The cash-in-advance constraints for the foreign agent are

$$m_t^* = P_t c_{xt}^*, \qquad (4.52)$$

$$n_t^* = P_t^* c_{yt}^*. \qquad (4.53)$$

In addition, we have the adding-up constraints

$$1 = \psi_{Mt} + \psi_{Mt}^*,$$

$$1 = \psi_{Nt} + \psi_{Nt}^*,$$

$$x_t = c_{xt} + c_{xt}^*,$$

$$y_t = c_{yt} + c_{yt}^*,$$

$$M_t = m_t + m_t^*,$$

$$N_t = n_t + n_t^*.$$

Together, the adding-up constraints and the cash-in-advance constraints give a unit-velocity quantity equation for each country:

$$M_t = P_t x_t,$$

$$N_t = P_t^* y_t,$$

which can be used to eliminate the endogenous nominal price levels from the Euler equations.

The equilibrium where people are able to pool and insure against their country-specific risks is given by

$$\omega_{xt} = \omega_{xt}^* = \omega_{yt} = \omega_{yt}^* = \psi_{Mt} = \psi_{Mt}^* = \psi_{Nt} = \psi_{Nt}^* = \tfrac{1}{2}.$$

Both the domestic and foreign representative households own half of the domestic endowment stream, half of the foreign endowment stream, half of all future domestic monetary transfers, and half of all future foreign monetary transfers. In short, they split the world's resources in half so the pooling equilibrium supports the symmetric allocation $c_{xt} = c_{xt}^* = x_t/2$ and $c_{yt} = c_{yt}^* = y_t/2$.

To solve for the nominal exchange rate S_t, we know from (4.47) that the real exchange rate is

$$\frac{u_2(c_{xt}, c_{yt})}{u_1(c_{xt}, c_{yt})} = \frac{S_t P_t^*}{P_t} = \frac{S_t N_t x_t}{M_t y_t}. \tag{4.54}$$

Rearranging (4.54) gives the nominal exchange rate:

$$S_t = \frac{u_2(c_{xt}, c_{yt})}{u_1(c_{xt}, c_{yt})} \frac{M_t}{N_t} \frac{y_t}{x_t}. \tag{4.55}$$

As in the monetary approach, the fundamental determinants of the nominal exchange rate are relative money supplies and relative GDPs. The two major differences are, first, that in the Lucas model the exchange rate depends on preferences (utility) and, second, that it does not depend explicitly on expectations of the future.

The solution under constant relative risk-aversion utility. Using the utility function (4.22), the equilibrium real exchange rate is $q_t = ((1-\theta)/\theta)(x_t/y_t)$. The income terms cancel out and the exchange rate is

$$S_t = \frac{(1-\theta)}{\theta} \frac{M_t}{N_t}. \tag{4.56}$$

The Euler equations are

$$\frac{e_t}{x_t} = \beta E_t \left[\left(\frac{C_{t+1}}{C_t} \right)^{(1-\gamma)} \left(\frac{M_t}{M_{t+1}} + \frac{e_{t+1}}{x_{t+1}} \right) \right], \tag{4.57}$$

$$\frac{e_t^*}{q_t y_t} = \beta E_t \left[\left(\frac{C_{t+1}}{C_t} \right)^{(1-\gamma)} \left(\frac{N_t}{N_{t+1}} + \frac{e_{t+1}^*}{q_{t+1} y_{t+1}} \right) \right], \tag{4.58}$$

$$\frac{r_t}{x_t} = \beta E_t \left[\left(\frac{C_{t+1}}{C_t} \right)^{(1-\gamma)} \left(\frac{\Delta M_{t+1}}{M_{t+1}} + \frac{r_{t+1}}{x_{t+1}} \right) \right], \tag{4.59}$$

$$\frac{r_t^*}{x_t} = \beta E_t \left[\left(\frac{C_{t+1}}{C_t} \right)^{(1-\gamma)} \left(\frac{1-\theta}{\theta} \frac{\Delta N_{t+1}}{N_{t+1}} + \frac{r_{t+1}^*}{x_{t+1}} \right) \right]. \tag{4.60}$$

Just as you can calculate the equilibrium price of nominal bonds even though they are not traded in equilibrium, you can compute the equilibrium forward exchange rate even though there is no explicit forward market. To do this, let b_t be the date-t dollar price of a one-period nominal discount bond that pays one dollar at the beginning of period $t+1$, and let b_t^* be the date-t euro price of a one-period nominal discount bond that pays one euro at the beginning of period $t+1$. By covered interest parity (1.2), the one-period-ahead forward exchange rate is

$$F_t = S_t \frac{b_t^*}{b_t}. \tag{4.61}$$

The equilibrium bond prices are

$$b_t = \beta E_t \left[\left(\frac{C_{t+1}}{C_t} \right)^{1-\gamma} \frac{M_t}{M_{t+1}} \right], \tag{4.62}$$

$$b_t^* = \beta E_t \left[\left(\frac{C_{t+1}}{C_t} \right)^{1-\gamma} \frac{N_t}{N_{t+1}} \right]. \tag{4.63}$$

4.4 AN INTRODUCTION TO THE CALIBRATION METHOD

The Lucas model plays a central role in asset-pricing research. Chapter 6 covers some tests of its predictions using time-series econometric methods. At this point, we introduce an alternative and popular methodology called *calibration*. In the calibration method, the researcher simulates the model given "reasonable" values of the underlying taste and technology parameters, and looks to see whether the simulated observations match various features of the real-world data.

Table 4.1 Notation for the Lucas model

x_t	The domestic good
y_t	The foreign good
q_t	The relative price of y in terms of x
c_{xt}	The home consumption of the home good
c_{yt}	The home consumption of the foreign good
C_t	The domestic Cobb–Douglas consumption index, $c_{xt}^{\theta} c_y^{(1-\theta)}$
C_t^*	The foreign Cobb–Douglas consumption index, $c_x^{*\theta} c_y^{*(1-\theta)}$
c_{xt}^*	The foreign consumption of the home good
c_{yt}^*	The foreign consumption of the foreign good
ω_{xt}	The shares of the home firm held by the home agent
ω_{yt}	The shares of the foreign firm held by the home agent
ω_{xt}^*	The shares of the home firm held by the foreign agent
ω_{yt}^*	The shares of the foreign firm held by the foreign agent
S_t	The nominal exchange rate; dollar price of the euro
e_t	The price of home firm equity in terms of x
e_t^*	The price of foreign firm equity in terms of x
P_t	The nominal price of x in dollars
P_t^*	The nominal price of y in euros
M_t	Dollars in circulation
N_t	Euros in circulation
λ_{tx}	The rate of growth of M
λ_{tx}^*	The rate of growth of N
m_t	Dollars held by the domestic household
m_t^*	Dollars held by the foreign household
n_t	Euros held by the domestic household
n_t^*	Euros held by the foreign household
r_t	The price of a claim to future dollar transfers in terms of x
r_t^*	The price of a claim to future euro transfers in terms of x
ψ_{Mt}	The shares of the dollar transfer stream held by the home agent
ψ_{Nt}	The shares of the euro transfer stream held by the home agent
ψ_{Mt}^*	The shares of the dollar transfer stream held by the foreign agent
ψ_{Nt}^*	The shares of the euro transfer stream held by the foreign agent
b_t	The price of a one-period nominal bond with a one-dollar payoff

Because there is no capital accumulation or production, the technology in the Lucas model is a stochastic process that governs the evolution of x_t and y_t. The reasonably simple mechanics underlying the model makes its calibration relatively straightforward. Our work here will set the stage for the next chapter, as real business cycle researchers rely heavily on the calibration method to evaluate the performance of their models.

Cooley and Prescott [32] set out the ingredients for the calibration method as follows:

1. Obtain a set of measurements from real-world data that you want to explain. These are typically a set of sample moments such as the mean, the standard deviation, and autocorrelations of a time-series. Special emphasis is often placed on the cross-correlations between two series, which measure the extent of their *co-movements*.

2. Solve and calibrate a candidate model. That is, assign values to the *deep parameters* of tastes (the utility function) and technology (the production function) that make sense or that have been estimated by others.

3. *Run (simulate)* the model by computer and generate time-series of the variables that you want to explain.

4. Decide whether the computer-generated time-series implied by the model "look like" the observations that you want to explain.[6]

4.5 CALIBRATING THE LUCAS MODEL

Measurement. The measurements that we ask the Lucas model to match are the volatility (standard deviation) and first-order autocorrelation of the gross rate of depreciation, S_{t+1}/S_t, the forward premium, F_t/S_t, the realized forward profit, $(F_t - S_{t+1})/S_t$, and the slope coefficient from regressing the gross depreciation on the forward premium. Using quarterly data for the US and Germany from 1973.1 to 1997.1, the measurements are given in the row labeled "Data" in table 4.2.

The implied forward and spot exchange rates exhibit the so-called forward premium puzzle – that the forward premium predicts the future depreciation, but with a negative sign. Recall that the uncovered interest parity condition implies that the forward premium predicts the future depreciation with a coefficient of 1. The depreciation and the realized profit exhibit volatilities of similar magnitude, which are much larger than the volatility of the forward premium. The forward premium exhibits substantial serial dependence.

Calibration. Let random variables be denoted with a tilde ("~"). The "technology" that underlies the model consists of the exogenous monetary growth rates $\tilde{\lambda}, \tilde{\lambda}^*$, and the exogenous output growth rates $\tilde{g}, \tilde{g}^*$. Let the state vector be $\underline{\tilde{\phi}} = (\tilde{\lambda}, \tilde{\lambda}^*, \tilde{g}, \tilde{g}^*)$. The process governing the state vector is a finite-state Markov chain with stationary probabilities (see the appendix). Each element

Table 4.2 Measured and implied moments, US–Germany

		Volatility			Autocorrelation		
	Slope	S_{t+1}/S_t	F_t/S_t	$(F_t - S_{t+1})/S_t$	S_{t+1}/S_t	F_t/S_t	$(F_t - S_{t+1})/S_t$
Data	−0.293	0.060	0.008	0.061	0.007	0.888	0.026
Model	−1.444	0.014	0.006	0.029	0.105	0.006	0.628

Model values generated with $\gamma = 10$, $\theta = 0.5$.

---

[6] The standard analysis is not based on classical statistical inference, although Cecchetti et al. [23], Burnside [17], and Gregory and Smith [64] show how calibration methods can be combined with classical statistical inference, but the practice has not caught on.

of the state vector is allowed to be in either one of two possible states – high or low. A "1" subscript indicates that the variable is in the high-growth state and a "2" subscript indicates that the variable is in the low-growth state. Therefore, $\lambda = \lambda_1$ indicates high domestic money growth, while $\lambda = \lambda_2$ indicates low domestic money growth. Analogous designations hold for the other variables. The 16 possible states of the world are as follows:

$$
\begin{aligned}
&\underline{\phi}_1 = (\lambda_1, \lambda_1^*, g_1, g_1^*), &\quad &\underline{\phi}_2 = (\lambda_1, \lambda_1^*, g_1, g_2^*), \\
&\underline{\phi}_3 = (\lambda_1, \lambda_1^*, g_2, g_1^*), &\quad &\underline{\phi}_4 = (\lambda_1, \lambda_1^*, g_2, g_2^*), \\
&\underline{\phi}_5 = (\lambda_1, \lambda_2^*, g_1, g_1^*), &\quad &\underline{\phi}_6 = (\lambda_1, \lambda_2^*, g_1, g_2^*), \\
&\underline{\phi}_7 = (\lambda_1, \lambda_2^*, g_2, g_1^*), &\quad &\underline{\phi}_8 = (\lambda_1, \lambda_2^*, g_2, g_2^*), \\
&\underline{\phi}_9 = (\lambda_2, \lambda_1^*, g_1, g_1^*), &\quad &\underline{\phi}_{10} = (\lambda_2, \lambda_1^*, g_1, g_2^*), \\
&\underline{\phi}_{11} = (\lambda_2, \lambda_1^*, g_2, g_1^*), &\quad &\underline{\phi}_{12} = (\lambda_2, \lambda_1^*, g_2, g_2^*), \\
&\underline{\phi}_{13} = (\lambda_2, \lambda_2^*, g_1, g_1^*), &\quad &\underline{\phi}_{14} = (\lambda_2, \lambda_2^*, g_1, g_2^*), \\
&\underline{\phi}_{15} = (\lambda_2, \lambda_2^*, g_2, g_1^*), &\quad &\underline{\phi}_{16} = (\lambda_2, \lambda_2^*, g_2, g_2^*).
\end{aligned}
$$

We will denote the 16×16 probability transition matrix for the state by $\mathbf{P}$, where $p_{ij} = P[\tilde{\underline{\phi}}_{t+1} = \underline{\phi}_j \mid \tilde{\underline{\phi}}_t = \underline{\phi}_i]$ is the ijth element.

The prices of the domestic and foreign currency bonds are $b_t = \beta E_t[(g_{t+1}^\theta g_{t+1}^{*(1-\theta)})^{1-\gamma}]/\lambda_{t+1}$ and $b_t^* = \beta E_t[(g_{t+1}^\theta g_{t+1}^{*(1-\theta)})^{1-\gamma}]/\lambda_{t+1}^*$, under the constant relative risk-aversion utility function (4.22). Since their values depend on the state of the world, we say that these are *state-contingent* bond prices. Next, define $G = [(g^\theta g^{*(1-\theta)})^{1-\gamma}]/\lambda$ and $G^* = [(g^\theta g^{*(1-\theta)})^{1-\gamma}]/\lambda^*$, and let $d = \lambda/\lambda^*$ be the gross rate of depreciation of the home currency. The possible values of G, G^*, and d are given in table 4.3.

Suppose that the current state is $\underline{\phi}_k$. By (4.56), the spot exchange rate is given by $(1 - \theta)d_k/\theta$. The domestic bond price is $b_k = \beta \sum_{i=1}^{16} p_{k,i} G_i$, the foreign bond price is $b_k^* = \beta \sum_{i=1}^{16} p_{k,i} G_i^*$, the expected gross change in the nominal exchange rate is $\sum_{i=1}^{16} p_{k,i} d_i$, and the state-$k$ contingent risk premium is

$$
rp_k = \sum_{i=1}^{16} p_{k,i} d_i - \frac{\left(\sum_{i=1}^{16} p_{k,i} G_i^* \right)}{\left(\sum_{i=1}^{16} p_{k,i} G_i \right)}.
$$

Next, we must estimate the probability transition matrix. The first question is whether we should use consumption data or GDP. In the Lucas model, consumption equals GDP, so there is no theoretical presumption as to which series we should use. Since prices depend on utility, which in turn depends on consumption, it might make sense to use consumption data. This is in fact what we do. The consumption and money data are from the *International Financial Statistics* and are in per capita terms.

The next question is what estimation technique to use. Using generalized method of moments or simulated method of moments (see sections 2.2.2 and 2.2.3) to estimate the transition matrix might be good choices if the dimensionality of the problem were smaller. Since we don't have a very long time span of data,

Table 4.3 Possible state values

$$G_1 = [(g_1^\theta g_1^{*(1-\theta)})^{1-\gamma}]/\lambda_1 \qquad G_1^* = [(g_1^\theta g_1^{*(1-\theta)})^{1-\gamma}]/\lambda_1^* \qquad d_1 = \lambda_1/\lambda_1^*$$

$$G_2 = [(g_1^\theta g_2^{*(1-\theta)})^{1-\gamma}]/\lambda_1 \qquad G_2^* = [(g_1^\theta g_2^{*(1-\theta)})^{1-\gamma}]/\lambda_1^* \qquad d_2 = \lambda_1/\lambda_1^*$$

$$G_3 = [(g_2^\theta g_1^{*(1-\theta)})^{1-\gamma}]/\lambda_1 \qquad G_3^* = [(g_2^\theta g_1^{*(1-\theta)})^{1-\gamma}]/\lambda_1^* \qquad d_3 = \lambda_1/\lambda_1^*$$

$$G_4 = [(g_2^\theta g_2^{*(1-\theta)})^{1-\gamma}]/\lambda_1 \qquad G_4^* = [(g_2^\theta g_2^{*(1-\theta)})^{1-\gamma}]/\lambda_1^* \qquad d_4 = \lambda_1/\lambda_1^*$$

$$G_5 = [(g_1^\theta g_1^{*(1-\theta)})^{1-\gamma}]/\lambda_1 \qquad G_5^* = [(g_1^\theta g_1^{*(1-\theta)})^{1-\gamma}]/\lambda_2^* \qquad d_5 = \lambda_1/\lambda_2^*$$

$$G_6 = [(g_1^\theta g_2^{*(1-\theta)})^{1-\gamma}]/\lambda_1 \qquad G_6^* = [(g_1^\theta g_2^{*(1-\theta)})^{1-\gamma}]/\lambda_2^* \qquad d_6 = \lambda_1/\lambda_2^*$$

$$G_7 = [(g_2^\theta g_1^{*(1-\theta)})^{1-\gamma}]/\lambda_1 \qquad G_7^* = [(g_2^\theta g_1^{*(1-\theta)})^{1-\gamma}]/\lambda_2^* \qquad d_7 = \lambda_1/\lambda_2^*$$

$$G_8 = [(g_2^\theta g_2^{*(1-\theta)})^{1-\gamma}]/\lambda_1 \qquad G_8^* = [(g_2^\theta g_2^{*(1-\theta)})^{1-\gamma}]/\lambda_2^* \qquad d_8 = \lambda_1/\lambda_2^*$$

$$G_9 = [(g_1^\theta g_1^{*(1-\theta)})^{1-\gamma}]/\lambda_2 \qquad G_9^* = [(g_1^\theta g_1^{*(1-\theta)})^{1-\gamma}]/\lambda_1^* \qquad d_9 = \lambda_2/\lambda_1^*$$

$$G_{10} = [(g_1^\theta g_2^{*(1-\theta)})^{1-\gamma}]/\lambda_2 \qquad G_{10}^* = [(g_1^\theta g_2^{*(1-\theta)})^{1-\gamma}]/\lambda_1^* \qquad d_{10} = \lambda_2/\lambda_1^*$$

$$G_{11} = [(g_2^\theta g_1^{*(1-\theta)})^{1-\gamma}]/\lambda_2 \qquad G_{11}^* = [(g_2^\theta g_1^{*(1-\theta)})^{1-\gamma}]/\lambda_1^* \qquad d_{11} = \lambda_2/\lambda_1^*$$

$$G_{12} = [(g_2^\theta g_2^{*(1-\theta)})^{1-\gamma}]/\lambda_2 \qquad G_{12}^* = [(g_2^\theta g_2^{*(1-\theta)})^{1-\gamma}]/\lambda_1^* \qquad d_{12} = \lambda_2/\lambda_1^*$$

$$G_{13} = [(g_1^\theta g_1^{*(1-\theta)})^{1-\gamma}]/\lambda_2 \qquad G_{13}^* = [(g_1^\theta g_1^{*(1-\theta)})^{1-\gamma}]/\lambda_2^* \qquad d_{13} = \lambda_2/\lambda_2^*$$

$$G_{14} = [(g_1^\theta g_2^{*(1-\theta)})^{1-\gamma}]/\lambda_2 \qquad G_{14}^* = [(g_1^\theta g_2^{*(1-\theta)})^{1-\gamma}]/\lambda_2^* \qquad d_{14} = \lambda_2/\lambda_2^*$$

$$G_{15} = [(g_2^\theta g_1^{*(1-\theta)})^{1-\gamma}]/\lambda_2 \qquad G_{15}^* = [(g_2^\theta g_1^{*(1-\theta)})^{1-\gamma}]/\lambda_2^* \qquad d_{15} = \lambda_2/\lambda_2^*$$

$$G_{16} = [(g_2^\theta g_2^{*(1-\theta)})^{1-\gamma}]/\lambda_2 \qquad G_{16}^* = [(g_2^\theta g_2^{*(1-\theta)})^{1-\gamma}]/\lambda_2^* \qquad d_{16} = \lambda_2/\lambda_2^*$$

it turns out that estimating the transition probability matrix **P** by GMM or by the SMM does not work well. Instead, we "estimate" the transition probabilities by counting the relative frequency of the transition events.

Let's classify the growth rate of a variable as being high-growth whenever it lies above its sample mean and being low-growth otherwise. Then set high-growth states λ_1, λ_1^*, g_1, and g_1^* to the average of the high-growth rates found in the data. Similarly, assign the low-growth states λ_2, λ_2^*, g_2, and g_2^* to the average of the low-growth rates found in the data. Using per capita consumption and money data for the US and Germany, and viewing the US as the home country, the estimates of the high- and low-growth state values are as follows:

$\lambda_1 = 1.010$ – average US money growth good state,
$\lambda_2 = 0.990$ – average US money growth bad state,
$\lambda_1^* = 1.011$ – average German money growth good state,
$\lambda_2^* = 0.991$ – average German money growth bad state,
$g_1 = 1.009$ – average US consumption growth good state,
$g_2 = 0.998$ – average US consumption growth bad state,
$g_1^* = 1.012$ – average German consumption growth good state,
$g_2^* = 0.993$ – average German consumption growth bad state.

Now classify the data into the ϕ states according to whether the observations lie above or below the mean, and then set the transition probabilities p_{jk} equal to the relative frequency of transitions from state ϕ_j to ϕ_k found in the data. The **P** estimated in this fashion, rounded to two significant digits, is

$$
\begin{bmatrix}
0.00 & 0.00 & 0.20 & 0.00 & 0.40 & 0.00 & 0.00 & 0.00 & 0.20 & 0.00 & 0.00 & 0.00 & 0.20 & 0.00 & 0.00 & 0.00 \\
0.20 & 0.20 & 0.20 & 0.20 & 0.00 & 0.20 & 0.00 & 0.00 & 0.00 & 0.00 & 0.00 & 0.00 & 0.00 & 0.00 & 0.00 & 0.00 \\
0.17 & 0.17 & 0.00 & 0.17 & 0.17 & 0.00 & 0.00 & 0.00 & 0.00 & 0.00 & 0.00 & 0.00 & 0.00 & 0.00 & 0.17 & 0.17 \\
0.00 & 0.00 & 0.00 & 0.00 & 0.17 & 0.00 & 0.00 & 0.00 & 0.00 & 0.17 & 0.33 & 0.17 & 0.00 & 0.00 & 0.17 & 0.00 \\
0.08 & 0.08 & 0.08 & 0.08 & 0.15 & 0.08 & 0.08 & 0.08 & 0.15 & 0.08 & 0.08 & 0.00 & 0.00 & 0.00 & 0.00 & 0.00 \\
0.20 & 0.00 & 0.00 & 0.00 & 0.20 & 0.00 & 0.00 & 0.00 & 0.00 & 0.00 & 0.20 & 0.00 & 0.00 & 0.20 & 0.20 & 0.00 \\
0.00 & 0.00 & 0.00 & 0.20 & 0.40 & 0.00 & 0.00 & 0.20 & 0.00 & 0.00 & 0.00 & 0.00 & 0.20 & 0.00 & 0.00 & 0.00 \\
0.25 & 0.00 & 0.00 & 0.00 & 0.00 & 0.50 & 0.00 & 0.00 & 0.00 & 0.00 & 0.00 & 0.00 & 0.00 & 0.00 & 0.00 & 0.25 \\
0.00 & 0.14 & 0.00 & 0.00 & 0.00 & 0.00 & 0.14 & 0.00 & 0.14 & 0.14 & 0.00 & 0.00 & 0.00 & 0.14 & 0.14 & 0.14 \\
0.00 & 0.00 & 0.00 & 0.00 & 0.00 & 0.00 & 0.25 & 0.00 & 0.25 & 0.00 & 0.00 & 0.25 & 0.25 & 0.00 & 0.00 & 0.00 \\
0.00 & 0.00 & 0.20 & 0.00 & 0.20 & 0.00 & 0.00 & 0.00 & 0.20 & 0.20 & 0.00 & 0.20 & 0.00 & 0.00 & 0.00 & 0.00 \\
0.00 & 0.25 & 0.00 & 0.25 & 0.25 & 0.00 & 0.00 & 0.00 & 0.00 & 0.00 & 0.00 & 0.00 & 0.00 & 0.25 & 0.00 & 0.00 \\
0.00 & 0.00 & 0.00 & 0.00 & 0.13 & 0.00 & 0.00 & 0.13 & 0.13 & 0.00 & 0.13 & 0.13 & 0.25 & 0.00 & 0.13 & 0.00 \\
0.00 & 0.00 & 0.20 & 0.00 & 0.00 & 0.00 & 0.00 & 0.00 & 0.00 & 0.00 & 0.00 & 0.00 & 0.20 & 0.00 & 0.40 & 0.20 \\
0.00 & 0.00 & 0.00 & 0.00 & 0.25 & 0.00 & 0.25 & 0.13 & 0.00 & 0.00 & 0.00 & 0.00 & 0.13 & 0.13 & 0.00 & 0.13 \\
0.00 & 0.00 & 0.00 & 0.20 & 0.00 & 0.20 & 0.00 & 0.00 & 0.00 & 0.00 & 0.00 & 0.00 & 0.20 & 0.20 & 0.20 & 0.00
\end{bmatrix}.
$$

Results. We set the share of home goods in consumption to be $\theta = 1/2$, the coefficient of relative risk aversion to be $\gamma = 10$, and the subjective discount factor to be $\beta = 0.99$, and simulate the model as follows.

Draw a sequence of T realizations of the gross change in the exchange rate, the forward premium, and the risk premium, with the initial state vector drawn from probabilities of the initial probability vector, $\underline{v}$. Let u_t be a *iid* uniform random variable on $[0, 1]$. The rule for determining the initial state is

$$
\begin{array}{ll}
\underline{\phi}_1 & \text{if } u_t < v_1, \\
\underline{\phi}_2 & \text{if } v_1 < u_t < \sum_{j=1}^{2} v_j, \\
\underline{\phi}_3 & \text{if } \sum_{j=1}^{2} v_j < u_t < \sum_{j=1}^{3} v_j, \\
\;\;\vdots & \;\;\vdots \\
\underline{\phi}_{16} & \text{if } \sum_{j=1}^{15} v_j < u_t < 1.
\end{array}
$$

For subsequent observations, suppose that at $t = 1$ we are in state k. Then the state at $t = 2$ is determined by

$$
\begin{array}{ll}
\underline{\phi}_1 & \text{if } u_t < p_{k1}, \\
\underline{\phi}_2 & \text{if } p_{k1} < u_t < \sum_{j=1}^{2} p_{kj}, \\
\underline{\phi}_3 & \text{if } \sum_{j=1}^{2} p_{kj} < u_t < \sum_{j=1}^{3} p_{kj}, \\
\;\;\vdots & \;\;\vdots \\
\underline{\phi}_{16} & \text{if } \sum_{j=1}^{15} p_{kj} < u_t < 1.
\end{array}
$$

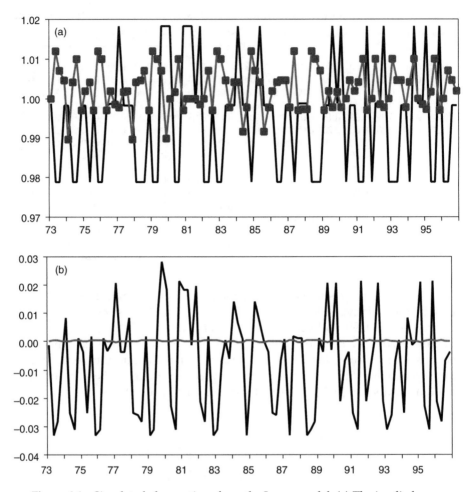

Figure 4.1 Simulated observations from the Lucas model. (a) The implied gross
one-period-ahead change in nominal exchange rate S_{t+1}/S_t and current forward
premium F_t/S_t (in boxes). (b) The implied *ex post* forward payoff $(S_{t+1} - F_t)/S_t$ (jagged
line) and risk premium $E_t(S_{t+1} - F_t)/S_t$ (smooth line).

Figure 4.1(a) shows 97 simulated values of S_{t+1}/S_t and F_t/S_t generated from
the model. Notice that these two series appear to be negatively correlated. This
certainly is not what you would expect to see if uncovered interest parity held.
But we know from chapter 1 that market participation of risk-averse agents is
potentially a key reason behind the failure of UIP.

Figure 4.1(b) shows the simulated values of the predicted forward payoff
$E_t(S_{t+1} - F_t)/S_t$ and the realized payoff $(S_{t+1} - F_t)/S_t$. The thing to notice here is
that the predicted payoff or risk premium seems too small to explain the data.
The largest predicted state contingent risk premium is actually only 0.14 percent
on a quarterly basis.

Now we generate 10,000 time-series observations from the model and use them to calculate slope coefficient, volatility, and autocorrelation coefficients shown in the row labeled "Model" in table 4.2. As can be seen, the implied volatility of the depreciation and of the realized profit is much too small. The implied persistence of the depreciation and the forward premium is also too low to be consistent with the data.

The model does predict that the forward rate is a biased predictor of the future spot rate due to the presence of a risk premium. However, the size of the implied risk premium appears to be too small to provide an adequate explanation for the data. We study the forward premium puzzle in greater detail in chapter 6.

▶ Chapter Summary

1. The Lucas model is a flexible-price, complete markets, dynamic general equilibrium model with optimizing agents. It is logically consistent and provides the microfoundations for international asset pricing.
2. The model provides a framework for pricing assets, including the exchange rate, in an international setting. The exchange rate depends on the same set of fundamental variables as predicted by the monetary model. (The empirical predictions of the model will be developed more fully in chapter 6.)
3. There is no trading volume for any of the assets. The prices derived in the model are shadow values, under which the existing stock of assets are willingly held by the agents.
4. Output is taken to be exogenous, so the model is not well equipped to explain quantities such as the current account.
5. The Lucas model is designed to help us understand the determination of the prices of assets – exchange rates, bonds, and stocks – that are consistent with equilibrium choices of consumption. Because it is an endowment model, the dynamics of consumption (or, alternatively, output) are taken exogeneously. This is actually a virtue of the model, since a model with production, while perhaps more "realistic," does not change the underlying asset pricing formulae, which are based on the Euler equations for the consumer's problem, but complicates the job by forcing us to write down a model where equilibrium decisions of the firm generate not only realistic asset price movements but also realistic output dynamics. It is therefore not necessary, or even desirable, to introduce production in order to understand equilibrium asset pricing issues.

▶ Appendix: Markov Chains

Let X_t be a random variable and let x_t be a particular realization of X_t. A Markov chain is a stochastic process $\{X_t\}_{t=0}^{\infty}$ with the property that the information in the current realized value of $X_t = x_t$ summarizes the entire past history of the process. That is,

$$\Pr[X_{t+1} = x_{t+1} | X_t = x_t, X_{t-1} = x_{t-1}, \ldots, X_0 = x_0]$$
$$= \Pr[X_{t+1} = x_{t+1} | X_t = x_t]. \tag{4.64}$$

A key result that simplifies probability calculations of Markov chains is the following.

Property 1   If $\{X_t\}_{t=0}^{\infty}$ is a Markov chain, then

$$\Pr[X_t = x_t \cap X_{t-1} = x_{t-1} \cap \cdots \cap X_0 = x_0]$$
$$= \Pr[X_t = x_t | X_{t-1} = x_{t-1}] \cdots \Pr[X_1 = x_1 | X_0 = x_0]\Pr[X_0 = x_0]. \tag{4.65}$$

Proof. Let A_j be the event $(X_j = x_j)$. You can write the left-hand side of (4.65) as

$$\Pr\left(A_t \cap A_{t-1} \cap \cdots \cap A_0\right)$$

$$= \Pr\left(A_t | \bigcap_{j=0}^{t-1} A_j\right) \Pr\left(\bigcap_{j=0}^{t-1} A_j\right) \quad \text{(multiplication rule)}$$

$$= \Pr(A_t | A_{t-1}) \Pr\left(\bigcap_{j=0}^{t-1} A_j\right) \quad \text{(Markov chain property)}$$

$$= \Pr(A_t | A_{t-1}) \Pr\left(A_{t-1} | \bigcap_{j=0}^{t-2} A_j\right) \Pr\left(\bigcap_{j=0}^{t-2} A_j\right) \quad \text{(multiplication rule)}$$

$$= \Pr\left(A_t | A_{t-1}\right) \Pr\left(A_{t-1} | A_{t-2}\right) \Pr\left(\bigcap_{j=0}^{t-2}\right) \quad \text{(Markov chain)}$$

$$\vdots$$

$$= \Pr(A_t | A_{t-1})\Pr(A_{t-1} | A_{t-2}) \cdots \Pr(A_1 | A_0)\Pr(A_0) \qquad \blacksquare$$

Let λ_j, $j = 1, \ldots, N$ denote the possible states for X_t. A Markov chain has stationary probabilities if the transition probabilities from state λ_i to λ_j are time-invariant. That is,

$$\Pr[X_{t+1} = \lambda_j \mid X_t = \lambda_i] = p_{ij}.$$

Notice that in Markov chain analysis the first subscript denotes the state on which you condition. For concreteness, consider a Markov chain with two possible states, λ_1 and λ_2, with transition matrix.

$$\mathbf{P} = \left[\begin{array}{cc} p_{11} & p_{12} \\ p_{21} & p_{22} \end{array} \right],$$

where the rows of $\mathbf{P}$ sum to 1.

Property 2   The transition matrix over k steps is

$$\mathbf{P}^k = \underbrace{\mathbf{PP} \cdots \mathbf{P}}_{k}.$$

Proof. For the two-state process, define

$$
\begin{aligned}
p_{ij}^{(2)} &= \Pr[X_{t+2} = \lambda_j \mid X_t = \lambda_i] \\
&= \Pr[X_{t+2} = \lambda_j \cap X_{t+1} = \lambda_1 | X_t = \lambda_i] + \Pr[X_{t+1} = \lambda_j \cap X_{t+1} = \lambda_2 | X_t = \lambda_i] \\
&= \sum_{k=1}^{2} \Pr[X_{t+1} = \lambda_j \cap X_{t+1} = \lambda_k | X_t = \lambda_i] \\
&= \frac{\Pr[X_{t+1} = \lambda_j \cap X_{t+1} = \lambda_k \cap X_t = \lambda_i]}{\Pr(X_t = \lambda_i)}.
\end{aligned}
\tag{4.66}
$$

Now, by property 1, the numerator in the last equality can be decomposed as

$$\Pr[X_{t+2} = \lambda_j | X_{t+1} = \lambda_k] \Pr[X_{t+1} = \lambda_k | X_t = \lambda_i] \Pr[X_t = \lambda_i]. \tag{4.67}$$

Substituting (4.67) into (4.66) gives

$$
\begin{aligned}
p_{ij}^{(2)} &= \sum_{k=1}^{2} \Pr[X_{t+1} = \lambda_j | X_{t+1} = \lambda_k] \Pr[X_{t+1} = \lambda_k | X_t = \lambda_i] \\
&= \sum_{k=1}^{2} p_{kj} p_{ik},
\end{aligned}
$$

which is seen to be the ijth element of the matrix $\mathbf{PP}$. The extension to any arbitrary number of steps forward follows analogously. ∎

▶ Problems

1. *Risk-sharing in the Lucas model* (Cole and Obstfeld [30]). Let the period
   utility function be $u(c_x, c_y) = \theta \ln c_x + (1 - \theta) \ln c_y$ for the home agent
   and $u(c_x^*, c_y^*) = \theta \ln c_x^* + (1 - \theta) \ln c_y^*$ for the foreign agent. Suppose that
   capital is internationally immobile. The home agent owns all of the x-
   endowment ($\omega_x = 1$) and the foreign agent owns all of the y-endowment
   ($\omega_y^* = 1$). Show that in the equilibrium under portfolio autarchy, trade in
   goods alone is sufficient to achieve efficient risk-sharing.

2. Now consider the single-good model. Let x_t be the home endowment and
   x_t^* be the foreign endowment of the same good. The planner's problem
   is to maximize

   $$\phi \ln c_t + (1 - \phi) \ln c_t^*,$$

   subject to $c_t + c_t^* = x_t + x_t^*$. Under zero capital mobility, the home agent's
   problem is to maximize $\ln(c_t)$ subject to $c_t = x_t$. The foreign agent maximizes $\ln(c_t^*)$ subject to $c_t^* = x_t^*$. Show that asset trade is necessary in this
   case to achieve efficient risk-sharing.

3. *Nontradable goods.* Let x and y be traded as in the model of this chapter. In
   addition, let N be a nonstorable, nontradable domestic good generated
   by an exogenous endowment, and let N^* be a nonstorable, nontraded
   foreign good also generated by exogenous endowment. Let the domestic
   agent's utility function be $u(c_{xt}, c_{yt}, c_N) = (C^{1-\gamma})/(1 - \gamma)$, where $C =$
   $c_x^{\theta_1} c_y^{\theta_2} c_N^{\theta_3}$ with $\theta_1 + \theta_2 + \theta_3 = 1$. The foreign agent has the same utility
   function. Show that trade in goods under zero capital mobility does not
   achieve efficient risk-sharing.

4. Derive the exchange rate in the Lucas model under log utility, $U(c_{xt}, c_{yt}) =$
   $\theta \ln(c_{xt}) + (1 - \theta) \ln(c_{yt})$ and compare it with the solution under constant
   relative risk-aversion utility.

5. Use the high- and low-growth states and the transition matrix given in
   section 4.5 to solve for the price–dividend ratios for equities. What does
   the Lucas model have to say about the volatility of stock prices? How
   does the behavior of equity prices in the monetary economy differ from
   the behavior of equity prices in the barter economy?

5

International Real Business Cycles

In this chapter, we continue our study of models with perfect markets in the absence of nominal rigidities, but turn our attention to understanding how business cycles originate, and how they are propagated and transmitted from one country to another through current account imbalances. For this purpose, we will study *real business cycle* models. These are stochastic growth models that have been employed to address business cycle fluctuations. As their name suggests, real business cycle models deal with the real side of the economy. They are Arrow–Debreu models in which there is no role for money, and their solution typically focuses on solving the social planner's problem.

Analytic solutions to the stochastic growth model are available only under special specifications – for example, when utility is time-separable and logarithmic and when capital fully depreciates each period. Complications beyond these very simple structures require that the model be solved and evaluated numerically. We will work with durable capital, along with the log utility specification. The resulting models are simple enough for us to retain our intuition for what is going on, but complicated enough so that we must solve them using numerical and approximation methods.

Real business cycle researchers evaluate their models using the calibration method, which was outlined in section 4.4.

5.1 CALIBRATING THE ONE-SECTOR GROWTH MODEL

We begin simply enough, with the closed economy stochastic growth model, with log utility and durable capital. Then we will construct an international real business cycle model by piecing two one-country models together.

⬤ MEASUREMENT

The job of real business cycle models is to explain *business cycles* but the data typically contains both *trend* and *cyclical* components.[1] We will think of a macroeconomic time-series, such as GDP, as being built up of the two components $y_t = y_{\tau t} + y_{ct}$, where $y_{\tau t}$ is the long-run trend component and y_{ct} is the cyclical component. Since business cycle theory is typically not well equipped to explain the trend, the first thing that real business cycle theorists do is to remove the noncyclical components by *filtering* the data.

There are many ways to filter out the trend component. Two very crude methods are either to work with first-differenced data or to use least-squares residuals from a linear or quadratic trend. Most real business cycle theorists, however, choose to work with Hodrick–Prescott [74] filtered data. This technique, along with background information on the spectral representation of time-series, is covered in chapter 2.

Our measurements are based on quarterly log real output, consumption of nondurables plus services, and gross business fixed investment in per capita terms for the US from 1973.1 to 1996.4. The output measure is GDP minus government expenditures. The raw data and Hodrick–Prescott trends are displayed in figure 5.1. The Hodrick–Prescott cyclical components are displayed in figure 5.2. Investment is the most volatile of the series and consumption is the smoothest, but all three are evidently highly correlated. That is, they display a high degree of "co-movement."

Table 5.1 displays some descriptive statistics of the filtered (cyclical part) data. Each series displays substantial persistence and a high degree of co-movement with output.

The Model

We will work with a version of the King, Plosser, and Rebelo [81] model that abstracts from the labor–leisure choice. The consumer has logarithmic period utility defined over the single consumption good $u(C) = \ln(C)$. Lifetime utility is $\sum_{j=0}^{\infty} \beta^j u(C_{t+j})$, where $0 < \beta < 1$ is the subjective discount factor.

The representative firm produces output, Y_t, by combining labor N_t and capital K_t according to a Cobb–Douglas production function. Technical change is driven by two components – through changes in labor productivity, X_t, and through changes in total factor productivity, A_t. Individuals are compelled to provide a fixed amount of N hours of labor to the firm each period. The number of *effective* labor units is NX_t. Labor productivity is assumed to evolve exogeneously and deterministically at the gross rate $\gamma = X_{t+1}/X_t$ and represents permanent changes to the technology. The second component that governs technology is a transient stochastic shock to total factor productivity. The production

---

[1]   The data also contains seasonal and irregular components, which we will ignore.

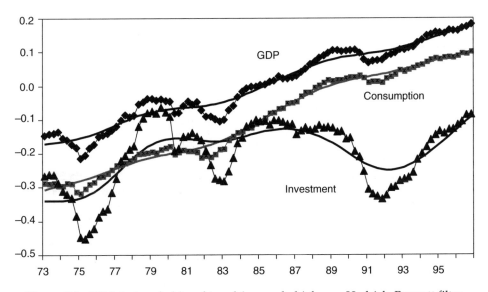

Figure 5.1 US data (symbols) and trend (no symbols) from a Hodrick–Prescott filter. Observations are quarterly per capita logarithms of GDP, consumption, and investment from 1973.1 to 1996.4.

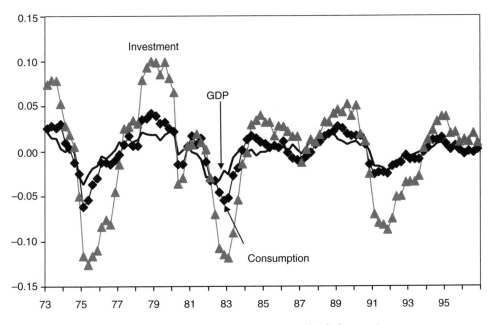

Figure 5.2 Hodrick–Prescott filtered cyclical observations.

Table 5.1 Closed-economy measurements

	Std. Dev.	Autocorrelations				
		1	*2*	*3*	*4*	*6*
y_t	0.022	0.86	0.66	0.46	0.27	0.02
c_t	0.013	0.85	0.72	0.57	0.38	0.14
i_t	0.056	0.89	0.73	0.56	0.40	0.08

	Cross-correlation with y_{t-k} at k					
	6	*4*	*1*	*0*	*−1*	*−4*	*−6*
c_t	0.09	0.20	0.72	0.87	0.87	0.46	0.14
i_t	0.01	0.43	0.91	0.94	0.81	0.20	0.10

All variables are logarithms of real per capita data for the US from 1973.1 to 1996.4 and have been passed through the Hodrick–Prescott filter with $\lambda = 1,600$. y_t is gross domestic product less government spending, c_t is consumption of nondurables plus services, and i_t is gross business fixed investment.
Source: International Financial Statistics

function is

$$Y_t = A_t K_t^\alpha (NX_t)^{1-\alpha}.$$

α is capital's share. Most estimates for the US place $0.33 \le \alpha \le 0.40$.

Output can be consumed or saved. Savings (or investment I_t) are used to replace worn capital and to augment the current capital stock. Capital depreciates at a rate δ and evolves according to

$$K_{t+1} = I_t + (1 - \delta)K_t.$$

There is no government and no foreign sector. There are also no market imperfections, so we can work with the fictitious social planner's problem, as we did with the Lucas model.

Problem 1.   The social planner wants to maximize

$$\mathrm{E}_t \sum_{j=0}^{\infty} \beta^j U(C_{t+j}), \tag{5.1}$$

subject to

$$Y_t = A_t K_t^\alpha (NX_t)^{1-\alpha}, \tag{5.2}$$

$$K_{t+1} = I_t + (1 - \delta)K_t, \tag{5.3}$$

$$Y_t = C_t + I_t, \tag{5.4}$$

$$U(C_t) = \ln(C_t). \tag{5.5}$$

The model allows for one normalization, so you can set $N = 1$.

In the steady state, you will want the economy to evolve along a balanced growth path in which all quantities except for N grow at the same gross rate:

$$\gamma = \frac{X_{t+1}}{X_t} = \frac{Y_{t+1}}{Y_t} = \frac{C_{t+1}}{C_t} = \frac{I_{t+1}}{I_t} = \frac{K_{t+1}}{K_t}.$$

The steady state is reasonably straightforward to obtain. However, if capital lasts more than one period, $\delta < 1$, the dynamics of the model must be solved by approximation methods. We'll first solve for the steady state and then take a linear approximation of the model around its steady state. The exogenous growth factor γ gives the model a moving steady state, which is inconvenient. To fix this, you can first transform the model to get a fixed steady state by normalizing all the variables by labor efficiency units. Let lower case letters denote these normalized values:

$$y_t = \frac{Y_t}{X_t}, \quad k_t = \frac{K_t}{X_t}, \quad i_t = \frac{I_t}{X_t}, \quad c_t = \frac{C_t}{X_t}.$$

Dividing (5.2) by X_t gives $y_t = A_t k_t^\alpha$. Dividing (5.3) by X_t gives $\gamma k_{t+1} = i_t + (1 - \delta)k_t$. To normalize lifetime utility (5.1), note that $\sum_{j=0}^\infty \beta^j \ln X_{t+j} = \sum_{j=0}^\infty \beta^j \ln(\gamma^j X_t) = \ln(X_t)/(1-\beta) + \ln(\gamma) \sum_{j=0}^\infty j\beta^j = \ln(X_t)/(1-\beta) + \ln(\gamma)\beta/(1-\beta)^2 < \infty$. Using this fact, adding and subtracting $\sum_{j=0}^\infty \beta^j \ln(X_{t+j})$ to (5.1) gives $E_t \sum_{j=0}^\infty \beta^j U(C_{t+j}) = \Omega_t + E_t \sum_{j=0}^\infty \beta^j U(c_{t+j})$, where $U(c_t) = \ln(c_t)$ and $\Omega_t = \ln(X_t)/(1-\beta) + \beta \ln(\gamma)/(1-\beta)^2$. Since Ω_t is exogenous, we can ignore it when solving the planner's problem. We will refer to the transformed problem as problem 2. This is the one that we will solve.

Problem 2. It will be useful to use the notation $f(A_t, k_t) = A_t k_t^\alpha$. Since Ω is a constant, the social planner's growth problem normalized by labor efficiency units is to maximize

$$E_t \sum_{j=0}^\infty \beta^j U(c_{t+j}), \tag{5.6}$$

subject to

$$y_t = f(A_t, k_t) = A_t k_t^\alpha, \tag{5.7}$$

$$\gamma k_{t+1} = i_t + (1 - \delta)k_t, \tag{5.8}$$

$$y_t = c_t + i_t, \tag{5.9}$$

$$U(c_t) = \ln(c_t). \tag{5.10}$$

It will be useful to make the notation more compact. Let $\underline{\lambda}_t = (k_{t+1}, k_t, A_t)'$ and combine the constraints (5.7)–(5.9) to form the consolidated budget constraint

$$c_t = g(\underline{\lambda}_t) = f(A_t, k_t) - \gamma k_{t+1} + (1 - \delta)k_t$$
$$= A_t k_t^\alpha - \gamma k_{t+1} + (1 - \delta)k_t. \tag{5.11}$$

Under Cobb–Douglas production and log utility, you have

$$f_k = \frac{\alpha y}{k}, \quad f_{kk} = \alpha(\alpha - 1)\frac{y}{k^2}, \quad u_c = \frac{1}{c}, \quad u_{cc} = \frac{-1}{c^2}.$$

Letting $g_j = \partial c_t / \partial \lambda_{jt}$ be the partial derivative of $g(\underline{\lambda}_t)$ with respect to the jth element of $\underline{\lambda}_t$ and letting $g_{ij} = \partial^2 c_t / (\partial \lambda_{it} \partial \lambda_{jt})$ be the second cross-partial derivative, for future reference you have

$$g_1 = -\gamma,$$
$$g_2 = f_k(A, k) + (1 - \delta),$$
$$g_3 = y/A,$$
$$g_{11} = g_{12} = g_{21} = g_{13} = g_{31} = g_{33} = 0,$$
$$g_{22} = f_{kk}(A, k),$$
$$g_{23} = g_{32} = \alpha k^{\alpha - 1}.$$

Now substitute (5.11) into (5.6) to transform the constrained optimization problem into an unconstrained problem. You want to maximize

$$E_t \sum_{j=0}^{\infty} \beta^j u[g(\underline{\lambda}_{t+j})], \tag{5.12}$$

where $g(\underline{\lambda}_t)$ is given in (5.11). At date t, k_t is predetermined and the only choice variable is i_t – and choosing i_t is equivalent to choosing k_{t+1}. The first-order conditions for all t are

$$-\gamma u_c(c_t) + \beta E_t u_c(c_{t+1})[f_k(A_{t+1}, k_{t+1}) + (1 - \delta)] = 0. \tag{5.13}$$

Notice that c_t must obey the consolidated budget constraint (5.11). It follows that (5.13) is a nonlinear stochastic difference equation in k_t. Analytic solutions to such equations are not easy to obtain, so we resort to approximation methods.

The Steady State

We will compute the approximate solution around the model's steady state. In order to do that, we need first to find the steady state. Denote the steady state values of output, consumption, investment, and capital by y, c, i, and k, without the time subscript, and let the steady state value of $A = 1$.

Since $f_k = \alpha k^{\alpha - 1} = \alpha(y/k)$, (5.13) becomes $\gamma = \beta[\alpha(y/k) + (1 - \delta)]$, from which we obtain the steady state output to capital ratio $y/k = (\gamma/\beta + \delta - 1)/\alpha$. Now divide the production function (5.7) by k and rearrange to get $k = (y/k)^{1/(\alpha-1)} = [(\gamma/\beta + \delta - 1)/\alpha]^{1/(\alpha-1)}$. Now that we know k, we can obtain y. From the accumulation equation (5.8), we have $i/k = \gamma + \delta - 1$ and, in turn,

$c/k = y/k - i/k$. Again, given k, we can solve for c. To summarize, in the steady state we have

$$y/k = (\gamma/\beta + \delta - 1)/\alpha, \tag{5.14}$$

$$i/k = \gamma + \delta - 1, \tag{5.15}$$

$$c/k = y/k - i/k, \tag{5.16}$$

$$k = (y/k)^{1/(\alpha-1)}. \tag{5.17}$$

Calibrating the Model

Each time period corresponds to a quarter. We set $\alpha = 0.33$, $\beta = 0.99$, $\delta = 0.10$, and $\gamma = 1.0038$.[2] The transient technology shock evolves according to the first-order autoregression

$$A_t = (1 - \rho) + \rho A_{t-1} + \epsilon_t, \tag{5.18}$$

where $\rho = 0.93$ and $\epsilon_t \overset{iid}{\sim} N(0, 0.010224^2)$.

Approximate Solution Near the Steady State

Many methods have been applied to solve real business cycle models. One option for solving the model is to take a first-order Taylor expansion of the nonlinear first-order condition (5.13) in the neighborhood around the steady state.[3] This yields the second-order stochastic difference equation in $k_t - k$:

$$a_0 + a_1(k_{t+2} - k) + a_2(k_{t+1} - k)$$
$$+ a_3(k_t - k) + a_4(A_{t+1} - 1) + a_5(A_t - 1) = 0, \tag{5.19}$$

where

$$a_0 = U_c g_1 + \beta U_c g_2 = 0,$$

$$a_1 = \beta U_{cc} g_1 g_2,$$

$$a_2 = U_{cc} g_1^2 + \beta U_{cc} g_2^2 + \beta U_c g_{22},$$

$$a_3 = U_{cc} g_1 g_2,$$

$$a_4 = \beta U_c g_{32} + \beta U_{cc} g_2 g_3,$$

$$a_5 = U_{cc} g_1 g_3.$$

The derivatives are evaluated at steady state values.

---

[2] This is the depreciation rate used by Backus, Kehoe, and Kydland [5]. Cooley and Prescott [32] recommend $\delta = 0.048$. γ is the value used by Cooley and Prescott and by King, Plosser, and Rebelo [81].

[3] This is the method of King, Plosser, and Rebelo [81].

A second, but equivalent, option is to take a second-order Taylor approximation to the objective function around the steady state and to solve the resulting
quadratic optimization problem. The second option is equivalent to the first
because it yields linear first-order conditions around the steady state. To pursue
the second option, recall that $\underline{\lambda}_t = (k_{t+1}, k_t, A_t)'$. Write the period utility function
in the unconstrained optimization problem as

$$R(\underline{\lambda}_t) = U[g(\underline{\lambda}_t)]. \tag{5.20}$$

Let $R_j = \partial R(\underline{\lambda}_t)/\partial \lambda_{jt}$ be the partial derivative of $R(\underline{\lambda}_t)$ with respect to the jth element of $\underline{\lambda}_t$ and let $R_{ij} = \partial^2 R(\underline{\lambda}_t)/(\partial \lambda_{it}\partial \lambda_{jt})$ be the second cross-partial derivative.
Since $R_{ij} = R_{ji}$, the relevant derivatives are

$$R_1 = U_c g_1,$$
$$R_2 = U_c g_2,$$
$$R_3 = U_c g_3,$$

$$R_{11} = U_{cc} g_1^2,$$
$$R_{22} = U_{cc} g_2^2 + U_c g_{22},$$
$$R_{33} = U_{cc} g_3^2,$$
$$R_{12} = U_{cc} g_1 g_2,$$
$$R_{13} = U_{cc} g_1 g_3,$$
$$R_{23} = U_{cc} g_2 g_3 + U_c g_{23}.$$

The second-order Taylor expansion of the period utility function is

$$\begin{aligned}
R(\underline{\lambda}_t) = R(\underline{\lambda}) &+ R_1(k_{t+1} - k) + R_2(k_t - k) \\
&+ R_3(A_t - A) + \tfrac{1}{2}R_{11}(k_{t+1} - k)^2 \\
&+ \tfrac{1}{2}R_{22}(k_t - k)^2 + \tfrac{1}{2}R_{33}(A_t - A)^2 + R_{12}(k_{t+1} - k)(k_t - k) \\
&+ R_{13}(k_{t+1} - k)(A_t - A) + R_{23}(k_t - k)(A_t - A).
\end{aligned}$$

Suppose that we let $\underline{q} = (R_1, R_2, R_3)'$ be the 3×1 row vector of partial derivatives
(the gradient) of R, and that we let $\mathbf{Q}$ be the 3×3 matrix of second partial derivatives (the Hessian) multiplied by $1/2$, where $Q_{ij} = R_{ij}/2$. Then the approximate
period utility function can be compactly written in matrix form as

$$R(\underline{\lambda}_t) = R(\underline{\lambda}) + [\underline{q} + (\underline{\lambda}_t - \underline{\lambda})'\mathbf{Q}](\underline{\lambda}_t - \underline{\lambda}). \tag{5.21}$$

The problem is now to maximize

$$E_t \sum_{j=0}^{\infty} \beta^j R(\underline{\lambda}_{t+j}). \tag{5.22}$$

The first-order conditions are, for all t,

$$
\begin{aligned}
0 = {} & (\beta R_2 + R_1) + \beta R_{12}(k_{t+2} - k) \\
& + (R_{11} + \beta R_{22})(k_{t+1} - k) + R_{12}(k_t - k) \\
& + \beta R_{23}(A_{t+1} - 1) + R_{13}(A_t - 1).
\end{aligned}
\tag{5.23}
$$

If you compare (5.23) to (5.19), you'll see that $a_0 = \beta R_2 + R_1$, $a_1 = \beta R_{12}$, $a_2 = R_{11} + \beta R_{22}$, $a_3 = R_{12}$, $a_4 = \beta R_{23}$, and $a_5 = R_{13}$. This verifies that the two approaches are indeed equivalent.

Now, to solve the linearized first-order conditions, work with (5.19). Since the data that we want to explain are in logarithms, you can convert the first-order conditions into near-logarithmic form. Let $\tilde{a}_i = ka_i$, for $i = 1, 2, 3$, and let a "hat" denote the approximate log difference from the steady state, so that $\hat{k}_t = (k_t - k)/k \simeq \ln(k_t/k)$ and $\hat{A}_t = A_t - 1$ (since the steady state value of $A = 1$). Now let $b_1 = -\tilde{a}_2/\tilde{a}_1$, $b_2 = -\tilde{a}_3/\tilde{a}_1$, $b_3 = -a_4/\tilde{a}_1$, and $b_4 = -a_4/\tilde{a}_1$.

The second-order stochastic difference equation (5.19) can be written as

$$
(1 - b_1 L - b_2 L^2)\hat{k}_{t+1} = W_t,
\tag{5.24}
$$

where

$$
W_t = b_3 \hat{A}_{t+1} + b_4 \hat{A}_t.
$$

The roots of the polynomial $(1 - b_1 z - b_2 z^2) = (1 - \omega_1 L)(1 - \omega_2 L)$ satisfy $b_1 = \omega_1 + \omega_2$ and $b_2 = -\omega_1 \omega_2$. Using the quadratic formula and evaluating at the parameter values that we used to calibrate the model, the roots are $z_1 = (1/\omega_1) = [-b_1 - \sqrt{b_1^2 + 4b_2}]/(2b_2) \simeq 1.23$ and $z_2 = (1/\omega_2) = [-b_1 + \sqrt{b_1^2 + 4b_2}]/(2b_2) \simeq 0.81$. There is a stable root, $|z_1| > 1$, that lies outside the unit circle, and an unstable root, $|z_2| < 1$, that lies inside the unit circle. The presence of an unstable root means that the solution is a saddle path. If you try to simulate (5.24) directly, the capital stock will diverge.

To solve the difference equation, exploit the *certainty equivalence* property of quadratic optimization problems. That is, you first get the *perfect-foresight* solution to the problem by solving the stable root backwards and the unstable root forwards. Then, replace future random variables with their expected values conditional upon the time-t information set. Begin by rewriting (5.24) as

$$
\begin{aligned}
W_t &= (1 - \omega_1 L)(1 - \omega_2 L)\hat{k}_{t+1} \\
&= (-\omega_2 L)(-\omega_2^{-1} L^{-1})(1 - \omega_2 L)(1 - \omega_1 L)\hat{k}_{t+1} \\
&= (-\omega_2 L)(1 - \omega_2^{-1} L^{-1})(1 - \omega_1 L)\hat{k}_{t+1},
\end{aligned}
$$

and rearrange to give

$$(1 - \omega_1 L)\hat{k}_{t+1} = \frac{-\omega_2^{-1}L^{-1}}{1 - \omega_2^{-1}L^{-1}}W_t$$

$$= -\left(\frac{1}{\omega_2}L^{-1}\right)\sum_{j=0}^{\infty}\left(\frac{1}{\omega_2}\right)^j W_{t+j}$$

$$= -\sum_{j=1}^{\infty}\left(\frac{1}{\omega_2}\right)^j W_{t+j}. \tag{5.25}$$

The autoregressive specification (5.18) implies the prediction formulae

$$E_t W_{t+j} = b_3 E_t \hat{A}_{t+j+1} + b_4 E_t \hat{A}_{t+j} = [b_3\rho + b_4]\rho^j \hat{A}_t.$$

Use this forecasting rule in (5.25), to give

$$\sum_{j=1}^{\infty}\left(\frac{1}{\omega_2}\right)^j E_t W_{t+j} = [b_3\rho + b_4]\hat{A}_t \sum_{j=1}^{\infty}\left(\frac{\rho}{\omega_2}\right)^j = \left[\frac{\rho}{\omega_2 - \rho}\right](b_3\rho + b_4)\hat{A}_t.$$

It follows that the solution for the capital stock is

$$\hat{k}_{t+1} = \omega_1\hat{k}_t - \left[\frac{\rho}{\omega_2 - \rho}\right][b_3\rho + b_4]\hat{A}_t. \tag{5.26}$$

To recover $\hat{y}_t$, note that the first-order expansion of the production function gives $y_t = f(A, k) + f_A\hat{A}_t + f_k k\hat{k}_t$, where $f_A = 1$ and $f_k = (\alpha y)/k$. Rearrangement gives $\hat{y}_t = \hat{A}_t + \hat{k}_t$. To recover $\hat{i}_t$, subtract the steady state value $\gamma k = i + (1 - \delta)k$ from (5.8) and rearrange to get $\hat{i}_t = (k/i)[\gamma\hat{k}_{t+1} - (1 - \delta)\hat{k}_t]$. Finally, obtain $\hat{c}_t = \hat{y}_t - \hat{i}_t$ from the adding-up constraint (5.9). The log-levels of the variables can be recovered by

$$\ln(Y_t) = \hat{y}_t + \ln(X_t) + \ln(y),$$
$$\ln(C_t) = \hat{c}_t + \ln(X_t) + \ln(c),$$
$$\ln(I_t) = \hat{i}_t + \ln(X_t) + \ln(i),$$
$$\ln(X_t) = \ln(X_0) + t\ln(\gamma).$$

Simulating the Model

We'll use the calibrated model to generate 96 time-series observations that correspond to the number of observations in the data. From these pseudo-observations, we can recover the implied log-levels and pass them through the Hodrick–Prescott filter. The steady state values are

$$y = 1.717, \quad k = 5.147, \quad c = 1.201, \quad i/k = 0.10.$$

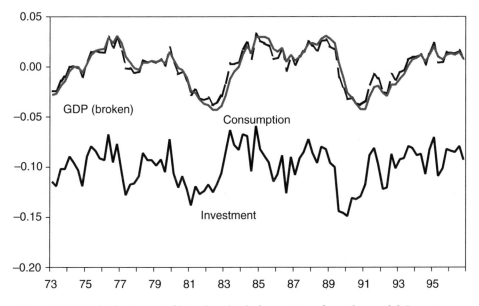

Figure 5.3 Hodrick–Prescott filtered cyclical observations from the model. Investment has been shifted down by 0.10 for visual clarity.

Table 5.2 Calibrated closed-economy model

	Std. Dev.	Autocorrelations				
		1	2	3	4	6
y_t	0.022	0.90	0.79	0.67	0.53	0.23
c_t	0.023	0.97	0.89	0.77	0.63	0.31
i_t	0.034	0.70	0.50	0.36	0.19	−0.04

	Cross-correlation with y_{t-k} at k						
	6	4	1	0	−1	−4	−6
c_t	0.49	0.77	0.96	0.90	0.79	0.33	0.04
i_t	0.29	0.11	0.41	0.74	0.73	0.61	0.44

Plots of the filtered log income, consumption, and investment observations are given in figure 5.3, and the associated descriptive statistics are given in table 5.2. The autoregressive coefficient and the error variance of the technology shock were selected to match the volatility of output exactly. From the figure, you can see that both consumption and investment exhibit high co-movements with output, and all three series display persistence. However, from table 5.2 the implied investment series is seen to be more volatile than the output, but is less volatile than that found in the data. The consumption implied by the model is more volatile than the output, which is counterfactual.

This coarse overview of the one-sector real business cycle model shows that there are some aspects of the data that the model does not explain. This is not surprising. Perhaps it is more surprising how well it actually does in generating "realistic" time-series dynamics of the data. In any event, this perfect markets – no nominal rigidities Arrow–Debreu model serves as a useful benchmark against which refinements can be judged.

5.2 CALIBRATING A TWO-COUNTRY MODEL

We now add a second country. This two-country model is a special case of Backus et al. [5]. Each county produces the same good, so we will not be able to study terms of trade or real exchange rate issues. The presence of country-specific idiosyncratic shocks gives an incentive to individuals in the two countries to trade as a means to insure each other against a bad relative technology shock, so we can examine the behavior of the current account.

● MEASUREMENT

We will call the first country the "US" and the second country "Europe." The data for European output, government spending, investment, and consumption are the aggregate of observations for the UK, France, Germany, and Italy. The aggregate of their current account balances suffers from double counting and does not make sense because of intra-European trade. Therefore, we examine only the US current account, which is measured as a fraction of real GDP.

Table 5.3 displays the features of the data that we will attempt to explain – their volatility, their persistence (characterized by their autocorrelations) and their co-movements (characterized by cross-correlations). Notice that the US and European consumption correlation is lower than their output correlation.

● THE TWO-COUNTRY MODEL

Both countries experience identical rates of depreciation of physical capital and long-run technological growth $X_{t+1}/X_t = X_{t+1}^*/X_t^* = \gamma$; they have the same capital shares and Cobb–Douglas form of the production function, and identical utility. Let the social planner attach a weight of ω to the domestic agent and a weight of $1 - \omega$ to the foreign agent. In terms of efficiency units, the social planner's problem is now to maximize

$$E_t \sum_{j=0}^{\infty} \beta^j [\omega U(c_{t+j}) + (1 - \omega)U(c_{t+j}^*)], \tag{5.27}$$

Table 5.3 Open-economy measurements

	Std. Dev.	Autocorrelations				
		1	*2*	*3*	*4*	*6*
ex_t	0.01	0.61	0.50	0.40	0.40	0.12
y_t^*	0.014	0.84	0.62	0.36	0.15	−0.15
c_t^*	0.010	0.68	0.47	0.30	0.04	−0.15
i_t^*	0.030	0.89	0.75	0.57	0.40	0.07

	Cross-correlations at lag *k*						
	6	*4*	*1*	*0*	*−1*	*−4*	*6*
$y_t ex_{t-k}$	0.43	0.42	0.41	0.41	0.37	0.03	0.32
$y_t y_{t-k}^*$	0.28	0.22	0.21	0.36	0.43	0.36	0.22
$c_t c_{t-k}^*$	0.26	0.39	0.28	0.25	0.05	0.15	0.26

ex_t is US net exports divided by GDP. Foreign country aggregates data from France, Germany, Italy, and the UK. All variables are real per capita from 1973.1 to 1996.4 and have been passed through the Hodrick–Prescott filter with $\lambda = 1,600$.

subject to

$$y_t = f(A_t, k_t) = A_t k_t^\alpha, \tag{5.28}$$

$$y_t^* = f(A_t^*, k_t^*) = A_t^* k_t^{*\alpha}, \tag{5.29}$$

$$\gamma k_{t+1} = i_t + (1 - \delta)k_t, \tag{5.30}$$

$$\gamma k_{t+1}^* = i_t^* + (1 - \delta)k_t^*, \tag{5.31}$$

$$y_t + y_t^* = c_t + c_t^* + (i_t + i_t^*). \tag{5.32}$$

In the market economy interpretation, we can view ω to indicate the size of the home country in the world economy. Equations (5.28) and (5.29) are the Cobb–Douglas production functions for the home and foreign counties, with normalized labor input $N = N^* = 1$. Equations (5.30) and (5.31) are the domestic and foreign capital accumulation equations, and (5.31) is the new form of the resource constraint. Both countries have the same technology, but are subject to heterogeneous transient shocks to total productivity according to

$$\begin{bmatrix} A_t \\ A_t^* \end{bmatrix} = \begin{bmatrix} 1 - \rho - \delta \\ 1 - \rho - \delta \end{bmatrix} + \begin{bmatrix} \rho & \delta \\ \delta & \rho \end{bmatrix} \begin{bmatrix} A_{t-1} \\ A_{t-1}^* \end{bmatrix} + \begin{bmatrix} \epsilon_t \\ \epsilon_t^* \end{bmatrix}, \tag{5.33}$$

where $(\epsilon_t, \epsilon_t^*)' \overset{iid}{\sim} N(\underline{0}, \Sigma)$. We set $\rho = 0.906$, $\delta = 0.088$, $\Sigma_{11} = \Sigma_{22} = 2.40e - 4$, and $\Sigma_{12} = \Sigma_{21} = 6.17e - 5$. The contemporaneous correlation of the innovations is 0.26.

Apart from the objective function, the main difference between the two-county and one-country models is the resource constraint (5.32). World output can either be consumed or saved, but a country's net saving, which is the current account balance, can be nonzero ($y_t - c_t - i_t = -(y_t^* - c_t^* - i_t^*) \neq 0$).

Let $\underline{\lambda}_t = (k_{t+1}, k_{t+1}^*, k_t, k_t^*, A_t, A_t^*, c_t^*)$ be the state vector, and indicate the dependence of consumption on the state by $c_t = g(\underline{\lambda}_t)$ and $c_t^* = h(\underline{\lambda}_t)$ (which equals c_t^* trivially). Substitute (5.28)–(5.31) into (5.32) and rearrange, to give

$$c_t = g(\underline{\lambda}_t) = f(A_t, k_t) + f(A_t^*, k_t^*) - \gamma(k_{t+1} + k_{t+1}^*)$$
$$+ (1 - \delta)(k_t + k_t^*) - c_t^*, \tag{5.34}$$
$$c_t^* = h(\underline{\lambda}_t) = c_t^*. \tag{5.35}$$

For future reference, the derivatives of g and h are

$$g_1 = g_2 = -\gamma,$$
$$g_3 = f_k(A, k) + (1 - \delta),$$
$$g_4 = f_k(A^*, k^*) + (1 - \delta),$$
$$g_5 = f(A, k)/A,$$
$$g_6 = f(A^*, k^*)/A^*,$$
$$g_7 = -1,$$
$$h_1 = h_2 = \cdots = h_6 = 0,$$
$$h_7 = 1.$$

Next, transform the constrained optimization problem into an unconstrained problem by substituting (5.34) and (5.35) into (5.27). The problem is now to maximize

$$\omega E_t(u[g(\underline{\lambda}_t)] + \beta U[g(\underline{\lambda}_{t+1})] + \beta^2 U[g(\underline{\lambda}_{t+2})] + \cdots)$$
$$+ (1 - \omega) E_t(u[h(\underline{\lambda}_t)] + \beta U[h(\underline{\lambda}_{t+1})] + \beta^2 U[h(\underline{\lambda}_{t+2})] + \cdots). \tag{5.36}$$

At date t, the choice variables available to the planner are k_{t+1}, k_{t+1}^*, and c_t^*. Differentiating (5.36) with respect to these variables and rearranging results in the Euler equations:

$$\gamma U_c(c_t) = \beta E_t U_c(c_{t+1})[g_3(\underline{\lambda}_{t+1})], \tag{5.37}$$
$$\gamma U_c(c_t) = \beta E_t U_c(c_{t+1})[g_4(\underline{\lambda}_{t+1})], \tag{5.38}$$
$$U_c(c_t) = [(1 - \omega)/\omega] U_c(c_t^*). \tag{5.39}$$

Equation (5.39) is the Pareto-optimal risk-sharing rule, which sets home marginal utility proportional to foreign marginal utility. Under log utility, home and foreign per capita consumption are perfectly correlated: $c_t = [\omega/(1 - \omega)]c_t^*$.

The Two-Country Steady State

From (5.37) and (5.38) we obtain $y/k = y^*/k^* = (\gamma/\beta + \delta - 1)/\alpha$. We've already determined that $c = [\omega/(1-\omega)]c^* = \omega c^w$, where $c^w = c + c^*$ is world consumption. From the production functions (5.28)–(5.29) we get $k = (y/k)^{1/(\alpha-1)}$ and $k^* = (y^*/k^*)^{1/(\alpha-1)}$. From (5.30)–(5.31) we get $i = i^* = (\gamma + \delta - 1)k$. It follows that $c = \omega c^w = \omega[y + y^* - (i + i^*)] = 2\omega[y - i]$.

Thus $y - c - i = (1 - 2\omega)(y - i)$, and unless $\omega = 1/2$, the current account will not be balanced in the steady state. If $\omega > 1/2$ the home country spends in excess of GDP and runs a current account deficit. How can this be? In the market (competitive equilibrium) interpretation, the excess absorption is financed by interest income earned on past lending to the foreign country. Foreigners need to produce in excess of their consumption and investment to service the debt. In a sense, they have "over-invested" in physical capital.

In the planning problem, the social planner simply takes away some of the foreign output and gives it to domestic agents. Due to the concavity of the production function, optimality requires that the world capital stock be split up between the two countries, so as to equate the marginal product of capital at home and abroad. Since technology is identical in the two countries, this implies equalization of national capital stocks, $k = k^*$, and income levels, $y = y^*$, even if consumption differs, $c \neq c^*$.

Quadratic Approximation

You can solve the model by taking the quadratic approximation of the unconstrained objective function about the steady state. Let R be the period weighted average of home and foreign utility:

$$R(\underline{\lambda}_t) = \omega U[g(\underline{\lambda}_t)] + (1 - \omega)U[h(\underline{\lambda}_t)].$$

Let $R_j = \omega U_c(c)g_j + (1 - \omega)U_c(c^*)h_j, j = 1, \ldots, 7$, be the first partial derivative of R with respect to the j – the element of $\underline{\lambda}_t$. Denote the second partial derivative of R by

$$R_{jk} = \frac{\partial R(\lambda)}{\partial \lambda_j \partial \lambda_k} = \omega[U_c(c)g_{jk} + U_{cc}g_j g_k] + (1 - \omega)[U_c(c^*)h_{jk} + U_{cc}(c^*)h_j h_k]. \quad (5.40)$$

Let $\underline{q} = (R_1, \ldots, R_7)'$ be the gradient vector, and let $\mathbf{Q}$ be the Hessian matrix of second partial derivatives, whose (j, k)th element is $Q_{jk} = (1/2)R_{j,k}$. Then the second-order Taylor approximation to the period utility function is

$$R(\underline{\lambda}_t) = [\underline{q} + (\underline{\lambda}_t - \underline{\lambda})'\mathbf{Q}](\underline{\lambda}_t - \underline{\lambda}),$$

and you can rewrite (5.36) as

$$\max E_t \sum_{j=0}^{\infty} \beta^j [\underline{q} + (\underline{\lambda}_{t+j} - \underline{\lambda})'\mathbf{Q}](\underline{\lambda}_{t+j} - \underline{\lambda}). \quad (5.41)$$

Let $Q_{j\bullet}$ be the jth row of the matrix $\mathbf{Q}$. The first-order conditions are

$$(k_{t+1}): \quad 0 = R_1 + \beta R_3 + Q_{1\bullet}(\underline{\lambda}_t - \underline{\lambda}) + \beta Q_{3\bullet}(\underline{\lambda}_{t+1} - \underline{\lambda}), \tag{5.42}$$

$$(k_{t+1}^*): \quad 0 = R_2 + \beta R_4 + Q_{2\bullet}(\underline{\lambda}_t - \underline{\lambda}) + \beta Q_{4\bullet}(\underline{\lambda}_{t+1}\underline{\lambda}), \tag{5.43}$$

$$(c_t^*): \quad 0 = R_7 + Q_{7\bullet}(\underline{\lambda}_t - \underline{\lambda}). \tag{5.44}$$

Now let a "tilde" denote the deviation of a variable from its steady state value, so that $\tilde{k}_t = k_t - k$, and write these equations out as

$$0 = a_1 \tilde{k}_{t+2} + a_2 \tilde{k}_{t+2}^* + a_3 \tilde{k}_{t+1} + a_4 \tilde{k}_{t+1}^* + a_5 \tilde{k}_t + a_6 \tilde{k}_t^* + a_7 \tilde{A}_{t+1}$$
$$+ a_8 \tilde{A}_{t+1}^* + a_9 \tilde{A}_t + a_{10} \tilde{A}_t^* + a_{11} \tilde{c}_{t+1}^* + a_{12} \tilde{c}_t^* + a_{13}, \tag{5.45}$$

$$0 = b_1 \tilde{k}_{t+2} + b_2 \tilde{k}_{t+2}^* + b_3 \tilde{k}_{t+1} + b_4 \tilde{k}_{t+1}^* + b_5 \tilde{k}_t + b_6 \tilde{k}_t^* + b_7 \tilde{A}_{t+1}$$
$$+ b_8 \tilde{A}_{t+1}^* + b_9 \tilde{A}_t + b_{10} \tilde{A}_t^* + b_{11} \tilde{c}_{t+1}^* + b_{12} \tilde{c}_t^* + b_{13}, \tag{5.46}$$

$$0 = d_3 \tilde{k}_{t+1} + d_4 \tilde{k}_{t+1}^* + d_5 \tilde{k}_t + d_6 \tilde{k}_t^* + d_9 \tilde{A}_t + d_{10} \tilde{A}_t^*$$
$$+ d_{12} \tilde{c}_t^* + d_{13}, \tag{5.47}$$

where the coefficients are given in the following table:

j	a_j	b_j	d_j
1	βQ_{31}	βQ_{41}	0
2	βQ_{32}	βQ_{42}	0
3	$\beta Q_{33} + Q_{11}$	$\beta Q_{43} + Q_{21}$	Q_{71}
4	$\beta Q_{34} + Q_{12}$	$\beta Q_{44} + Q_{22}$	Q_{72}
5	Q_{13}	Q_{23}	Q_{73}
6	Q_{14}	Q_{24}	Q_{74}
7	βQ_{35}	βQ_{45}	0
8	βQ_{36}	βQ_{46}	0
9	Q_{15}	Q_{25}	Q_{75}
10	Q_{16}	Q_{26}	Q_{76}
11	Q_{37}	Q_{47}	0
12	Q_{17}	Q_{27}	Q_{77}
13	$R_1 + \beta R_3$	$R_2 + \beta R_4$	R_7

Mimicking the algorithm developed for the one-country model and using (5.47) to substitute out c_t^* and c_{t+1}^* in (5.45) and (5.46) gives

$$0 = \tilde{a}_1 \tilde{k}_{t+2} + \tilde{a}_2 \tilde{k}_{t+2}^* + \tilde{a}_3 \tilde{k}_{t+1} + \tilde{a}_4 \tilde{k}_{t+1}^* + \tilde{a}_5 \tilde{k}_t + \tilde{a}_6 \tilde{k}_t^* + \tilde{a}_7 \tilde{A}_{t+1}$$
$$+ \tilde{a}_8 \tilde{A}_{t+1}^* + \tilde{a}_9 \tilde{A}_t + \tilde{a}_{10} \tilde{A}_t^* + \tilde{a}_{11}, \tag{5.48}$$

$$0 = \tilde{b}_1 \tilde{k}_{t+2} + \tilde{b}_2 \tilde{k}_{t+2}^* + \tilde{b}_3 \tilde{k}_{t+1} + \tilde{b}_4 \tilde{k}_{t+1}^* + \tilde{b}_5 \tilde{k}_t + \tilde{b}_6 \tilde{k}_t^* + \tilde{b}_7 \tilde{A}_{t+1}$$
$$+ \tilde{b}_8 \tilde{A}_{t+1}^* + \tilde{b}_9 \tilde{A}_t + \tilde{b}_{10} \tilde{A}_t^* + \tilde{b}_{11}. \tag{5.49}$$

At this point, the marginal benefit from looking at analytic expressions for the coefficients is probably negative. For the specific calibration of the model, the numerical values of the coefficients are as follows:

$$\begin{array}{ll}
\tilde{a}_1 = 0.105, & \tilde{b}_1 = 0.105, \\
\tilde{a}_2 = 0.105, & \tilde{b}_2 = 0.105, \\
\tilde{a}_3 = -0.218, & \tilde{b}_3 = -0.212, \\
\tilde{a}_4 = -0.212, & \tilde{b}_4 = -0.218, \\
\tilde{a}_5 = 0.107, & \tilde{b}_5 = 0.107, \\
\tilde{a}_6 = 0.107, & \tilde{b}_6 = 0.107, \\
\tilde{a}_7 = -0.128, & \tilde{b}_7 = -0.161, \\
\tilde{a}_8 = -0.159, & \tilde{b}_8 = -0.130, \\
\tilde{a}_9 = 0.158, & \tilde{b}_9 = 0.158, \\
\tilde{a}_{10} = 0.158, & \tilde{b}_{10} = 0.158, \\
\tilde{a}_{11} = 0.007, & \tilde{b}_{11} = 0.007.
\end{array}$$

You can see that $\tilde{a}_3 + \tilde{a}_4 = \tilde{b}_3 + \tilde{b}_4$ and $\tilde{a}_7 + \tilde{b}_7 = \tilde{a}_8 + \tilde{b}_8$, which means that there is a singularity in this system. To deal with this singularity, let $\tilde{A}_t^w = \tilde{A}_t + \tilde{A}_t^*$ denote the "world" technology shock and add (5.48) to (5.49), to give

$$\tilde{a}_1 \tilde{k}_{t+2}^w + \frac{\tilde{a}_3 + \tilde{a}_4}{2} \tilde{k}_{t+1}^w + \tilde{a}_5 \tilde{k}_t^w + \frac{\tilde{a}_7 + \tilde{b}_7}{2} \tilde{A}_{t+1}^w + \tilde{a}_9 \tilde{A}_t^w + \frac{\tilde{a}_{11} + \tilde{b}_{11}}{2} = 0. \quad (5.50)$$

Equation (5.50) is a second–order stochastic difference equation in $\tilde{k}_t^w = \tilde{k}_t + \tilde{k}_t^*$, which can be rewritten compactly as[4]

$$\tilde{k}_{t+2}^w - m_1 \tilde{k}_{t+1}^w - m_2 \tilde{k}_t^w = W_{t+1}^w, \quad (5.51)$$

where $W_{t+1}^w = m_3 \tilde{A}_{t+1}^w + m_4 \tilde{A}_t^w$, and

$$m_1 = -(\tilde{a}_3 + \tilde{a}_4)/(2\tilde{a}_1),$$
$$m_2 = -\tilde{a}_5/\tilde{a}_1,$$
$$m_3 = -(\tilde{a}_7 + \tilde{b}_7)/(2\tilde{a}_1),$$
$$m_4 = -\tilde{a}_9/\tilde{a}_1,$$
$$m_5 = -\frac{\tilde{a}_{11} + \tilde{b}_{11}}{2\tilde{a}_{11}}.$$

You can write second-order stochastic difference equation (5.51) as $(1 - m_1 L - m_2 L^2)\hat{k}_{t+1}^w = W_t^w$. The roots of the polynomial $(1 - m_1 z - m_2 z^2) = (1 - \omega_1 L)(1 - \omega_2 L)$ satisfy $m_1 = \omega_1 + \omega_2$ and $m_2 = -\omega_1 \omega_2$. Under the parameter values used to

---

[4]   Unlike the one-country model, we don't want to write the model in logs, because we have to be able to recover $\tilde{k}$ and $\tilde{k}^*$ separately.

calibrate the model, and using the quadratic formula, the roots are $z_1 = (1/\omega_1) = [-m_1 - \sqrt{m_1^2 + 4m_2}]/(2m_2) \simeq 1.17$ and $z_2 = (1/\omega_2) = [-m_1 + \sqrt{m_1^2 + 4m_2}]/(2m_2) \simeq 0.84$. The stable root $|z_1| > 1$ lies outside the unit circle, and the unstable root $|z_2| < 1$ lies inside the unit circle.

From the law of motion governing the technology shocks (5.33), you have

$$\tilde{A}_{t+1}^w = (\rho + \delta)\tilde{A}_t^w + \epsilon_t^w, \tag{5.52}$$

where $\epsilon_t^w = \epsilon_t + \epsilon_t^*$. Now $E_t W_{t+k} = m_3 \tilde{A}_{t+1}^w + m_4 \tilde{A}_t^w + m_5 = [m_3(\rho + \delta) + m_4](\rho + \delta)^k \tilde{A}_t^w + m_5$. As in the one-country model, use these forecasting formulae to solve the unstable root forwards and the stable root backwards. The solution for the world capital stock is

$$\tilde{k}_{t+1}^w = \omega_1 \tilde{k}_t^w - \frac{(\rho + \delta)}{\omega_2 - (\rho + \delta)}\left([m_3(\rho + \delta) + m_4]\tilde{A}_t^w + m_5\right). \tag{5.53}$$

Now you need to recover the domestic and foreign components of the world capital stock. Subtract (5.49) from (5.48), to get

$$\tilde{k}_{t+1} - \tilde{k}_{t+1}^* = \left(\frac{\tilde{b}_7 - \tilde{a}_7}{\tilde{a}_3 - \tilde{a}_4}\right)\tilde{A}_{t+1} + \left(\frac{\tilde{b}_8 - \tilde{a}_8}{\tilde{a}_3 - \tilde{a}_4}\right)\tilde{A}_{t+1}^*. \tag{5.54}$$

Add (5.53) to (5.54), to give

$$\tilde{k}_{t+1} = \tfrac{1}{2}[\tilde{k}_{t+1}^w + (\tilde{k}_{t+1} - \tilde{k}_{t+1}^*)]. \tag{5.55}$$

The date $t + 1$ world capital stock is predetermined at date t. How that capital is allocated between the home and foreign country depends on the realization of the idiosyncratic shocks $\tilde{A}_{t+1}$ and $\tilde{A}_{t+1}^*$.

Given $\tilde{k}_t$ and $\tilde{k}_t^*$, it follows from the production functions that the outputs are

$$\tilde{y}_t = f_A \tilde{A}_t + f_k \tilde{k}_t = y\tilde{A}_t + \alpha\frac{y}{k}\tilde{k}_t, \tag{5.56}$$

$$\tilde{y}_t^* = f_A^* \tilde{A}_t^* + f_k^* \tilde{k}_t^* = y^*\tilde{A}_t^* + \alpha\frac{y^*}{k^*}\tilde{k}_t^*, \tag{5.57}$$

and the investment rates are

$$\tilde{i}_t = \gamma\tilde{k}_{t+1} - (1 - \delta)\tilde{k}_t, \tag{5.58}$$

$$\tilde{i}_t^* = \gamma\tilde{k}_{t+1}^* - (1 - \delta)\tilde{k}_t^*. \tag{5.59}$$

Let world consumption be $\tilde{c}_t^w = \tilde{c}_t + \tilde{c}_t^* = \tilde{y}_t + \tilde{y}_t^* - (\tilde{i}_t + \tilde{i}_t^*)$. By the optimal risk-sharing rule (5.39), $\tilde{c}_t^* = [(1 - \omega)/\omega]\tilde{c}_t$, which can be used to determine

$$\tilde{c}_t = \omega\tilde{c}_t^w. \tag{5.60}$$

It follows that $\tilde{c}_t^* = \tilde{c}_t^w - \tilde{c}_t$. The log-level of consumption is recovered by

$$\ln(C_t) = \ln(X_t) + \ln(\tilde{c}_t + c).$$

Log-levels of the other variables can be obtained in an analogous manner.

● SIMULATING THE TWO-COUNTRY MODEL

The steady state values are

$$y = y^* = 1.53, \qquad k = k^* = 3.66, \qquad i = i^* = 0.42, \qquad c = c^* = 1.11.$$

The model is used to generate 96 time-series observations. Descriptive statistics calculated with the Hodrick–Prescott filtered cyclical parts of the log-levels of the simulated observations are displayed in table 5.4. Figure 5.4 shows the simulated current account balance.

The simple model of this chapter makes many realistic predictions. It produces time-series that are persistent and that display coarse co-movements that are broadly consistent with the data. But there are also several features of the model that are inconsistent with the data. First, consumption in the two-country model is much smoother than output. Second, domestic and foreign consumption are perfectly correlated, due to the perfect risk-sharing, whereas the correlation in the data is much lower than 1. A related point is that home and foreign output

Table 5.4 The calibrated open-economy model

	Std. Dev.	Autocorrelations				
		1	2	3	4	6
y_t	0.022	0.66	0.40	0.15	0.07	0.04
c_t	0.017	0.63	0.42	0.18	0.12	−0.04
i_t	0.114	0.05	−0.13	−0.09	−0.10	0.03
ex_t	0.038	0.09	−0.09	−0.09	−0.10	−0.00
y_t^*	0.021	0.65	0.32	0.07	−0.15	−0.27
c_t^*	0.017	0.63	0.42	0.18	0.12	−0.04
i_t^*	0.116	0.03	−0.15	−0.07	−0.08	0.00

	Cross-correlations at k						
	6	4	1	0	−1	−4	−6
$ex_t y_{t-k}$	0.00	0.18	0.41	0.44	0.21	0.15	0.15
$y_t^* y_{t-k}$	0.10	0.06	0.27	0.18	0.06	0.28	0.05

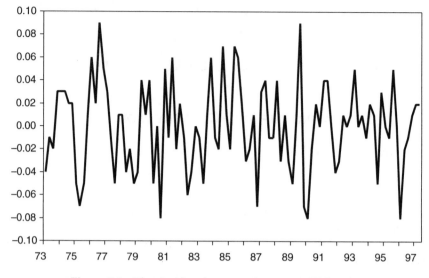

Figure 5.4   The simulated current account to GDP ratio.

are predicted to display a lower degree of co-movement than home and foreign consumption, which also is not borne out in the data.

▶ Chapter Summary

1. The workhorses of real business cycle research are dynamic stochastic general equilibrium models. They can be viewed as Arrow–Debreu models, and solved by exploiting the social planner's problem. They feature perfect markets and fully flexible prices. The models are fully articulated and have solidly grounded microfoundations.

2. Real business cycle researchers employ the calibration method to quantitatively evaluate their models. Typically, the researcher takes a set of moments, such as correlations between actual time-series, and asks if the theory is capable of replicating these *co-movements*. The calibration style of research stands in contrast with econometric methodology as articulated in the Cowles commission tradition. In standard econometric practice, one begins by achieving model identification, progressing to estimation of the structural parameters, and finally by conducting hypothesis tests of the model's overidentifying restrictions, but how one determines whether or not the model is successful in the calibration tradition is not entirely clear.

Foreign Exchange Market Efficiency

In his second review article on efficient capital markets, Fama [47] writes

> "I take the market efficiency hypothesis to be the simple statement that security prices fully reflect all available information."

He goes on to say

> "..., market efficiency per se is not testable. It must be tested jointly with some model of equilibrium, an asset-pricing model."

Market efficiency does not mean that asset returns are serially uncorrelated, nor does it mean that the financial markets present zero expected profits. The crux of market efficiency is that there are no unexploited *excess* profit opportunities. What is considered to be excessive depends on the model of market equilibrium.

This chapter is an introduction to the economics of foreign exchange market efficiency. We begin with an evaluation of the simplest model of international currency and money-market equilibrium – uncovered interest parity. Econometric analyses show that it is strongly rejected by the data. The ensuing challenge is then to understand why uncovered interest parity fails.

We cover three possible explanations. The first is that the forward foreign exchange rate contains a risk premium. This argument is developed using the Lucas model of chapter 4. The second explanation is that the true underlying structure of the economy is subject to change occasionally, but economic agents only learn about these structural changes over time. During this transitional learning period, market participants have an incomplete understanding of the economy and make systematic prediction errors even though they are behaving rationally. This is called the "peso-problem" approach. The third explanation is that some market participants are actually irrational in the sense that they believe that the value of an asset depends on extraneous information in addition to the economic fundamentals. The individuals who take actions based on these pseudo-signals are called "noise" traders.

The notational convention followed in this chapter is to let upper case letters denote variables in levels and lower case letters denote their logarithms, with the exception of interest rates, which are always denoted in lower case. As usual, stars are used to denote foreign country variables.

6.1 DEVIATIONS FROM UIP

Let s be the log spot exchange rate, let f be the log one-period-forward rate, let i be the one-period nominal interest rate on a domestic currency (dollar) asset, and let i^* be the nominal interest rate on the foreign currency (euro) asset. If uncovered interest parity holds, $i_t - i_t^* = E_t(s_{t+1}) - s_t$ but, by covered interest parity, $i_t - i_t^* = f_t - s_t$. Therefore, unbiasedness of the forward exchange rate as a predictor of the future spot rate $f_t = E_t(s_{t+1})$ is equivalent to uncovered interest parity.

We begin by covering the basic econometric analyses used to detect these deviations.

HANSEN AND HODRICK'S TESTS OF UIP

Hansen and Hodrick [68] use generalized method of moments (GMM) to test uncovered interest parity. The GMM method is covered in section 2.2. The Hansen–Hodrick *problem* is that a moving-average serial correlation is induced into the regression error when the prediction horizon exceeds the sampling interval of the data.

The Hansen–Hodrick Problem

To see how the problem arises, let $f_{t,3}$ be the log 3-month-forward exchange rate at time t, let s_t be the log spot rate, let I_t be the time t information set available to market participants, and let J_t be the time t information set available to you, the econometrician. Even though you are working with 3-month-forward rates, you will sample the data monthly. You want to test the hypothesis

$$H_0: E(s_{t+3}|I_t) = f_{t,3}.$$

In setting up the test, you note that I_t is not observable, but since J_t is a subset of I_t and since $f_{t,3}$ is contained in J_t, you can use the law of iterated expectations to test

$$H_0': E(s_{t+3}|J_t) = f_{t,3},$$

which is implied by H_0. You do this by taking a vector of economic variables $\underline{z}_{t-3}$ in J_{t-3}, running the regression

$$s_t - f_{t-3,3} = \underline{z}'_{t-3}\underline{\beta} + \epsilon_{t,3},$$

and doing a joint test that the slope coefficients are zero.

Under the null hypothesis, the forward rate is the market's forecast of the spot rate 3 months ahead, $f_{t-3,3} = E(s_t|J_{t-3})$. The observations, however, are collected every month. Let $J_t = (\epsilon_t, \epsilon_{t-1}, \ldots, \underline{z}_t, \underline{z}_{t-1}, \ldots)$. The regression error formed at time $t-3$ is $\epsilon_t = s_t - E(s|J_{t-3})$. At $t-3$, $E(\epsilon_t|J_{t-3}) = E(s_t - E(s_t|J_{t-3})) = 0$, so the error term is unpredictable at time $t-3$ when it is formed. But at time $t-2$ and $t-1$ you get new information and you cannot say that $E(\epsilon_t|J_{t-1}) = E(s_t|J_{t-1}) - E[E(s_t|J_{t-3})|J_{t-1}]$ is zero. Using the law of iterated expectations, the first autocovariance of the error, $E(\epsilon_t\epsilon_{t-1}) = E(\epsilon_{t-1}E(\epsilon_t|J_{t-1}))$, need not be zero. You can't say that $E(\epsilon_t\epsilon_{t-2})$ is zero either. You can, however, say that $E(\epsilon_t\epsilon_{t-k}) = 0$ for $k \geq 3$. When the forecast horizon of the forward exchange rate is three sampling periods, the error term is potentially correlated with two lags of itself and follows an MA(2) process. If you work with a *k-period* forward rate, you must be prepared for the error term to follow an MA($k-1$) process.

Generalized least-squares procedures, such as Cochrane–Orcutt or Hildreth–Lu, covered in elementary econometrics texts cannot be used to handle these serially correlated errors, because these estimators are inconsistent if the regressors are not econometrically exogenous. Researchers usually follow Hansen and Hodrick by estimating the coefficient vector by least squares and then calculating the asymptotic covariance matrix assuming that the regression error follows a moving average process. Least squares is consistent because the regression error, ϵ_t, being a rational expectations forecast error under the null, is uncorrelated with the regressors, $\underline{z}_{t-3}$.[1]

Hansen–Hodrick Regression Tests of UIP

Hansen and Hodrick ran two sets of regressions. In the first set, the independent variables were the lagged forward exchange rate forecast errors $(s_{t-3} - f_{t-6,3})$ of the own currency plus those of cross-rates. In the second set, the independent variables were the own forward premium and those of cross-rates $(s_{t-3} - f_{t-3,3})$. They rejected the null hypothesis at very small significance levels.

[1] To compute the asymptotic covariance matrix of the least-squares vector, follow the GMM interpretation of least squares developed in section 2.2. Assume that ϵ_t is conditionally homoskedastic, and let $\underline{w}_t = \underline{z}_{t-3}\epsilon_t$. We have $E(\underline{w}_t\underline{w}'_t) = E(\epsilon_t^2\underline{z}_{t-3}\underline{z}'_{t-3}) = E(E[\epsilon_t^2\underline{z}_{t-3}\underline{z}'_{t-3}|\underline{z}_{t-3}]) = \gamma_0 E(\underline{z}_{t-3}\underline{z}'_{t-3}) = \gamma_0\mathbf{Q}_0$, where $\gamma_0 = E(\epsilon_t^2)$ and $\mathbf{Q} = E(\underline{z}_{t-3}\underline{z}'_{t-3})$. Now, $E(\underline{w}_t\underline{w}'_{t-1}) = E(\epsilon_t\epsilon_{t-1}\underline{z}_{t-3}\underline{z}'_{t-4}) = E(E[\epsilon_t\epsilon_{t-1}\underline{z}_{t-3}\underline{z}'_{t-4}|\underline{z}_{t-3},\underline{z}_{t-4}]) = E(\underline{z}_{t-3}\underline{z}'_{t-4}E[\epsilon_t\epsilon_{t-1}|\underline{z}_{t-3},\underline{z}_{t-4}]) = \gamma_1\mathbf{Q}_1$, where $\gamma_1 = E(\epsilon_t\epsilon_{t-1})$, and $\mathbf{Q}_1 = E(\underline{z}_{t-3}\underline{z}_{t-4})$. By an analogous argument, $E(\underline{w}_t\underline{w}'_{t-2}) = \gamma_2\mathbf{Q}_2$ and $E(\underline{w}_t\underline{w}'_{t-k}) = 0$, for $k \geq 3$. Now, $\mathbf{D} = E(\partial(\underline{z}_t\epsilon_t)/\partial\underline{\beta}') = \mathbf{Q}_0$, so the asymptotic covariance matrix for the least-squares estimator is $(\mathbf{Q}'_0\mathbf{W}^{-1}\mathbf{Q}_0)^{-1}$, where $\mathbf{W} = \gamma_0\mathbf{Q}_0 + \sum_{j=1}^2 \gamma_j(\mathbf{Q}_j + \mathbf{Q}'_j)$. Actually, Hansen and Hodrick used weekly observations with the 3-month forward rate, which leads the regression error to follow an MA(11) process.

Table 6.1 Hansen–Hodrick tests of UIP

	US–BP	US–JY	US–DM	DM–BP	DM–JY	BP–JY
Wald(NW[6])	16.23	400.47	5.701	66.77	46.35	294.31
p-value	0.001	0.000	0.127	0.000	0.000	0.000
Wald(HH[2])	16.44	324.85	4.299	57.81	32.73	300.24
p-value	0.001	0.000	0.231	0.000	0.000	0.000

Regression $s_t - f_{t-3,3} = \underline{z}'_{t-3}\beta + \epsilon_{t,3}$ estimated on monthly observations from 1973,3 to 1999,12. Wald is the Wald statistic for the test that $\beta = 0$. Asymptotic covariance matrix estimated by Newey–West with six lags (NW[6]) and by Hansen–Hodrick with two lags (HH[2]).

Let's run their second set of regressions using the dollar (US), pound (BP), yen (JY), and deutschemark (DM). The dependent variable is the realized forward contract profit, which is regressed on the own and cross forward premia. The 350 monthly observations are formed by taking observations from every fourth Friday. From March 1973 to December 1991, the data are from the Harris Bank Foreign Exchange *Weekly Review* extending from March 1973 to December 1991. From 1992 to 1999, the data are from *Datastream*. The Wald test that the slope coefficients are jointly zero with p-values are given in table 6.1. The Wald statistics are asymptotically χ_3^2 under the null hypothesis. Two versions of the asymptotic covariance matrix are estimated: Newey and West with six lags (denoted Wald(NW[6])), and Hansen–Hodrick with two lags (denoted Wald(HH[2])). In these data, UIP is rejected at reasonable levels of significance for every currency except for the dollar–deutschemark rate.

The Advantage of Using Overlapping Observations

The Hansen–Hodrick correction involves some extra work. Are the benefits obtained by using the extra observations worth the extra costs? After all, you can avoid inducing the serial correlation into the regression error by using nonoverlapping quarterly observations, but then you would only have 111 data points. Using the overlapping monthly observations increases the nominal sample size by a factor of three, but the *effective* increase in sample size may be less than this if the additional observations are highly dependent.

The advantage that one gains by going to monthly data are illustrated in table 6.2, which shows the results of a small Monte Carlo experiment that compares the two (overlapping versus nonoverlapping) strategies. The data-generating process is

$$y_{t+3} = x_t + \epsilon_{t+3}, \quad \epsilon_t \overset{iid}{\sim} N(0,1),$$

$$x_t = 0.8x_{t-1} + u_t, \quad u_t \overset{iid}{\sim} N(0,1),$$

Table 6.2 The Monte Carlo distribution of OLS slope coefficients and *T*-ratios using overlapping and nonoverlapping observations

T	Overlapping observations		Percentiles			Relative range
			2.5	50	97.5	
50	Yes	Slope	0.778	0.999	1.207	0.471
		t_{NW}	(− 2.738)	(− 0.010)	(2.716)	1.207
		t_{HH}	[−2.998]	[−0.010]	[3.248]	1.383
16	No	Slope	0.543	0.998	1.453	
		t_{OLS}	((− 2.228))	((− 0.008))	((2.290))	
100	Yes	Slope	0.866	0.998	1.126	0.474
		t_{NW}	(− 2.286)	(− 0.025)	(2.251)	1.098
		t_{HH}	[−2.486]	[−0.020]	[2.403]	1.183
33	No	Slope	0.726	0.996	1.274	
		t_{OLS}	((− 2.105))	((− 0.024))	((2.026))	
300	Yes	Slope	0.929	1.001	1.074	0.509
		t_{NW}	(− 2.071)	(0.021)	(2.177)	1.041
		t_{HH}	[−2.075]	[−0.016]	[2.065]	1.014
100	No	Slope	0.858	1.003	1.143	
		t_{OLS}	((− 2.030))	((0.032))	((2.052))	

True slope = 1. t_{NW}, Newey–West *t*-ratio; t_{HH}, Hansen–Hodrick *t*-ratio; t_{OLS}, OLS *t*-ratio. The relative range is the ratio of the distance between the 97.5 and 2.5 percentiles in the Monte Carlo distribution for the statistic constructed using overlapping observations to that constructed using nonoverlapping observations.

where T is the number of overlapping (monthly) observations. y_{t+3} is regressed on x_t and Newey–West *t*-ratios t_{NW} are reported in parentheses. Five lags were used for $T = 50, 100$ and six lags were used for $T = 300$. Hansen–Hodrick *t*-ratios t_{HH} are given in square brackets and OLS *t*-ratios t_{OLS} are given in double parentheses. The relative range is the 2.5–97.5 percentiles of the distribution with overlapping observations divided by the 2.5–97.5 percentiles of the distribution with nonoverlapping observations.[2] The empirical distribution of each statistic is based on 2,000 replications.

You can see that there definitely is an efficiency gain to using overlapping observations. The range encompassing the 2.5–97.5 percentiles of the Monte Carlo distribution of the OLS estimator shrinks approximately by half when going from nonoverlapping (quarterly) to overlapping (monthly) observations. The tradeoff is that, for very small samples, the distribution of the *t*-ratios under overlapping observations are more fat-tailed and look less like the standard normal distribution than the OLS *t*-ratios.

---

[2] For example, we get the row 1 relative range value 0.471 for the slope coefficient from (1.207 − 0.778)/(1.453 − 0.543).

● FAMA DECOMPOSITION REGRESSIONS

Although the preceding Monte Carlo experiment suggested that you can achieve efficiency gains by using overlapping observations, in the interests of simplicity we will go back to working with the log one-period, forward rate, $f_t = f_{t,1}$ – to avoid inducing moving average errors.

Define the expected excess nominal forward foreign exchange payoff to be

$$p_t \equiv f_t - E_t[s_{t+1}], \tag{6.1}$$

where $E_t[s_{t+1}] = E[s_{t+1}|I_t]$. You already know from the Hansen–Hodrick regressions that p_t is nonzero and that it evolves over time as a random process. Adding and subtracting s_t from both sides of (6.1) gives

$$f_t - s_t = E_t(s_{t+1} - s_t) + p_t. \tag{6.2}$$

Fama [46] shows how to deduce some properties of p_t using the analysis of omitted variables bias in regression problems. First, consider the regression of the *ex post* forward profit $f_t - s_{t+1}$ on the current-period forward premium $f_t - s_t$. Second, consider the regression of the one-period-ahead depreciation $s_{t+1} - s_t$ on the current-period forward premium. The regressions are

$$f_t - s_{t+1} = \alpha_1 + \beta_1(f_t - s_t) + \varepsilon_{1t+1}, \tag{6.3}$$

$$s_{t+1} - s_t = \alpha_2 + \beta_2(f_t - s_t) + \varepsilon_{2t+1}. \tag{6.4}$$

Equations (6.3) and (6.4) are not independent, because when you add them together you get

$$\alpha_1 + \alpha_2 = 0,$$
$$\beta_1 + \beta_2 = 1, \tag{6.5}$$
$$\varepsilon_{1t+1} + \varepsilon_{2t+1} = 0. \tag{6.6}$$

In addition, these regressions have no structural interpretation. So why was Fama interested in running them? Because it allowed him to estimate moments and functions of moments that characterize the joint distribution of p_t and $E_t(s_{t+1} - s_t)$.

The population value of the slope coefficient in the first regression (6.3) is $\beta_1 = \text{Cov}[(f_t - s_{t+1}), (f_t - s_t)]/\text{Var}[f_t - s_t]$. Using the definition of p_t, it follows that the forward premium can be expressed as $f_t - s_t = p_t + E(\Delta s_{t+1}|I_t)$, whose variance is $\text{Var}(f_t - s_t) = \text{Var}(p_t) + \text{Var}[E(\Delta s_{t+1}|I_t)] + 2\text{Cov}[p_t, E(\Delta s_{t+1}|I_t)]$. Now add and subtract $E(s_{t+1}|I_t)$ to the realized profit, to get $f_t - s_{t+1} = p_t - u_{t+1}$, where $u_{t+1} = s_{t+1} - E(s_{t+1}|I_t) = \Delta s_{t+1} - E(\Delta s_{t+1}|I_t)$ is the unexpected depreciation. Now you have $\text{Cov}[(f_t - s_{t+1}), (f_t - s_t)] = \text{Cov}[(p_t - u_{t+1}), (p_t + E(\Delta s_{t+1}|I_t))] = \text{Var}(p_t) + \text{Cov}[p_t, E(\Delta s_{t+1}|I_t))]$. With the aid of these calculations, the slope coefficient from the first regression can be expressed as

$$\beta_1 = \frac{\text{Var}(p_t) + \text{Cov}[p_t, E_t(\Delta s_{t+1})]}{\text{Var}(p_t) + \text{Var}[E_t(\Delta s_{t+1})] + 2\text{Cov}[p_t, E_t(\Delta s_{t+1})]}. \tag{6.7}$$

Table 6.3 Estimates of regression equations (6.3) and (6.4)

	US–BP	US–JY	US–DM	DM–BP	DM–JY	BP–JY
$\hat{\beta}_2$	−3.481	−4.246	−0.796	−1.645	−2.731	−4.295
$t(\beta_2 = 0)$	(−2.413)	(−3.635)	(−0.542)	(−1.326)	(−1.797)	(−2.626)
$t(\beta_2 = 1)$	(−3.107)	(−4.491)	(−1.222)	(−2.132)	(−2.455)	(−3.237)
$\hat{\beta}_1$	4.481	5.246	1.796	2.645	3.731	5.295

Nonoverlapping quarterly observations from 1976.1 to 1999.4. $t(\beta_2 = 0)\,(t(\beta_2 = 1))$ is the t-statistic to test $\beta_2 = 0\,(\beta_2 = 1)$.

In the second regression (6.4), the population value of the slope coefficient is $\beta_2 = \text{Cov}[(\Delta s_{t+1}), (f_t - s_t)]/\text{Var}(f_t - s_t)$. Making the analogous substitutions yields

$$\beta_2 = \frac{\text{Var}[E_t(\Delta s_{t+1})] + \text{Cov}[p_t, E_t(\Delta s_{t+1})]}{\text{Var}(p_t) + \text{Var}[E_t(\Delta s_{t+1})] + 2\text{Cov}[p_t, E_t(\Delta s_{t+1})]}. \tag{6.8}$$

Let's run the Fama regressions using nonoverlapping quarterly observations from 1976.1 to 1999.4 for the British pound (BP), yen (JY), deutschemark (DM), and dollar (US). We get the results shown in table 6.3.

There is ample evidence that the forward premium contains useful information for predicting the future depreciation in the (generally) significant estimates of β_2. Since $\hat{\beta}_2$ is significantly less than 1, uncovered interest parity is rejected. The anomalous result is not that $\beta_2 \neq 1$, but that it is negative. The forward premium evidently predicts the future depreciation, but with the "wrong" sign from the UIP perspective. Recall that the calibrated Lucas model in chapter 4 also predicts a negative β_2 for the dollar–deutschemark rate.

The anomaly is driven by the dynamics in p_t. We have evidence that it is statistically significant. The next question that Fama asks is whether p_t is economically significant. Is it big enough to be economically interesting? To answer this question, we use the estimates and the slope-coefficient decompositions (6.7) and (6.8) to get information about the relative volatility of p_t.

First, note that $\hat{\beta}_2 < 0$. From (6.8) it follows that p_t must be negatively correlated with the expected depreciation, $\text{Cov}[p_t, E(\Delta s_{t+1}|I_t)] < 0$. By (6.5), the negative estimate of β_2 implies that $\hat{\beta}_1 > 0$. By (6.7), it must be the case that $\text{Var}(p_t)$ is large enough to offset the negative $\text{Cov}(p_t, E_t(\Delta s_{t+1}))$. Since $\hat{\beta}_1 - \hat{\beta}_2 > 0$, it follows that $\text{Var}(p_t) > \text{Var}(E(\Delta s_{t+1}|I_t))$, which at least places a lower bound on the size of p_t.

● ESTIMATING p_t

We have evidence that $p_t = f_t - E(s_{t+1}|I_t)$ evolves as a random process, but what does it look like? You can get a quick estimate of p_t by projecting the realized profit $f_t - s_{t+1} = p_t - u_{t+1}$ on a vector of observations $\underline{z}_t$, where $u_{t+1} = s_{t+1} -$ E$(s_{t+1}|I_t)$ is the rational prediction error. Using the law of iterated expectations and the property that E$(u_{t+1}|\underline{z}_t) = 0$, you have E$(f_t - s_{t+1}|\underline{z}_t) =$ E$(p_t|\underline{z}_t)$. If you run the regression

$$f_t - s_{t+1} = \underline{z}_t'\beta + u_{t+1},$$

you can use the fitted value of the regression as an estimate of the *ex ante* payoff, $\hat{p}_t = \underline{z}_t'\hat{\beta}$.

A slightly more sophisticated estimate can be obtained from a vector error correction representation that incorporates the joint dynamics of the spot and forward rates. Here, the log spot and forward rates are assumed to be unit-root processes and the forward premium is assumed to be stationary. The spot and forward rates are cointegrated, with cointegration vector $(1, -1)$. As shown in section 2.6, s_t and f_t have a vector error correction representation, which can be represented equivalently as a bivariate vector autoregression in the forward premium $(f_t - s_t)$ and the depreciation Δs_t.

Let's pursue the VAR option. Let $\underline{y}_t = (f_t - s_t, \Delta s_t)'$ follow the kth order VAR

$$\underline{y}_t = \sum_{j=1}^{k} \mathbf{A}_j \underline{y}_{t-j} + \underline{v}_t.$$

Let $\underline{e}_2 = (0, 1)$ be a selection vector such that $\underline{e}_2 \underline{y}_t = \Delta s_t$ picks off the depreciation, and let $\underline{H}_t = (\underline{y}_t, \underline{y}_{t-1}, \dots)$ be the current and lagged values of $\underline{y}_t$. Then E$(\Delta s_{t+1}|\underline{H}_t) = \underline{e}_2E(\underline{y}_{t+1}|\underline{H}_t) = \underline{e}_2 \left[\sum_{j=1}^{k} \mathbf{A}_j \underline{y}_{t+1-j}\right]$, and you can estimate p_t with

$$\hat{p}_t = (f_t - s_t) - \underline{e}_2 \left[\sum_{j=1}^{k} \hat{\mathbf{A}}_j \underline{y}_{t+1-j}\right]. \qquad (6.9)$$

Mark and Wu [100] used the VAR method to obtain quarterly estimates of p_t for the US dollar relative to the deutschemark, pound, and yen. Their estimates, shown in figure 6.1, show that E$(\Delta s_{t+1}|\underline{H}_t)$ are persistent for the pound and yen. Both $\hat{p}_t$ and $\hat{\text{E}}(\Delta s_{t+1}|\underline{H}_t)$ alternate between positive and negative values, but they change sign infrequently. The cross-sectional correlation across the three exchange rates is also evident. Each of the series peaks in early 1980 and 1981, and the $\hat{p}_t$s are generally positive during the period of dollar strength from mid-1980 to 1985 and are generally negative from 1990 to late 1993. You can also see in the figures the negative covariance between $\hat{p}_t$ and $\hat{\text{E}}_t(\Delta s_{t+1})$ deduced by Fama's regressions.

Deviations from uncovered interest parity are a stylized fact of the foreign exchange market landscape. But whether the stochastic p_t term floating around is the byproduct of an inefficient market is an unresolved issue. As per Fama's definition, we say that the foreign exchange market is efficient if the relevant prices are determined in accordance with a model of market equilibrium. One possibility is that p_t is a risk premium. At this point, we revisit the Lucas model and use it to place some structure on p_t.

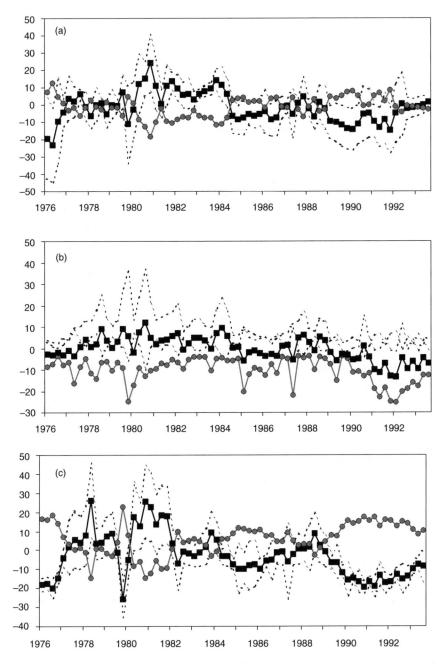

Figure 6.1 Time-series point estimates of p_t (boxes), plus and minus two standard errors (dotted) and point estimates of $E_t(\Delta s_{t+1})$ (circles). (a) US–UK; (b) US–Germany; (c) US–Japan.

| 6.2 RATIONAL RISK PREMIA

Hodrick [73] and Engel [42] show how to use the Lucas model to price forward foreign exchange. We follow their use of the Lucas model to understand
deviations from uncovered interest parity.

Recall that forward foreign exchange contracts are like nominal bonds in the
Lucas model in that they are not actually traded. We are calculating shadow
prices that keep them off the market. Let S_t be the nominal spot exchange rate
expressed as the home currency price of a unit of foreign currency, and let F_t be
the price of the foreign currency for one-period-ahead delivery.

The *intertemporal marginal rate of substitution* will play a key role. In aggregate
asset-pricing applications, it is common to work with per capita consumption
data. One way to justify using such data in the utility function in Lucas's two-
country model is to assume that the period utility function is homothetic and
that the relative price between the home good and the foreign good (the real
exchange rate) is constant. This allows you to write the representative agent's
intertemporal marginal rate of substitution between t and $t + 1$ as

$$\mu_{t+1} = \frac{\beta u'(C_{t+1})}{u'(C_t)}, \tag{6.10}$$

where $u'(C_t)$ is the representative agent's marginal utility evaluated at equilibrium consumption.[3]

Let P_t be the domestic price level and let β be the subjective discount factor. A
speculative position in a forward contract requires no investment at time t. If the
agent is behaving optimally, the expected marginal utility from the real payoff
from buying the foreign currency forward is $E_t [u'(c_{t+1})(F_t - S_{t+1})/P_{t+1}] = 0$.
To express the Euler equation in terms of stationary random variables, so that
their unconditional variances and unconditional covariances between random
variables exist, multiply both sides by β and divide by $u'(c_t)$, to give

$$E_t \left[\mu_{t+1} \frac{F_t - S_{t+1}}{P_{t+1}} \right] = 0. \tag{6.11}$$

Equation (6.11) is key to understanding the demand for forward foreign
exchange risk premia in the intertemporal asset pricing framework. Keep in
mind that the intertemporal marginal rate of substitution varies inversely with
consumption growth, so that when the agent experiences the good state, consumption growth is high and the intertemporal marginal rate of substitution is
low.

---

[3] If the period utility function in Lucas's two-good model is $u(C_t) = C_t^{1-\gamma}/(1 - \gamma)$, with
$C_t = C_{xt}^\theta C_{yt}^{1-\theta}$, the intertemporal marginal rate of substitution is $\beta(C_{t+1}/C_t)^{1-\gamma}(C_{xt}/C_{xt+1})$. But if
the relative price between X and Y is constant, the growth rate of consumption of X is the same
as the growth rate of the consumption index and the intertemporal marginal rate of substitution
becomes that given in (6.10).

Covariance decomposition and Euler equations. We will use the property that the covariance between any two random variables, X_{t+1} and Y_{t+1}, can be decomposed as

$$\text{Cov}_t(X_{t+1}, Y_{t+1}) = E_t(X_{t+1}Y_{t+1}) - E_t(X_{t+1})E_t(Y_{t+1}).$$

For a particular definition of X and Y, the theory, embodied in (6.11), restricts $E_t(X_{t+1}Y_{t+1}) = 0$. Using this restriction in the covariance decomposition and rearranging gives

$$E_t(Y_{t+1}) = \frac{-\text{Cov}_t(X_{t+1}, Y_{t+1})}{E_t(X_{t+1})}. \tag{6.12}$$

 ## THE REAL RISK PREMIUM

Set $Y_{t+1} = (F_t - S_{t+1})/P_{t+1}$ and $X_{t+1} = \mu_{t+1}$ in (6.11) and use (6.12), to give

$$E_t[F_t - S_{t+1}/P_{t+1}] = \frac{-\text{Cov}_t\left[((F_t - S_{t+1})/P_t), \mu_{t+1}\right]}{E_t\mu_{t+1}}. \tag{6.13}$$

The forward rate is in general not the rationally expected future spot in the Lucas model. The expected forward contract payoff is proportional to the conditional covariance between the payoff and the intertemporal marginal rate of substitution. The factor of proportionality is $-1/E_t(\mu_{t+1})$, which is the *ex ante* gross real interest rate multiplied by -1.

How do we make sense of (6.13)? Suppose that $E_t[(F_t - S_{t+1})/P_{t+1}] < 0$. Then the covariance on the right-hand side is positive. You expect to generate a profit by buying the foreign currency (euros) forward and reselling them in the spot market at $E_t(S_{t+1})$. A corresponding strategy that exploits the deviation from uncovered interest parity is to borrow the home currency (dollars) and lend uncovered in the foreign currency (euros). The market pays a premium to those investors who are willing to hold euro-denominated assets. It follows that the euro must be the risky currency. If you are holding the euro forward, the high payoff states occur when $[(F_t - S_{t+1})/P_{t+1}]$ is negative. By the covariance term in (6.13), these states are associated with low realizations of μ_{t+1}. But μ_{t+1} is low when consumption growth is high. What it boils down to is this. Holding the euro forward pays off well in good states of the world, but you don't need an asset to pay off well in the good state. You want assets to pay off well in the bad state – when you really need it. But the forward euro will pay off poorly in the bad state, and in that sense it is risky.

If the euro is risky, the dollar is safe. If $E_t[(F_t - S_{t+1})/P_{t+1}] < 0$ and you buy the dollar forward, you expect to realize a loss. It might seem like a strange idea to buy an asset with an expected negative payoff, but this is something that risk-averse individuals are willing to do if the asset provides consumption insurance by providing high payoffs in bad (low-growth) consumption states. The expected negative payoff can be viewed as an insurance premium.

To summarize, in Lucas's intertemporal asset-pricing model, the risk of an asset lies in the covariance of its payoff with something that individuals care about – namely consumption. Assets that generate high payoffs in the bad state offer insurance against these bad states and are considered safe. A high payoff during the good state is less valuable to the individual than it is during the bad state, due to the concavity of the utility function. Risk-averse individuals require compensation by way of a risk premium to hold the risky assets.

Risk-neutral forward exchange.   If individuals are risk neutral, the intertemporal marginal rate of substitution μ_{t+1} is constant. Since the covariance of any random variable with a constant is zero, (6.13) becomes

$$E_t \left(\frac{F_t}{P_{t+1}} \right) = E_t \left(\frac{S_{t+1}}{P_{t+1}} \right). \tag{6.14}$$

So even under risk-neutrality the forward rate is not the rationally expected future spot rate, because you need to divide by the future and stochastic price level. To see more clearly how covariance risk is related to the fundamentals, it is useful to take a look at expected nominal speculative profits.

● THE NOMINAL RISK PREMIUM

Multiply (6.11) by P_t and divide through by S_t, to give

$$E_t \left[\left(\mu_{t+1} \frac{P_t}{P_{t+1}} \right) \left(\frac{F_t - S_{t+1}}{S_t} \right) \right] = 0.$$

Let

$$\mu_{t+1}^m = \mu_{t+1} \frac{P_t}{P_{t+1}}. \tag{6.15}$$

Since $1/P_t$ is the purchasing power of one domestic currency unit and $u'(C_t)/P_t$ is the marginal utility of money, we will call μ_{t+1}^m the intertemporal marginal rate of substitution of money. In chapter 4 (equation (4.62)), we found that the price of a one-period riskless domestic currency nominal bond is $(1+i_t)^{-1} = E_t(\mu_{t+1}^m)$.

Using (6.12), set $Y_{t+1} = (F_t - S_{t+1})/P_{t+1}$ and $X_{t+1} = \mu_{t+1}^m$. Because F_t/S_t is known at date t, it can be treated as a constant, and you have

$$E_t \left[\frac{F_t - S_{t+1}}{S_t} \right] = (1 + i_t) \text{Cov}_t \left[\mu_{t+1}^m, \frac{S_{t+1}}{S_t} \right]. \tag{6.16}$$

Perhaps now you can see more clearly why the foreign currency (euro) is risky when the forward euro contract offers an expected profit. If $E_t[(F_t - S_{t+1})/P_{t+1}] < 0$, the covariance in (6.16) must be negative. In the bad state, μ_{t+1}^m is high because consumption growth is low. This is associated with a weakening of the euro (low values of S_{t+1}/S_t). The euro is risky because its value is positively correlated with consumption. Agents consume both the domestic and the foreign goods, but the foreign currency buys fewer foreign goods in the bad state of nature and is therefore a bad hedge against low consumption states.

Pitfalls in pricing nominal contracts. Suppose that individuals are risk neutral. Then $\mu_{t+1}^m = \beta P_t/P_{t+1}$ and the covariance in (6.16) need not be zero – and again you can see that the forward rate is not necessarily the rationally expected future spot rate. Agents care about real profits, not nominal profits. Under risk neutrality, equilibrium expected real profits are zero, but in order to achieve zero expected real profits, the forward rate may have to be a biased predictor of the future spot.

This is why market efficiency does not mean that the exchange rate must follow a random walk, or that uncovered interest parity must hold. The Lucas model predicts that, in equilibrium, it is the *marginal utility* of the forward contract payoff that is unpredictable, and that deviations from UIP can emerge as compensation for risk-bearing.

6.3 TESTING EULER EQUATIONS

Using the methods of Hansen and Singleton [70], Mark [98] estimated and tested the Euler equation restrictions using 1-month forward exchange rates. Modjtahedi [104] goes a step further and tests implied Euler equation restrictions across the entire term structure available for forward rates (1, 3, 6, and 12 months). The strategy is to estimate the coefficient of relative risk aversion, γ, and test the orthogonality conditions implied by the Euler equation (6.11) using GMM.

Here, we use nonoverlapping quarterly observations on dollar rates of the pound, deutschemark, and yen from 1973.1 to 1997.1 and revisit Mark's analysis. To write the problem compactly, let $\underline{r}_{t+1}$ be the 3 × 1 forward foreign exchange payoff vector

$$\underline{r}_{t+1} = \begin{bmatrix} (F_{1t} - S_{1t+1})/(S_{1t}) \\ (F_{2t} - S_{2t+1})/(S_{2t}) \\ (F_{3t} - S_{3t+1})/(S_{3t}) \end{bmatrix},$$

and let the 3 × 1 vector $\underline{w}_{t+1}$ be

$$\underline{w}_{t+1} = \mu_{t+1}^m \underline{r}_{t+1}, \tag{6.17}$$

where μ_{t+1}^m is the US representative investor's intertemporal marginal rate of substitution of money under CRRA utility, $u(C) = C^{1-\gamma}/(1-\gamma)$.

Using the notation developed here to rewrite the Euler equations (6.11), you get

$$E[\underline{w}_{t+1}|I_t] = 0. \tag{6.18}$$

Divide both sides by β, so that you only need to estimate γ. Equation (6.18) says that $\underline{w}_{t+1}$ is uncorrelated with any time-t information. Let $\underline{z}_t$ be a k-dimensional vector of time-t "instrumental variables," available to you, the econometrician. Then (6.18) implies the following $3 \times k$ estimable and testable equations[4]

$$E[\underline{w}_{t+1} \otimes \underline{z}_t] = E[(\mu^m_{t+1}\underline{r}_{t+1}) \otimes \underline{z}_t] = 0. \tag{6.19}$$

Now, the question is what to choose for $\underline{z}_t$. It is not a good idea to use too many variables, because the estimation problem will become intractable and the small sample properties of the GMM estimator will suffer. A good candidate is the forward premium, since we know that it is directly relevant to the problem at hand. Furthermore, it is not necessary to use *all* of the possible orthogonality conditions. To reduce the dimensionality of the estimation problem further, for each currency i, let

$$\underline{z}_{it} = \begin{bmatrix} 1 \\ (F_{it} - S_{it})/S_{it} \end{bmatrix}$$

be a vector of instrumental variables consisting of the constant 1 and the normalized forward premium. Estimating γ from the system of six equations

$$E \begin{bmatrix} \underline{w}_{1t+1}\underline{z}_{1t} \\ \underline{w}_{2t+1}\underline{z}_{2t} \\ \underline{w}_{3t+1}\underline{z}_{3t} \end{bmatrix} = 0 \tag{6.20}$$

gives $\hat{\gamma} = 48.66$, with an asymptotic standard error of 79.36. The coefficient of relative risk aversion is uncomfortably large and imprecisely estimated. However, the test of the five overidentifying restrictions gives a chi-square statistic of 7.20 (p-value $= 0.206$), which is not rejected at standard levels of significance.

Why does the data force $\hat{\gamma}$ to be so big? We can gain some intuition by recasting the problem as a regression. Suppose that you look at just one currency. If $[C_t/C_{t+1}, P_t/P_{t+1}, (F_t - S_{t+1})/S_t]$ are jointly log-normally distributed then w_{t+1} is also log-normal.[5] Taking logs, of both sides of (6.17), you obtain

$$\ln\left(\frac{F_t - S_{t+1}}{S_t}\right) + \ln\left(\frac{P_t}{P_{t+1}}\right) = -\gamma \ln\left(\frac{C_t}{C_{t+1}}\right) + \ln w_{t+1}.$$

$\ln(C_t/C_{t+1})$ is correlated with $\ln \underline{w}_{t+1}$, so you don't get consistent estimates with OLS – but you do get consistency with instrumental variables, and this is what GMM does. However, the regression analogy tells us that the large estimate of γ and its large standard error can be attributed to high variability in the excess

---

[4] $\otimes$ denotes the Kronecker product. Let

$$A = \begin{pmatrix} a_{11} & a_{12} \\ a_{21} & a_{22} \end{pmatrix}$$

and let **B** be any $n \times k$ matrix. Then

$$A \otimes B = \begin{pmatrix} a_{11}B & a_{12}B \\ a_{21}B & a_{22}B \end{pmatrix}.$$

[5]   A random variable X is said to be log-normally distributed if $\ln(X)$ is normally distributed.

return combined with low variability in consumption growth. The difficulty that the Lucas model under CRRA utility faces in explaining the data with small values of γ is not confined to the foreign exchange market. The corresponding difficulty for the model to simultaneously explain historical stock and bond returns is what Mehra and Prescott [103] call the "equity premium puzzle."

● VOLATILITY BOUNDS

Hansen and Jagannathan [69] propose a framework to evaluate the extent to which the Euler equations from representative agent asset-pricing models satisfy volatility restrictions on the intertemporal marginal rate of substitution.

We will first derive a lower bound on the volatility of the intertemporal marginal rate of substitution predicted by the Euler equations of the intertemporal asset-pricing model. Let $\underline{r}_{t+1}$ be an N-dimensional vector of holding period *returns* from t to $t + 1$ available to the agent, and let $\mu_{t+1} = \beta u'(C_{t+1})/u'(C_t)$ be the intertemporal marginal rate of substitution.

We need to write the Euler equations in returns form. For equities, they take the form $1 = E_t(\mu_{t+1}r^e_{t+1})$, where r^e_{t+1} is the gross return.[6] This reads as follows: an asset with expected payoff $E_t(\mu_{t+1}r^e_{t+1})$ costs one unit of the consumption good. An analogous returns form of the Euler equation holds for bonds. In the case of forward foreign exchange contracts, there is no investment required in the current period, so the returns form for the Euler equation is $0 = E_t\mu_{t+1}(F_t - S_{t+1})/P_t$. Thus, the returns form of the Euler equations for asset pricing can generically be represented as

$$\underline{v} = E_t(\mu_{t+1}\underline{r}_{t+1}),\qquad(6.21)$$

where $\underline{v}$ is a vector of constants whose ith element $v_i = 1$ if asset i is a stock or bond, and $v_i = 0$ if asset i is a forward foreign exchange contract.

Taking the unconditional expectation on both sides of (6.21) and using the law of iterated expectations gives

$$\underline{v} = E(\mu_{t+1}\underline{r}_{t+1}).\qquad(6.22)$$

Let $\theta_\mu \equiv E(\mu_t)$, $\sigma^2_\mu \equiv E(\mu_t - \theta_\mu)^2$, $\underline{\theta}_r \equiv E(r_t)$, and $\Sigma_r \equiv E(\underline{r}_t - \underline{\theta}_r)(\underline{r}_t - \underline{\theta}_r)'$. Project $(\mu_t - \theta_\mu)$ on to $(r_t - \underline{\theta}_r)$, to obtain

$$(\mu_t - \theta_\mu) = (\underline{r}_t - \underline{\theta}_r)'\underline{\beta}_\mu + u_t,\qquad(6.23)$$

where $\underline{\beta}_\mu$ is a vector of least-squares projection coefficients, u_t is the least-squares projection error, and

$$\underline{\beta}_\mu = \Sigma_r^{-1}E(\underline{r}_t - \underline{\theta}_r)(\mu_t - \theta_\mu).\qquad(6.24)$$

---

[6] Take the equity Euler equation (4.12) and divide both sides by $e_t u_{1,t+1}$. Let $r^e_{t+1} = (e_{t+1} + x_{t+1})/e_t$ to get the expression in the text.

Furthermore, you know that

$$E(\underline{r}_t - \underline{\theta}_r)(\mu_t - \theta_\mu) = \underbrace{E(\underline{r}_t \mu_t)}_{\underline{v}} - \underline{\theta}_r \theta_\mu, \tag{6.25}$$

where $E(\underline{r}_t \mu_t) = \underline{v}$ comes from the returns form of the Euler equations. Upon substituting (6.25) into (6.24), we have $\underline{\beta}_\mu = \Sigma_r^{-1}(\underline{v} - \underline{\theta}_r \theta_\mu)$.

Computing the variance of the intertemporal marginal rate of substitution gives

$$\begin{aligned}
\sigma_\mu^2 &= E(\mu_t - \theta_\mu)^2 \\
&= E(\mu_t - \theta_\mu)'(\mu_t - \theta_\mu) \\
&= E[(\underline{r}_t - \underline{\theta}_r)'\underline{\beta}_\mu + u_t]'[(\underline{r}_t - \underline{\theta}_r)'\underline{\beta}_\mu + u_t] \\
&= E[\underline{\beta}_\mu'(\underline{r}_t - \underline{\theta}_r)(\underline{r}_t - \underline{\theta}_r)'\underline{\beta}_\mu] + \sigma_u^2 \\
&\quad + \underbrace{\underline{\beta}_\mu' E(\underline{r}_t - \underline{\theta}_r)u_t + Eu_t(\underline{r}_t - \underline{\theta}_r)'\beta_\mu}_{(a)} \\
&= E(\mu_t \underline{r}_t - \theta_\mu \underline{\theta}_r)'\Sigma_r^{-1}\Sigma_r\Sigma_r^{-1}E(\mu_t \underline{r}_t - \theta_\mu \underline{\theta}_r) + \sigma_u^2 \\
&= (\underline{v} - \theta_\mu \underline{\theta}_r)'\Sigma_r^{-1}(\underline{v} - \theta_\mu \underline{\theta}_r) + \sigma_u^2. \tag{6.26}
\end{aligned}$$

The term labeled (a) above is zero because u_t is the least-squares projection error and is by construction orthogonal to $\underline{r}_t$. Since $\sigma_u^2 \geq 0$, the volatility or standard deviation of the intertemporal marginal rate of substitution must lie above σ_r, where

$$\sigma_\mu \geq \sigma_r \equiv \sqrt{(\underline{v} - \theta_\mu \underline{\theta}_r)' \Sigma_r^{-1}(\underline{v} - \theta_\mu \underline{\theta}_r)}. \tag{6.27}$$

The right-hand side of (6.27) is the lower bound on the volatility of the intertemporal marginal rate of substitution. If the assets are all equities or bonds, $\underline{v}$ is a vector of ones and the volatility bound is a parabola in (θ_μ, σ_μ) space. If the assets are all forward foreign exchange contracts, $\underline{v}$ is a vector of zeros and the lower volatility bound is a ray from the origin:

$$\sigma_r = \theta_\mu \left[\underline{\theta}_r' \Sigma_r^{-1} \underline{\theta}_r \right]^{1/2}. \tag{6.28}$$

How does one construct and use the volatility bound in practice? First, determine $\underline{v}$ and calculate $\underline{\theta}_r$ and Σ_r from asset-price data. Then, using (6.28), trace out σ_r as a function of θ_μ. Next, for a given functional form of the utility function, use consumption data to calculate the volatility of the intertemporal marginal rate of substitution, σ_μ. Compare this estimate to the volatility bound and determine whether the bound is satisfied.

When we do this using quarterly US consumption and CPI data and dollar exchange rates for the pound, deutschemark, and yen from 1973.1 to 1997.1, we get $\sqrt{\underline{\theta}'_r \Sigma^{-1} \underline{\theta}_r} = 0.309$. Now let the utility function be CRRA, with relative risk-aversion coefficient γ. As we vary γ, we generate the entries in the following table:

γ	θ_μ	σ_μ	σ_r
2	0.982	0.015	0.303
4	0.974	0.031	0.301
10	0.953	0.078	0.294
20	0.923	0.159	0.285
30	0.901	0.248	0.278
40	0.886	0.349	0.273
50	0.879	0.469	0.272
60	0.881	0.615	0.272

You can see that $\sigma_\mu < \sigma_r$ for values of γ below 30. This means that exchange rate payoffs are too volatile relative to the fundamentals (the intertemporal marginal rate of substitution) over this range of γ. Note how the GMM estimate of $\gamma = 48$ obtained earlier in this chapter is consistent with this result. In order to explain the data, the Lucas model with CRRA utility requires people to be very risk averse. Many people feel that the degree of risk aversion associated with $\gamma = 48$ is unrealistically high, and would rule out many observed risky gambles undertaken by economic agents.

The mean and volatility of the intertemporal marginal rate of substitution (θ_μ, σ_μ) for alternative values of γ and the lower volatility bound $(\sigma_r = 0.309\theta_\mu)$ implied by the data are illustrated in figure 6.2.[7]

6.4 APPARENT VIOLATIONS OF RATIONALITY

We've seen that there are important dimensions of the data that the Lucas model with CRRA utility cannot explain.[8] What other approaches have been taken to explain deviations from uncovered interest parity? This section covers the

---

[7] Backus, Gregory, and Telmer [4] investigate the lower volatility bound (6.28) implied by data on the US dollar prices of the Canadian dollar, the deutschemark, the French franc, the pound, and the yen. They compute the bound for an investor who chases positive expected profits by defining forward exchange payoffs on currency i as $I_{it}(F_{i,t} - S_{i,t+1})/S_{i,t}$, where $I_{it} = 1$ if $E_t(f_{i,t} - s_{i,t+1}) > 0$ and $I_{it} = 0$ otherwise. The bound computed in the text does not make this adjustment, because it is not a prediction of the Lucas model, where investors may be willing to take a position that earns expected negative profit if it provides consumption insurance. Using the indicator adjustment on returns lowers the volatility bound, making it more difficult for the asset-pricing model to match this quarterly data set.

[8] The failure of the model to generate sufficiently variable risk premia to explain the data cannot be blamed on the CRRA utility function. Bekaert [8] obtains similar results with utility specifications where consumption exhibits durability and when utility displays "habit persistence."

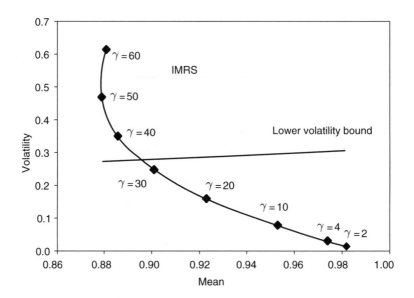

Figure 6.2 Mean and volatility estimates of the intertemporal marginal rate of substitution (IMRS) with $\beta = 0.99$ and alternative values of γ under constant relative risk-aversion utility and a lower bound implied by forward exchange payoffs of the pound, deutschemark, and yen, 1973.1 to 1997.1.

peso-problem approach and the noise-trader paradigm. Both approaches predict that market participants make systematic forecast errors. In the peso-problem approach, agents have rational expectations but don't know the true economic environment with certainty. In the noise-trading approach, some agents are irrational.

Before tackling these issues, we want to have some evidence that market participants actually do make systematic forecast errors. So we first look at a line of research that studies the properties of exchange rate forecasts compiled by surveys of actual foreign exchange market participants. The subjective expectations of market participants are key to any theory in international finance. The *rational expectations* assumption conveniently allows the economic analyst to model these subjective expectations without having to collect data on people's expectations *per se*. If the rational expectations assumption is wrong, its violation may what underlies asset-pricing anomalies such as the deviation from uncovered interest parity.

● PROPERTIES OF SURVEY EXPECTATIONS

Instead of modeling the subjective expectations of market participants as mathematical conditional expectations, why not just ask people what they think? One

line of research has used surveys of exchange rate forecasts by market participants to investigate the forward premium bias (deviation from UIP). Froot and
Frankel [62] study surveys conducted by the *Economist's Financial Report* from
June 1981 to December 1985, Money Market Services from March 1983 to October
1984, and American Express Banking Corporation from January 1976 to July
1985; Frankel and Chinn [56] employ a survey compiled monthly by *Currency
Forecasters' Digest* from February 1988 through February 1991; and Cavaglia et
al. [22] analyze forecasts on ten USD bilateral rates and eight deutschemark bilateral rates surveyed by Business International Corporation from January 1986
to December 1990. The survey respondents were asked to provide forecasts at
horizons of 3, 6, and 12 months into the future.

The salient properties of the survey expectations are captured in two regressions. Let $\hat{s}^e_{t+1}$ be the median of the survey forecast of the log spot exchange rate
s_{t+1} reported at date t. The first equation is the regression of the survey forecast
error on the forward premium:

$$\Delta \hat{s}^e_{t+1} - \Delta s_{t+1} = \alpha_1 + \beta_1(f_t - s_t) + \epsilon_{1t+1}. \tag{6.29}$$

If survey respondents have rational expectations, the survey forecast error realized at date $t + 1$ will be uncorrelated with any publicly available at time t, and
the slope coefficient β_1 in (6.29) will be zero.

The second regression is the counterpart to Fama's decomposition, and measures the weight that market participants attach to the forward premium in their
forecasts of the future depreciation:

$$\Delta \hat{s}^e_{t+1} = \alpha_2 + \beta_2(f_t - s_t) + \epsilon_{2,t+1}. \tag{6.30}$$

Survey respondents perceive there to be a risk premium to the extent that β_2
deviates from one. That is because if a risk premium exists, it will be impounded
in the regression error, and through the omitted variables bias will cause β_2 to
deviate from one.

Table 6.4 reports selected estimation results drawn from the literature. Two
main points can be drawn from the table:

1. The survey forecast regressions generally yield estimates of β_1 that are significantly
   different from zero, which provides evidence against the rationality of the survey
   expectations. In addition, the slope estimates typically exceed 1, which indicates
   that survey respondents evidently place too much weight on the forward rate
   when predicting the future spot. That is, an increase in the forward premium
   predicts that the survey forecast will exceed the future spot rate.
2. Estimates of β_2 are generally insignificantly different from 1. This suggests that
   survey respondents do not believe that there is a risk premium in the forward
   foreign exchange rate. Respondents use the forward rate as a predictor of the future
   spot. They are putting too much weight on the forward rate, and are forming their
   expectations irrationally in light of the empirically observed forward rate bias.

We should point out that some economists are skeptical about the accuracy
of survey data and therefore about the robustness of results obtained from the

Table 6.4 Empirical estimates from studies of survey forecasts

	Data set					
	Economist	*MMS*	*AMEX*	*CFD*	*BIC–USD*	*BIC–DEM*
Horizon: 3 months						
β_1	2.513	6.073	—	—	5.971	1.930
$t(\beta_1 = 1)$	1.945	2.596	—	—	1.921	−0.452
$t(\beta_2 = 1)$	1.304	−0.182	—	0.423	1.930	0.959
t-test	1.188	−2.753	—	−2.842	5.226	−1.452
Horizon: 6 months						
β_1	2.986	—	3.635	—	5.347	1.841
$t(\beta_1 = 1)$	1.870	—	2.705	—	2.327	−0.422
β_2	1.033	—	1.216	—	1.222	0.812
$t(\beta_2 = 1)$	0.192	—	1.038	—	1.461	−4.325
Horizon: 12 months						
β_1	0.517	—	3.108	—	5.601	1.706
$t(\beta_1 = 1)$	0.421	—	2.400	—	3.416	0.832
β_2	0.929	—	0.877	1.055	1.046	0.502
$t(\beta_2 = 1)$	−0.476	—	−0.446	0.297	0.532	−6.594

Estimates from the *Economist*, Money Market Services, and American Express surveys are from Froot and Frankel [62]. Estimates from the *Currency Forecasters' Digest* survey are from Frankel and Chinn [56], and estimates from the Business International Corporation (BIC) survey from Cavaglia et al. [22]. BIC–USD is the average of individual estimates for ten dollar exchange rates. BIC–DEM is the average over eight deutschemark exchange rates.

analyses of these data. They question whether there are sufficient incentives for survey respondents to truthfully report their predictions, and believe that you should study what market participants do, not what they say.

6.5 THE "PESO PROBLEM"

On the surface, systematic forecast errors suggests that market participants are repeatedly making the same mistake. It would seem that people cannot be rational if they do not learn from their past mistakes. The "peso problem" is a rational expectations explanation for persistent and serially correlated forecast errors, as typified in the survey data. Until this point, we have assumed that economic agents know with complete certainty, the model that describes the economic environment. That is, they know the processes, including the parameter values governing the exogenous state variables, the forms of the utility functions and production functions, and so forth. In short, they know and understand everything that we write down about the economic environment.

In "peso-problem" analyses, agents may have imperfect knowledge about some aspects of the underlying economic environment. Like applied econometricians, rational agents have observed an insufficient number of data points from which to exactly determine the true structure of the economic environment. Systematic forecast errors can arise as a small-sample problem.

A SIMPLE "PESO-PROBLEM" EXAMPLE

The "peso problem" was originally studied by Krasker [85], who observed a persistent interest differential in favor of Mexico even though the nominal exchange rate was fixed by the central bank. By covered interest arbitrage, there would also be a persistent forward premium, since if i is the US interest rate and i^* is the Mexican interest rate, $i_t - i_t^* = f_t - s_t < 0$. If the fix is maintained at $t + 1$, we have a realization of $f_t < s_{t+1}$, and repeated occurrence suggests systematic forward rate forecast errors.

Suppose that the central bank fixes the exchange rate at s_0, but the peg is not completely credible. Each period that the fix is in effect, there is a probability p that the central bank will abandon the peg and devalue the currency to $s_1 > s_0$ and a probability $1 - p$ that the s_0 peg will be maintained. The process governing the exchange rate is

$$s_{t+1} = \begin{cases} s_1 & \text{with probability } p, \\ s_0 & \text{with probability } 1 - p. \end{cases} \qquad (6.31)$$

The one-period-ahead rationally expected future spot rate is $E_t(s_{t+1}) = ps_1 + (1 - p)s_0$. As long as the peg is maintained and $p > 0$, we will observe the sequence of systematic, serially correlated, but rational forecast errors

$$s_0 - E_t(s_{t+1}) = p(s_0 - s_1) < 0. \qquad (6.32)$$

If the forward exchange rate is the market's expected future spot rate, we have a rational explanation for the forward premium bias. Although the forecast errors are serially correlated, they are not useful in predicting the future depreciation.

LEWIS'S "PESO PROBLEM" WITH BAYESIAN LEARNING

Lewis [91] studies an exchange rate pricing model in the presence of the peso problem. The stochastic process governing the fundamentals undergoes a shift, but economic agents are initially unsure as to whether a shift has actually occurred. Such a regime shift may be associated with changes in the economic, policy, or political environment. One example of such a phenomenon occurred in 1979, when the Federal Reserve switched its policy from targeting interest rates to one of targeting monetary aggregates. In hindsight, we now know that the Fed actually did change its operating procedures but, at the time, one may not have been completely sure. Even when policy-makers announce a change, there is always the possibility that they are not being truthful.

Lewis works with the monetary model of exchange rate determination. The switch in the stochastic process that governs the fundamentals occurs unexpectedly. Agents update their prior probabilities about the underlying process as Bayesians and learn about the regime shift, but this learning takes time. The resulting rational forecast errors are systematic and serially correlated during the learning period.

As in chapter 3, we let the fundamentals be $f_t = m_t - m_t^* - \phi(y_t - y_t^*)$, where m is money, y is real income, and ϕ is the interest semi-elasticity of money demand.[9] For convenience, the basic difference equation (3.9) that characterizes the model is reproduced here:

$$s_t = \gamma f_t + \psi E_t(s_{t+1}), \tag{6.33}$$

where $\gamma = 1/(1 + \lambda)$, $\psi = \lambda\gamma$, and λ is the interest semi-elasticity of money demand. The process that governs the fundamentals is known by foreign exchange market participants and evolves according to a random walk with drift term δ_0:

$$f_t = \delta_0 + f_{t-1} + v_t, \tag{6.34}$$

where $v_t \overset{iid}{\sim} N\left(0, \sigma_v^2\right)$.

We will obtain the no-bubbles solution using the *method of undetermined coefficients* (MUC). Beginning with (6.33), we see from the first term that s_t depends on f_t. s_t also depends on $E_t(s_{t+1})$, which is a function of the currently available information set, I_t. Since f_t is the only exogenous variable and the model is linear, it is reasonable to conjecture that the solution has the form

$$s_t = \pi_0 + \pi_1 f_t. \tag{6.35}$$

Now you need to determine the coefficients π_0 and π_1 that make (6.35) the solution. From (6.34), the one-period-ahead forecast of the fundamentals is $E_t f_{t+1} = \delta_0 + f_t$. If (6.35) is the solution, you can advance time by one period and take the conditional expectation as of date t, to give

$$E_t(s_{t+1}) = \pi_0 + \pi_1(\delta_0 + f_t). \tag{6.36}$$

Substitute (6.35) and (6.36) into (6.33), to obtain

$$\pi_0 + \pi_1 f_t = \gamma f_t + \psi(\pi_0 + \pi_1 \delta_0 + \pi_1 f_t). \tag{6.37}$$

In order for (6.37) to be a solution, the coefficients on the constant and on f_t on both sides must be equal. Upon equating coefficients, you see that the equation holds only if $\pi_0 = \lambda\delta_0$ and $\pi_1 = 1$. The no-bubbles solution for the exchange rate when the fundamentals follow a random walk with drift δ_0 is therefore

$$s_t = \lambda\delta_0 + f_t. \tag{6.38}$$

---

[9] Note that f denotes the fundamentals here, not the forward exchange rate.

A possible regime shift. Now suppose that market participants are told at date t_0 that the drift of the process governing the fundamentals *may* have increased to $\delta_1 > \delta_0$. Agents attach a probability $p_{0t} = \mathrm{Pr}(\delta = \delta_0|I_t)$ that there has been no regime change and a probability $p_{1t} = \mathrm{Pr}(\delta = \delta_1|I_t)$ that there has been a regime change, where I_t is the information set available to agents at date t. Agents use new information as it becomes available to update their beliefs about the true drift. At time t, they form expectations of the future values of the fundamental according to

$$E_t(f_{t+1}) = p_{0t}E(\delta_0 + v_t + f_t) + p_{1t}E(\delta_1 + v_t + f_t)$$
$$= p_{0t}\delta_0 + p_{1t}\delta_1 + f_t. \tag{6.39}$$

Use the MUC again to solve for the exchange rate under the new assumption about the fundamentals, by conjecturing the solution to depend on f_t and on the two possible drift parameters δ_0 and δ_1:

$$s_t = \pi_1 f_t + \pi_2 \delta_0 p_{0t} + \pi_3 \delta_1 p_{1t}. \tag{6.40}$$

The new information available to agents is the current-period realization of the fundamentals, which evolves according to a random walk. Since the new information is not predictable, the conditional expectation of the next period probability at date t is the current probability, $E_t(p_{0t+1}) = p_{0t}$.[10] Using this information, advance time by one period in (6.40) and take date-t expectations, to give

$$E_t s_{t+1} = \pi_1(f_t + p_{0t}\delta_0 + p_{1t}\delta_1) + \pi_2 \delta_0 p_{0t} + \pi_3 \delta_1 p_{1t}$$
$$= \pi_1 f_t + (\pi_1 + \pi_2)p_{0t}\delta_0 + (\pi_1 + \pi_3)p_{1t}\delta_1. \tag{6.41}$$

Substitute (6.40) and (6.41) into (6.33), to give

$$\pi_1 f_t + \pi_2 \delta_0 p_{0t} + \pi_3 \delta_1 p_{1t} = \gamma f_t + \psi \pi_1(p_{0t}\delta_0 + p_{1t}\delta_1 + f_t)$$
$$+ \psi \pi_2 \delta_0 p_{0t} + \psi \pi_3 \delta_1 p_{1t}, \tag{6.42}$$

and equate coefficients, to obtain $\pi_1 = 1$, $\pi_2 = \pi_3 = \lambda$. This gives the solution

$$s_t = f_t + \lambda(p_{0t}\delta_0 + p_{1t}\delta_1). \tag{6.43}$$

Now we want to calculate the forecast errors so that we can see how they behave during the learning period. To do this, advance the time subscript in (6.43) by one period, to give

$$s_{t+1} = f_{t+1} + \lambda(p_{0t+1}\delta_0 + p_{1t+1}\delta_1).$$

and take time-t expectations, to get

$$E_t s_{t+1} = f_t + p_{0t}\delta_0 + p_{1t}\delta_1 + \lambda p_{0t}\delta_0 + \lambda p_{1t}\delta_1$$
$$= f_t + (1 + \lambda)(p_{0t}\delta_0 + p_{1t}\delta_1). \tag{6.44}$$

---

[10] This claim is verified in problem 6 at the end of the chapter.

The time-$(t+1)$ rational forecast error is

$$s_{t+1} - E_t(s_{t+1}) = \lambda[\delta_0(p_{0t+1} - p_{0t}) + \delta_1(p_{1t+1} - p_{1t})] + \Delta f_{t+1} - \underbrace{(p_{0t}\delta_0 + p_{1t}\delta_1)]}_{E_t \Delta f_{t+1}}$$

$$= \lambda(\delta_1 - \delta_0)[p_{1t+1} - p_{1t}] + \delta_1 + v_{t+1} - [\delta_0 + (\delta_1 - \delta_0)p_{1t}]. \tag{6.45}$$

The regime probabilities p_{1t} and the updated probabilities $p_{1t+1} - p_{1t}$ are serially correlated during the learning period. The rational forecast error therefore contains systematic components and is serially correlated, but the forecast errors are not useful for predicting the future depreciation. To determine explicitly the sequence of the agent's belief probabilities, we use Bayes' rule.

Bayes' rule.   For events $A_i, i = 1, \ldots, N$, that partition the sample space S, and any event B with $\Pr(B) > 0$,

$$\Pr(A_i|B) = \frac{\Pr(A_i)\Pr(B|A_i)}{\sum_{j=1}^{N} \Pr(A_j)\Pr(B|A_j)}.$$

To apply Bayes' rule to the problem at hand, let news of the possible regime shift be released at $t = 0$. Agents begin with the unconditional probability, $p_0 = \Pr(\delta = \delta_0)$, and $p_1 = \Pr(\delta = \delta_1)$. In the period after the announcement, $t = 1$, apply Bayes' rule by setting $B = (\Delta f_1)$, $A_1 = \delta_1$, $A_2 = \delta_0$ to get the updated probabilities

$$p_{0,1} = \Pr(\delta = \delta_0|\Delta f_1) = \frac{p_0\Pr(\Delta f_1|\delta_0)}{p_0\Pr(\Delta f_1|\delta_0) + p_1\Pr(\Delta f_1|\delta_1)}. \tag{6.46}$$

As time evolves and observations on Δf_t are acquired, agents update their beliefs according to

$$p_{0,2} = \Pr(\delta_0|\Delta f_2, \Delta f_1)$$
$$= \frac{p_0\Pr(\Delta f_2, \Delta f_1|\delta_0)}{p_0\Pr(\Delta f_2, \Delta f_1|\delta_0) + p_1\Pr(\Delta f_2, \Delta f_1|\delta_1)},$$
$$p_{0,3} = \Pr(\delta_0|\Delta f_3, \Delta f_2, \Delta f_1)$$
$$= \frac{p_0\Pr(\Delta f_3, \Delta f_2, \Delta f_1|\delta_0)}{p_0\Pr(\Delta f_3, \Delta f_2, \Delta f_1|\delta_0) + p_1\Pr(\Delta f_3, \Delta f_2, \Delta f_1|\delta_1)},$$
$$\vdots$$
$$p_{0,T} = \Pr(\delta_0|\Delta f_T, \ldots, \Delta f_1)$$
$$= \frac{p_0\Pr(\Delta f_T, \ldots, \Delta f_1|\delta_0)}{p_0\Pr(\Delta f_T, \ldots, \Delta f_1|\delta_0) + p_1\Pr(\Delta f_T, \ldots, \Delta f_1|\delta_1)}.$$

The updated probabilities $p_{0t} = \Pr(\delta_0 | \Delta f_t, \ldots, \Delta f_1)$ are called the *posterior probabilities*. An equivalent way to obtain the posterior probabilities is

$$p_{0,1} = \frac{p_0 \Pr(\Delta f_1 | \delta_0)}{p_0 \Pr(\Delta f_1 | \delta_0) + p_1 \Pr(\Delta f_1 | \delta_1)},$$

$$p_{0,2} = \frac{p_{0,1} \Pr(\Delta f_2 | \delta_0)}{p_{0,1} \Pr(\Delta f_2 | \delta_0) + p_{1,1} \Pr(\Delta f_2 | \delta_1)},$$

$$\vdots$$

$$p_{0,t} = \frac{p_{0,t-1} \Pr(\Delta f_t | \delta_0)}{p_{0,t-1} \Pr(\Delta f_t | \delta_0) + p_{1,t-1} \Pr(\Delta f_t | \delta_1)}.$$

How long is the learning period? To start things off, you need to specify an initial *prior* probability, $p_0 = \Pr(\delta = \delta_0)$.[11] Let $\delta_0 = 0, \delta_1 = 1$, and let v have a discrete probability distribution with the probabilities

$$\Pr(v = -5) = 3/66, \quad \Pr(v = -4) = 3/66, \quad \Pr(v = -3) = 3/66,$$
$$\Pr(v = -2) = 1/11, \quad \Pr(v = -1) = 2/11, \quad \Pr(v = 0) = 2/11,$$
$$\Pr(v = 1) = 2/11, \quad \Pr(v = 2) = 1/11, \quad \Pr(v = 3) = 3/66,$$
$$\Pr(v = 4) = 3/66, \quad \Pr(v = 5) = 3/66$$

We generate the distribution of posterior probabilities, learning times, and forecast error autocorrelations by simulating the economy 2,000 times. Figure 6.3 shows the *median* of the posterior probability distribution when the initial prior is 0.95. The distribution of learning times and autocorrelations is not sensitive to the initial prior. The learning time distribution is quite skewed, with the 5, 50, and 95 percentiles of the distribution of learning times being 1, 14, and 66 periods respectively. Judging from the median of the distribution, Bayesian updaters quickly learn about the true economy. Since the forecast errors are serially correlated only during the learning period, we calculate the autocorrelation of the forecast errors only during the learning period. The median autocorrelations at lags one through four of the forecast errors computed from the first 14 periods are -0.130, -0.114, -0.098, and -0.078.

This simple example serves as an introduction to rational learning in peso problems. However, the rapid rate at which learning takes place suggests that a single regime switch is insufficient to explain systematic forecast errors observed over long periods of time, as might be the case in foreign exchange rates. If the peso problem is to provide a satisfactory explanation of the data, a model with richer dynamics, and with recurrent regime shifts, as outlined in Evans [45], is needed.

---

[11] Lewis's approach is to assume that learning is complete by some date $T > t_0$ in the future, at which time $p_{0,T} = 0$. Having pinned down the endpoint, she can work backwards to find the implied value of p_0 that is consistent with learning having been completed by T.

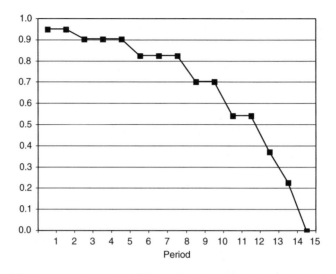

Figure 6.3   Median posterior probabilities of $\delta = \delta_0$ when truth is $\delta = \delta_1$ with an initial prior of 0.95.

6.6 NOISE TRADERS

We now consider the possibility that some market participants are not fully rational. Mark and Wu [100] present a model in which a mixture of rational and irrational agents produce spot and forward exchange dynamics that are consistent with the findings from survey data. The model adapts the overlapping-generations noise-trader model of De Long et al. [37] to study the pricing of foreign currencies in an environment where heterogeneous beliefs across agents generate trading volume and excess currency returns.

The irrational "noise" traders are motivated by Black's [13] suggestion that the real world is so complex that some (noise) traders are unable to distinguish between pseudo-signals and news. These individuals think that the pseudo-signals contain information about asset returns. Their beliefs regarding prospective investment returns seem distorted by waves of excessive optimism and pessimism. The resulting trading dynamics produce transitory deviations of the exchange rate from its fundamental value. Short-horizon rational investors bear the risk that they may be required to liquidate their positions at a time when noise traders have pushed asset prices even farther away from the fundamental value than they were when the investments were initiated.

● THE MODEL

We consider a two-country constant-population partial equilibrium model. It is an *overlapping-generations* model, where people live for two periods. When people are born, they have no assets, but they do have a full stomach and they do not consume in the first period of life. People make portfolio decisions to maximize the expected utility of second-period wealth, which is used to finance consumption when old.

The home-country currency unit is called the "dollar" and the foreign country currency unit is called the "euro." In each country, there is a one-period nominally safe asset in terms of the local currency. Both assets are available in perfectly elastic supply so that, in period t, people can borrow or lend any amount they desire at the gross dollar rate of interest, $R_t = (1 + i_t)$, or at the gross euro rate of interest, $R_t^* = (1 + i_t^*)$. The nominal interest rate differential – and hence, by covered interest parity, the forward premium – is exogenous.

In order for financial wealth to have value, it must be denominated in the currency of the country in which the individual resides. Thus, in the second period, the domestic agent must convert wealth to dollars and the foreign agent must convert wealth to euros. We also assume that the price level in each country is fixed at unity. Individuals therefore evaluate wealth in national currency units. The portfolio problem is to decide whether to borrow the local currency and to lend uncovered in the foreign currency or vice versa, in an attempt to exploit deviations from uncovered interest parity, as described in section 1.1.

The domestic young decide whether to borrow dollars and lend euros or vice versa. Let λ_t be the dollar value of the portfolio position taken. If the home agent borrows dollars and lends euros, the individual has taken a long euro position, which we represent with positive values of λ_t. To take a long euro position, the young trader borrows λ_t dollars at the gross interest rate R_t and invests λ_t/S_t euros at the gross rate R_t^*. When old, the euro payoff $R_t^*(\lambda_t/S_t)$ is converted into $(S_{t+1}/S_t)R_t^*\lambda_t$ dollars. If the agent borrows euros and lends dollars, the individual has taken a long dollar position, which we represent with negative λ_t. A long position in dollars is achieved by borrowing $-\lambda_t/S_t$ euros and investing the proceeds in the dollar asset at R_t. In the second period, the domestic agent sells $-(S_{t+1}/S_t)R_t^*\lambda_t$ dollars in order to repay the euro debt $-R_t^*(\lambda_t/S_t)$. In either case, the net payoff is the number of dollars at stake multiplied by the deviation from uncovered interest parity, $[(S_{t+1}/S_t)R_t^* - R_t]\lambda_t$. We use the approximations $(S_{t+1}/S_t) \simeq (1 + \Delta s_{t+1})$ and $(R_t/R_t^*) = (F_t/S_t) \simeq 1 + x_t$ to express the net payoff as[12]

$$[\Delta s_{t+1} - x_t]R_t^*\lambda_t. \tag{6.47}$$

The foreign agent's portfolio position is denoted by λ_{*t}, with positive values indicating long euro positions. To take a long euro position, the foreign young borrows λ_{*t} dollars and invests (λ_{*t}/S_t) euros at the gross interest rate R_t^*. Next period's net euro payoff is $(R_t^*/S_t - R_t/S_{t+1})\lambda_{*t}$. A long dollar position is achieved by borrowing $-(\lambda_{*t}/S_t)$ euros and investing $-\lambda_{*t}$ dollars. The net euro payoff in the second period is $-(R_t/S_{t+1} - R_t^*/S_t)\lambda_{*t}$. Using the approximation

---

[12] These approximations are necessary in order to avoid dealing with Jensen inequality terms when evaluating the foreign wealth position which render the model intractable. Jensen's inequality is $E(1/X) > 1/(EX)$. So we have $[(S_{t+1}/S_t)R_t^* - R_t]\lambda_t = [(1 + \Delta s_{t+1})R_t^* - (1 + x_t)R_t^*]\lambda_t$, which is (6.47).

$(F_t S_t)/(S_t S_{t+1}) \simeq 1 + x_t - \Delta s_{t+1}$, the net euro payoff is[13]

$$[\Delta s_{t+1} - x_t] R_t^* \frac{\lambda_{*t}}{S_t}. \tag{6.48}$$

The foreign exchange market clears when net dollar sales of the current young equal the net dollar purchases of the current old:

$$\lambda_t + \lambda_{*t} = \frac{S_t}{S_{t-1}} R_{t-1}^* \lambda_{t-1} + R_{t-1} \lambda_{*t-1}. \tag{6.49}$$

⬤ FUNDAMENTAL AND NOISE TRADERS

A fraction μ of the domestic and foreign traders are fundamentalists who have rational expectations. The remaining fraction $1 - \mu$ are noise traders, whose beliefs concerning future returns from their portfolio investments are distorted. Let the speculative positions of home fundamentalist and home noise traders be given by λ_t^f and λ_t^n respectively. Similarly, let the foreign fundamentalist and foreign noise-trader positions be λ_{*t}^f and λ_{*t}^n. The total portfolio position of domestic residents is $\lambda_t = \mu \lambda_t^f + (1 - \mu) \lambda_t^n$ and that of foreign residents is $\lambda_{*t} = \mu \lambda_{*t}^f + (1 - \mu) \lambda_{*t}^n$.

We denote subjective date-t conditional expectations generically as $\mathcal{E}_t(\cdot)$. When it is necessary to make a distinction, we will denote the expectations of fundamentalists by $E_t(\cdot)$. Similarly, the conditional variance is generically denoted by $\mathcal{V}_t(\cdot)$, with the conditional variance of fundamentalists denoted by $V_t(\cdot)$.

Utility displays constant absolute risk aversion with coefficient γ. The young construct a portfolio to maximize the expected utility of next-period wealth:

$$\mathcal{E}_t \left(-e^{-\gamma W_{t+1}} \right). \tag{6.50}$$

Both fundamental and noise traders believe that, conditional on time-t information, W_{t+1} is normally distributed. As shown in section 1.1.1, maximizing (6.50) with a (perceived) normally distributed W_{t+1} is equivalent to maximizing

$$\mathcal{E}_t(W_{t+1}) - \frac{\gamma}{2} \mathcal{V}_t(W_{t+1}). \tag{6.51}$$

The relevant uncertainty in the model shows up in the forward premium, which in turn inherits its uncertainty from the interest rates R_t and R_t^*, through the covered interest parity condition. The randomness of one of the interest rates is redundant. Therefore, the algebra can be simplified without loss of generality by letting the uncertainty be driven by R_t alone and we can fix $R^* = 1$.

---

[13] To obtain (6.48), $-(R_t/S_{t+1} - R_t^*/S_t)\lambda_{*t} = -\lambda_{*t}[(R_t^* F_t)/(S_t S_{t+1}) - (R_t^*/S_t)] = -\lambda_{*t}(R_t^*/S_t) \times [(S_t F_t)/(S_t S_{t+1}) - 1] = -\lambda_{*t} R_t^*/S_t[1 + x_t - \Delta s_{t+1}].$

● A FUNDAMENTALS ($\mu = 1$) ECONOMY

Suppose that everyone is rational ($\mu = 1$), so that $\mathcal{E}_t(\cdot) = E_t(\cdot)$ and $\mathcal{V}_t(\cdot) = V_t(\cdot)$. The second-period wealth of the fundamentalist domestic agent is the portfolio payoff plus c dollars of exogenous "labor" income, which is paid in the second period.[14] The forward premium, $(F_t/S_t) = (R_t/R^*) = R_t \simeq 1 + x_t$, inherits its stochastic properties from R_t, which evolves according to the AR(1) process:

$$x_t = \rho x_{t-1} + v_t, \tag{6.52}$$

with $0 < \rho < 1$ and $v_t \overset{iid}{\sim} (0, \sigma_v^2)$. Second-period wealth can now be written as

$$W_{t+1}^f = [\Delta s_{t+1} - x_t]\lambda_t^f + c. \tag{6.53}$$

People evaluate the conditional mean and variance of the next-period wealth as

$$E_t(W_{t+1}^f) = [E_t(\Delta s_{t+1}) - x_t]\lambda_t^f + c, \tag{6.54}$$

$$V_t(W_{t+1}^f) = \sigma_s^2(\lambda_t^f)^2, \tag{6.55}$$

where $\sigma_s^2 = V_t(\Delta s_{t+1})$. The domestic fundamental trader's problem is to choose λ_t^f to maximize

$$[E_t(\Delta s_{t+1}) - x_t]\lambda_t^f + c - \frac{\gamma}{2}\left(\lambda_t^f\right)^2 \sigma_s^2, \tag{6.56}$$

which is attained by setting

$$\lambda_t^f = \frac{[E_t(\Delta s_{t+1}) - x_t]}{\gamma \sigma_s^2}. \tag{6.57}$$

Equation (6.57) displays the familiar property of constant absolute risk-aversion utility, in which portfolio positions are proportional to the expected asset payoff. The factor of proportionality is inversely related to the individual's absolute risk-aversion coefficient. Recall that individuals undertake zero-net-investment strategies. The portfolio position in our setup does not depend on wealth, because traders are endowed with zero initial wealth.

The foreign fundamental trader faces an analogous problem. The second-period euro-wealth of fundamentalist foreign agents is the payoff from portfolio investments plus an exogenous euro payment of "labor" income c_*, $W_{*t+1}^f = [\Delta s_{t+1} - x_t](\lambda_{*t}^f/S_t) + c_*$. The solution is to choose $\lambda_{*t}^f = S_t\lambda_t^f$. Because individuals at home and abroad have identical tastes but evaluate wealth in national currency units, they will pursue identical investment strategies by taking positions of the same size as measured in monetary units of the country of residence.

---

[14]   The exogenous income is introduced to lessen the likelihood of negative second-period wealth realizations but, as in De Long et al., we cannot rule out such a possibility.

These portfolios combined with the market clearing condition (6.49) imply the difference equation[15]

$$E_t \Delta s_{t+1} - x_t = \Gamma_t (E_{t-1} \Delta s_t - x_{t-1}), \tag{6.58}$$

where $\Gamma_t \equiv [(S_t/S_{t-1}) + S_{t-1}R_{t-1}]/(1 + S_t)$. The level of the exchange rate is indeterminate, but it is easily seen that a solution for the rate of depreciation is

$$\Delta s_t = \frac{1}{\rho}x_t = x_{t-1} + \frac{1}{\rho}v_t. \tag{6.59}$$

The independence of v_t and x_{t-1} implies that $E_t(\Delta s_{t+1}) = x_t$, and the fundamentals solution therefore does not generate a forward premium bias, because uncovered interest parity holds in the fundamentals equilibrium even when agents are risk averse. The reason is that, under homogeneous expectations and common knowledge, you demand the same risk premium as I do, and we want to do the same transaction. Since we cannot find a counterparty to take the opposite side of the transaction, no trades take place. The only way that no trades will occur in equilibrium is for uncovered interest parity to hold.

⬤ A NOISE-TRADER ($\mu < 1$) ECONOMY

Now let's introduce noise traders, whose beliefs about expected returns are distorted by the stochastic process $\{n_t\}$. Noise traders can compute $E_t(x_{t+1})$, but they believe that asset returns are influenced by other factors ($\{n_t\}$). The distortion in noise-trader beliefs occurs only in evaluating first moments of returns. Their evaluation of second moments coincides with that of fundamentalists. The current young domestic noise trader evaluates the conditional mean and variance of next-period wealth as

$$\mathcal{E}_t \left(W_{t+1}^n \right) = [E_t(\Delta s_{t+1}) - x_t] \lambda_t^n + n_t \lambda_t^n + c, \tag{6.60}$$

$$\mathcal{V}_t \left(W_{t+1}^n \right) = \left(\lambda_t^n \right)^2 \sigma_s^2. \tag{6.61}$$

Recall that a positive value of λ_t represents a long position in euros. Equation (6.60) implies that noise traders appear to over-react to news. They exhibit excess dollar pessimism when $n_t > 0$, for they believe that the dollar will be weaker in the future than is justified by the fundamentals.

We specify the noise distortion to conform with the evidence from survey expectations, in which respondents appear to place excessive weight on the forward premium when predicting future changes in the exchange rate:

$$n_t = kx_t + u_t, \tag{6.62}$$

[15] The left-hand side of the market clearing condition (6.49) is $\lambda_t + \lambda_{*t} = (1 + S_t)\lambda_t = (1 + S_t)/(\gamma \sigma_s)[E_t \Delta s_{t+1} - x_t]$. The right-hand side is $(S_t/S_{t-1})R^* \lambda_{t-1} + R_{t-1}S_{t-1}\lambda_{t-1} = [(S_t/S_{t-1}) + (1 + x_{t-1})S_{t-1}]\lambda_{t-1}$. Finally, using $\lambda_{t-1} = [E_{t-1}\Delta s_t - x_{t-1}]/(\gamma \sigma_s^2)$, we obtain (6.58).

where $k > 0, u_t \overset{iid}{\sim} N\left(0, \sigma_u^2\right)$. The domestic noise trader's problem is to maximize $\lambda_t^n \left(E_t \Delta s_{t+1} - x_t + n_t\right) - \gamma \left(\lambda_t^n\right)^2 \sigma_s^2/2$. The solution is to choose

$$\lambda_t^n = \lambda_t^f + \frac{n_t}{\gamma \sigma_s^2}. \tag{6.63}$$

The noise trader's position deviates from that of the fundamentalist by a term that depends on the distortion in his or her beliefs, n_t.

The foreign noise trader holds similar beliefs, solves an analogous problem, and chooses

$$\lambda_{*t}^n = S_t \lambda_t^n. \tag{6.64}$$

Substituting these optimal portfolio positions into the market clearing condition (6.49) yields the stochastic difference equation

$$[E_t \Delta s_{t+1} - x_t] + (1 - \mu)n_t = \Gamma_t([E_{t-1}\Delta s_t - x_{t-1}] + (1 - \mu)n_{t-1}). \tag{6.65}$$

Using the method of undetermined coefficients, you can verify that

$$\Delta s_t = \frac{1}{\rho}x_t - \frac{(1 - \mu)}{\rho}n_t - (1 - \mu)u_{t-1} \tag{6.66}$$

is a solution.

PROPERTIES OF THE SOLUTION

First, fundamentalists and noise traders both believe, *ex ante*, that they will earn positive profits from their portfolio investments. It is the differences in their beliefs that lead them to take opposite sides of the transaction. When noise traders are excessively pessimistic and take short positions in the dollar, fundamentalists take the offsetting long position. In equilibrium, the expected payoff of fundamentalists and noise traders are, respectively,

$$E_t \Delta s_{t+1} - x_t = -(1 - \mu)n_t, \tag{6.67}$$

$$\mathcal{E}_t \Delta s_{t+1} - x_t = \mu n_t. \tag{6.68}$$

On average, the forward premium is the subjective predictor of the future depreciation: $\mu E_t \Delta s_{t+1} + (1 - \mu)\mathcal{E}_t \Delta s_{t+1} = x_t$. As the measure of noise traders approaches zero ($\mu \to 1$), the fundamentals solution with no trading is restored. Foreign exchange risk, excess currency movements, and trading volume are induced entirely by noise traders. Neither type of trader is guaranteed to earn profits or losses, however. The *ex post* profit depends on the sign of

$$\Delta s_{t+1} - x_t = -(1-\mu)n_t + \frac{1}{\rho}[1 - k(1-\mu)]v_{t+1} - \frac{1-\mu}{\rho}u_{t+1}, \qquad (6.69)$$

which can be positive or negative.

Matching Fama's regressions. To generate a negative forward premium bias, substitute (6.62) and (6.52) into (6.66), to give

$$\Delta s_{t+1} = [1 - k(1-\mu)]x_t + \xi_{t+1}, \qquad (6.70)$$

where $\xi_{t+1} \equiv (1/\rho)[1 - k(1-\mu)]v_{t+1} - (1-\mu)/\rho u_{t+1} - (1-\mu)u_t$ is an error term which is orthogonal to x_t. If $[1 - k(1-\mu)] < 0$, the implied slope coefficient in a regression of the future depreciation on the forward premium is negative.

Next, we compute the implied second moments of the deviation from uncovered interest parity and the expected depreciation:

$$\mathrm{Cov}([x_t - \mathrm{E}_t(\Delta s_{t+1})], \mathrm{E}_t(\Delta s_{t+1})) = k(1-\mu)(1 - k(1-\mu))\sigma_x^2 - (1-\mu)^2\sigma_u^2, \qquad (6.71)$$

$$\mathrm{Var}(x_t - \mathrm{E}_t(\Delta s_{t+1})) = (1-\mu)^2 \left[k^2\sigma_x^2 + \sigma_u^2\right], \qquad (6.72)$$

$$\mathrm{Var}(\mathrm{E}_t(\Delta s_{t+1})) = \mathrm{Var}(x_t - \mathrm{E}_t(\Delta s_{t+1})) + [1 - 2k(1-\mu)]\sigma_x^2. \qquad (6.73)$$

We see that $1 - k(1-\mu) < 0$ also implies that Fama's p_t covaries negatively with, and is more volatile than, the rationally expected depreciation. The noise-trader model is capable of matching the stylized facts of the data as summarized by Fama's regressions.

Matching the survey expectations. The survey research on expectations presents results on the behavior of the mean forecast from a survey of individuals. Let $\hat{\mu}$ be the fraction of the survey respondents comprised of fundamentalists and let $1 - \hat{\mu}$ be the fraction of the survey respondents made up of noise traders.

Suppose that the survey samples the proportion of fundamentalists and noise traders in the population without error ($\hat{\mu} = \mu$). Then the mean survey forecast of depreciation is $\Delta\hat{s}_{t+1}^e = \mu\mathrm{E}_t(\Delta s_{t+1}) + (1-\mu)\mathcal{E}_t(\Delta s_{t+1}) = \mu[1 - k(1-\mu)]x_t + \mu(\mu-1)u_t + (1-\mu)(1+\mu k)x_t + (1-\mu)\mu u_t = x_t$, which predicts that $\beta_2 = 1$. There is no risk premium if $\hat{\mu} = \mu$. In addition to $\beta_2 = 1$, we have $\beta = 1 - k(1-\mu) = 1 - \beta_1$ and $\beta_1 = k(1-\mu)$, which amounts to one equation in two unknowns, k and μ, so the coefficient of over-reaction k cannot be identified here.

We can "back out" the implied value of over-reaction k if we are willing to make an assumption about the survey measurement error. If $\hat{\mu} \neq \mu$, then $\Delta\hat{s}_{t+1}^e = \hat{\mu}\mathrm{E}_t(\Delta s_{t+1}) + (1 - \hat{\mu})\mathcal{E}_t(\Delta s_{t+1}) = [1 + k(\mu - \hat{\mu})]x_t + (\mu - \hat{\mu})u_t$, which implies $\beta_2 = 1 + k(\mu - \hat{\mu})$, $\beta_1 = k(1 - \hat{\mu})$, and $\beta = 1 - k(1 - \mu)$. For given values of $\hat{\mu}$, β_1, and β, we have $k = \beta_1/(1 - \hat{\mu})$ and $\mu = (\beta - 1 + k)/k$. For example, if we assume that $\hat{\mu} = 0.5$, the 3-month horizon BIC–US results in table 6.4 imply that $k = 11.94$ and $\mu = 0.579$.

Chapter Summary

1. The financial market is said to be efficient if no unexploited excess profit opportunities are available. What is excessive depends on a model of market equilibrium. Violations of uncovered interest parity in and of themselves do not mean that the foreign exchange market is inefficient.

2. The Lucas model – perhaps the most celebrated asset pricing model of the past 20 years – provides a qualitative and elegant explanation for why uncovered interest parity doesn't hold. The reason is that risk-averse agents must be compensated with a risk premium in order for them to hold forward contracts in a risky currency. The forward rate becomes a biased predictor of the future spot rate, because this risk premium is impounded into the price of a forward contract. But the Lucas model requires what many people regard as an implausible coefficient of relative risk aversion to generate sufficiently large and variable risk premia to be consistent with the volatility of exchange rate returns data.

3. Analyses of survey data from professional foreign exchange market participants, predictions of future exchange rates find that the survey forecast error is systematic. If you believe the survey data, these systematic prediction errors may be the reason why uncovered interest parity doesn't hold.

4. Market participants' systematic forecast errors can be consistent with rationality. A class of models called "peso-problem" models show how rational agents make systematic prediction errors when there is a positive probability that the underlying structure may undergo a regime shift.

5. On the other hand, it may be the case that some market participants are indeed irrational in the sense that they believe that pseudo-signals are important determinants of asset returns. The presence of such noise traders generates equilibrium asset prices that deviate from their fundamental values.

Problems

1. *Siegel's Paradox* [121]. Let S_t be the spot dollar price of the euro and let F_t be the one-period forward rate in dollars per euro. The claim is that if investors are risk-neutral and the forward foreign exchange market is efficient, the forward rate is the rational expectation of the future spot rate. From the US perspective, we write this as

$$E_t(S_{t+1}) = F_t.$$

From a European perspective, the risk-neutral, rational-expectations, efficient market statement is

$$(1/F_t) = E_t(1/S_{t+1}),$$

since the euro price of the dollar is the reciprocal of the dollar–euro rate. Both statements cannot possibly be true. Why not? (Hint: Use Jensen's inequality.)

2. Let the Euler equation for a domestic investor that speculates in forward foreign exchange be

$$F_t = \frac{E_t[u'(c_{t+1})(S_{t+1}/P_{t+1})]}{E_t[u'(c_t)/P_{t+1}]},$$

where $u'(c)$ is marginal utility of real consumption c and P is the domestic price level. From the foreign perspective, the Euler equation is

$$\frac{1}{F_t} = \frac{E_t[u'(c^*_{t+1}/(S_{t+1}P^*_{t+1}))]}{E_t[u'(c^*_t)/P^*_{t+1}]},$$

where c^* is foreign consumption and P^* is the foreign price level. Suppose further that both domestic and foreign agents are risk neutral. Show that Siegel's paradox does not pose a problem now that payoffs are stated in real terms.[16]

3. We saw that the slope coefficient in a regression of $s_t - s_{t-1}$ on $f_t - s_{t-1}$ is negative. McCallum [101] shows that regressing $s_t - s_{t-2}$ on $f_t - s_{t-2}$ yields a slope coefficient near 1. How can you explain McCallum's result?

4. (Kaminsky and Peruga [80]). Suppose that the data generating process for observations on consumption growth, inflation, and exchange rates is given by the log-normal distribution, and that the utility function is $u(c) = c^{1-\gamma}$. Let lower case letters denote variables in logarithms. We have $\Delta c_{t+1} = \ln(C_{t+1}/C_t)$ be the rate of consumption growth, $\Delta s_{t+1} = \ln(S_{t+1}/S_t)$ be the depreciation rate, $\Delta p_{t+1} = \ln(P_{t+1}/P_t)$ be the inflation rate, and $f_t = \ln(F_t)$ be the log one-period forward rate.

If $\ln(Y) \sim N(\mu, \sigma^2)$, then Y is said to be log-normally distributed and

$$E\left[e^{\ln(y)}\right] = E(Y) = e^{[\mu + \sigma^2/2]}. \tag{6.74}$$

Let J_t consist of lagged values of $c_t, s_t,$ and p_t, and let f_t be the date-t information set available to the econometrician. Conditional on J_t, let

---

[16] Engel's [41] empirical work showed that regression test results on forward exchange rate unbiasedness done with nominal exchange rates were robust to specifications in real terms, so evidently Siegel's paradox is not economically important.

$y_{t+1} = (\Delta s_{t+1}, \Delta c_{t+1}, \Delta p_{t+1})'$ be normally distributed with conditional mean $E(y_{t+1}|J_t) = (\mu_{st}, \mu_{ct}, \mu_{pt})'$ and conditional covariance matrix

$$\Sigma_t = \begin{bmatrix} \sigma_{sst} & \sigma_{sct} & \sigma_{spt} \\ \sigma_{cst} & \sigma_{cct} & \sigma_{cpt} \\ \sigma_{pst} & \sigma_{pct} & \sigma_{ppt} \end{bmatrix}. \tag{6.75}$$

Show that

$$\mu_{st} - f_t = \gamma \sigma_{cst} + \sigma_{spt} - \frac{\sigma_{sst}}{2}. \tag{6.76}$$

5. *Testing the volatility restrictions* (Cecchetti et al. [24]). This exercise develops the volatility bounds analysis so that we can do classical statistical hypothesis tests to compare the implied volatility of the intertemporal marginal rate of substitution and the lower volatility bound. Begin by defining ϕ as a vector of parameters that characterize the utility function, and ψ as a vector of parameters associated with the stochastic process governing consumption growth.

Stack the parameters that must be estimated from the data into the vector θ:

$$\theta = \begin{pmatrix} \underline{\mu}_r \\ \text{vec}(\Sigma_r) \\ \psi \end{pmatrix},$$

where $\text{vec}(\Sigma_r)$ is the vector obtained by stacking all of the unique elements of the symmetric matrix, Σ_r. Let θ_0 be the true value of θ, and let $\hat{\theta}$ be a consistent estimator of θ_0 such that

$$\sqrt{T}(\hat{\theta} - \theta_0) \xrightarrow{D} N(0, \Sigma_\theta).$$

Assume that consistent estimators of both θ_0 and Σ_θ are available.

Now make explicit the fact that the moments of the intertemporal marginal rate of substitution and the volatility bound depend on sample information. The estimated mean and standard deviation predicted by the model are $\hat{\mu}_\mu = \mu_\mu(\phi; \hat{\psi})$ and $\hat{\sigma}_\mu = \sigma_\mu(\phi; \hat{\psi})$, while the estimated volatility bound is

$$\hat{\sigma}_r = \sigma_r(\phi; \hat{\theta}) = \sqrt{\left(\hat{\underline{\mu}}_q - \mu_\mu(\phi; \hat{\psi})\hat{\underline{\mu}}_r \right)' \hat{\Sigma}_r^{-1} \left(\hat{\underline{\mu}}_q - \mu_\mu(\phi; \hat{\psi})\hat{\underline{\mu}}_r \right)}.$$

Let

$$\Delta(\phi; \hat{\theta}) = \sigma_{\mathcal{M}}(\phi; \hat{\psi}) - \sigma_r(\phi; \hat{\theta}),$$

be the difference between the estimated volatility bound and the estimated volatility of the intertemporal marginal rate of substitution. Using the "delta method" (a first-order Taylor expansion about the true parameter vector), show that

$$\sqrt{T}(\Delta(\phi; \hat{\theta}) - \Delta(\phi; \theta_0)) \xrightarrow{D} N\left(0, \sigma_\Delta^2\right),$$

where

$$\sigma_\Delta^2 = \left(\frac{\partial \Delta}{\partial \theta'}\right)_{\theta_0} (\hat{\theta} - \theta_0)(\hat{\theta} - \theta_0)' \left(\frac{\partial \Delta}{\partial \theta}\right)_{\theta_0}.$$

How can this result be used to conduct a statistical test of whether a particular model attains the volatility restrictions?

6. *Peso problem.* Let the fundamentals, $f_t = m_t - m_t^* - \lambda \left(y_t - y_t^*\right)$ follow the random walk with drift, $f_{t+1} = \delta_0 + f_t + v_{t+1}$, where $v_t \sim iid$ with $E(v_t) = 0$ and $E\left(v_t^2\right) = \sigma_v^2$. Agents know the fundamentals process with certainty. Forward iteration on (6.33) yields the present-value formula:

$$s_t = \gamma \sum_{j=1}^{\infty} E_t(f_{t+j}).$$

Verify the solution (6.38) by direct substitution of $E_t(f_{t+j})$.

Now let agents believe that the drift may have increased to $\delta = \delta_1$. Show that $E_t(f_{t+j}) = f_t + j(\delta_0 - \delta_1)p_{0t} + j\delta_1$. Use direct substitution of this forecasting formula in the present-value formula to verify the solution (6.43) in the text.

The Real Exchange Rate

In this chapter, we examine the behavior of the nominal exchange rate in relation to domestic and foreign goods prices in the short run and in the long run. A basic theoretical framework that underlies the empirical examination of these prices is the PPP doctrine, encountered in chapter 3. The flexible-price models of chapters 3–5 assume that the the "law of one price" holds internationally and, by implication, that purchasing-power parity holds. In empirical work, we define the (log) real exchange rate between two countries as the relative price between a domestic and foreign commodity basket:

$$q = s + p^* - p. \tag{7.1}$$

Under purchasing-power parity, the log real exchange rate is constant (specifically, $q = 0$).

The prediction that q_t is constant is clearly false – a fact we discovered after examining figure 3.1 in section 3.1. This result is not new. So, given the obvious short-run violations of PPP, the interesting things to study are whether these international pricing relationships hold in the long run and, if so, to see how much time it takes to get to the long run.

Why would we want to know this? Because real exchange rate fluctuations can have important allocative effects. A prolonged real appreciation may have an adverse effect on a country's competitiveness, as the appreciation raises the relative price of home goods and induces expenditures to switch from home goods toward foreign goods. Domestic output might then be expected to fall in response. Although the domestic tradable-goods sector is hurt, consumers evidently benefit. On the other hand, a real depreciation may be beneficial to the tradable-goods sector and harmful to consumers. The foreign debt of many developing countries is denominated in US dollars, however, so a real depreciation reflects a real increase in debt servicing costs. These expenditure-switching effects are absent in the flexible-price theories that we have covered thus far.

So what leads you to conclude that PPP does not hold in the long run? Would this make any sense? What theory predicts that PPP does not hold?

The Balassa [6] – Samuelson [117] model, which is developed in this chapter, provides one such theory. The Balassa–Samuelson model predicts that the long-run real exchange rate depends on relative productivity trends between the home and foreign countries. If relative productivity is governed by a stochastic trend, the real exchange rate will similarly be driven and will not exhibit any mean-reverting behavior.

The research on real exchange rate behavior raises many questions but, as we will see, offers few concrete answers.

7.1 SOME PRELIMINARY ISSUES

The first issue that you confront in real exchange rate research is that data on price levels are generally not available. Instead, you typically have access to a price index P_t^I, which is the ratio of the price level P_t in the measurement year to the price level in a base year P_0. Letting stars denote foreign-country variables and lower case letters denote variables in logarithms, the empirical log real exchange rate uses price indices, and amounts to

$$q_t = (p_0 - p_0^*) + s_t + p_t^* - p_t. \tag{7.2}$$

$s_t + p_t^* - p_t$ is the relative price of the foreign commodity basket in terms of the domestic basket. This term is zero if PPP holds instantaneously, and is mean-reverting about zero if PPP is violated in the short run but holds in the long run. Tests of whether PPP holds in the long run typically ask whether q_t is stationary about a fixed mean, because even if PPP holds, measured q_t will be $(p_0 - p_0^*)$, which need not be zero due to the base-year normalization of the price indices.

In the older literature, the distinction was made between absolute PPP ($s_t + p_t^* - p_t = 0$) and relative PPP ($\Delta s_t + \Delta p_t^* - \Delta p_t = 0$). By taking first differences of the observations, the arbitrary base-year price levels drop out under relative PPP. In this chapter, when we talk about PPP, we mean absolute PPP.

A second issue that you confront in this line of research is that there are as many empirical real exchange rates as there are price indices. As discussed in section 3.1, you might use the CPI if your main interest is to investigate the Casselian view of PPP, because the CPI includes prices of a broad range of both tradable and nontradable final goods. The PPI has a higher tradable-goods component than the CPI and is viewed by some as a crude measure of tradable-goods prices. If a story about aggregate production forms the basis of your investigation, the gross domestic product deflator may make better sense.

7.2 DEVIATIONS FROM THE "LAW OF ONE PRICE"

The root cause of deviations from PPP must be violations of the "law of one price." Such violations are easy to find. Just check out the price of unleaded regular gasoline at two gas stations, located at different corners of the same intersection. More puzzling, however, is that international violations of the "law of one price" are several orders of magnitude larger than intranational violations. There is a large empirical literature that studies international violations of the "law of one price." We will consider two of the many contributions that have attracted the attention of international macroeconomists.

ISARD'S STUDY OF THE "LAW OF ONE PRICE"

Isard [77] collected unit export and unit import transactions prices for the US, Germany, and Japan from 1970 to 1975 at four- and five-digit standard international trade classification (SITC) levels for machined items. Isard defines the relative export price to be the ratio of the US dollar price of German exports of these items to the dollar price of US exports of the same items. Between 1970 and 1975, the dollar fell by 55.2 percent, while at the same time the relative export price of internal combustion engines, office calculating machinery, and forklift trucks increased by 48.1 percent, 47.7 percent, and 39.1 percent, respectively, in spite of the fact that German and US prices are both measured in dollars. Evidently, nominal exchange rate changes over this five-year period had a big effect on the real exchange rate.

In a separate regression analysis, he obtains seven-digit export commodities, which he matches to seven-digit import unit values, in which the imports are distinguished by country of origin. The dependent variable is the US import unit value from Canada, Japan, and Germany, respectively, divided by the unit values of US exports to the rest of the world, both measured in dollars. If the "law of one price" held, this ratio would be 1. Instead, when the ratio is regressed on the DM price of the dollar, the slope coefficient is positive, but is significantly different from 1 for Germany and Japan. The slope coefficients and implied standard errors for Germany and Japan are reproduced in table 7.1.[1] The estimates for Germany indicate that import and export prices exhibit insufficient dependence on the exchange rate to be consistent with the "law of one price," whereas the estimates for Japan suggest that there is too much dependence.

While Isard's study provides evidence of striking violations of the "law of one price," it is important to bear in mind that these results were drawn from a very short time-series sample taken from the 1970s. This was a time period of substantial international macroeconomic uncertainty, and one in which people may have been relatively unfamiliar with the workings of the flexible exchange rate system.

---

[1]   A potential econometric problem in Isard's analysis is that he runs the regression $R_t = a_0 + a_1 S_t + a_2 D_t + e_t + \rho e_{t-1}$, where R_t is the ratio of import to export prices, S_t is the DM price of the dollar, and D_t is a dummy variable that splits up the sample. The problem is that the regression is run by Cochrane–Orcutt to control for serial correlation in the error term, e_t, which is inconsistent if the regressors are not strictly (econometrically) exogenous.

Table 7.1 Slope coefficients in Isard's regression of the US import to export price ratio on the nominal exchange rate

Imports from Germany			Imports from Japan		
Soap	Tires	Wallpaper	Soap	Tires	Wallpaper
0.094	0.04	0.03	15.49	6.28	6.79
(0.04)	(0.02)	(0.01)	(13.8)	(1.04)	(1.28)

ENGEL AND ROGERS ON THE BORDER

Engel and Rogers [44] ask what determines the volatility of the percentage change in the price of 14 categories of consumer prices sampled in various US and Canadian cities from September 1978 through December 1994.[2] Let p_{ijt} be the price of good i in city j at time t, measured in US dollars. Let σ_{ijk} be the volatility of the percentage change in the relative price of good i in cities j and k. That is, σ_{ijk} is the time-series sample standard deviation of $\Delta \ln (p_{ijt}/p_{ikt})$. In addition, define D_{jk} as the logarithm of the distance between cities j and k. The idea of the distance variable is to capture potential effects of transportation costs that may cause violations of the "law of one price" between two locations. Let B_{jk} be a dummy variable that is 1 if cities j and k are separated by the US–Canadian border and 0 otherwise, and let X_i' be a vector of control variables, such as a separate dummy variable for each good i and/or for each city in the sample. Engel and Rogers run restricted cross-section regressions

$$\sigma_{ijk} = \alpha D_{jk} + \beta B_{jk} + X_i' \underline{\gamma}_i + u_{ijk},$$

and obtain $\hat{\beta} = 10.6 \times 10^{-4}$ (s.e. $= 3.25 \times 10^{-4}$), $\hat{\alpha} = 11.9 \times 10^{-3}$ (s.e. $= 0.42 \times 10^{-3}$), and $\bar{R}^2 = 0.77$. The regression estimates imply that the border adds 11.9×10^{-3} to the average volatility (standard deviation) of prices between two pairs of cities. Based on the estimate of α, this is equivalent to an additional 75,000 miles of distance between two cities in the *same* country. In addition, the border was found to account for 32.4 percent of the variation in the σ_{ijk}, while log distance was found to explain 20.3 percent.

The striking differences between within-country violations of the "law of one price" and across-country violations raise, but do not answer, the question "Why is the border is so important?" This is still an open question but possible explanations include the following:

1. Barriers to international trade, such as tariffs and quotas, and non tariff barriers such as bureaucratic red tape imposed on foreign businesses. The Engel–Rogers

[2] The cities are Baltimore, Boston, Chicago, Dallas, Detroit, Houston, Los Angeles, Miami, New York, Philadelphia, Pittsburgh, San Francisco, St. Louis, Washington D.C., Calgary, Edmonton, Montreal, Ottawa, Quebec, Regina, Toronto, Vancouver, and Winnipeg.

sample spans both pre- and post-trade liberalization periods between the US and Canada. In sub-sample analysis, they reject the trade barrier hypothesis.

2. Labor markets are more integrated and homogeneous within countries than they are across countries. This might explain why there would be less volatility in per-unit costs of production across cities within the same country and more per-unit cost volatility across countries.

3. Nominal price stickiness. Goods prices seem to respond to macroeconomic shocks and news with a lag, and behave more sluggishly than asset prices and nominal exchange rates. Engel and Rogers find that this hypothesis does not explain all of the relative price volatility.[3]

4. Pricing-to-market. This is a term used to describe how firms with monopoly power engage in price discrimination between segmented domestic and foreign markets characterized by different elasticities of demand.

 ## WHAT ABOUT THE LONG RUN?

Since the international "law of one price" and purchasing-power parity have firmly been shown to break down in the short run, the next step might be to ask whether purchasing-power parity holds in the long run. Recent work on this issue proceeds by testing for a unit root in the log real exchange rate. The null hypothesis in popular unit-root tests is that the series being examined contains a unit root. But before we jump in, we should ask whether these tests are interesting from an economic perspective. In order for unit-root tests on the real exchange rate to be interesting, the null hypothesis (that the real exchange rate has a unit root) should have a firm theoretical foundation. Otherwise, if we do not reject the unit root, we learn only that the test has insufficient power to reject a null hypothesis that we know to be false, and if we do reject the unit root, we have only confirmed what we believed to be true in the first place.

The next section covers the Balassa–Samuelson model, which provides a theoretical justification for PPP to be violated even in the long run.

7.3 LONG-RUN DETERMINANTS OF THE REAL EXCHANGE RATE

We study a two-sector small open economy. The sectors are a tradable-goods sector and a nontradable-goods sector. The terms of trade (the relative price of exports in terms of imports) are given by world conditions and are assumed to be fixed. Before formally developing the model, it will be useful to consider the following sectoral decomposition of the real exchange rate.

---

[3] The experiment that they run here is as follows. Instead of measuring the relative inter-city price as $p_{ijt}/(S_t p^*_{ikt})$, where S is the nominal exchange rate, p is the US dollar price, and p^* is the Canadian dollar price, replace it with $(p_{ijt}/P_t)/(P^*_t/p^*_{ikt})$, where P and P^* are the overall price levels in the US and Canada respectively. If the border effect is entirely due to sticky prices, the border should be insignificant when the alternative price measure is used. But in fact, the border remains significant, so sticky nominal prices can provide only a partial explanation.

⬤ SECTORAL REAL EXCHANGE RATE DECOMPOSITION

Let P_T be the price of the tradable good, let P_N be the price of the nontradable good, and let the general price level be given by the Cobb–Douglas form

$$P = (P_T)^\theta (P_N)^{1-\theta}, \tag{7.3}$$

$$P^* = (P_T^*)^\theta (P_N^*)^{1-\theta}, \tag{7.4}$$

where the shares of the tradable and nontradable goods are identical at home and abroad ($\theta^* = \theta$). The log real exchange rate can be decomposed as

$$q = (s + p_T^* - p_T) + (1 - \theta)(p_N^* - p_T^*) - (1 - \theta)(p_N - p_T), \tag{7.5}$$

where lower case letters denote variables in logarithms. We adopt the commodity arbitrage view of PPP (section 3.1) and assume that the "law of one price" holds for tradable goods. It follows that the first term on the right-hand side of (7.5), which is the deviation from PPP for the tradable good, is zero. The dynamics of the real exchange rate is then completely driven by the relative price of the tradable good in terms of the nontradable good.

⬤ THE BALASSA–SAMUELSON MODEL

Now, we need a theory to understand the behavior of the relative price of tradables in terms of nontradables. It turns out that if (i) factor markets and final goods markets are competitive, (ii) production takes place under constant returns to scale, (iii) capital is perfectly mobile internationally, and (iv) labor is internationally immobile but mobile between the tradable and nontradable sectors, then the relative price of nontradable goods in terms of tradable goods is determined entirely by the production technology. Demand (preferences) does not matter at all.

The theory is viewed as holding in the long run: therefore we omit the time subscripts. To fix ideas, let there be only one tradable good and one nontradable good. Capital and labor are supplied elastically. Let $L_T(L_N)$ and $K_T(K_N)$ be the labor and capital employed in the production of the tradable Y_T (nontradable Y_N) good. A_T (A_N) is the technology level in the tradable (nontradable) sector. The two goods are produced according to Cobb–Douglas production functions

$$Y_T = A_T L_T^{(1-\alpha_T)} K_T^{(\alpha_T)}, \tag{7.6}$$

$$Y_N = A_N L_N^{(1-\alpha_N)} K_N^{(\alpha_N)}. \tag{7.7}$$

The balance of trade is assumed to be zero, which must be true in the long run. Let the tradable good be the numeraire. The small open economy takes the price of tradable goods as given. We'll set $P_T = 1$. R is the rental rate on capital, W is the wage rate, and P_N is the price of nontradable goods, all stated in terms of the tradable good.

Competitive firms take factor and output prices as given and choose K and L to maximize profits. The intersectoral mobility of labor and capital equalizes factor prices paid in the tradable and nontradable sectors. The tradable-good firm chooses K_T and L_T to maximize profits:

$$A_T L_T^{(1-\alpha_T)} K_T^{\alpha_T} - (WL_T + RK_T). \tag{7.8}$$

The nontradable-good firm's problem is to choose K_N and L_N to maximize

$$P_N A_N L_N^{(1-\alpha_N)} K_N^{\alpha_N} - (WL_N + RK_N). \tag{7.9}$$

Let $k \equiv (K/L)$ denote the capital–labor ratio. It follows from the first-order conditions that

$$R = A_T \alpha_T (k_T)^{\alpha_T - 1}, \tag{7.10}$$
$$R = P_N A_N \alpha_N (k_N)^{\alpha_N - 1}, \tag{7.11}$$
$$W = A_T (1 - \alpha_T)(k_T)^{\alpha_T}, \tag{7.12}$$
$$W = P_N A_N (1 - \alpha_N)(k_N)^{\alpha_N}. \tag{7.13}$$

The international mobility of capital combined with the small-country assumption implies that R is exogenously given by the world rental rate on capital. Equations (7.10)–(7.13) form four equations in the four unknowns (P_N, W, k_T, k_N).

To solve the model, first obtain the tradable-goods sector capital–labor ratio from (7.10):

$$k_T = \left[\frac{\alpha_T A_T}{R} \right]^{1/(1-\alpha_T)}. \tag{7.14}$$

Next, substitute (7.14) into (7.12) to get the wage rate:

$$W = (1 - \alpha_T)(A_T)^{1/(1-\alpha_T)} \left[\frac{\alpha_T}{R} \right]^{\alpha_T/(1-\alpha_T)}. \tag{7.15}$$

Substituting (7.15) into (7.13), you have

$$k_N = \left(\frac{(1 - \alpha_T)}{(1 - \alpha_N)} \frac{A_T^{1/(1-\alpha_T)} (\alpha_T/R)^{\alpha_T/(1-\alpha_T)}}{P_N A_N} \right)^{1/\alpha_N}. \tag{7.16}$$

Finally, plug (7.16) into (7.11), to give the solution for the relative price of the nontradable good in terms of the tradable good:

$$P_N = \frac{A_T^{(1-\alpha_N)/(1-\alpha_T)}}{A_N} C R^{(\alpha_N - \alpha_T)/(1-\alpha_T)}, \tag{7.17}$$

where C is a positive constant. Now let $a = \ln(A)$, $r = \ln(R)$, and $c = \ln(C)$, and take logs of (7.17) to get the solution for the log relative price of nontradable goods in terms of tradable goods:

$$p_N = \left(\frac{1 - \alpha_N}{1 - \alpha_T}\right) a_T - a_N + \left(\frac{(\alpha_N - \alpha_T)}{(1 - \alpha_T)}\right) r + c. \qquad (7.18)$$

Over time, the evolution of the log relative price of nontradables depends only on the technology and the exogenous rental rate on capital. We see that there are at least two reasons why the relative price of nontradables in terms of tradables should increase with a country's income.

First, suppose that the economy experiences unbiased technological growth, where a_N and a_T increase at the same rate. p_N will rise over time if tradable-goods production is relatively capital intensive ($\alpha_N < \alpha_T$). A standard argument is that tradables are manufactured goods whose production is relatively capital intensive, whereas nontradable goods are mainly services, which are relatively labor intensive. Second, p_N will increase over time if technological growth is biased toward the capital-intensive sector. In this case, a_T actually grows at a faster rate than a_N. If either of these scenarios are correct, it follows that fast growing economies will experience a rising relative price of nontradables and, by (7.5), a real appreciation over time.

The implications for the behavior of the real exchange rate are as follows. If the productivity factors grow deterministically, the deviation of the real exchange rate from a deterministic trend should be a stationary process. But if the productivity factors contain a stochastic trend (section 2.6), the log real exchange rate will inherit the random walk behavior and will be unit-root nonstationary. In either case, PPP will not hold in the long run.

When we take the Balassa–Samuelson model to the data, it is tempting to think of services as being nontradable. It is also tempting to think that services are relatively labor intensive. While this may be true of some services, such as haircuts, it is not true that all services are nontradable or that they are labor intensive. Financial services are sold at home and abroad by international banks, which makes them tradable, and transportation and housing services are evidently capital intensive.

7.4 LONG-RUN ANALYSES OF REAL EXCHANGE RATES

Empirical research into the long-run behavior of real exchange rates has employed econometric analyses of nonstationary time-series and is aimed at testing the hypothesis that the real exchange rate has a unit root. This research can potentially provide evidence to distinguish between the Casselian and the Balassa–Samuelson views of the world.

UNIVARIATE TESTS OF PPP OVER THE FLOAT

To test whether PPP holds in the long run, you can use the augmented Dickey–Fuller test (section 2.4.3) to test the hypothesis that the real exchange rate contains a unit root. Using quarterly observations of the CPI-defined real exchange rate from 1973.1 to 1997.4 for 19 high-income countries, table 7.2 shows the results of univariate unit-root tests for US and German real exchange rates. Four lags of Δq_t and a constant were included in the test equation. The p-values are the proportion of the Dickey–Fuller distribution that lies to the left (below) τ_c. Including a trend in the test regressions yields qualitatively similar results and these are not reported.

Statistical versus economic significance. Classical hypothesis testing is designed to establish statistical significance. Given a sufficiently long time-series, it may be possible to establish statistical significance of the Studentized coefficients to reject the unit root, but if the true value of the dominant root is 0.98, the half-life of a shock is still over 34 years, and this stationary process may not be significantly different from a true unit-root process in the economic sense.

If that is indeed the case, then in light of the statistical difficulties surrounding unit-root tests, it can be argued that we should not even care whether the real exchange rate has a unit root, but that we should instead focus on measuring the economic implications of the real exchange rate's behavior. What market participants care about is the degree of persistence in the real exchange rate and one measure of persistence is the half-life.

The annualized half-lives reported in table 7.2 are based on estimates adjusted for bias by Kendall's formula (2.81).[4] The average half-life is 3.7 years when the US is the numeraire country. That is, on average, it takes 3.7 years – quite a long time since the business cycle frequency ranges from 1.25 to 8 years – for half of a shock to the log real exchange rate to disappear. The average half-life is 2.6 years when Germany is the numeraire county.

Univariate tests using data from the post Bretton Woods float typically cannot reject the hypothesis that the real exchange rate is driven by a unit-root process. Using the US as the home country, only two of the tests can reject the unit root at the 10 percent level of significance.

The results are somewhat sensitive to the choice of the home (numeraire) country.[5] Part of the persistence exhibited in the real value of the dollar comes from the very large swings during the 1980s. The real appreciation in the early 1980s and the subsequent depreciation was largely a dollar phenomenon, not shared by cross-rates. To illustrate, the evidence for purchasing-power parity is a little stronger when Germany is used as the home country since, here, the unit root can be rejected at the 10 percent level of significance for German real exchange rates with several European countries.

---

[4] Christiano and Eichenbaum [26] put forth this argument in the context of the unit root in GNP.
[5] A point made by Papell and Theodoridis [114].

Table 7.2 Augmented Dickey–Fuller tests for a unit root in post-1973 real exchange rates

	Relative to US			Relative to Germany		
Country	τ_c	*(p-value)*	*Half-life*	τ_c	*(p-value)*	*Half-life*
Australia	−1.895	(0.329)	4.582	−2.444	(0.124)	2.095
Austria	−2.434	(0.126)	3.208	**−3.809**	(0.004)	5.516
Belgium	−2.369	(0.138)	4.223	**−2.580**	(0.093)	2.914
Canada	−1.342	(0.621)	—	−2.423	(0.127)	2.914
Denmark	−2.319	(0.155)	3.733	**−3.212**	(0.017)	1.759
Finland	−2.919	(0.039)	2.421	**−2.589**	(0.089)	3.208
France	−2.526	(0.105)	2.761	**−4.540**	(0.001)	0.695
Germany	−2.470	(0.118)	3.025	—	—	—
Greece	−2.276	(0.169)	4.336	−2.360	(0.140)	1.278
Italy	−2.511	(0.107)	2.580	−1.855	(0.351)	5.709
Japan	−2.057	(0.252)	9.251	−1.930	(0.314)	11.919
Korea	−1.235	(0.677)	3.274	−2.125	(0.215)	1.165
Netherlands	**−2.576**	(0.094)	2.623	**−2.676**	(0.075)	2.969
Norway	−2.184	(0.193)	2.668	**−2.573**	(0.095)	2.539
Spain	−2.358	(0.140)	5.006	−2.488	(0.113)	2.861
Sweden	−2.042	(0.257)	5.516	−2.534	(0.103)	1.719
Switzerland	**−2.670**	(0.076)	2.215	**−3.389**	(0.011)	1.759
UK	−2.484	(0.113)	2.313	−2.272	(0.169)	3.274

Half-lives are adjusted for bias and are measured in years. The significance at the 10 percent level is indicated in bold face.

● UNIVARIATE TESTS FOR PPP OVER LONG TIME SPANS

One reason why the evidence against a unit root in q_t is weak may be that the power of the test is low with only 100 quarterly observations.[6] One way to get more observations is to go back in time and examine real exchange rates over long historical timespans. This was the strategy of Lothian and Taylor [92], who constructed annual real exchange rates between the US and the UK from 1791 to 1990, and between the UK and France from 1803 to 1990, using wholesale price indices.

Figure 7.1 displays the log nominal and log real exchange rate (multipled by 100) for the US–UK rate using CPIs. Using the "eyeball metric," the real exchange rate appears to be mean-reverting over this long historical period. Table 7.3 presents ADF unit-root tests on annual data for the US and UK. The real exchange rates defined over producer prices extend from 1791 to 1990 and are Lothian and Taylor's data.[7] The real exchange rates defined over consumer prices extend from 1871 to 1997. Half-lives are adjusted for bias with Kendall's formula (2.81). Using long-timespan data, the augmented Dickey–Fuller test can

---

[6] The power of a test is the probability that the test correctly rejects the null hypothesis when it is false.

[7] David Papell kindly provided me with Lothian and Taylor's data.

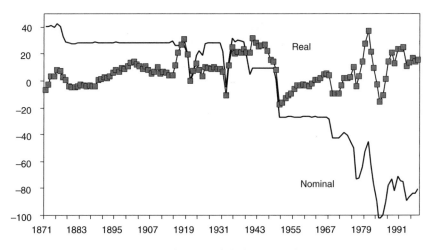

Figure 7.1 The real and nominal dollar–pound rate, 1871–1997.

Table 7.3 ADF test and annual half-life estimates using over a century of real dollar–pound real exchange rates

	Lags	τ_c	(p-value)	Half-life	τ_{ct}	(p-value)	Half-life
PPIs	4	**−3.074**	(0.028)	6.911	**−4.906**	(0.001)	2.154
	8	−2.122	(0.238)	10.842	**−4.104**	(0.007)	2.126
	12	−1.559	(0.510)	16.720	−2.754	(0.229)	2.785
CPIs	4	**−3.148**	(0.031)	3.659	**−3.201**	(0.096)	3.520
	8	**−3.087**	(0.037)	3.033	−3.101	(0.124)	2.982
	12	**−2.722**	(0.073)	2.917	−2.720	(0.243)	2.885

Bold face indicates significance at the 10 percent level.

reject the hypothesis that the real dollar–pound rate has a unit root. However, the test is sensitive to the number of lagged Δq_t values included in the test regression. The Studentized coefficients are significant when a trend is included in the test equation which rejects the hypothesis that the deviation from trend has a unit root. This result is consistent with the Balassa–Samuelson model in which sectoral productivity differentials evolved deterministically.

⬤ VARIANCE RATIOS OF REAL EXCHANGE RATES

We can use the variance-ratio statistic (see section 2.4) to examine the relative contribution to the overall variance of the real depreciation from a permanent component and a temporary component. Table 7.4 shows variance ratios calculated on the Lothian–Taylor data along with asymptotic standard errors.[8]

---

[8] Huizinga [75] calculated variance-ratio statistics for the real exchange rate from 1974 to 1986, while Grilli and Kaminisky [65] did so for the real dollar–pound rate from 1884 to 1986, as well as over various subperiods.

Table 7.4 Variance ratios and asymptotic standard errors of real dollar–sterling exchange rates. Lothian–Taylor data using PPIs

k	VR_k	s.e.
1	1.00	—
2	1.07	0.152
3	0.951	0.156
4	0.906	0.166
5	0.841	0.169
10	0.457	0.124
15	0.323	0.106
20	0.232	0.0872

The point estimates display a "hump" shape. They initially rise above 1 at short horizons, and then fall below 1 at the longer horizons. This is a pattern often found with financial data. The variance ratio falls below 1 because of a preponderance of negative autocorrelations at the longer horizons. This means that a current jump in the real exchange rate tends to be offset by future changes in the opposite direction. Such movements are characteristic of mean-reverting processes.

Even at the 20-year horizon, however, the point estimates indicate that 23 percent of the variance of the dollar–pound real exchange rate can be attributed to a permanent (random walk) component. The asymptotic standard errors tend to overstate the precision of the variance ratios in small samples. That being said, even at the 20-year horizon, VR_{20} for the dollar–pound rate is (using the asymptotic standard error) significantly greater than zero which implies the presence of a permanent component in the real exchange rate. This conclusion contradicts the results in table 7.3 that rejected the unit-root hypothesis.

Summary of univariate unit-root tests.   We get conflicting evidence about PPP from univariate unit-root tests. From post Bretton Woods data, there is not much evidence that PPP holds in the long run when the US serves as the numeraire country. The evidence for PPP with Germany as the numeraire currency is stronger. Using long-timespan data, the tests can reject the unit root, but the results are dependent on the number of lags included in the test equation. On the other hand, the pattern of the variance-ratio statistic is consistent with there being a unit root in the real exchange rate.

The time period covered by the historical data span across the fixed exchange rate regimes of the gold standard and the Bretton Woods adjustable peg system, as well as over flexible exchange rate periods of the inter-war years and after 1973. Thus, even if the results on the long-span data uniformly rejected the unit root, we still do not have direct evidence that PPP holds during a pure floating regime.

PANEL TESTS FOR A UNIT ROOT IN THE REAL EXCHANGE RATE

Let's return specifically to the question of whether long-run PPP holds over the float. Suppose we think that univariate tests have low power because the available time-series are so short. We will revisit the question by combining observations across the 19 countries that we examined in the univariate tests into a panel data set. We thus have $N = 18$ real exchange rate observations over $T = 100$ quarterly periods.

The results from the popular Levin–Lin test (section 2.5) are presented in table 7.5.[9] Nonparametric bootstrap p-values are in parentheses and parametric bootstrap p-values are in square brackets. τ_{ct} indicates that a linear trend is included in the test equations. τ_c indicates that only a constant is included in the test equations. τ_c^* and τ_{ct}^* are the adjusted Studentized coefficients (see section 2.5).When we account for the common time effect, the unit root is rejected at the 10 percent level both when a time trend is and is not included in the test equations when the dollar is the numeraire currency. Using the deutschemark as the numeraire currency, the unit root cannot be rejected when a trend is included. The asymptotic evidence against the unit root is very weak.

Next, we test the unit root when the common time effect is omitted. Here, the evidence against the unit root is strong when the deutschemark is the numeraire currency, but not for the dollar. The bias-adjusted approximate half-life to convergence ranges from 1.7 to 5.3 years, which many people still consider to be a surprisingly long time.

Table 7.6 shows panel tests of PPP using the Im–Pesaran–Shin test and the Maddala–Wu test. Here, I did not remove the common time effect. These tests are consistent with the Levin–Lin test results. When the dollar is the numeraire, we cannot reject the hypothesis that the deviation from trend is a unit root. When the deutschemark is the numeraire currency, the unit root is rejected whether or not a trend is included. The evidence against a unit root is generally stronger when the deutschemark is used as the numeraire currency.

CANZONERI, CUMBY, AND DIBA'S TEST OF BALASSA–SAMUELSON

Canzoneri, Cumby, and Diba [20] employ IPS to test implications of the Balassa–Samuelson model. They examine sectoral OECD data for the US, Canada, Japan, France, Italy, UK, Belgium, Denmark, Sweden, Finland, Austria, and Spain. They define output by the "manufacturing" and "agricultural, hunting forestry and fishing" sectors to be tradable goods. Nontradable goods are produced by the "wholesale and retail trade," "restaurants and hotels," "transport,

---

[9] Frankel and Rose [57], MacDonald [94], Wu [127], and Papell conduct Levin–Lin tests on the real exchange rate.

Table 7.5   The Levin–Lin test of PPP

Numeraire	Time effect	τ_c	Half-life	τ_{ct}	Half-life	τ_c^*	τ_{ct}^*
US	Yes	**−8.593**	2.953	**−9.927**	1.796	−1.878	**−0.920**
		(0.021)		(0.070)		(0.164)	(0.093)
		[0.009]		[0.074]		[0.117]	[0.095]
	No	−6.954	5.328	−7.415	3.943	—	—
		(0.115)		(0.651)			
		[0.168]		[0.658]			
Germany	Yes	**−8.017**	3.764	**−9.701**	1.816	−1.642	−0.628
		(0.018)		(0.106)		(0.154)	(0.421)
		[0.022]		[0.127]		[0.158]	[0.442]
	No	**−10.252**	3.449	**−11.185**	1.859	—	—
		(0.000)		(0.007)			
		[0.001]		[0.006]			

Bold face indicates significance at the 10 percent level. Half-lives are based on bias-adjusted $\hat{\rho}$ by Nickell's formula (2.82) and are stated in years. Nonparametric bootstrap *p*-values are in parentheses. Parametric bootstrap *p*-values are in square brackets.

Table 7.6   Im–Pesaran–Shin and Maddala–Wu tests of PPP

Numeraire	$\bar{\tau}_c$	(p-value)	[p-value]	$\bar{\tau}_{ct}$	(p-value)	[p-value]
Im–Pesaran–Shin						
US	**−2.259**	(0.047)	[0.052]	−2.385	(0.302)	[0.307]
Germany	**−2.641**	(0.000)	[0.000]	**−3.119**	(0.000)	[0.001]
Maddala-Wu						
US	**66.902**	(0.083)	[0.088]	40.162	(0.351)	[0.346]
Germany	**101.243**	(0.000)	[0.000]	**102.017**	(0.000)	[0.000]

Nonparametric bootstrap *p*-values are in parentheses. Parametric bootstrap *p*-values are in square brackets. Bold face indicates significance at the 10 percent level.

storage and communications," "finance, insurance, real estate and business," "community social and personal services," and "nonmarket services" sectors.

Their analysis begins with the first-order conditions for profit-maximizing firms. Equating (7.12) to (7.13), the relative price of nontradables in terms of tradables can be expressed as

$$\frac{P_N}{P_T} = \frac{1 - \alpha_T}{1 - \alpha_N} \frac{A_T}{A_N} \frac{k_T^{\alpha_T}}{k_N^{\alpha_N}}, \tag{7.19}$$

where $k = K/L$ is the capital–labor ratio. By virtue of the Cobb–Douglas form of the production function, $Ak^{\alpha} = Y/L$ is the average product of labor. Let

Table 7.7 Canzoneri et al.'s IPS tests of Balassa–Samuelson

Variable	All countries	G-7	European countries
$(p_N - p_T) - (x_T - x_N)$	**-3.762**	-2.422	—
$s_t - (p_T - p_T^*)$ (dollar)	-2.382	**-5.319**	—
$s_t - (p_T - p_T^*)$ (DM)	-1.775	—	-1.565

Bold face indicates asymptotic significance at the 10 percent level.

$x_T \equiv \ln(Y_T/L_T)$ and let $x_N \equiv \ln(Y_N/L_N)$ denote the log average product of labor. We rewrite (7.19) in logarithmic form as

$$p_N - p_T = \ln\left(\frac{1-\alpha_T}{1-\alpha_N}\right) + x_T - x_N. \tag{7.20}$$

Table 7.7 shows the standardized $\bar{t}$ calculated by Canzoneri, Cumby, and Diba. All calculations control for common time effects. Their results support the Balassa–Samuelson model. They find evidence that there is a unit root in $p_N - p_T$ and in $x_T - x_N$, and that they are cointegrated, and there is reasonably strong evidence that PPP holds for tradable goods.

SIZE DISTORTION IN UNIT-ROOT TESTS

Empirical researchers are typically worried that unit-root tests may have low statistical power in applications due to the relatively small number of time-series observations that are available. Low power means that the null hypothesis that the real exchange rate has a unit root will be difficult to reject even if it is false. Low power is a fact of life because, for any finite sample size, a stationary process can be arbitrarily well approximated by a unit-root process, and vice versa.[10] The conflicting evidence from post-1973 data and the long-timespan data are consistent with the hypothesis that the real exchange rate is stationary, but the tests suffer from low statistical power.

The flip side to the power problem is that the tests suffer size distortion in small samples. Engel [43] suggests that the observational equivalence problem lies behind the inability to reject the unit root during the post Bretton Woods float and the rejections of the unit root in the Lothian–Taylor data, and argues that these empirical results are plausibly generated by a permanent–transitory components process with a slow-moving permanent component. Engel's point is that the unit-root tests have more power as T grows and are more likely to

[10] Think of the permanent–transitory components decomposition. $T < \infty$ observations from a stationary AR(1) process will be observationally equivalent to T observations of a permanent–transitory components model with judicious choice of the size of the innovation variances to the permanent and the transitory parts. This is the argument laid forth in papers by Blough [15], Cochrane [29], and Faust [48].

reject with the historical data than over the float. But if the truth is that the real exchange rate contains a small unit-root process, the size of the test, which is approximately equal to the power of the test, is also higher when T is large. That is, the probability of committing a type I error also increases with sample size, and the unit-root tests suffer from size distortion with the sample sizes available.

▶ Chapter Summary

1. Purchasing-power parity is a simple theory that links domestic and foreign prices. It is not valid as a short-run proposition, but most international economists believe that some variant of PPP holds in the long run.
2. There are several explanations for why PPP does not hold. The Balassa–Samuelson view focuses on the role of nontradable goods. Another view, that we will exploit in the next chapter, is that the persistence exhibited in the real exchange rate is due to nominal rigidities in the macroeconomy, where firms are reluctant to change nominal prices immediately following shocks of reasonably small magnitude.

▶ Problem

Heterogeneous commodity baskets. Suppose that there are two goods, both of which are internationally tradable, and for whom the "law of one price" holds:

$$p_{1t} = s_t + p_{1t}^*, \quad p_{2t} = s_t + p_{2t}^*,$$

where p_i is the home currency price of good i, p_i^* is the foreign currency price, and s is the nominal exchange rate, all in logarithms. Assume further that the nominal exchange rate follows a unit-root process, $s_t = s_{t-1} + v_t$, where v_t is a stationary process, and that foreign prices are driven by a common stochastic trend, z_t^*:

$$p_{1t}^* = z_t^* + \epsilon_{1t}^*, \quad p_{2t}^* = z_t^* + \epsilon_{2t}^*,$$

where $z_t^* = z_{t-1}^* + u_t$, ϵ_{it}^* $(i = 1, 2)$ are stationary processes, and u_t is iid with $E(u_t) = 0$ and $E(u_t^2) = \sigma_u^2$. Show that even if the price levels are constructed as

$$p_t = \phi p_{1t} + (1 - \phi)p_{2t}, \quad p_t^* = \phi^* p_{1t}^* + (1 - \phi^*)p_{2t}^*,$$

with $\phi \neq \phi^*$, $p_t - (s_t + p_t^*)$ is a stationary process.

8

The Mundell–Fleming Model

This chapter covers models based on Mundell [105] and Fleming [52], who adapted the IS–LM framework to analyze the open economy. Although the framework is rather old and *ad hoc*, the basic framework continues to be used in policy-related research (Williamson [126], Hinkle and Montiel [72], MacDonald and Stein [95]). The hallmark of the Mundell–Fleming framework is that goods prices exhibit stickiness, whereas asset markets – including the foreign exchange market – are continuously in equilibrium. The actions of policy-makers play a major role in these models, because the presence of nominal rigidities opens the way for nominal shocks to have real effects. We begin with a simple static version of the model. Next, we present the dynamic but deterministic Mundell–Fleming model due to Dornbusch [38]. Third, we present a stochastic Mundell–Fleming model based on Obstfeld [106].

8.1 A STATIC MUNDELL–FLEMING MODEL

This is a Keynesian model where goods prices are fixed for the duration of the analysis. The home country is small in the sense that it takes foreign variables as fixed. All variables except the interest rate are in logarithms.

Equilibrium in the goods market is given by an open-economy version of the IS curve. There are three determinants of the demand for domestic goods. First, expenditures depend positively on own income y through the absorption channel. An increase in income leads to higher consumption, most of which is spent on domestically produced goods. Second, domestic goods demand depends negatively on the interest rate i through the investment-saving channel. Since goods prices are fixed, the nominal interest rate is identical to the real interest rate. Higher interest rates reduce investment spending and may encourage a reduction of consumption and an increase in saving. Third, demand for home goods depends positively on the real exchange rate $s + p^* - p$. An increase in the real exchange rate lowers the price of domestic goods relative to foreign goods, leading expenditures by residents of the home country as well as residents of the rest of the world to switch toward domestically produced goods. We call this the *expenditure-switching* effect of exchange rate fluctuations. In equilibrium, output equals expenditures, which is given by the IS curve

$$y = \delta(s + p^* - p) + \gamma y - \sigma i + g, \tag{8.1}$$

where g is an exogenous shifter, which we interpret as changes in fiscal policy. The parameters δ, γ, and σ are defined to be positive with $0 < \gamma < 1$.

As in the monetary model, log real money demand, $m^d - p$, depends positively on log income y and negatively on the nominal interest rate i, which measures the opportunity cost of holding money. Since the price level is fixed, the nominal interest rate is also the real interest rate, r. In logarithms, equilibrium in the money market is represented by the LM curve:

$$m - p = \phi y - \lambda i. \tag{8.2}$$

The country is small and takes the world price level and world interest rate as given. For simplicity, we fix $p^* = 0$. The domestic price level is also fixed, so we might as well set $p = 0$.

Capital is perfectly mobile across countries.[1] International capital market equilibrium is given by uncovered interest parity with *static expectations*:[2]

$$i = i^*. \tag{8.3}$$

Substitute (8.3) into (8.1) and (8.2). Totally differentiate the result and rearrange to obtain the two-equation system

$$dm = \frac{\phi\delta}{1-\gamma}\,ds - \left[\lambda + \frac{\phi\sigma}{1-\gamma}\right]di^* + \frac{\phi}{1-\gamma}\,dg, \tag{8.4}$$

$$dy = \frac{\delta}{1-\gamma}\,ds - \frac{\sigma}{1-\gamma}\,di^* + \frac{dg}{1-\gamma}. \tag{8.5}$$

All of our comparative statics results come from these two equations.

ADJUSTMENT UNDER FIXED EXCHANGE RATES

Domestic credit expansion. Assume that the monetary authorities are credibly committed to fixing the exchange rate. In this environment, the exchange

---

[1] Given the rapid pace at which international financial markets are becoming integrated, analyses under conditions of imperfect capital mobility are becoming less relevant. However, one can easily allow for imperfect capital mobility by modeling both the current account and the capital account and setting the balance of payments to zero (the external balance constraint) as an equilibrium condition. See the end-of-chapter problems.
[2] Agents expect no change in the exchange rate.

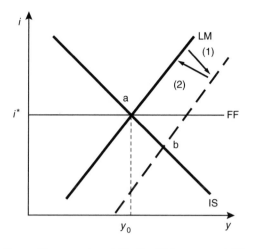

Figure 8.1 Domestic credit expansion shifts the LM curve out. The central bank loses reserves to accommodate the resulting capital outflow, which shifts the LM curve back in.

rate is a policy variable. As long as the fix is in effect, we set $ds = 0$. Income y and the money supply m are endogenous variables.

Suppose that the authorities expand the domestic credit component of the money supply. Recall from (1.22) that the monetary base is made up of the sum of domestic credit and international reserves. In the absence of any other shocks ($di^* = 0, dg = 0$), we see from (8.4) that there is no long-run change in the money supply $dm = 0$ and, from (8.5), there is no long-run change in output. The initial attempt to expand the money supply by increasing domestic credit results in an offsetting loss of international reserves. Upon the initial expansion of domestic credit, the money supply does increase. The interest rate must remain fixed at the world rate, however, and domestic residents are unwilling to hold additional money at i^*. They eliminate the excess money by accumulating foreign interest bearing assets and run a temporary balance-of-payments deficit. The domestic monetary authorities evidently have no control over the money supply in the long run, and monetary policy is said to be ineffective as a stabilization tool under a fixed exchange rate regime with perfect capital mobility.

The situation is depicted graphically in figure 8.1. First, the expansion of domestic credit shifts the LM curve out. To maintain interest parity there is an incipient capital outflow. The central bank defends the exchange rate by selling reserves. This loss of reserves causes the LM curve to shift back to its original position.

Domestic currency devaluation. From (8.4) and (8.5), you have $dy = [\delta/(1 - \gamma)]\,ds > 0$ and $dm = [\phi\delta/(1 - \gamma)]\,ds > 0$. The expansionary effects of a devaluation are shown in figure 8.2. The devaluation makes domestic goods more competitive and expenditures switch toward domestic goods. This has

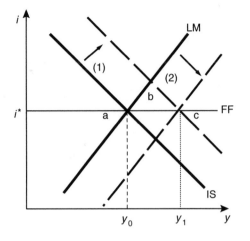

Figure 8.2 Devaluation shifts the IS curve out. The central bank accumulates reserves to accommodate the resulting capital inflow, which shifts the LM curve out.

a direct effect on aggregate expenditures. In a closed economy, the expansion would lead to an increase in the interest rate, but in the open economy under perfect capital mobility, the expansion generates a capital inflow. To maintain the new exchange rate, the central bank accommodates the capital flows by accumulating foreign exchange reserves, with the result that the LM curve shifts out.

One feature that the model misses is that, in real-world economies, the country's foreign debt is typically denominated in the foreign currency, so the devaluation increases the country's real foreign debt burden.

Fiscal policy shocks. The results of an increase in government spending are $dy = [1/(1-\gamma)]\,dg$ and $dm = [\phi/(1-\gamma)]\,dg$, which is expansionary. The increase in g shifts the IS curve to the right and has a direct effect on expenditures. Fiscal policy works in the same way as a devaluation, and is said to be an effective stabilization tool under fixed exchange rates and perfect capital mobility.

Foreign interest rate shocks. An increase in the foreign interest rate has a contractionary effect on domestic output and the money supply: $dy = -(\sigma/(1-\gamma))\,di^*$ and $dm = -(\lambda + \phi\sigma/(1-\gamma))\,di^*$. The increase i^* creates an incipient capital outflow. To defend the exchange rate, the monetary authorities sell foreign exchange reserves, which causes the money supply to contract. The situation is depicted graphically in figure 8.3.

Implied international transmissions. Although we are working with the small-country version of the model, we can qualitatively deduce how policy shocks would be transmitted internationally in a two-country model. If the increase in i^* was the result of monetary tightening in the large foreign country, output would also contract abroad. We say that monetary shocks are *positively*

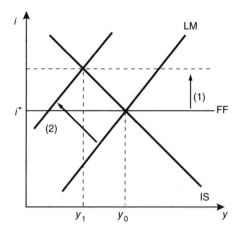

Figure 8.3 An increase in i^* generates a capital outflow, a loss of central bank reserves, and a contraction of the domestic money supply.

transmitted internationally, as they lead to positive output co-movements at home and abroad. If the increase in i^* was the result of expansionary foreign government spending, foreign output would expand, whereas domestic output would contract. Aggregate expenditure shocks are said to be *negatively transmitted* internationally under a fixed exchange rate regime.

A currency devaluation has negative transmission effects. The devaluation of the home currency is equivalent to a revaluation of the foreign currency. Since the domestic currency devaluation has an expansionary effect on the home country, it must have a contractionary effect on the foreign country. A devaluation that expands the home country at the expense of the foreign country is referred to as a *beggar-thy-neighbor policy.*

⬤ FLEXIBLE EXCHANGE RATES

When the authorities do not intervene in the foreign exchange market, s and y are endogenous in the system (8.4)–(8.5) and the authorities regain control over m, which is treated as exogenous.

Domestic credit expansion. An expansionary monetary policy generates an incipient capital outflow, which leads to a depreciation of the home currency: $ds = [(1 - \gamma)/\phi\delta]\,dm > 0$. The expenditure-switching effect of the depreciation increases expenditures on the home good and has an expansionary effect on output: $dy = (1/\phi)\,dm > 0$.

The situation is represented graphically in figure 8.4, where the expansion of domestic credit shifts the LM curve to the right. In the closed economy, the home interest rate would fall, but in the small open economy with perfect

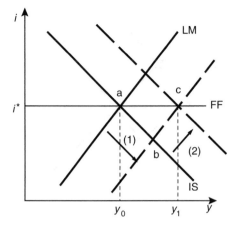

Figure 8.4 Expansion of domestic credit shifts the LM curve out. Incipient capital outflow is offset by depreciation of domestic currency, which shifts the IS curve out.

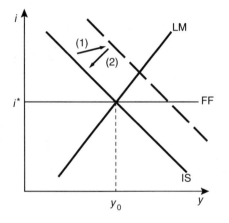

Figure 8.5 Expansionary fiscal policy shifts the IS curve out. Incipient capital inflow generates an appreciation that shifts the IS curve back to its original position.

capital mobility, the result is an incipient capital outflow, which causes the home currency to depreciate (s increases) and the IS curve to shift to the right. The effectiveness of monetary policy is restored under flexible exchange rates.

Fiscal policy. Fiscal policy becomes ineffective as a stabilization tool under flexible exchange rates and perfect capital mobility. The situation is depicted in figure 8.5. An expansion of government spending is represented by an initial outward shift in the IS curve, which leads to an incipient capital inflow and an appreciation of the home currency: $ds = -(1/\delta)\,dg < 0$. The resulting expenditure switch forces a subsequent inward shift of the IS curve. The contractionary effects of the induced appreciation offset the expansionary effect of the

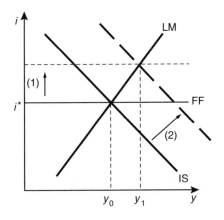

Figure 8.6　An increase in the world interest rate generates an incipient capital outflow, leading to a depreciation and an outward shift in the IS curve.

government spending, leaving output unchanged $dy = 0$. The model predicts an international version of crowding out. Recipients of government spending expand at the expense of the tradable goods sector.

Interest rate shocks.　An increase in the foreign interest rate leads to an incipient capital outflow and a depreciation given by $ds = [(\lambda(1-\gamma)+\sigma\phi)/\phi\delta] \, di^* > 0$. The expenditure-switching effect of the depreciation causes the IS curve in figure 8.6 to shift out. The expansionary effect of the depreciation more than offsets the contractionary effect of the higher interest rate, resulting in an expansion of output: $dy = (\lambda/\phi) \, di^* > 0$.

International transmission effects.　If the interest rate shock was caused by a contraction in foreign money, the expansion of domestic output would be associated with a contraction of foreign output, and monetary policy shocks would be negatively transmitted from one country to another under flexible exchange rates. Government spending, on the other hand, would be positively transmitted. If the increase in the foreign interest rate was precipitated by an expansion of foreign government spending, we would observe expansion in output both abroad and at home.

8.2　DORNBUSCH'S DYNAMIC MUNDELL–FLEMING MODEL

As we saw in chapter 3, the exchange rate in a free float behaves much like stock prices. In particular, it exhibits more volatility than macroeconomic fundamentals such as the money supply and real GDP. Dornbusch [38] presents a dynamic version of the Mundell–Fleming model that explains excess exchange rate volatility in a deterministic perfect foresight setting. The key feature of the model is that the asset market adjusts to shocks instantaneously, while goods market adjustment takes time.

The money market is continuously in equilibrium, which is represented by the LM curve, restated here as

$$m - p = \phi y - \lambda i. \tag{8.6}$$

To allow for possible disequilibrium in the goods market, let y denote actual output, which is assumed to be *fixed*, and let y^d denote the demand for home output. The demand for domestic goods depends on the real exchange rate $s + p^* - p$, real income y, and the interest rate i. The small open-economy version of the IS curve is[3]

$$y^d = \delta(s - p) + \gamma y - \sigma i + g, \tag{8.7}$$

where we have set $p^* = 0$.

Denote the time derivative of a function x of time with a "dot": $\dot{x}(t) = dx(t)/dt$. Price-level dynamics are governed by the rule

$$\dot{p} = \pi(y^d - y), \tag{8.8}$$

where the parameter $0 < \pi < \infty$ indexes the speed of goods market adjustment.[4] Equation (8.8) says that the rate of inflation is proportional to excess demand for goods. Because excess demand is always finite, the rate of change in goods prices is always finite, so there are *no jumps* in price level. If the price level cannot jump, then at any point in time it is instantaneously fixed. The adjustment of the price level toward its long-run value must occur over time, and it is in this sense that goods prices are sticky in the Dornbusch model.

International capital market equilibrium is given by the uncovered interest parity condition

$$i = i^* + \dot{s}^e, \tag{8.9}$$

where $\dot{s}^e$ is the expected instantaneous depreciation rate. Let $\bar{s}$ be the steady state nominal exchange rate. The model is completed by specifying the forward-looking expectations

$$\dot{s}^e = \theta(\bar{s} - s). \tag{8.10}$$

Market participants believe that the instantaneous depreciation is proportional to the gap between the current exchange rate and its long-run value but, to be model consistent, agents must have perfect foresight. This means that the factor of proportionality θ must be chosen to be consistent with values of the other parameters of the model. This perfect-foresight value of θ can be solved

---

[3] Making demand depend on the real interest rate results in the same qualitative conclusions, but messier algebra.

[4] Low values of π indicate slow adjustment. Letting $\pi \to \infty$ allows goods prices to adjust instantaneously, which allows the goods market to be in continuous equilibrium.

for directly (as in the appendix) or by the method of undetermined coefficients.[5] Since we can understand most of the interesting predictions of the model without explicitly solving for the equilibrium, we will do so and simply assume that we have available the model consistent value of θ such that

$$\dot{s}^e = \dot{s}. \tag{8.11}$$

STEADY STATE EQUILIBRIUM

Let an "overbar" denote the steady state value of a variable. The model is characterized by a fixed steady state with $\dot{s} = \dot{p} = 0$ and

$$\bar{i} = i^*, \tag{8.12}$$

$$\bar{p} = m - \phi y + \lambda \bar{i}, \tag{8.13}$$

$$\bar{s} = \bar{p} + \frac{1}{\delta}[(1 - \gamma)y + \sigma\bar{i} - g]. \tag{8.14}$$

Differentiating these long-run values with respect to m yields $d\bar{p}/dm = 1$ and $d\bar{s}/dm = 1$. The model exhibits the sensible characteristic that money is neutral in the long run. Differentiating the long-run values with respect to g yields $d\bar{s}/dg = -1/\delta = d(\bar{s} - \bar{p})/dg$. Nominal exchange rate adjustments in response to aggregate expenditure shocks are entirely real in the long run and PPP does not hold if there are permanent shocks to the composition of aggregate expenditures, even in the long run.

EXCHANGE RATE DYNAMICS

The hallmark of this model is the interesting exchange rate dynamics that follow an unanticipated monetary expansion.[6] Totally differentiating (8.6), but noting that p is instantaneously fixed and y is always fixed, the monetary expansion produces a liquidity effect:

$$di = -\frac{1}{\lambda}\, dm < 0. \tag{8.15}$$

Differentiate (8.9) while holding i^* constant and use $d\bar{s} = dm$ to get $di = \theta(dm - ds)$. Use this expression to eliminate di in (8.15). Solving for the

---

[5]   The perfect-foresight solution is

$$\theta = \tfrac{1}{2}[\pi(\delta + \sigma/\lambda) + \sqrt{\pi^2(\delta + \sigma/\lambda)^2 + 4\pi\delta/\lambda}].$$

[6]   This often used experiment brings up an uncomfortable question. If agents have perfect foresight, how can a shock be unanticipated?

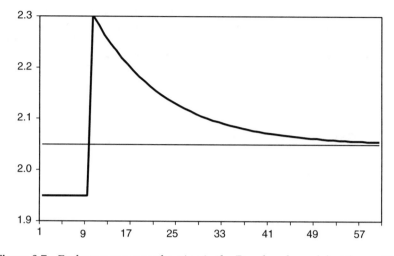

Figure 8.7   Exchange rate overshooting in the Dornbusch model with $\pi = 0.15$, $\delta = 0.15, \sigma = 0.02$, and $\lambda = 5$.

instantaneous depreciation yields

$$ds = \left(1 + \frac{1}{\lambda\theta}\right)dm > d\bar{s}. \tag{8.16}$$

This is the famous *overshooting result*. Upon impact, the instantaneous depreciation exceeds the long-run depreciation, so the exchange rate overshoots its long-run value. During the transition to the long run, $i < i^*$ so that, by (8.11), people expect the home currency to appreciate. Given that there is a long-run depreciation, the only way that people can rationally expect this to occur is for the exchange rate to initially overshoot the long-run level, so that it declines during the adjustment period. This result is significant, because the model predicts that the exchange rate is more volatile than the underlying economic fundamentals, even when agents have perfect foresight. The implied dynamics are illustrated in figure 8.7.

If there were instantaneous adjustment ($\pi = \infty$), we would immediately go to the long run and we would continuously be in equilibrium. So long as $\pi < \infty$, the goods market spends some time in disequilibrium and the economy-wide adjustment to the long-run equilibrium occurs gradually. The transition paths, which we did not solve for explicitly but which are treated in the appendix, describe the disequilibrium dynamics. It is in comparison to the flexible-price (long-run) equilibrium that the transitional values are viewed to be in disequilibrium.

There is no overshooting nor any associated excess volatility in response to fiscal policy shocks. You are invited to explore this further in the end-of-chapter problems.

8.3   A STOCHASTIC MUNDELL–FLEMING MODEL

Let's extend the Mundell–Fleming model to a stochastic environment, following Obstfeld [106]. Let y_t^d be aggregate demand, let s_t be the nominal exchange rate, let p_t be the domestic price level, let i_t be the domestic nominal interest rate, let m_t be the nominal money stock, and let $E_t(X_t)$ be the mathematical expectation of the random variable X_t, conditioned on date-t information. All variables except interest rates are in natural logarithms. Foreign variables are taken as given, so without loss of generality we set $p^* = 0$ and $i^* = 0$.

The IS curve in the stochastic Mundell–Fleming model is

$$y_t^d = \eta(s_t - p_t) - \sigma[i_t - E_t(p_{t+1} - p_t)] + d_t, \tag{8.17}$$

where d_t is an aggregate demand shock and $i_t - E_t(p_{t+1} - p_t)$ is the *ex ante* real interest rate. The LM curve is

$$m_t - p_t = y_t^d - \lambda i_t, \tag{8.18}$$

where the income elasticity of money demand is assumed to be 1. Capital market equilibrium is given by uncovered interest parity:

$$i_t - i^* = E_t(s_{t+1} - s_t). \tag{8.19}$$

The long-run or the steady state is not conveniently characterized in a stochastic environment, because the economy is constantly being hit by shocks to the nonstationary exogenous state variables. Instead of a long-run equilibrium, we will work with an equilibrium concept given by the solution formed under hypothetically fully flexible prices. Then, as long as there is some degree of price-level stickiness that prevents complete instantaneous adjustment, the disequilibium can be characterized by the gap between sticky-price solution and the shadow flexible-price equilibrium.

Let the shadow values associated with the flexible-price equilibrium be denoted with a "tilde." The predetermined part of the price level is $E_{t-1}\tilde{p}_t$, which is a function of time $-(t-1)$ information. Let $\theta(\tilde{p}_t - E_{t-1}\tilde{p}_t)$ represent the extent to which the actual price level p_t responds at date-t to new information, where θ is an adjustment coefficient. The sticky-price adjustment rule is

$$p_t = E_{t-1}\tilde{p}_t + \theta(\tilde{p}_t - E_{t-1}\tilde{p}_t). \tag{8.20}$$

According to this rule, goods prices display rigidity for at most one period. Prices are instantaneously perfectly flexible if $\theta = 1$, and they are completely fixed one period in advance if $\theta = 0$. Intermediate degrees of price fixity are characterized by $0 < \theta < 1$, which allows the price level at t to partially adjust from its one-period-in-advance predetermined value $E_{t-1}(\tilde{p}_t)$ in response to period-t information regarding prices, $\tilde{p}_t - E_{t-1}\tilde{p}_t$.

The exogenous state variables are output, money, and the aggregate demand shock, and they are governed by unit-root processes. Output and the money supply are driven by the driftless random walks

$$y_t = y_{t-1} + z_t, \tag{8.21}$$

$$m_t = m_{t-1} + v_t, \tag{8.22}$$

where $z_t \overset{iid}{\sim} N(0, \sigma_z^2)$ and $v_t \overset{iid}{\sim} N(0, \sigma_v^2)$. The demand shock d_t is also a unit-root process:

$$d_t = d_{t-1} + \delta_t - \gamma \delta_{t-1}, \tag{8.23}$$

where $\delta_t \overset{iid}{\sim} N(0, \sigma_\delta^2)$. Demand shocks are permanent, as represented by d_{t-1}, but also display transitory dynamics in which some portion $0 < \gamma < 1$ of any shock δ_t is reversed in the next period.[7] To solve the model, the first thing you need is to get the shadow flexible-price solution.

⬤ FLEXIBLE-PRICE SOLUTION

Under fully flexible prices, $\theta = 1$ and the goods market is continuously in equilibrium: $y_t = y_t^d$. Let $q_t = s_t - p_t$ be the real exchange rate. Substitute (8.19) into the IS curve (8.17), and rearrange to give

$$\tilde{q}_t = \frac{y_t - d_t}{\eta + \sigma} + \left(\frac{\sigma}{\eta + \sigma}\right) E_t \tilde{q}_{t+1}. \tag{8.24}$$

This is a stochastic difference equation in $\tilde{q}$. It follows that the solution for the flexible-price equilibrium real exchange rate is given by the present-value formula, which you can get by iterating forward on (8.24). But we won't do that here. Instead, we will use the method of undetermined coefficients. We begin by conjecturing a guess solution in which $\tilde{q}$ depends linearly on the available date-t information:

$$\tilde{q}_t = a_1 y_t + a_2 m_t + a_3 d_t + a_4 \delta_t. \tag{8.25}$$

We then deduce conditions on the a-coefficients such that (8.25) solves the model. Since m_t does not appear explicitly in (8.24), it probably is the case that $a_2 = 0$. To see if this is correct, take time-t conditional expectations on both sides of (8.25), to give

$$E_t \tilde{q}_{t+1} = a_1 y_t + a_2 m_t + a_3 (d_t - \gamma \delta_t). \tag{8.26}$$

Substitute (8.25) and (8.26) into (8.24), to get

$$a_1 y_t + a_2 m_t + a_3 d_t + a_4 \delta_t = \frac{y_t - d_t}{\eta + \sigma} + \frac{\sigma}{\eta + \sigma}[a_1 y_t + a_2 m_t + a_3 (d_t - \gamma \delta_t)].$$

---

[7]   Recursive backward substitution in (8.23) gives $d_t = \delta_t + (1 - \gamma)\delta_{t-1} + (1 - \gamma)\delta_{t-2} + \cdots$. Thus the demand shock is a quasi-random walk without drift, in that a shock δ_t has a permanent effect on d_t, but the effect on future values $(1 - \gamma)$ is smaller than the current effect.

Now equate the coefficients on the variables, to give

$$a_1 = \frac{1}{\eta} = -a_3,$$

$$a_2 = 0,$$

$$a_4 = \frac{\gamma}{\eta}\left(\frac{\sigma}{\eta + \sigma}\right).$$

The flexible-price solution for the real exchange rate is

$$\tilde{q}_t = \frac{y_t - d_t}{\eta} + \frac{\gamma}{\eta}\left(\frac{\sigma}{\eta + \sigma}\right)\delta_t, \tag{8.27}$$

where, indeed, nominal (monetary) shocks have no effect on $\tilde{q}_t$. The real exchange rate is driven only by real factors – supply and demand shocks.

Since both of these shocks were assumed to evolve according to unit-root processes, there is a presumption that $\tilde{q}_t$ also is a unit-root process. A permanent shock to supply y_t leads to a real depreciation. Since $\gamma\sigma/(\eta(\eta + \sigma)) < (1/\eta)$, a permanent shock to demand δ_t leads to a real appreciation.[8]

To get the shadow price level, start from (8.18) and (8.19), to get $\tilde{p}_t = m_t - y_t + \lambda E_t(s_{t+1} - s_t)$. If you add $\lambda\tilde{p}_t$ to both sides, add and subtract $\lambda E_t\tilde{p}_{t+1}$ from the right side and rearrange, you have

$$(1 + \lambda)\tilde{p}_t = m_t - y_t + \lambda E_t(\tilde{q}_{t+1} - \tilde{q}_t) + \lambda E_t\tilde{p}_{t+1}. \tag{8.28}$$

By (8.27), $E_t(\tilde{q}_{t+1} - \tilde{q}_t) = [\gamma/(\eta + \sigma)]\delta_t$, which you can substitute back into (8.28) to obtain the stochastic difference equation

$$\tilde{p}_t = \frac{m_t - y_t}{1 + \lambda} + \frac{\lambda\gamma}{(\eta + \sigma)(1 + \lambda)}\delta_t + \frac{\lambda}{1 + \lambda}E_t\tilde{p}_{t+1}. \tag{8.29}$$

Now solve (8.29) by the MUC. Let

$$\tilde{p}_t = b_1 m_t + b_2 y_t + b_3 d_t + b_4 \delta_t \tag{8.30}$$

be the guess solution. Taking expectations conditional on time-t information gives

$$E_t\tilde{p}_{t+1} = b_1 m_t + b_2 y_t + b_3(d_t - \gamma\delta_t). \tag{8.31}$$

Substitute (8.31) and (8.30) into (8.29), to give

$$b_1 m_t + b_2 y_t + b_3 d_t + b_4 \delta_t = \frac{m_t - y_t}{1 + \lambda} + \frac{\lambda\gamma}{(1 + \lambda)(\eta + \sigma)}\delta_t$$

$$+ \frac{\lambda}{1 + \lambda}[b_1 m_t + b_2 y_t + b_3(d_t - \gamma\delta_t)]. \tag{8.32}$$

---

[8]   Here is another way to motivate the null hypothesis that the real exchange rate follows a unit-root process in tests of long-run PPP, covered in chapter 7.

Equate coefficients on the variables, to give

$$b_1 = 1 = -b_2,$$

$$b_3 = 0,$$

$$b_4 = \frac{\lambda\gamma}{(1+\lambda)(\eta+\sigma)}. \tag{8.33}$$

Write the flexible-price equilibrium solution for the price level as

$$\tilde{p}_t = m_t - y_t + \alpha\delta_t, \tag{8.34}$$

where

$$\alpha = \frac{\lambda\gamma}{(1+\lambda)(\eta+\sigma)}.$$

A supply shock y_t generates shadow deflationary pressure, whereas demand shocks δ_t and money shocks m_t generate shadow inflationary pressure.

The shadow nominal exchange rate can now be obtained by adding $\tilde{q}_t + \tilde{p}_t$:

$$\tilde{s}_t = m_t + \left(\frac{1-\eta}{\eta}\right)y_t - \frac{d_t}{\eta} + \left(\frac{\gamma\sigma}{\eta(\eta+\sigma)} + \alpha\right)\delta_t. \tag{8.35}$$

Positive monetary shocks unambiguously lead to a nominal depreciation, but the effect of a supply shock on the shadow nominal exchange rate depends on the magnitude of the expenditure-switching elasticity, η. You are invited to verify that a positive demand shock δ_t lowers the nominal exchange rate.

Collecting the equations that form the flexible-price solution, we have

$$y_t = y_{t-1} + z_t = y(z_t),$$

$$\tilde{q}_t = \frac{y_t - d_t}{\eta} + \frac{\gamma\sigma}{\eta(\eta+\sigma)}\delta_t = \tilde{q}(z_t, \delta_t),$$

$$\tilde{p}_t = m_t - y_t + \alpha\delta_t = \tilde{p}(z_t, \delta_t, v_t).$$

The system displays a *triangular* structure in the exogenous shocks. Only supply shocks affect output; demand and supply shocks affect the real exchange rate; while supply, demand, and monetary shocks affect the price level. We will revisit the implications of this triangular structure in section 8.4.

⬤ DISEQUILIBRIUM DYNAMICS

To obtain the sticky-price solution with $0 < \theta < 1$, substitute the solution (8.34) for $\tilde{p}_t$ into the price adjustment rule (8.20), to get $p_t = m_{t-1} - y_{t-1} + \theta[v_t - z_t + \alpha\delta_t]$. Next, add and subtract $(v_t - z_t + \alpha\delta_t)$ from the right-hand side and rearrange, to give

$$p_t = \tilde{p}_t - (1-\theta)[v_t - z_t + \alpha\delta_t]. \tag{8.36}$$

The gap between p_t and $\tilde{p}_t$ is proportional to current information $(v_t - z_t + \alpha\delta_t)$, which we'll call news. You will see below that the gaps between all disequilibrium values and their shadow values are proportional to this news variable. Monetary shocks v_t and demand shocks δ_t cause the price level to lie below its equilibrium value $\tilde{p}_t$, while supply shocks z_t cause the current price level to lie above its equilibrium value.[9] Since the solution for p_t does not depend on lagged values of the shocks, the deviation from full-price flexibility values generated by current-period shocks last for only one period.

Next, solve for the real exchange rate. Substitute (8.36) and aggregate demand from the IS curve (8.17) into the LM curve (8.18), to give

$$m_t - \tilde{p}_t + (1-\theta)[v_t - z_t + \alpha\delta_t] = d_t + \eta q_t - (\sigma + \lambda)(E_t q_{t+1} - q_t) - \lambda E_t(p_{t+1} - p_t). \tag{8.37}$$

By (8.36) and (8.34), you know that

$$E_t(p_{t+1} - p_t) = -\alpha\delta_t + (1 - \theta)[v_t - z_t + \alpha\delta_t]. \tag{8.38}$$

Substitute (8.38) and $\tilde{p}_t$ into (8.37) to obtain the stochastic difference equation in q_t:

$$(\eta + \sigma + \lambda)q_t = y_t - d_t + (1-\theta)(1+\lambda)(v_t - z_t) - \theta(1+\lambda)\alpha\delta_t + (\sigma + \lambda)E_t q_{t+1}. \tag{8.39}$$

Let the conjectured solution be

$$q_t = c_1 y_t + c_2 d_t + c_3 \delta_t + c_4 v_t + c_5 z_t. \tag{8.40}$$

It follows that

$$E_t q_{t+1} = c_1 y_t + c_2(d_t - \gamma\delta_t). \tag{8.41}$$

Substitute (8.40) and (8.41) into (8.39), to give

$$(\eta + \sigma + \lambda)[c_1 y_t + c_2 d_t + c_3 \delta_t + c_4 v_t + c_5 z_t]$$
$$= y_t - d_t + (1 - \theta)(1 + \lambda)(v_t - z_t) - \theta(1 + \lambda)\alpha\delta_t + (\sigma + \lambda)[c_1 y_t + c_2(d_t - \gamma\delta_t)].$$

Equating coefficients gives

$$c_1 = \frac{1}{\eta} = -c_2,$$

$$c_3 = \frac{\gamma(\sigma + \lambda) - \eta\alpha\theta(1 + \lambda)}{\eta(\eta + \sigma + \lambda)},$$

$$c_4 = \frac{(1 - \theta)(1 + \lambda)}{\eta + \sigma + \lambda} = -c_5,$$

and the solution is

$$q_t = \frac{y_t - d_t}{\eta} + \frac{\gamma(\sigma + \lambda) - \alpha\eta\theta(1 + \lambda)}{\eta(\eta + \sigma + \lambda)}d_t + \frac{(1 - \theta)(1 + \lambda)}{\eta + \sigma + \lambda}(v_t - z_t).$$

[9]   The price-level responses to the various shocks conform precisely to the predictions from the aggregate-demand, aggregate-supply model as taught in principles of macroeconomics.

Using the definition of α and (8.27) to eliminate $(y_t - d_t)/\eta$, rewrite the solution in terms of $\tilde{q}_t$ and news

$$q_t = \tilde{q}_t + \frac{(1+\lambda)(1-\theta)}{\eta + \sigma + \lambda}[v_t - z_t + \alpha\delta_t]. \tag{8.42}$$

Nominal shocks have an effect on the real exchange rate due to the rigidity in price adjustment. Disequilibrium adjustment in the real exchange rate runs in the direction opposite to price-level adjustment. Monetary shocks and demand shocks cause the real exchange rate to temporarily rise above its equilibrium value, whereas supply shocks cause the real exchange rate to temporarily fall below its equilibrium value.

To get the nominal exchange rate $s_t = q_t + p_t$, add the solutions for q_t and p_t:

$$s_t = \tilde{s}_t + (1 - \eta - \sigma)\frac{(1-\theta)}{(\eta + \sigma + \lambda)}[v_t - z_t + \alpha\delta_t]. \tag{8.43}$$

The solution displays a modified form of exchange-rate overshooting, under the presumption that $\eta + \sigma < 1$ in that a monetary shock causes the exchange rate to rise above its shadow value $\tilde{s}_t$. In contrast to the Dornbusch model, both nominal and real shocks generate modified exchange-rate overshooting. Positive demand shocks cause s_t to rise above $\tilde{s}_t$, whereas supply shocks cause s_t to fall below $\tilde{s}_t$.

To determine excess goods demand, you know that aggregate demand is

$$y_t^d = \eta q_t - \sigma E_t(\Delta q_{t+1}) + d_t.$$

Taking expectations of (8.42) yields

$$E_t(\Delta q_{t+1}) = \frac{\gamma}{\eta + \sigma}\delta_t - \frac{(1+\lambda)(1-\theta)}{(\eta + \sigma + \lambda)}[v_t - z_t + \alpha\delta_t].$$

Substitute this and q_t from (8.42) back into aggregate demand, and rearrange to give

$$y_t^d = y_t + \frac{(1+\lambda)(1-\theta)(\eta+\sigma)}{(\eta + \sigma + \lambda)}[v_t - z_t + \alpha\delta_t]. \tag{8.44}$$

Goods market disequilibrium is proportional to the news $v_t - z_t + \alpha\delta_t$. Monetary shocks have a short-run effect on aggregate demand, which is the stochastic counterpart to the statement that monetary policy is an effective stabilization tool under flexible exchange rates.

8.4 VAR ANALYSIS OF MUNDELL–FLEMING

Even though it required tons of algebra to solve it, the stochastic Mundell–Fleming with one-period nominal rigidity is still too stylized to take seriously in formulating econometric specifications. Modeling lag dynamics in price adjustment is problematic, because we don't have a good theory for how prices adjust or for why they are sticky. Tests of overidentifying restrictions implied by dynamic versions of the Mundell–Fleming model are frequently rejected, but the investigator does not know whether it is the Mundell–Fleming theory that is being rejected or one of the auxiliary assumptions associated with the parametric econometric representation of the theory.[10]

Sims [122] views the restrictions imposed by explicitly formulated macro-econometric models to be incredible and proposes the unrestricted VAR method to investigate macroeconomic theory without having to assume very much about the economy. In fact, just about the only thing that you need to assume is which variables to include in the analysis. Unrestricted VAR estimation and accounting methods are described in section 2.1.

THE EICHENBAUM AND EVANS VAR

Eichenbaum and Evans [40] employed the Sims VAR method to the five-dimensional vector time-series consisting of (i) US industrial production, (ii) US CPI, (iii) a US monetary policy variable, (iv) a US–foreign nominal interest rate differential, and (v) the US real exchange rate. They considered two measures of monetary policy. The first was the ratio of the logarithm of nonborrowed reserves to the logarithm of total reserves. The second was the federal funds rate. They estimated separate VARs using exchange rates and interest rates for each of five countries – Japan, Germany, France, Italy, and the UK – with monthly observations from 1974.1 through 1990.5.

Here, we will re-estimate the Eichenbaum–Evans VAR and do the associated VAR accounting using monthly observations for the US, UK, Germany, and Japan from 1973.1 to 1998.1. All variables except interest rates are in logarithms. Let y_t be US industrial production, let p_t be the US consumer price index, let nbr_t be the log of nonborrowed bank reserves divided by the log of total bank reserves, let $i_t - i_t^*$ be the three-month US–foreign nominal interest rate differential, let q_t be the real exchange rate, and let s_t be the nominal exchange rate.[11] For each US–foreign country pair, two separate VARs were run – one using the real exchange rate and one with the nominal exchange rate. In the first system, the VAR is estimated for the five-dimensional vector $\underline{x}_t = (y_t, p_t, nbr_t, i_t - i_t^*, q_t)'$. In the second system, we used $\underline{x}_t = (y_t, p_t, nbr_t, i_t - i_t^*, s_t)'$.[12]

The first row of plots in figure 8.8 shows the impulse response of the log real exchange rates for US–UK, US–Germany, and US–Japan, following a one-standard deviation shock to nbr_t. An increase in nbr_t corresponds to a positive monetary shock. The second row shows the responses of the log nominal exchange rate with the same countries to a one-standard-deviation shock to nbr_t.

---

10 See Papell [112].
11 Interest rates for the US and UK are the secondary market three-month Treasury Bill rate. For Germany, I used the inter-bank deposit rate. For Japan, the interest rate is the Japanese lending rate from the beginning of the sample to 1981.8, and is the private bill rate from 1981.9 to 1998.1.
12 Using BIC (chapter 2, equation (2.3)) with the updated data indicated that the VARs required three lags. To conform with Eichenbaum and Evans, I included six lags and a linear trend.

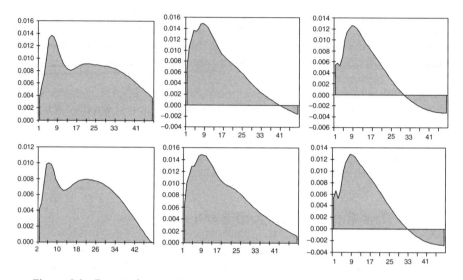

Figure 8.8 Row 1: the impulse response of log real US–UK, US–German, and US–Japan exchange rates to an orthogonalized one-standard-deviation shock to nbr_t. Row 2: the impulse responses of the log nominal exchange rate.

Both the real and nominal exchange rates are found to depreciate upon impact, but the maximal nominal depreciation occurs some months after the initial shock. The impulse response of both exchange rates is hump-shaped. There is evidently evidence of overshooting, but it is different from Dornbusch overshooting, which is instantaneous. This unrestricted VAR response pattern has come to be known as *delayed overshooting*.

Long-horizon (36 months ahead) forecast-error variance decompositions of nominal exchange rates attributable to orthogonalized monetary shocks are 16 percent for the UK, 24 percent for Germany, and 10 percent for Japan. For real exchange rates, the percentage of variance attributable to monetary shocks is 23 percent for the UK and Germany, and 9 percent for Japan. Evidently, nominal shocks are pretty important in driving the dynamics of the real exchange rate.

● CLARIDA–GALI STRUCTURAL VAR

In section 2.1, we discussed some potential pitfalls associated with the unrestricted VAR methodology. The main problem is that the unrestricted VAR analyzes a reduced form of a structural model, so we don't necessarily learn anything about the effect of policy interventions on the economy. For example, when we examine impulse responses from an innovation in y_t, we do not know whether the underlying cause was due to a shock to aggregate demand or to aggregate supply, or an expansion of domestic credit.

Blanchard and Quah [14] show how to use economic theory to place identifying restrictions on the VAR, resulting in so-called structural VARs.[13] Clarida and Gali [27] employ the Blanchard–Quah structural VAR method, using restrictions implied by the stochastic Mundell–Fleming model. To see how this works, consider the three-dimensional vector, $\underline{x}_t = (\Delta(y_t - y_t^*), \Delta(p_t - p_t^*), \Delta q_t)'$, where y is log industrial production, p is the log price level, and q is the log real exchange rate, and the starred variables are for the foreign country. Given the processes that govern the exogenous variables (8.21) and (8.22), the stochastic Mundell–Fleming model predicts that income and the real exchange rate are unit-root processes, so the VAR should be specified in terms of first-differenced observations. The triangular structure also informs us that the variables are not cointegrated, since each of the variables is driven by a different unit-root process.[14]

As described in section 2.1, first fit a pth-order VAR for $\underline{x}_t$ and get the Wold moving-average representation

$$\underline{x}_t = \sum_{j=0}^{\infty} (\mathbf{C}_j L^j)\underline{\epsilon}_t = \mathbf{C}(L)\underline{\epsilon}_t, \tag{8.45}$$

where $E(\underline{\epsilon}_t \underline{\epsilon}_t') = \Sigma$, $\mathbf{C}_0 = \mathbf{I}$, and $\mathbf{C}(L) = \sum_{j=0}^{\infty} \mathbf{C}_j L^j$ is the one-sided matrix polynomial in the lag operator L. The theory predicts that, in the long run, $\underline{x}_t$ is driven by the three-dimensional vector of aggregate supply, aggregate demand, and monetary shocks, $\underline{v}_t = (z_t, \delta_t, v_t)'$.

The economic structure embodied in the stochastic Mundell–Fleming model is represented by

$$\underline{x}_t = \sum_{j=0}^{\infty} (\mathbf{F}_j L^j)\underline{v}_t = \mathbf{F}(L)\underline{v}_t. \tag{8.46}$$

Because the underlying structural innovations are not observable, you are allowed to make one normalization. Take advantage of it by setting $E(\underline{v}_t \underline{v}_t' = \mathbf{I})$. The orthogonality between the various structural shocks is an identifying assumption. To map the innovations $\underline{\epsilon}_t$ from the unrestricted VAR into structural innovations $\underline{v}_t$, compare (8.45) and (8.46). It follows that

$$\underline{\epsilon}_t = \mathbf{F}_0 \underline{v}_t \quad \Rightarrow \quad \underline{\epsilon}_{t-j} = \mathbf{F}_0 \underline{v}_{t-j} \quad \Rightarrow \quad \mathbf{C}_j \underline{\epsilon}_{t-j} = \mathbf{C}_j \mathbf{F}_0 \underline{v}_{t-j} = \mathbf{F}_j \underline{v}_{t-j}.$$

To summarize,

$$\mathbf{F}_j = \mathbf{C}_j \mathbf{F}_0 \text{ for all } j \quad \Rightarrow \quad \mathbf{F}(1) = \mathbf{C}(1)\mathbf{F}_0. \tag{8.47}$$

Given the $\mathbf{C}_j$, which you get from unrestricted VAR accounting, (8.47) says that you only need to determine $\mathbf{F}_0$, after which the remaining $\mathbf{F}_j$ follow.

In our three-dimensional system, $\mathbf{F}_0$ is a 3×3 matrix with nine unique elements. To identify $\mathbf{F}_0$, you need nine pieces of information. Start with $\Sigma = \mathbf{G}'\mathbf{G} = E(\underline{\epsilon}_t \underline{\epsilon}_t') = \mathbf{F}_0 E(\underline{v}_t \underline{v}_t')\mathbf{F}_0' = \mathbf{F}_0 \mathbf{F}_0'$, where $\mathbf{G}$ is the unique upper triangular Choleski

---

[13]   They are only identifying restrictions, however, and cannot be tested.
[14]   Cointegration is discussed in section 2.6.

decomposition of the error covariance matrix Σ. To summarize,

$$\Sigma = G'G = F_0 F_0'. \tag{8.48}$$

Let g_{ij} be the ijth element of G and let $f_{ij,0}$ be the ijth element of F_0. Writing (8.48) out gives

$$g_{11}^2 = f_{11,0}^2 + f_{12,0}^2 + f_{13,0}^2, \tag{8.49}$$

$$g_{11}g_{12} = f_{11,0}f_{21,0} + f_{12,0}f_{22,0} + f_{13,0}f_{23,0}, \tag{8.50}$$

$$g_{11}g_{13} = f_{11,0}f_{31,0} + f_{12,0}f_{32,0} + f_{13,0}f_{33,0}, \tag{8.51}$$

$$g_{12}^2 + g_{22}^2 = f_{21,0}^2 + f_{22,0}^2 + f_{23,0}^2, \tag{8.52}$$

$$g_{12}g_{13} + g_{22}g_{23} = f_{21,0}f_{31,0} + f_{22,0}f_{32,0} + f_{23,0}f_{33,0}, \tag{8.53}$$

$$g_{13}^2 + g_{23}^2 + g_{33}^2 = f_{31,0}^2 + f_{32,0}^2 + f_{33,0}^2. \tag{8.54}$$

G has six unique elements, so this decomposition gives you six equations in nine unknowns. You still need three additional pieces of information. Get them from the long-run predictions of the theory.

Stochastic Mundell–Fleming predicts that neither demand shocks nor monetary shocks have a long-run effect on output, which we represent by setting $f_{12}(1) = 0$ and $f_{13}(1) = 0$, where $f_{ij}(1)$ is the ijth element of $F(1) = \sum_{j=0}^{\infty} F_j$. The model also predicts that money has no long-run effect on the real exchange rate $f_{33}(1) = 0$. Since $F(1) = C(1)F_0$, impose these three restrictions by setting

$$f_{13}(1) = 0 = c_{11}(1)f_{13,0} + c_{12}(1)f_{23,0} + c_{13}(1)f_{33,0}, \tag{8.55}$$

$$f_{12}(1) = 0 = c_{11}(1)f_{12,0} + c_{12}(1)f_{22,0} + c_{13}(1)f_{32,0}, \tag{8.56}$$

$$f_{33}(1) = 1 = c_{31}(1)f_{13,0} + c_{32}(1)f_{23,0} + c_{33}(1)f_{33,0}. \tag{8.57}$$

Equations (8.49)–(8.57) form a system of nine equations in nine unknowns and implicitly define F_0. Once the F_j are obtained, you can do impulse–response analyses and forecast error variance decompositions using the "structural" response matrices F_j.

Clarida and Gali estimated a structural VAR using quarterly data from 1973.3 to 1992.4 for the US, Germany, Japan, and Canada. Their impulse–response analysis revealed that following a one-standard-deviation nominal shock, the real exchange rate displayed a hump shape, initially depreciating and then subsequently appreciating. Real exchange rate dynamics were found to display delayed overshooting.

We'll re-estimate the structural VAR using four lags and monthly data for the US, UK, Germany, and Japan from 1976.1 through 1997.4. The structural impulse–response dynamics of the levels of the variables are displayed in figure 8.9. As predicted by the theory, supply shocks lead to a permanent real depreciation and demand shocks lead to a permanent real appreciation. The US–UK real exchange rate does not exhibit delayed overshooting in response to monetary shocks. The real dollar–pound rate initially appreciates

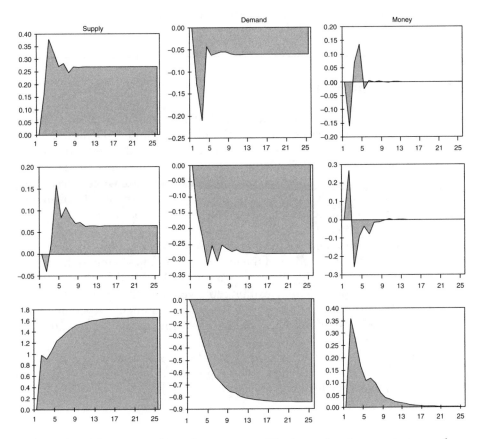

Figure 8.9　The structural impulse response of the log real exchange rate to supply, demand, and money shocks. Row 1, US–UK; row 2, US–Germany; row 3, US–Japan.

Table 8.1　Structural VAR forecast error variance decompositions for real exchange rate depreciation

	1 month			36 months		
	Supply	Demand	Money	Supply	Demand	Money
UK	0.378	0.240	0.382	0.331	0.211	0.458
Germany	0.016	0.234	0.750	0.066	0.099	0.835
Japan	0.872	0.011	0.117	0.810	0.071	0.119

and then subsequently depreciates following a positive monetary shock. The real dollar–deutschemark rate displays overshooting by first depreciating and then subsequently appreciating. The real dollar–yen displays Dornbusch-style overshooting. Money shocks are found to contribute a large fraction of the forecast error variance in both the long run as well as the short run for the real exchange rate. The decompositions at the 1-month and 36-month forecast horizons are reported in table 8.1.

> ▶ **Chapter Summary**
>
> 1. The hallmark of Mundell–Fleming models is that they assume that goods prices are sticky. Many people think of Mundell–Fleming models synonymously with sticky-price models. Because there exist nominal rigidities, these models invite an assessment of monetary (and fiscal) policy interventions under both fixed and flexible exchange rates. The models also provide predictions regarding the international transmission of domestic shocks and co-movements of macroeconomic variables at home and abroad.
> 2. The Dornbusch version of the model exploits the slow adjustment in the goods market combined with the instantaneous adjustment in the asset markets to explain why the exchange rate, which is the relative price of two monies (assets), may exhibit more volatility than the fundamentals in a deterministic and perfect-foresight environment. Explaining the excess volatility of the exchange rate is a recurring theme in international macroeconomics.
> 3. The dynamic stochastic version of the model is amenable to empirical analysis. The model provides a useful guide for doing unrestricted and structural VAR analysis.

▶ Appendix: Solving the Dornbusch Model

From (8.9) and (8.11), we see that the behavior of $i(t)$ is completely determined by that of $s(t)$. This means that we need only determine the differential equations governing the exchange rate and the price level to obtain a complete characterization of the system's dynamics.

Substitute (8.9) and (8.11) into (8.6). Make use of (8.13) and rearrange, to obtain

$$\dot{s}(t) = \frac{1}{\lambda}[p(t) - \bar{p}]. \tag{8.58}$$

To obtain the differential equation for the price level, begin by substituting (8.58) into (8.9), and then substitute the result into (8.8), to give

$$\dot{p}(t) = \pi[\delta(s(t) - p(t)) + (\gamma - 1)y - \sigma i^* - \frac{\sigma}{\lambda}(p(t) - \bar{p}) + g]. \tag{8.59}$$

However, in the long run,

$$0 = \pi[\delta(\bar{s} - \bar{p}) + (\gamma - 1)y - \sigma r^* + g], \tag{8.60}$$

the price dynamics are more conveniently characterized by

$$\dot{p}(t) = \pi \left[\delta(s(t) - \bar{s}) - \left(\delta + \frac{\sigma}{\lambda} \right) (p(t) - \bar{p}) \right], \tag{8.61}$$

which is obtained by subtracting (8.60) from (8.59).

Now write (8.58) and (8.61) as the system

$$\begin{pmatrix} \dot{s}(t) \\ \dot{p}(t) \end{pmatrix} = A \begin{pmatrix} s(t) - \bar{s} \\ p(t) - \bar{p} \end{pmatrix}, \tag{8.62}$$

where

$$A = \begin{pmatrix} 0 & 1/\lambda \\ \pi\delta & -\pi(\delta + \sigma/\lambda) \end{pmatrix}.$$

Equation (8.62) is a system of two linear homogeneous differential equations. We know that the solutions to these systems take the form

$$s(t) = \bar{s} + \alpha e^{\theta t}, \tag{8.63}$$

$$p(t) = \bar{p} + \beta e^{\theta t}. \tag{8.64}$$

We will next substitute (8.63) and (8.64) into (8.62) and solve for the unknown coefficients, α, β, and θ. First, taking time derivatives of (8.63) and (8.64) yields

$$\dot{s} = \theta \alpha e^{\theta t}, \tag{8.65}$$

$$\dot{p} = \theta \beta e^{\theta t}. \tag{8.66}$$

Substitution of (8.65) and (8.66) into (8.62) yields

$$(A - \theta I_2) \begin{pmatrix} \alpha \\ \beta \end{pmatrix} = 0. \tag{8.67}$$

In order for (8.67) to have a solution *other* than the trivial one $(\alpha, \beta) = (0, 0)$, we require that

$$0 = |A - \theta I_2| \tag{8.68}$$

$$= \theta^2 - Tr(A)\theta + |A|, \tag{8.69}$$

where $Tr(A) = -\pi(\delta + \sigma/\lambda)$ and $|A| = -\pi\delta/\lambda$ otherwise. $(A - \theta I_2)^{-1}$ exists, which means that the unique solution is the trivial one, which isn't very interesting. Imposing the restriction that (8.69) is true, we find that its roots are

$$\theta_1 = \tfrac{1}{2} \left[Tr(A) - \sqrt{Tr^2(A) - 4|A|} \right] < 0, \tag{8.70}$$

$$\theta_2 = \tfrac{1}{2} \left[Tr(A) + \sqrt{Tr^2(A) - 4|A|} \right] > 0. \tag{8.71}$$

The general solution is

$$s(t) = \bar{s} + \alpha_1 e^{\theta_1 t} + \alpha_2 e^{\theta_2 t}, \tag{8.72}$$

$$p(t) = \bar{p} + \beta_1 e^{\theta_1 t} + \beta_2 e^{\theta_2 t}. \tag{8.73}$$

This solution is explosive, however, because of the eventual dominance of the positive root. We can view an explosive solution as a bubble, in which the exchange rate and the price level diverge from values of the economic fundamentals. While there are no restrictions within the model to rule out explosive solutions, we will simply assume that the economy follows the stable solution by setting $\alpha_2 = \beta_2 = 0$, and study the solution with the stable root

$$\theta \equiv -\theta_1 \tag{8.74}$$

$$= \tfrac{1}{2} \left[\pi(\delta + \sigma/\lambda) + \sqrt{\pi^2(\delta + \sigma/\lambda)^2 + 4\pi\delta/\lambda} \right]. \tag{8.75}$$

Now, to find the stable solution, we solve (8.67) with the stable root

$$0 = (A - \theta_1 I_2) \begin{pmatrix} \alpha \\ \beta \end{pmatrix}$$

$$= \begin{pmatrix} -\theta_1 & 1/\lambda \\ \pi\delta & -\theta_1 - \pi(\delta + \sigma/\lambda) \end{pmatrix} \begin{pmatrix} \alpha \\ \beta \end{pmatrix}. \tag{8.76}$$

When this is multiplied out, we have

$$0 = -\theta_1 \alpha + \beta/\lambda, \tag{8.77}$$

$$0 = \pi\delta\alpha - \left[\theta_1 + \pi \left(\delta + \frac{\sigma}{\lambda} \right) \right] \beta. \tag{8.78}$$

It follows that

$$\alpha = \beta/\theta_1 \lambda. \tag{8.79}$$

Because α is proportional to β, we need to impose a normalization. Let this normalization be $\beta = p_0 - \bar{p}$, where $p_0 \equiv p(0)$. Then $\alpha = (p_0 - \bar{p})/\theta_1\lambda = -[p_0 - \bar{p}]/\theta\lambda$, where $\theta \equiv -\theta_1$. Using these values of α and β in (8.63) and (8.64), yields

$$p(t) = \bar{p} + [p_0 - \bar{p}]e^{-\theta t}, \tag{8.80}$$

$$s(t) = \bar{s} + [s_0 - \bar{s}]e^{-\theta t}, \tag{8.81}$$

where $(s_0 - \bar{s}) = -[p_0 - \bar{p}]/\theta\lambda$. This solution gives the time paths for the price level and the exchange rate.

To characterize the system and its response to monetary shocks, we will want to phase diagram the system. Going back to (8.58) and (8.61), we see that $\dot{s}(t) = 0$ if and only if $p(t) = \bar{p}$, while $\dot{p}(t) = 0$ if and only if $s(t) - \bar{s} = (1 + \sigma/\lambda\delta)(p(t) - \bar{p})$.

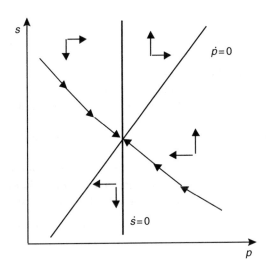

Figure 8.10 The phase diagram for the Dornbusch model.

These points are plotted in figure 8.10. The system displays a saddle path solution.

Problems

1. *Static Mundell–Fleming with imperfect capital mobility.* Let the trade balance be given by $\alpha(s + p^* - p) - \psi y$. A real depreciation raises exports and raises the trade balance, whereas an increase in income leads to higher imports, which lowers the trade balance. Let the capital account be given by $\theta(i - i^*)$, where $0 < \theta < \infty$ indexes the degree of capital mobility. We replace (8.3) with the *external balance* condition,

$$\alpha(s + p^* - p) - \psi y + \theta(i - i^*) = 0,$$

that the balance of payments is zero. (We are ignoring the service account.) When capital is completely immobile, $\theta = 0$ and the balance of payments reduces to the trade balance. Under perfect capital mobility, $\theta = \infty$ implies $i = i^*$, which is (8.3).

   (a) Call the external balance condition the FF curve. Draw the FF curve in r, y space along with the LM and IS curves.

   (b) Repeat the comparative statics experiments covered in this chapter, using the modified external balance condition. Are any of the results sensitive to the degree of capital mobility? In particular, how do the results depend on the slope of the FF curve in relation to the LM curve?

2. How would the Mundell–Fleming model with perfect capital mobility explain the international co-movements of macroeconomic variables in chapter 5?

3. Consider the Dornbusch model.

(a) What is the instantaneous effect on the exchange rate of a shock to aggregate demand? Why does an aggregate demand shock not produce overshooting?

(b) Suppose that output can change in the short run by replacing the IS curve (8.7) with $y = \delta(s - p) + \gamma y - \sigma i + g$, and replacing the price adjustment rule (8.8) with $\dot{p} = \pi(y - \bar{y})$, where long-run output is given by $\bar{y} = \delta(\bar{s} - \bar{p}) + \gamma\bar{y} - \sigma i^* + g$. Under what circumstances is the overshooting result (in response to a change in money) robust?

9
The New International Macroeconomics

The *new international macroeconomics* is a class of theories that embed imperfect competition and nominal rigidities in a dynamic general equilibrium open-economy setting. In these models, producers have monopoly power and charge at prices above marginal cost. Since it is optimal in the short run for producers to respond to small fluctuations by changing output, these models explain why output is demand determined in the short run when current prices are predetermined due to some nominal rigidity. It follows from the imperfectly competitive environment that equilibrium output lies below the socially optimal level. We will see that this feature is instrumental in producing results that are very different from Mundell–Fleming models. Because Mundell–Fleming predictions can be overturned, it is perhaps inaccurate to characterize these models as providing the microfoundations for Mundell–Fleming.

These models also, and not surprisingly, are sharply distinguished from the Arrow–Debreu style real business cycle models. Both classes of theories are set in dynamic general equilibrium, with optimizing agents and well-specified tastes and technology. Instead of being set in a perfect real business cycle world, the presence of market imperfections and nominal rigidities permits international transfers of wealth in equilibrium and prevents equilibrium welfare from reaching the socially optimal level of welfare. It therefore makes sense here to examine the welfare effects of policy interventions; whereas it does not make sense in real business cycle models, since all real business cycle dynamics are Pareto efficient.

The genesis of this literature is the Obstfeld and Rogoff [108] Redux model. This model makes several surprising predictions that are contrary to Mundell–Fleming. The model is somewhat fragile, however, as we will see when we cover the pricing-to-market refinement by Betts and Devereux [10].

In this chapter, stars denote foreign country variables, but lower case letters *do not* automatically mean logarithms. Unless explicitly noted, variables are in levels. There is also a good deal of notation. For ease of reference, table 9.1 (see page 210) summarizes the notation for the Redux model and table 9.2

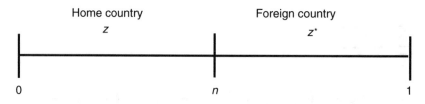

Figure 9.1   Home and foreign households lined up on the unit interval.

(see page 230) lists the notation for the pricing-to-market model. The terms "household," "agent," "consumer," and "individual" are used interchangeably. The home currency unit is the "dollar" and the foreign currency is the "euro."

9.1   THE REDUX MODEL

We are set in a deterministic environment and agents have perfect foresight. There are two countries, each populated by a continuum of consumer–producers. There is no physical capital. Each household produces a *distinct* and *differentiated* good using only its labor and the production of each household is completely specialized. Households are arranged on the unit interval $[0,1]$, with a fraction n living in the home country and a fraction $1-n$ living in the foreign country. We will index domestic agents by z, where $0 < z < n$, and foreign agents by z^*, where $n < z^* < 1$. Figure 9.1 displays the partitioning between domestic and foreign agents. When we refer to both home and foreign agents, we will use the index u, where $0 < u < 1$.

Preferences.   Households derive utility from consumption, leisure, and real cash balances. Higher output means more income, which is good, but it also means less leisure, which is bad. Money is introduced through the utility function, where agents value the real cash balances of their *own* country's money. Money does not have intrinsic value, but provides individuals with indirect utility because higher levels of real cash balances help to lower shopping (transactions) costs.

We assume that households have identical utility functions.

The household in the Redux model.   Let $c_t(z)$ be the home representative agent's consumption of the domestic good z, and let $c_t(z^*)$ be the agent's consumption of the foreign good z^*. People have tastes for all varieties of goods and the household's consumption basket is a constant elasticity of substitution (CES) index that aggregates across the available varieties of goods:

$$
\begin{aligned}
C_t &= \left[\int_0^1 c_t(u)^{(\theta-1)/\theta} \, du \right]^{\theta/(\theta-1)} \\
&= \left[\int_0^n c_t(z)^{(\theta-1)/\theta} \, dz + \int_n^1 c_t(z^*)^{\frac{\theta-1}{\theta}} \, dz^* \right]^{\theta/(\theta-1)},
\end{aligned}
\tag{9.1}
$$

where $\theta > 1$ is the elasticity of substitution between the varieties.[1]

Let $y_t(z)$ be the time-t output of individual z, let M_t be the domestic per capita money stock, and let P_t be the domestic price level. The lifetime utility of the domestic household z is given by

$$
U_t = \sum_{j=0}^{\infty} \beta^j \left[\ln C_{t+j} + \frac{\gamma}{1-\epsilon} \left(\frac{M_{t+j}}{P_{t+j}} \right)^{1-\epsilon} - \frac{\rho}{2} y_{t+j}^2(z) \right],
\tag{9.2}
$$

where $0 < \beta < 1$ is the subjective discount factor, C_{t+j} is the CES index given in (9.1), and M_t/P_t are real balances. The costs of forgone leisure associated with work are represented by the term $(-\rho/2)y_t^2(z)$.

Let $p_t(z)$ be the domestic price of good z, let S_t be the nominal exchange rate, and let $p_t^*(z)$ be the foreign-currency price of good z. A key assumption is that prices are set in the *producer's currency*. It follows that the "law of one price" holds for every good, $0 < u < 1$:

$$
p_t(u) = S_t p_t^*(u).
\tag{9.3}
$$

The pricing assumption also implies that there is complete *pass-through* of nominal exchange rate fluctuations. That is, an x percent depreciation of the dollar is fully passed through, resulting in an x percent increase in the dollar price of the imported good.

Since utility of consumption is a monotone transformation of the CES index, we can begin with some standard results from consumer theory under CES

---

[1] In the discrete commodity formulation with N goods, the index can be written as $C = \left[\sum_{z=1}^N c_z^{(\theta-1)/\theta} \Delta z \right]^{\theta/(\theta-1)}$, where $\Delta z = 1$. The representation under a continuum of goods takes the limit of the sums given by the integral formulation in (9.1).

utility.[2] First, the correct domestic price index is

$$P_t = \left[\int_0^1 p_t(u)^{1-\theta} \, du \right]^{1/(1-\theta)}$$

$$= \left[\int_0^n p_t(z)^{1-\theta} \, dz + \int_n^1 \left[S_t p_t^*(z^*) \right]^{1-\theta} \, dz^* \right]^{1(1-\theta)}. \tag{9.4}$$

Second, household demand for the domestic good z, and for the foreign good z^*, are

$$c_t(z) = \left[\frac{p_t(z)}{P_t} \right]^{-\theta} C_t, \tag{9.5}$$

$$c_t(z^*) = \left[\frac{S_t p_t^*(z^*)}{P_t} \right]^{-\theta} C_t. \tag{9.6}$$

Analogously, foreign-household z^* lifetime utility is

$$U_t^* = \sum_{j=0}^{\infty} \beta^j \left[\ln C_{t+j}^* + \frac{\gamma}{1-\epsilon} \left(\frac{M_{t+j}^*}{P_{t+j}^*} \right)^{1-\epsilon} - \frac{\rho}{2} y_{t+j}^{*2}(z^*) \right], \tag{9.7}$$

with consumption and price indices

$$C_t^* = \left[\int_0^n c_t^*(z)^{(\theta-1)/\theta} \, dz + \int_n^1 c_t^*(z^*)^{(\theta-1)/\theta} \, dz^* \right]^{\theta/(\theta-1)}, \tag{9.8}$$

$$P_t^* = \left[\int_0^n \left(\frac{p_t(z)}{S_t} \right)^{(1-\theta)} \, dz + \int_n^1 [p_t^*(z^*)]^{(1-\theta)} \, dz^* \right]^{1/(1-\theta)}, \tag{9.9}$$

and individual demand for z and z^* goods

$$c_t^*(z) = \left[\frac{p_t(z)}{S_t P_t^*} \right]^{-\theta} C_t^*,$$

$$c_t^*(z^*) = \left[\frac{p_t^*(z^*)}{P_t^*} \right]^{-\theta} C_t^*.$$

---

[2] In the static problem facing a consumer who wants to maximize

$$U = \left(x_1^{(\theta-1)/\theta} + x_2^{(\theta-1)/\theta} \right)^{\theta/(\theta-1)} \qquad \text{subject to } I = p_1 x_1 + p_2 x_2,$$

where I is a given level of nominal income, the indirect utility function is

$$v(p_1, p_2; I) = \frac{I}{[p_1^{(1-\theta)} + p_2^{(1-\theta)}]^{1/(1-\theta)}},$$

the appropriate price index is $P = [p_1^{(1-\theta)} + p_2^{(1-\theta)}]^{1/(1-\theta)}$, and the individual's demand for good $j = 1, 2$ is $x_j^d = [p_j/P]^{-\theta}(I/P)$, where (I/P) is real income.

Every good is equally important in home and foreign-household utility. It follows that the elasticity of demand $1/\theta$ – in all goods markets, whether at home or abroad – is identical. Every producer has the identical technology in production. In equilibrium, all domestic producers behave identically to each other, and all foreign producers behave identically to each other, in the sense that they produce the same level of output and charge the same price. Thus it will be the case that, for any two domestic producers, $0 < z < z' < n$,

$$y_t(z) = y_t(z'),$$
$$p_t(z) = p_t(z'),$$

and that, for any two foreign producers, $n < z^* < z^{*'} < 1$,

$$y_t^*(z^*) = y_t^*(z^{*'}),$$
$$p_t^*(z^*) = p_t^*(z^{*'}).$$

It follows that the home and foreign price levels, (9.4) and (9.9), simplify to

$$P_t = \left[np_t(z)^{1-\theta} + (1-n)(S_t p_t^*(z^*))^{1-\theta} \right]^{1/(1-\theta)}, \tag{9.10}$$

$$P_t^* = \left[n(p_t(z)/S_t)^{1-\theta} + (1-n)p_t^*(z^*)^{1-\theta} \right]^{1/(1-\theta)}, \tag{9.11}$$

and that PPP holds for the correct CES price index:

$$P_t = S_t P_t^*. \tag{9.12}$$

Notice that PPP will hold for GDP deflators only if $n = 1/2$.

Asset markets. The world capital market is fully integrated. There is an internationally tradable one-period real discount bond, which is denominated in terms of the *composite* consumption good C_t. r_t is the real interest rate paid by the bond between t and $t+1$. The bond is available in *zero net supply*, so that bonds held by foreigners are issued by home residents. The gross nominal interest rate is given by the Fisher equation,

$$1 + i_t = \frac{P_{t+1}}{P_t}(1 + r_t), \tag{9.13}$$

and is related to the foreign nominal interest rate by uncovered interest parity:

$$1 + i_t = \frac{S_{t+1}}{S_t}(1 + i_t^*). \tag{9.14}$$

Let B_t be the stock of bonds held by the domestic agent and let B_t^* be the stock of bonds held by the foreign agent. By the zero-net-supply constraint, $0 = nB_t + (1-n)B_t^*$, it follows that

$$B_t^* = -\frac{n}{1-n}B_t. \tag{9.15}$$

Table 9.1   Notation for the Redux model

n	The fraction of the world population in home country
u	The index across all individuals of the world, $0 < u < 1$
z, z^*	The index of domestic and foreign individuals, $0 < z < n < z^* < 1$
$y_t(z)$	The home output of good z
$c_t(u)$	The home representative household consumption of good u
C_t	The home CES consumption goods aggregator
$y_t^*(z^*)$	The foreign output of good z^*
$c_t^*(u)$	The foreign representative household consumption of good u
C_t^*	The foreign CES consumption goods aggregator
$p_t(u)$	The dollar price of good u
P_t	The home price index
$p_t^*(u)$	The euro price of good u
P_t^*	The foreign price index
S_t	The dollar price of euro
$g_t(u)$	The home-government consumption of good u
G_t	The home-government CES consumption goods aggregator
T_t	Home tax receipts
M_t	The home money supply
B_t	The home-household holdings of international real bonds
$g_t(u)$	Home-government consumption of good u
G_t^*	The foreign-government CES consumption goods aggregator
T_t^*	Foreign tax receipts
M_t^*	The foreign money supply
B_t^*	The foreign-household holdings of international real bonds
r_t	The real interest rate
i_t	The home nominal interest rate
θ	Elasticity of substitution between varieties of goods ($\theta > 1$)
$1/\epsilon$	Consumption elasticity of money demand
γ, ρ	Parameters of the utility function:
	$\hat{b}_t = \Delta B_t / C_0^w$
	$\hat{b}_t^* = \Delta B_t^* / C_0^w$
	$\hat{g}_t = \Delta G_t / C_0^w$
	$\hat{g}_t^* = \Delta G_t^* / C_0^w$
C_t^w	The average world private consumption ($C_t^w = nC_t + (1 - n)C_t^*$)
G_t^w	The average world government consumption ($G_t^w = nG_t + (1 - n)G_t^*$)
M_t^w	The average world money supply ($M_t^w = nM_t + (1 - n)M_t^*$)

The government.   For $0 < u < 1$, let $g_t(u)$ be home-government consumption of good u. Total home- and foreign-government consumption is given by the analogous CES aggregator over government purchases of all varieties:

$$G_t = \left[\int_0^1 g_t(u)^{(1-\theta)/\theta} \, du \right]^{\theta/(\theta-1)},$$

$$G_t^* = \left[\int_0^1 g_t^*(u)^{(1-\theta)/\theta} \, du \right]^{\theta/(\theta-1)}.$$

It follows that home-government demand for individual goods is given by replacing c_t with g_t and C_t with G_t in (9.5)–(9.6). The identical reasoning holds for the foreign-government demand function.

Governments issue no debt. They finance consumption either through money creation (seignorage) or by lump-sum taxes T_t and T_t^*. Negative values of T_t and T_t^* are lump-sum transfers from the government to residents. The budget constraints of the home and foreign governments are

$$G_t = T_t + \frac{M_t - M_{t-1}}{P_t}, \tag{9.16}$$

$$G_t^* = T_t^* + \frac{M_t^* - M_{t-1}^*}{P_t^*}. \tag{9.17}$$

Aggregate demand. Let the average world private and government consumption be the population-weighted average of the domestic and foreign counterparts:

$$C_t^w = nC_t + (1-n)C_t^*, \tag{9.18}$$

$$G_t^w = nG_t + (1-n)G_t^*. \tag{9.19}$$

Then $C_t^w + G_t^w$ is the world aggregate demand. The total demand for any home or foreign good is given by

$$y_t^d(z) = \left[\frac{p_t(z)}{P_t}\right]^{-\theta}(C_t^w + G_t^w), \tag{9.20}$$

$$y_t^{*d}(z^*) = \left[\frac{p_t^*(z^*)}{P_t^*}\right]^{-\theta}(C_t^w + G_t^w). \tag{9.21}$$

Budget constraints. Wealth that domestic agents take into the next period, $P_tB_t + M_t$, is derived from wealth brought into the current period ($[1 + r_{t-1}]P_tB_{t-1} + M_{t-1}$) plus current income ($p_t(z)y_t(z)$) less consumption and taxes ($P_t(C_t + T_t)$). Wealth is accumulated in a similar fashion by the foreign agent. The budget constraints for home and foreign agents are

$$P_tB_t + M_t = (1 + r_{t-1})P_tB_{t-1} + M_{t-1} + p_t(z)y_t(z) - P_tC_t - P_tT_t, \tag{9.22}$$

$$P_t^*B_t^* + M_t^* = (1 + r_{t-1})P_t^*B_{t-1}^* + M_{t-1}^* + p_t^*(z^*)y_t^*(z^*) - P_t^*C_t^* - P_t^*T_t^*. \tag{9.23}$$

We can simplify the budget constraints by eliminating $p(z)$ and $p^*(z^*)$. Because output is demand determined, rearrange (9.20) to get $p_t(z)y_t(z) = P_ty_t(z)^{(\theta-1)/\theta}[C_t^w + G_t^w]^{1/\theta}$, and substitute the result into (9.22). Do the same for the foreign household's budget constraint using the zero-net-supply constraint on bonds (9.15) to eliminate B^*, to give

$$C_t = (1 + r_{t-1})B_{t-1} - B_t - \frac{M_t - M_{t-1}}{P_t} - T_t$$

$$+ y_t(z)^{(\theta-1)/\theta} \left[C_t^w + G_t^w \right]^{1/\theta}, \tag{9.24}$$

$$C_t^* = (1 + r_{t-1})\frac{-nB_{t-1}}{1-n} + \frac{nB_t}{1-n} - \frac{M_t^* - M_{t-1}^*}{P_t^*} - T_t^*$$

$$+ y_t^*(z^*)^{(\theta-1)/\theta} \left[C_t^w + G_t^w \right]^{1/\theta}. \tag{9.25}$$

Euler equations. C_t, M_t, and B_t are the choice variables for the domestic agent and C_t^*, M_t^*, and B_t^* are the choice variables for the foreign agent. For the domestic household, substitute the budget constraint (9.22) into the lifetime utility function (9.2) to transform the problem into an unconstrained dynamic optimization problem. Do the same for the foreign household. The Euler equations associated with bond-holding choice are the familiar intertemporal optimality conditions:

$$C_{t+1} = \beta(1 + r_t)C_t, \tag{9.26}$$

$$C_{t+1}^* = \beta(1 + r_t)C_t^*. \tag{9.27}$$

The Euler equations associated with optimal cash holdings are the money demand functions

$$\frac{M_t}{P_t} = \left[\frac{\gamma(1 + i_t)}{i_t} C_t \right]^{1/\epsilon}, \tag{9.28}$$

$$\frac{M_t^*}{P_t^*} = \left[\frac{\gamma(1 + i_t^*)}{i_t^*} C_t^* \right]^{1/\epsilon}, \tag{9.29}$$

where $1/\epsilon$ is the consumption elasticity of money demand.[3] The Euler equations for optimal "labor supply" are[4]

$$\left[y_t(z) \right]^{(\theta+1)/\theta} = \left[\frac{\theta-1}{\rho\theta} \right] C_t^{-1} [C_t^w + G_t^w]^{1/\theta}, \tag{9.30}$$

$$\left[y_t(z^*)^* \right]^{(\theta+1)/\theta} = \left[\frac{\theta-1}{\rho\theta} \right] C_t^{*-1} [C_t^w + G_t^w]^{1/\theta}. \tag{9.31}$$

It will be useful to *consolidate* the budget constraints of the individual and the government by combining (9.22) and (9.16) for the home country and (9.17) and

---

[3]   The home-agent first-order condition is

$$\gamma \left(\frac{M_t}{P_t} \right)^{-\epsilon} \frac{1}{P_t} - \frac{1}{P_t C_t} + \frac{\beta}{P_{t+1}C_{t+1}} = 0.$$

Now, using (9.26) to eliminate β and the Fisher equation (9.13) to eliminate $(1 + r_t)$ produces (9.28).

[4]   "Supply" is placed in quotes since the monopolistically competitive firm doesn't have a supply curve.

(9.24) for the foreign country:

$$C_t = (1 + r_{t-1})B_{t-1} - B_t + \frac{p_t(z)y_t(z)}{P_t} - G_t, \tag{9.32}$$

$$C_t^* = -(1 + r_{t-1})\frac{n}{1 - n}B_{t-1} + \frac{n}{1 - n}B_t + \frac{p_t^*(z^*)y_t^*(z^*)}{P_t^*} - G_t^*. \tag{9.33}$$

Because of the monopoly distortion, equilibrium output lies below the socially optimal level. Therefore, we cannot use the planner's problem and we must solve for the market equilibrium. The solution method is to linearize the Euler equations around the steady state. To do so, we must first study the steady state.

 ## THE STEADY STATE

Consider the state to which the economy converges following a shock. Let these steady state values be denoted without a time subscript. We restrict the analysis to *zero-inflation* steady states. Then the government budget constraints (9.16) and (9.17) are $G = T$ and $G^* = T^*$. By (9.26), the steady state real interest rate is

$$r = \frac{(1 - \beta)}{\beta}. \tag{9.34}$$

From (9.32) and (9.33), the steady state consolidated budget constraints are

$$C = rB + \frac{p(z)y(z)}{P} - G, \tag{9.35}$$

$$C^* = -r\frac{nB}{1 - n} + \frac{p^*(z^*)y^*(z^*)}{P^*} - G^*. \tag{9.36}$$

The "0-steady state." We have just described the forward-looking steady state to which the economy eventually converges. We now specify the steady state from which we depart. This benchmark steady state has no international debt and no government spending. We call it the "0-steady state" and indicate it with a "0" subscript: $B_0 = G_0 = G_0^* = 0$. From the domestic agent's budget constraint (9.35), we have $C_0 = (p_0(z)/P_0)y_0(z)$. Since there is no international indebtedness, international trade must be balanced, which means that consumption equals income: $C_0 = y_0(z)$. It also follows from (9.35) that $p_0(z) = P_0$. Analogously, $C_0^* = y_0^*(z^*)$ and $p_0^*(z^*) = P_0^*$ in the foreign country. By PPP, $P_0 = S_0 P_0^*$, and from the foregoing $p_0(z) = S_0 p_0^*(z^*)$. That is, the dollar price of good z is equal to the dollar price of the foreign good z^* in the 0-equilibrium. It follows that, in the 0-steady state, world demand is

$$C_0^w = nC_0 + (1 - n)C_0^* = ny_0(z) + (1 - n)y_0^*(z^*).$$

Substitute this expression into the labor supply rules (9.30) and (9.31), to give

$$y_0(z)^{(2\theta+1)/\theta} = \left(\frac{\theta-1}{\rho\theta}\right)\left[ny_0(z) + (1-n)y_0^*(z^*)\right]^{1/\theta},$$

$$y_0^*(z^*)^{(2\theta+1)/\theta} = \left(\frac{\theta-1}{\rho\theta}\right)\left[ny_0(z) + (1-n)y_0^*(z^*)\right]^{1/\theta}.$$

Together, these relations tell us that 0-steady state output at home and abroad is equal to consumption:

$$y_0(z) = y_0^*(z^*) = \left[\frac{\theta-1}{\rho\theta}\right]^{1/2} = C_0 = C_0^* = C_0^w. \tag{9.37}$$

Nominal and real interest rates in the 0-steady state are equalized with $(1 + i_0)/i_0 = 1/(1-\beta)$. By (9.28) and (9.29), 0-steady state money demand is

$$\frac{M_0}{P_0} = \frac{M_0^*}{P_0^*} = \left[\frac{\gamma y_0(z)}{1-\beta}\right]^{1/\epsilon}. \tag{9.38}$$

Finally, by (9.38) and PPP, it follows that the 0-steady state nominal exchange rate is

$$S_0 = \frac{M_0}{M_0^*}. \tag{9.39}$$

Equation (9.39) looks pretty much like the Lucas-model solution (4.55).

● LOG-LINEAR APPROXIMATION ABOUT THE 0-STEADY STATE

We denote the approximate log deviation from the 0-steady state with a "hat," so that, for any variable, $\hat{X}_t = (X_t - X_0)/X_0 \simeq \ln(X_t/X_0)$. The consolidated budget constraints (9.32) and (9.33) with $B_{t-1} = B_0 = 0$ become

$$C_t = \frac{p_t(z)}{P_t}y_t(z) - B_t - G_t, \tag{9.40}$$

$$C_t^* = \frac{p_t^*(z^*)}{P_t^*}y_t^*(z^*) + \left(\frac{nB_t}{1-n}\right) - G_t^*. \tag{9.41}$$

Multiply (9.40) by n and (9.41) by $1 - n$, and add them together to get the consolidated world budget constraint:

$$C_t^w = n\left(\frac{p_t(z)}{P_t}\right)y_t(z) + (1-n)\left(\frac{p_t^*(z^*)}{P_t^*}\right)y_t^*(z^*) - G_t^w. \tag{9.42}$$

Log-linearizing (9.42) about the 0-steady state yields

$$\hat{C}_t^w = n[\hat{p}_t(z) + \hat{y}_t(z) - \hat{P}_t] + (1-n)\left[\hat{p}_t^*(z^*) + \hat{y}_t^*(z^*) - \hat{P}_t^*\right] - \hat{g}_t^w, \tag{9.43}$$

where $\hat{g}_t^w \equiv G_t^w / C_0^w.$[5] Do the same for PPP (9.12) and the domestic and foreign price levels (9.10)–(9.11), to give

$$\hat{S}_t = \hat{P}_t - \hat{P}_t^*, \tag{9.44}$$

$$\hat{P}_t = n\hat{p}_t(z) + (1-n)\left(\hat{S}_t + \hat{p}_t^*(z^*)\right), \tag{9.45}$$

$$\hat{P}_t^* = n(\hat{p}_t(z) - \hat{S}_t) + (1-n)\hat{p}_t^*(z^*). \tag{9.46}$$

Log-linearizing the world demand functions (9.20) and (9.21) gives

$$\hat{y}_t(z) = \theta[\hat{P}_t - \hat{p}_t(z)] + \hat{C}_t^w + \hat{g}_t^w, \tag{9.47}$$

$$\hat{y}_t^*(z^*) = \theta[\hat{P}_t^* - \hat{p}_t^*(z^*)] + \hat{C}_t^w + \hat{g}_t^w. \tag{9.48}$$

Log-linearizing the "labor supply rules" (9.30) and (9.31) gives

$$(1+\theta)\hat{y}_t(z) = -\theta\hat{C}_t + \hat{C}_t^w + \hat{g}_t^w, \tag{9.49}$$

$$(1+\theta)\hat{y}_t^*(z^*) = -\theta\hat{C}_t^* + \hat{C}_t^w + \hat{g}_t^w. \tag{9.50}$$

Log-linearizing the consumption Euler equations (9.26)–(9.27) gives

$$\hat{C}_{t+1} = \hat{C}_t + (1-\beta)\hat{r}_t, \tag{9.51}$$

$$\hat{C}_{t+1}^* = \hat{C}_t^* + (1-\beta)\hat{r}_t, \tag{9.52}$$

and, finally, log-linearizing the money demand functions (9.28) and (9.29) gives

$$\hat{M}_t - \hat{P}_t = \frac{1}{\epsilon}\left[\hat{C}_t - \beta\left(\hat{r}_t + \frac{\hat{P}_{t+1} - \hat{P}_t}{1-\beta}\right)\right], \tag{9.53}$$

$$\hat{M}_t^* - \hat{P}_t^* = \frac{1}{\epsilon}\left[\hat{C}_t^* - \beta\left(\hat{r}_t + \frac{\hat{P}_{t+1}^* - \hat{P}_t^*}{1-\beta}\right)\right]. \tag{9.54}$$

---

[5] The expansion of the first term about 0-steady state values is $\Delta n(p_t(z)/P_t)y_t(z) = n(y_0(z)/P_0)(p_t(z) - p_0(z)) + n(p_0(z)/P_0)(y_t(z) - y_0(z)) - n[(p_0(z)y_0(z))/P_0^2](P_t - P_0)$. When you divide by C_0^w, note that $C_0^w = y_0(z)$ and $P_0 = p_0(z)$ to get $n[\hat{p}_t(z) - \hat{P}_t + \hat{y}_t(z)]$. Expansion of the other terms follows in an analogous manner.

⬤ LONG-RUN RESPONSE

The economy starts out in the 0-steady state. We will solve for the new steady state following a permanent monetary or government spending shock. For any variable X, let $\hat{X} \equiv \ln(X/X_0)$, where X is the new (forward-looking) steady state value. Since log-linearized equations (9.43)–(9.50) hold for arbitrary t, they also hold across steady states and, from (9.43), (9.47), (9.48), (9.49), and (9.50), you have

$$\hat{C}^w = n[\hat{p}(z) + \hat{y}(z) - \hat{P}] + (1-n)[\hat{p}^*(z^*) + \hat{y}^*(z^*) - \hat{P}^*] - \hat{g}^w, \quad (9.55)$$

$$\hat{y}(z) = \theta[\hat{P} - \hat{p}(z)] + \hat{C}^w + \hat{g}^w, \quad (9.56)$$

$$\hat{y}^*(z^*) = \theta[\hat{P}^* - \hat{p}^*(z^*)] + \hat{C}^w + \hat{g}^w, \quad (9.57)$$

$$(1+\theta)\hat{y}(z) = -\theta\hat{C} + \hat{C}^w + \hat{g}^w, \quad (9.58)$$

$$(1+\theta)\hat{y}^*(z^*) = -\theta\hat{C}^* + \hat{C}^w + \hat{g}^w, \quad (9.59)$$

where $\hat{g} = G/C_0^w$ and $\hat{g}^* = G^*/C_0^w$. Log-linearizing the steady state budget constraints (9.35) and (9.36) and letting $\hat{b} = B/C_0^w$ yields

$$\hat{C} = r\hat{b} + \hat{p}(z) + \hat{y}(z) - \hat{P} - \hat{g}, \quad (9.60)$$

$$\hat{C}^* = -\left(\frac{n}{1-n}\right)r\hat{b} + \hat{p}^*(z^*) + \hat{y}^*(z^*) - \hat{P}^* - \hat{g}^*. \quad (9.61)$$

Together, (9.55)–(9.61) comprise seven equations in seven unknowns $(\hat{y}, \hat{y}^*, (\hat{p}(z)-\hat{P}), (\hat{p}^*(z^*)-\hat{P}^*), \hat{C}, \hat{C}^*, \hat{C}^w)$. There is no easy way to solve this system. To solve this system of equations, you must bite the bullet and do the tedious algebra.[6] The solution for the steady state changes is

$$\hat{C} = \frac{1}{2\theta}[(1+\theta)r\hat{b} + (1-n)\hat{g}^* - (1-n+\theta)\hat{g}], \quad (9.62)$$

$$\hat{C}^* = \frac{1}{2\theta}\left[-\frac{n(1+\theta)r}{(1-n)}\hat{b} + n\hat{g} - (n+\theta)\hat{g}^*\right], \quad (9.63)$$

$$\hat{C}^w = -\frac{\hat{g}^w}{2}, \quad (9.64)$$

$$\hat{y}(z) = \frac{1}{1+\theta}\left[\frac{\hat{g}^w}{2} - \theta\hat{C}\right], \quad (9.65)$$

---

[6] Or you can use a symbolic mathematics software package such as *Mathematica*™ or *Maple*™. I confess that I used *Maple*™.

$$\hat{y}^*(z^*) = \frac{1}{1+\theta}\left[\frac{\hat{g}^w}{2} - \theta\hat{C}^*\right],\tag{9.66}$$

$$\hat{p}(z) - \hat{P} = \frac{1}{2\theta}\left[(1-n)(\hat{g}^* - \hat{g}) + r\hat{b}\right],\tag{9.67}$$

$$\hat{p}^*(z^*) - \hat{P}^* = \frac{n}{(1-n)2\theta}\left[(1-n)(\hat{g} - \hat{g}^*) - r\hat{b}\right].\tag{9.68}$$

From (9.62) and (9.63) you can see that a steady state transfer of wealth in the amount of B, from the foreign country to the home country, raises home steady state consumption and lowers it abroad. The wealth transfer reduces steady state home work effort (9.65) and raises foreign steady state work effort (9.66). From (9.67), we see that this occurs along with $\hat{p}(z) - \hat{P} > 0$, so that the relative price is high in the high-wealth country. The underlying cause of the wealth redistribution has not yet been specified. It could have been induced either by government spending shocks or monetary shocks.

If the shock originates with an increase in home-government consumption, ΔG is spent on home and foreign goods, which has a direct effect on home and foreign output. At home, however, higher government consumption raises the domestic tax burden and this works to reduce domestic steady state consumption.

The relative price of exports in terms of imports is called the *terms of trade*. To get the steady state change in the terms of trade, subtract (9.68) from (9.67), add S_t to both sides, and note that PPP implies $\hat{P} - (\hat{S} + \hat{P}^*) = 0$, to give

$$\hat{p}(z) - (\hat{S} + \hat{p}^*(z^*)) = \frac{1}{\theta}(\hat{y}^* - \hat{y}) = \frac{1}{1+\theta}(\hat{C} - \hat{C}^*).\tag{9.69}$$

From (9.53) and (9.54), it follows that the steady state changes in the price levels are

$$\hat{P} = \hat{M} - \frac{1}{\epsilon}\hat{C},\tag{9.70}$$

$$\hat{P}^* = \hat{M}^* - \frac{1}{\epsilon}\hat{C}^*.\tag{9.71}$$

By PPP, (9.70), and (9.71), the long-run response of the exchange rate is

$$\hat{S} = \hat{M} - \hat{M}^* - \frac{1}{\epsilon}(\hat{C} - \hat{C}^*).\tag{9.72}$$

SHORT-RUN ADJUSTMENT UNDER STICKY PRICES

We assume that there is a one-period nominal rigidity in which nominal prices $p_t(z)$ and $p_t^*(z^*)$ are set one period in advance in the producer's currency.[7] This

---

[7] z-goods prices are set in dollars and z^*-goods prices are set in euros.

assumption is *ad hoc* and not the result of a clearly articulated optimization problem. The prices cannot be changed within the period, but are fully adjustable after one period. It follows that the dynamics of the model are fully described in three periods. At $t-1$, the economy is in the 0-steady state. The economy is shocked at t, and the variable X responds in the short run by $\hat{X}_t$. At $t+1$, we are in the new steady state and the long-run adjustment is $\hat{X}_{t+1} = \hat{X} \simeq \ln(X/X_0)$. Date-$(t+1)$ variables in the linearized model are the new steady state values and date-t hat values are the short-run deviations.

From (9.45) and (9.46), the price-level adjustments are

$$\hat{P}_t = (1-n)\hat{S}_t, \tag{9.73}$$

$$\hat{P}_t^* = -n\hat{S}_t. \tag{9.74}$$

In the short run, output is demand determined by (9.47) and (9.48). Substituting (9.73) into (9.47) and (9.74) into (9.48), and noting that individual goods prices are sticky, $\hat{p}_t(z) = \hat{p}_t^*(z^*) = 0$, you have

$$\hat{y}_t(z) = \theta(1-n)\hat{S}_t + \hat{C}_t^w + \hat{g}^w, \tag{9.75}$$

$$\hat{y}_t^*(z^*) = -\theta(n)\hat{S}_t + \hat{C}_t^w + \hat{g}^w. \tag{9.76}$$

The remaining equations that characterize the short run are (9.51)–(9.54), which are rewritten as

$$\hat{C} = \hat{C}_t + (1-\beta)\hat{r}_t, \tag{9.77}$$

$$\hat{C}^* = \hat{C}_t^* + (1-\beta)\hat{r}_t, \tag{9.78}$$

$$\hat{M}_t - \hat{P}_t = \frac{1}{\epsilon}\left[\hat{C}_t - \beta\left(\hat{r}_t + \frac{\hat{P} - \hat{P}_t}{1-\beta}\right)\right], \tag{9.79}$$

$$\hat{M}_t^* - \hat{P}_t^* = \frac{1}{\epsilon}\left[\hat{C}_t^* - \beta\left(\hat{r}_t + \frac{\hat{P}^* - \hat{P}_t^*}{1-\beta}\right)\right]. \tag{9.80}$$

Using the consolidated budget constraints, (9.40)–(9.41), and the price-level response (9.73) and (9.74), the current account responds by

$$\hat{b}_t = \hat{y}_t(z) - (1-n)\hat{S}_t - \hat{C}_t - \hat{g}_t, \tag{9.81}$$

$$\hat{b}_t^* = \hat{y}_t^*(z^*) + n\hat{S}_t - \hat{C}_t^* - \hat{g}_t^* = \frac{-n}{1-n}\hat{b}_t. \tag{9.82}$$

We have not specified the source of the underlying shocks, which may originate from either monetary or government spending shocks. Since the role of nominal rigidities is most clearly illustrated with monetary shocks, we will specialize the model to analyze an unanticipated and permanent monetary shock. The analysis of government spending shocks is treated in the end-of-chapter problems.

● MONETARY SHOCKS

Set $G_t = 0$ for all t in the preceding equations and subtract (9.78) from (9.77), (9.80) from (9.79), and use PPP to obtain the pair of equations

$$\hat{C} - \hat{C}^* = \hat{C}_t - \hat{C}_t^*, \tag{9.83}$$

$$\hat{M}_t - \hat{M}_t^* - \hat{S}_t = \frac{1}{\epsilon}(\hat{C}_t - \hat{C}_t^*) - \frac{\beta}{\epsilon(1-\beta)}(\hat{S} - \hat{S}_t). \tag{9.84}$$

Substitute $\hat{S}$ from (9.72) into (9.84), to give

$$\hat{S}_t = (\hat{M}_t - \hat{M}_t^*) - \frac{1}{\epsilon}(\hat{C}_t - \hat{C}_t^*). \tag{9.85}$$

This looks like the solution that we obtained for the monetary approach, except that consumption replaces output as the scale variable. Comparing (9.85) to (9.72) and using (9.83), you can see that the exchange rate jumps immediately to its long-run value:

$$\hat{S} = \hat{S}_t. \tag{9.86}$$

Even though goods prices are sticky, there is *no exchange rate overshooting* in the Redux model.

Equation (9.85) isn't a solution, because it depends on $\hat{C}_t - \hat{C}_t^*$, which is endogenous. To get the solution, first note from (9.83) that you only need to solve for $\hat{C} - \hat{C}^*$. Second, it must be the case that asset holdings immediately adjust to their new steady state values, $\hat{b}_t = \hat{b}$, because with one-period price stickiness, all variables must be at their new steady state values at time $t + 1$. The extent of any current account imbalance at $t + 1$ can only be due to steady state debt service – not to changes in asset holdings. It follows that bond stocks determined at t which are taken into $t + 1$ are already at their steady state values. So, to get the solution, start by subtracting (9.63) from (9.62), to give

$$\hat{C} - \hat{C}^* = \frac{(1+\theta)}{2\theta}\frac{r\hat{b}}{1-n}. \tag{9.87}$$

But $\hat{b}/(1-n) = \hat{y}_t(z) - \hat{y}_t^*(z^*) - \hat{S}_t - (\hat{C}_t - \hat{C}_t^*)$, which follows from subtracting (9.82) from (9.81) and noting that $\hat{b} = \hat{b}_t$. In addition, $\hat{y}_t(z) - \hat{y}_t^*(z^*) = \theta\hat{S}_t$, which you get by subtracting (9.48) from (9.47), using PPP, and noting that $\hat{p}_t(z) - \hat{p}_t^*(z^*) = 0$. Now you can rewrite (9.87) as

$$\hat{C} - \hat{C}^* = \frac{(\theta^2 - 1)r}{r(1+\theta) + 2\theta}\hat{S}_t, \tag{9.88}$$

and solve (9.85) and (9.88), to give

$$\hat{S}_t = \frac{\epsilon[r(1+\theta)+2\theta]}{r(\theta^2-1)+\epsilon[r(1+\theta)+2\theta]}(\hat{M}_t - \hat{M}_t^*), \tag{9.89}$$

$$\hat{C}_t - \hat{C}_t^* = \frac{\epsilon[r(\theta^2-1)]}{r(\theta^2-1)+\epsilon[r(1+\theta)+2\theta]}(\hat{M}_t - \hat{M}_t^*). \tag{9.90}$$

From (9.87) and (9.90), the solution for the current account is

$$\hat{b} = \frac{2\theta\epsilon(1-n)(\theta-1)}{r(\theta^2-1)+\epsilon[r(1+\theta)+2\theta]}(\hat{M}_t - \hat{M}_t^*). \tag{9.91}$$

Equations (9.83), (9.90), and (9.69) together give the steady state terms of trade:

$$\hat{p}(z) - \hat{p}^*(z^*) - \hat{S} = \frac{\epsilon r(\theta-1)}{r(\theta^2-1)+\epsilon[r(1+\theta)+2\theta]}(\hat{M}_t - \hat{M}_t^*). \tag{9.92}$$

We can now see that money is *not neutral* since, in (9.92), the monetary shock generates a long-run change in the terms of trade. A domestic money shock generates a home current account surplus (in (9.91)) and improves the home wealth position and therefore the terms of trade. Home agents enjoy more leisure in the new steady state.

From (9.89) it follows that the nominal exchange rate exhibits less volatility than the money supply. It also exhibits less volatility under sticky prices than under flexible prices, since if prices were perfectly flexible, money would be neutral and the effect of a monetary expansion on the exchange rate would be $\hat{S}_t = \hat{M}_t - \hat{M}_t^*$.

The short-run terms of trade decline by $\hat{S}_t$, since $\hat{p}_t(z) = \hat{p}_t^*(z^*) = 0$. Since there are no further changes in the exchange rate, it follows from (9.92) and (9.90) that the short-run increase in the terms of trade exceeds the long-run increase. The partial reversal means there is overshooting in the terms of trade.

To find the effect of permanent monetary shocks on the real interest rate, use the consumption Euler equations (9.51) and (9.52), to give

$$\hat{C}_t^w = -(1-\beta)\hat{r}_t. \tag{9.93}$$

To solve for $\hat{C}_t^w$, use (9.73)–(9.74) to substitute out the short-run price-level changes and (9.70)–(9.71) to substitute out the long-run price-level changes from the log-linearized money demand functions (9.53)–(9.54):

$$\hat{C}_t + \frac{\beta}{\epsilon(1-\beta)}\hat{C} - \left(\epsilon + \frac{\beta}{(1-\beta)}\right)\left[\hat{M}_t - (1-n)\hat{S}_t\right] = \beta\hat{r}_t,$$

$$\hat{C}_t^* + \frac{\beta}{\epsilon(1-\beta)}\hat{C}^* - \left(\epsilon + \frac{\beta}{(1-\beta)}\right)\left[\hat{M}_t^* + n\hat{S}_t\right] = \beta\hat{r}_t.$$

Multiply the first equation by n, the second by $1-n$, and then add them together, noting, by (9.64), that $\hat{C}^w = 0$. This gives

$$\beta \hat{r}_t = \hat{C}_t^w - \left(\epsilon + \frac{\beta}{(1-\beta)}\right)\hat{M}_t^w.$$

Now, solving for the real interest rate gives the liquidity effect:

$$\hat{r}_t = -\left(\epsilon + \frac{\beta}{(1-\beta)}\right)\hat{M}_t^w. \tag{9.94}$$

A home monetary expansion lowers the real interest rate and raises average world consumption. From the world demand functions (9.47) and (9.48), it follows that domestic output unambiguously increases following a domestic monetary expansion. The monetary shock raises home consumption. Part of the new spending falls on home goods, which raises home output. The other part of the new consumption is spent on foreign goods but, because $\hat{p}_t^*(z^*) = 0$, the increased demand for foreign goods generates a real appreciation for the foreign country and leads to an expenditure-switching effect away from foreign goods. As a result, it is possible (but unlikely for reasonable parameter values, as shown in the end-of-chapter problems) for foreign output to fall. Since the real interest rate falls in the foreign country, foreign consumption following the shock behaves identically to home-country consumption. Current-period foreign consumption must lie above foreign output. Foreigners go into debt to finance the excess consumption and run a current account deficit. There is a steady state transfer of wealth to the home country. To service the debt, foreign agents work harder and consume less in the new steady state. To determine whether the monetary expansion is – on balance – a good thing or a bad thing, we will perform a welfare analysis of the shock.

WELFARE ANALYSIS

We will drop the notational dependence on z and z^*. Beginning with the domestic household, break lifetime utility into the three components that arise from consumption, leisure, and real cash balances, $U_t = U_t^c + U_t^y + U_t^m$, where

$$U_t^c = \sum_{j=0}^{\infty} \beta^j \ln(C_{t+j}), \tag{9.95}$$

$$U_t^y = -\frac{\rho}{2}\sum_{j=0}^{\infty} \beta^j y_{t+j}^2, \tag{9.96}$$

$$U_t^m = \frac{\gamma}{1-\epsilon}\sum_{j=0}^{\infty} \beta^j \left(\frac{M_{t+j}}{P_{t+j}}\right)^{1-\epsilon}. \tag{9.97}$$

It is easy to see that the surprise monetary expansion raises U_t^m, so we need only concentrate on U_t^c and U_t^y.

Before the shock, $U_{t-1}^c = \ln(C_0) + (\beta/(1-\beta)) \ln(C_0)$. After the shock, $U_t^c = \ln(C_t) + (\beta/(1-\beta)) \ln(C)$. The change in utility due to changes in consumption is

$$\Delta U_t^c = \hat{C}_t + \frac{\beta}{1-\beta}\hat{C}. \tag{9.98}$$

To determine the effect on utility of leisure, in the 0-steady state, $U_{t-1}^y = -(\rho/2)[y_0^2 + (\beta/(1-\beta))y_0^2]$. Directly after the shock, $U_t^y = -(\rho/2)[y_t^2 + (\beta/(1-\beta))y^2]$. Using the first-order approximation, $y_t^2 = y_0^2 + 2y_0(y_t - y_0)$, it follows that $\Delta U_t^y = -(\rho/2)[(y_t^2 - y_0^2) + (\beta/(1-\beta))(y^2 - y_0^2)]$. Dividing through by y_0 yields

$$\Delta U_t^y = -\rho\left[y_0^2\hat{y}_t + \frac{\beta}{(1-\beta)}y_0^2\hat{y}\right]. \tag{9.99}$$

Now use the fact that $C_0 = y_0 = C_0^w = [(\theta - 1)/\rho\theta]^{1/2}$, to get

$$\Delta U_t^c + \Delta U_t^y = \hat{C}_t - \left(\frac{(\theta - 1)}{\theta}\right)\hat{y}_t + \frac{\beta}{(1-\beta)}\left[\hat{C} - \frac{(\theta - 1)}{\theta}\hat{y}\right]. \tag{9.100}$$

Analogously, in the foreign country,

$$\Delta U_t^{c*} + \Delta U_t^{y*} = \hat{C}_t^* - \left(\frac{(\theta - 1)}{\theta}\right)\hat{y}_t^* + \frac{\beta}{(1-\beta)}\left[\hat{C}^* - \frac{(\theta - 1)}{\theta}\hat{y}^*\right]. \tag{9.101}$$

To evaluate (9.101), first note that $\hat{y}_t = \theta(1 - n)\hat{S}_t + \hat{C}_t^w$, which follows from (9.75). From (9.89) and (9.90) it follows that $\hat{C}_t = b\hat{S}_t + \hat{C}_t^*$, where $b = [r(\theta^2 - 1)/(r(1+\theta)+2\theta)]$. Eliminate foreign consumption using $\hat{C}_t^* = (\hat{C}_t^w - n\hat{C}_t)/(1-n)$, to give

$$\hat{C}_t = \frac{(1-n)r(\theta^2 - 1)}{r(1+\theta) + 2\theta}\hat{S}_t + \hat{C}_t^w. \tag{9.102}$$

Now plug (9.102) and (9.93) into (9.77), to obtain the long-run effect on consumption:

$$\hat{C} = \frac{r(1-n)(\theta^2 - 1)}{r(1+\theta) + 2\theta}\hat{S}_t. \tag{9.103}$$

Substitute $\hat{C}$ into (9.65), to obtain the long-run effect on home output:

$$\hat{y} = \frac{-r\theta(1-n)(\theta - 1)}{r(1+\theta) + 2\theta}\hat{S}_t. \tag{9.104}$$

Now, substituting these results back into (9.100) gives

$$
\Delta U_t^c + \Delta U_t^y = \frac{(1-n)r(\theta^2-1)}{r(1+\theta)+2\theta}\hat{S}_t + \hat{C}_t^w - \left(\frac{\theta-1}{\theta}\right)\left[\theta(1-n)\hat{S}_t + \hat{C}_t^w\right]
$$

$$
+ \frac{\beta}{(1-\beta)}\left[\frac{r(1-n)(\theta^2-1)}{r(1+\theta)+2\theta}\right]\hat{S}_t
$$

$$
+ \left(\frac{\beta}{1-\beta}\right)\left(\frac{\theta-1}{\theta}\right)\frac{r\theta(1-n)(\theta-1)}{r(1+\theta)+2\theta}\hat{S}_t. \tag{9.105}
$$

After collecting terms, the coefficient on $\hat{S}_t$ is seen to be zero. Substituting $r = (1-\beta)/\beta$, you are left with

$$
\Delta U_t^c + \Delta U_t^y = \frac{\hat{C}_t^w}{\theta} = \frac{-(1-\beta)\hat{r}_t}{\theta} = \left(\frac{\beta + \epsilon(1-\beta)}{\theta}\right)\hat{M}_t^w > 0, \tag{9.106}
$$

where the first equality uses (9.93) and the second equality uses (9.94).

Due to the extensive symmetry built into the model, the solutions for the foreign variables $\hat{C}^*, \hat{C}_t^*, \hat{y}^*,$ and $\hat{y}_t^*$ are given by the same formulae derived for the home country, except that $1-n$ is replaced with $-n$. It follows that the effect on $\Delta U_t^{c*} + \Delta U_t^{y*}$ is identical to (9.106).

One of the striking predictions of Redux is that the exchange rate effects have no effect on welfare. All that is left of the monetary shock is the liquidity effect. The traditional terms of trade and current account effects that typically form the focus of international transmission analysis are of second order of importance in Redux. The reason is that, in the presence of sticky nominal prices, the monetary shock generates a surprise depreciation and lowers the price level to foreigners. Home producers produce and sell more output, but they also have to work harder, which means less leisure. These two effects offset each other.

The monetary expansion is *positively transmitted* abroad, as it raises the leisure and consumption components of welfare by equal amounts in the two countries. Due to the monopoly distortion, firms set price above marginal cost, which leads to a level of output that is less than the socially optimal level. The monetary expansion generates higher output in the short run, which moves both economies closer to the efficient frontier. The expenditure-switching effects of exchange rate fluctuations and associated beggar-thy-neighbor policies identified in the Mundell–Fleming model are unimportant in the Redux model environment.

It is possible, but unlikely for reasonable parameter values, that the domestic monetary expansion can lower welfare abroad through its effects on foreign real cash balances. The analysis of this aspect of foreign welfare is treated in the end-of-chapter problems.

Summary of Redux predictions. The "law of one price" holds for all goods and, as a consequence, PPP holds as well. A permanent domestic monetary shock raises domestic and foreign consumption. Domestic output increases and it is likely that foreign output increases, but by a lesser amount. The presumption is that home and foreign consumption exhibit a higher degree of co-movement than home and foreign output. Both home and foreign households experience the identical positive welfare effect from changes in consumption and leisure. The monetary expansion moves production closer to the efficient level, which is distorted in equilibrium by imperfect competition. There is no exchange rate overshooting. The nominal exchange rate jumps immediately to its long-run value. The exchange rate also exhibits less volatility than the money supply.

Many of these predictions are violated in the data. For example, Knetter [84] and Feenstra et al. [50] find that pass-through of the exchange rate onto the domestic prices of imports is far from complete, whereas there is complete pass-through in Redux.[8] Also, we saw in chapter 7 that deviations from PPP and deviations from the "law of one price" are persistent and can be quite large. Also, Redux does not explain why international consumption displays lower degrees of co-movements than output, as we saw in chapter 5.

We now turn to a refinement of the Redux model in which the price-setting rule is altered. The change in this one aspect of the model overturns many of the Redux model predictions and brings us back toward the Mundell–Fleming model.

9.2 PRICING-TO-MARKET

The integration of international commodity markets in the Redux model rules out deviations from the "law of one price" in equilibrium. Were such violations to occur, they presumably would induce consumers to take advantage of international price differences by crossing the border to buy the goods (or contracting with foreign consumers to do the shopping for them) in the lower-price country, which would result in the international price differences being bid away.

We will now modify the Redux model by assuming that domestic and foreign goods markets are *segmented*. Domestic (foreign) agents are unable to buy the domestically produced good in the foreign (home) country. The monopolistically competitive firm has the ability to engage in price discrimination by setting a dollar price for domestic sales that differs from the price that it sets for exports. This is called *pricing-to-market*.

For concreteness, let the home country be the "US" and the foreign country be "Europe." We assume that all domestic firms have the ability to price-to-market as do all foreign firms. This is called "full" pricing-to-market. Betts and Devereux [10] allow the degree of pricing-to-market – the fraction of firms that operate in internationally segmented markets – to vary from 0 to 1. Both the Redux model and the next model that we study are nested within their framework. The associated notation is summarized in table 9.2 (see page 230).

---

[8]   Pass-through is the extent to which the dollar price of US imports rises in response to a 1 percent depreciation in the dollar currency.

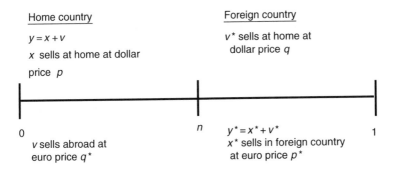

Figure 9.2 Pricing-to-market home and foreign households lined up on the unit interval.

FULL PRICING-TO-MARKET

We modify Redux in two ways. The first difference lies in the price-setting opportunities for monopolistically competitive firms. The goods market is integrated *within* the home country and *within* the foreign country, but not internationally. The second modification is in the menu of assets available to agents. Here, the internationally tradable asset is a nominal bond denominated in "dollars." The model is still set in a deterministic environment.

Goods markets. A US firm, z, sells $x_t(z)$ units of output in the home market and exports $v_t(z)$ to the foreign country. The total output of the US firm is $y_t(z) = x_t(z) + v_t(z)$. The per-unit dollar price of US sales is set at $p_t(z)$ and the per-unit *euro* price of exports is set at $q_t^*(z)$. The relationship among firms, their markets, and their pricing policies is illustrated in figure 9.2.

A European firm, z^*, sells $x_t^*(z^*)$ units of output in Europe at the preset euro price $p_t^*(z^*)$ and exports $v_t^*(z^*)$ to the US, which it sells at a preset *dollar* price of $q_t(z^*)$. The total output of the European firm is $y_t^*(z^*) = x_t^*(z^*) + v_t^*(z^*)$.

Asset markets. The internationally tradable asset is a one-period *nominal* bond, denominated in dollars. Restricting asset availability places potential limits on the degree of international risk-sharing that can be achieved. Since violations of the "law of one price" can now occur, so can violations of purchasing power parity. It follows that that real interest rates can diverge across countries. Since intertemporal optimality requires that agents set the growth of marginal utility (consumption in the log utility case) to be proportional to the real interest rate, the international inequality of real interest rates implies that home and foreign consumption will not be perfectly correlated.

The bond is sold at discount and has a face value of one dollar. Let B_t be the dollar value of bonds held by domestic households, and let B_t^* be the *dollar* value of bonds held by foreign households. Bonds outstanding are in zero-net-supply: $nB_t + (1 - n)B_t^* = 0$. The dollar price of the bond is

$$\delta_t \equiv \frac{1}{(1 + i_t)}.$$

The foreign nominal interest rate is given by uncovered interest parity:

$$(1 + i_t^*) = (1 + i_t)\left(\frac{S_t}{S_{t+1}}\right).$$

Households. We need to distinguish between hours worked, which is chosen by the household, and output, which is chosen by the firm. The utility function is similar to (9.2) in the Redux model, except that hours of work, $h_t(z)$, appears explicitly in place of output, $y_t(z)$:

$$U_t = \sum_{j=0}^{\infty} \beta^j \left[\ln C_{t+j} + \frac{\gamma}{1 - \epsilon}\left(\frac{M_{t+j}}{P_{t+j}}\right)^{1-\epsilon} - \frac{\rho}{2}h_{t+j}^2(z) \right]. \tag{9.107}$$

The associated price indices for the domestic and foreign households are

$$P_t = \left[\int_0^n p_t(z)^{1-\theta}\,dz + \int_n^1 q_t(z^*)^{1-\theta}\,dz^* \right]^{1/(1-\theta)}, \tag{9.108}$$

$$P_t^* = \left[\int_0^n q_t^*(z)^{1-\theta}\,dz + \int_n^1 p_t^*(z^*)^{1-\theta}\,dz^* \right]^{1/(1-\theta)}. \tag{9.109}$$

W_t is the home-country competitive nominal wage. The household derives income from selling labor to firm z, $W_t h_t(z)$. Household z also owns firm z, from which it earns profits $\pi_t(z)$. Nominal wealth taken into the next period consists of cash balances and bonds $(M_t + \delta_t B_t)$. This wealth is the result of wealth brought into the current period $(M_{t-1} + B_{t-1})$ plus current income $(W_t h_t(z) + \pi_t(z))$ less consumption and taxes $(P_t C_t + P_t T_t)$. The home and foreign budget constraints are given by

$$M_t + \delta_t B_t = W_t h_t(z) + \pi_t(z) + M_{t-1} + B_{t-1} - P_t C_t - P_t T_t, \tag{9.110}$$

$$M_t^* + \delta_t \frac{B_t^*}{S_t} = W_t^* h_t^*(z) + \pi_t^*(z) + M_{t-1}^* + \frac{B_{t-1}^*}{S_t} - P_t^* C_t^* - P_t^* T_t^*. \tag{9.111}$$

Households take prices and firm profits as given and choose B_t, M_t, and h_t. To derive the Euler equations implied by domestic household optimality, transform the household's problem into an unconstrained dynamic choice problem, by rewriting the budget constraint (9.110) in terms of consumption and substituting this result into the utility function (9.107). Do the same for the foreign agent. The resulting first-order conditions can be rearranged to yield[9]

$$\delta_t P_{t+1} C_{t+1} = \beta P_t C_t, \tag{9.112}$$

$$\delta_t P^*_{t+1} C^*_{t+1} \left(\frac{S_{t+1}}{S_t} \right) = \beta P^*_t C^*_t, \tag{9.113}$$

$$\frac{M_t}{P_t} = \left[\frac{\gamma C_t}{1 - \delta_t} \right]^{1/\epsilon}, \tag{9.114}$$

$$\frac{M^*_t}{P^*_t} = \left[\frac{\gamma C^*_t}{1 - \delta_t \frac{S_{t+1}}{S_t}} \right]^{1/\epsilon}, \tag{9.115}$$

$$h_t(z) = \frac{1}{\rho} \frac{W_t}{P_t C_t}, \tag{9.116}$$

$$h^*_t(z) = \frac{1}{\rho} \frac{W^*_t}{P^*_t C^*_t}. \tag{9.117}$$

The domestic household demand for domestic z-goods and that for foreign z^*-goods are

$$c_t(z) = \left[\frac{p_t(z)}{P_t} \right]^{-\theta} C_t, \tag{9.118}$$

$$c_t(z^*) = \left[\frac{q_t(z^*)}{P_t} \right]^{-\theta} C_t. \tag{9.119}$$

The foreign household demand for domestic z-goods and that for foreign z^*-goods are

$$c^*_t(z) = \left[\frac{q^*_t(z)}{P^*_t} \right]^{-\theta} C^*_t, \tag{9.120}$$

$$c^*_t(z^*) = \left[\frac{p^*_t(z^*)}{P^*_t} \right]^{-\theta} C^*_t. \tag{9.121}$$

---

[9]   Differentiating the utility function with respect to B_t gives

$$\frac{\partial U_t}{\partial B_t} = \frac{-\delta_t}{P_t C_t} + \frac{\beta}{P_{t+1} C_{t+1}} = 0,$$

which is rearranged as (9.112). Differentiating the utility function with respect to M_t gives

$$\frac{\partial U_t}{\partial M_t} = \frac{-1}{P_t C_t} + \frac{\beta}{P_{t+1} C_{t+1}} + \frac{\gamma}{P_t} \left(\frac{M_t}{P_t} \right)^{-\epsilon} = 0.$$

Rearranging this equation and using (9.112) to substitute out $P_{t+1} C_{t+1} = \beta P_t C_t / \delta_t$ results in (9.114). The first-order condition for hours is

$$\frac{\partial U_t}{\partial h_t} = \frac{W_t}{P_t C_t} - \rho h_t = 0,$$

from which (9.117) follows directly. Derivations of the Euler equations for the foreign country follow analogously.

Firms.   Firms only employ labor. There is no capital in the model. The domestic and foreign production technologies are identical and are linear in hours of work:

$$y_t(z) = h_t(z),$$

$$y_t^*(z) = h_t^*(z).$$

Domestic- and foreign-firm profits are

$$\pi_t(z) = p_t(z)x_t(z) + S_t q_t^*(z)v_t(z) - W_t h_t(z), \tag{9.122}$$

$$\pi_t^*(z^*) = p_t^*(z^*)x_t^*(z^*) + \frac{q_t(z^*)}{S_t}v_t^*(z^*) - W_t^* h_t^*(z^*). \tag{9.123}$$

The domestic z-firm sets prices at the beginning of the period before period-t shocks are revealed. The monopolistically competitive firm maximizes profits by choosing output to set marginal revenue equal to marginal cost. Given the demand functions (9.118)–(9.121), the rule for setting the price of home sales is the constant markup of price over costs,[10] $p_t(z) = [\theta/(\theta - 1)]W_t$. The z-firm also sets the *euro* price of its exports, $q_t^*(z)$. Before period-t monetary or fiscal shocks are revealed, the firm observes the exchange rate S_t, and sets the euro price according to the "law of one price," $S_t q_t^*(z) = p_t(z)$. This is optimal, conditional on the information available at the time prices are set, because home and foreign market elasticity of demand are identical. Although the firm has the power to set different prices for the foreign and home markets, it chooses not to do so. Once $p_t(z)$ and $q_t^*(z)$ are set, they are fixed for the remainder of the period. The foreign firm sets price according to a similar technology.

Since the elasticity of demand for all goods markets is identical and all firms have the identical technology, price-setting is identical among home firms and is identical among all foreign firms:

$$p_t(z) = S_t q_t^*(z) = \frac{\theta}{\theta - 1}W_t, \tag{9.124}$$

$$p_t^*(z^*) = \frac{q_t(z^*)}{S_t} = \frac{\theta}{\theta - 1}W_t^*. \tag{9.125}$$

Using (9.124) and (9.125), the formulae for the price indices (9.108) and (9.109) can be simplified to

$$P_t = \left[n p_t(z)^{(1-\theta)} + (1-n)q_t(z^*)^{(1-\theta)} \right]^{1/(1-\theta)}, \tag{9.126}$$

$$P_t^* = \left[n q_t^*(z)^{(1-\theta)} + (1-n)p_t^*(z^*)^{(1-\theta)} \right]^{1/(1-\theta)}. \tag{9.127}$$

---

[10]   The domestic demand function, $y = p^{-\theta}P^{\theta}C$, can be rewritten as $p = PC^{1/\theta}y^{-1/\theta}$. Multiply by y to get total revenue. Differentiating with respect to y yields marginal revenue, $[(\theta-1)/\theta]PC^{1/\theta}y^{-1/\theta} = [(\theta-1)/\theta]p$. Marginal cost is simply W. Equating marginal cost to marginal revenue gives the markup rule.

Output is demand determined in the short run and can either be sold to the domestic market or made available for export. The adding-up constraints on output, sales to the home market, and sales to the foreign market are

$$y_t(z) = x_t(z) + v_t(z), \tag{9.128}$$

$$x_t(z) = \left[\frac{p_t(z)}{P_t}\right]^{-\theta} nC_t, \tag{9.129}$$

$$v_t(z) = \left[\frac{p_t(z)}{S_t P_t^*}\right]^{-\theta} (1-n)C_t^*. \tag{9.130}$$

The analogous formulae for the foreign country are

$$y_t^*(z^*) = x_t^*(z^*) + v_t^*(z^*), \tag{9.131}$$

$$x_t^*(z^*) = \left[\frac{p_t^*(z^*)}{P_t^*}\right]^{-\theta} (1-n)C_t^*, \tag{9.132}$$

$$v_t^*(z^*) = \left[\frac{S_t p_t^*(z^*)}{P_t}\right]^{-\theta} (1-n)C_t. \tag{9.133}$$

Government. Government spending is financed by tax receipts and seignorage:

$$P_t G_t = P_t T_t + M_t - M_{t-1}, \tag{9.134}$$

$$P_t^* G_t^* = P_t^* T_t^* + M_t^* - M_{t-1}^*. \tag{9.135}$$

In characterizing the equilibrium, it will help to consolidate the individual's and the government's budget constraints. Substitute profits (9.122)–(9.123) and the government budget constraints (9.134)–(9.135) into the household budget constraints (9.110)–(9.111) and use the zero-net-supply constraint $B_t^* = -(n/(1-n))B_t$ from (9.137), to give

$$P_t C_t + P_t G_t + \delta_t B_t = p_t(z)x_t(z) + S_t q_t^*(z)v_t(z) + B_{t-1}, \tag{9.136}$$

$$P_t^* C_t^* + P_t^* G_t^* - \frac{n}{1-n}\frac{\delta_t B_t}{S_t} = p_t^*(z^*)x_t^*(z^*) + \frac{q_t(z^*)}{S_t}v_t^*(z^*) - \frac{n}{1-n}\frac{B_{t-1}}{S_t}. \tag{9.137}$$

The equilibrium is characterized by the Euler equations (9.112)–(9.117), the consolidated budget constraints (9.136) and (9.137) with $B_0 = G_0 = G_0^* = 0$, and the output equations (9.128)–(9.133).

From this point on, we will consider only *monetary* shocks. To simplify the algebra, set $G_t = G_t^* = 0$ for all t. We employ the same solution technique as we used in the Redux model. First, solve for the 0-steady state with zero international debt and zero government spending, and then take a log-linear approximation around that benchmark steady state.

Table 9.2 Notation for the pricing-to-market model

$p_t(z)$	The dollar price of home good z in the home country
$q_t^*(z)$	The euro price of home good z in the foreign country
$p_t^*(z^*)$	The euro price of foreign good z^* in the foreign country
$q_t(z^*)$	The dollar price of foreign good z^* in the home country
$y_t(z)$	The home goods output
$x_t(z)$	The home goods sold at home
$v_t(z)$	The home goods sold in the foreign country
$y_t^*(z^*)$	The foreign goods output
$x_t^*(z^*)$	The foreign goods sold in the foreign country
$r_t^*(z^*)$	The foreign goods sold in the home country
$\pi_t(z)$	Domestic firm profits
$\pi_t^*(z^*)$	Foreign firm profits
$h_t(z)$	Hours worked by a domestic individual
$h_t^*(z^*)$	Hours worked by a foreign individual
B_t	The dollar value of a nominal bond held by a domestic individual
B_t^*	The dollar value of a nominal bond held by a foreign individual
i_t	The nominal interest rate
δ_t	The nominal price of the nominal bond
W_t	The nominal wage in dollars
W_t^*	The nominal wage in euros
G_t	Home-government spending
G_t^*	Foreign-government spending
T_t	Home-government lump-sum tax receipts
T_t^*	Foreign-government lump-sum tax receipts
C_t	The home CES consumption index
C_t^*	The foreign CES consumption index
P_t	The home CES price index
P_t^*	The foreign CES price index
S_t	The nominal exchange rate

The 0-steady state. The 0-steady state under pricing-to-market is identical to that in the Redux model. Set $G_0 = G_0^* = B_0 = 0$. The dollar prices of z and z^* goods sold at home are identical: $p_0(z) = q_0(z^*)$. From the markup rules (9.124) and (9.125), it follows that, by the "law of one price," $p_0(z) = q_0(z^*) = S_0 q_0^*(z) = S_0 p_0^*(z^*)$. We also have

$$P_0 = S_0 P_0^*. \tag{9.138}$$

Steady state hours of work, output, and consumption are

$$h_0(z) = y_0(z) = h_0^*(z^*) = y_0^*(z^*) = C_0 = C_0^* = \left[\frac{\theta - 1}{\rho\theta}\right]^{1/2}. \tag{9.139}$$

From the money demand functions, it follows that the exchange rate is

$$S_0 = \frac{M_0}{M_0^*}. \tag{9.140}$$

Log-linearizing around the 0-steady state.

The log-expansion of (9.114) and (9.115) around 0-steady state values gives [11]

$$\hat{M}_t - \hat{P}_t = \frac{1}{\epsilon}\hat{C}_t + \frac{\beta}{\epsilon(1-\beta)}\hat{\delta}_t, \tag{9.141}$$

$$\hat{M}_t^* - \hat{P}_t^* = \frac{1}{\epsilon}\hat{C}_t^* + \frac{\beta}{\epsilon(1-\beta)}[\hat{\delta}_t + \hat{S}_{t+1} - \hat{S}_t]. \tag{9.142}$$

Log-linearizing the consolidated budget constraints (9.136) and (9.137) with $B_0 = G_0 = G_0^* = 0$ gives[12]

$$\hat{C}_t = n[\hat{p}_t(z) + \hat{x}_t(z) - \hat{P}_t] + (1-n)[\hat{q}_t^*(z) + \hat{S}_t + \hat{v}_t(z) - \hat{P}_t] - \beta\hat{b}_t, \tag{9.143}$$

$$\hat{C}_t^* = (1-n)[\hat{p}_t^*(z^*) + \hat{x}_t^*(z^*) - \hat{P}_t^*] + n[\hat{q}_t(z^*) - \hat{S}_t$$
$$+ \hat{v}_t^*(z^*) - \hat{P}_t^*] + \beta\frac{n}{1-n}\hat{b}_t. \tag{9.144}$$

Log-linearizing (9.128)–(9.133) gives

$$\hat{y}_t(z) = n\hat{x}_t(z) + (1-n)\hat{v}_t(z), \tag{9.145}$$

$$\hat{y}_t^*(z^*) = (1-n)\hat{x}_t^*(z^*) + n\hat{v}_t^*(z^*), \tag{9.146}$$

$$\hat{x}_t(z) = \theta[\hat{P}_t - \hat{p}_t(z)] + \hat{C}_t, \tag{9.147}$$

$$\hat{v}_t(z) = \theta[\hat{S}_t + \hat{P}_t^* - p_t(z)] + \hat{C}_t^*, \tag{9.148}$$

$$\hat{x}_t^*(z^*) = \theta[\hat{P}_t^* - \hat{p}_t^*(z^*)] + \hat{C}_t^*, \tag{9.149}$$

$$\hat{v}_t^*(z^*) = \theta[\hat{P}_t - \hat{S}_t - \hat{p}_t^*(z^*)] + \hat{C}_t. \tag{9.150}$$

Log-linearizing the labor supply rules (9.116) and (9.117) and using the price markup rules (9.124)–(9.125) to eliminate the wage yields

$$\hat{y}_t(z) = \hat{p}_t(z) - \hat{P}_t - \hat{C}_t, \tag{9.151}$$

$$\hat{y}_t^*(z^*) = \hat{p}_t^*(z^*) - \hat{P}_t^* - \hat{C}_t^*. \tag{9.152}$$

---

[11] Taking log-differences of the money demand function (9.114) gives $\hat{M}_t - \hat{P}_t = \frac{1}{\epsilon}[\hat{C}_t - (\ln(1-\delta_t) - \ln(1-\delta_0))]$. But

$$\Delta(\ln(1-\delta_t)) \simeq \frac{-\delta_0}{1-\delta_0}\left(\frac{\delta_t - \delta_0}{\delta_0}\right) = \frac{-\beta}{1-\beta}\hat{\delta}_t,$$

which together gives (9.141).

[12] Write (9.136) as $C_t = p_t(z)x_t(z)/P_t + S_tq_t^*(z)v_t(z)/P_t - \delta_tB_t/P_t$. It follows that $\Delta C_t = C_t - C_0 = \Delta[p_t(z)x_t(z)/P_t] + \Delta[S_tq_t^*(z)v_t(z)/P_t] - \Delta[\delta_tB_t/P_t]$. The expansion of the first term is $\Delta[p_t(z)x_t(z)/P_t] = x_0(z)[\hat{x}_t + \hat{p}_t - \hat{P}_t]$ because $P_0 = p_0(z)$. The expansion of the second term follows analogously. To expand the third term, note that $P_0 = 1$, $\delta_0 = \beta$, and $B_0 = 0$ gives $\Delta[\delta_tB_t/P_t] = \beta B_t$. After dividing through by $C_0^w = y_0(z)$, and noting that $x_0(z)/y_0(z) = n$, and $v_0(z)/y_0(z) = (1-n)$, you obtain (9.143).

Log-linearizing the intertemporal Euler equations (9.112) and (9.113) gives

$$\hat{P}_t + \hat{C}_t = \hat{\delta}_t + \hat{C}_{t+1} + \hat{P}_{t+1},$$ (9.153)

$$\hat{P}_t^* + \hat{C}_t^* = \hat{\delta}_t + \hat{C}_{t+1}^* + \hat{P}_{t+1}^* + \hat{S}_{t+1} - \hat{S}_t.$$ (9.154)

Long-Run Response

The log-linearized equations hold for arbitrary t and also hold in the new steady state. By the intertemporal optimality condition (9.112), $\delta = \beta$ in the new steady state, which implies $\hat{\delta} = 0$. Noting that the nominal exchange rate is constant in the new steady state, it follows from (9.141) and (9.142) that

$$\hat{M} - \hat{P} = \frac{1}{\epsilon}\hat{C},$$ (9.155)

$$\hat{M}^* - \hat{P}^* = \frac{1}{\epsilon}\hat{C}^*.$$ (9.156)

By the "law of one price," $\hat{p}(z) = \hat{q}^*(z) + \hat{S}$. Equations (9.143) and (9.144) become

$$\hat{C} = \hat{p}(z) + \hat{y}(z) - \hat{P} - \beta\hat{b},$$ (9.157)

$$\hat{C}^* = \hat{p}^*(z^*) + \hat{y}^*(z^*) - \hat{P}^* - \left[\frac{n\beta}{1-n}\right]\hat{b}.$$ (9.158)

Taking a weighted average of the log-linearized budget constraints (9.157) and (9.158) gives

$$\hat{C}^w = n[\hat{p}(z) - \hat{P} + \hat{y}(z)] + (1-n)[\hat{p}^*(z^*) - \hat{P}^* + \hat{y}^*(z^*)].$$ (9.159)

Recall that world demand for home goods is $y(z) = [p(z)/P]^{-\theta}C^w$ and world demand for foreign goods is $y^*(z^*) = [p^*(z^*)/P^*]^{-\theta}C^w$. The change in steady state demand is

$$\hat{y}(z) = -\theta[\hat{p}(z) - \hat{P}] + \hat{C}^w,$$ (9.160)

$$\hat{y}^*(z^*) = -\theta[\hat{p}^*(z^*) - \hat{P}^*] + \hat{C}^w.$$ (9.161)

By (9.151) and (9.152), the optimal labor supply changes by

$$\hat{y}(z) = \hat{p}(z) - \hat{P} - \hat{C},$$ (9.162)

$$\hat{y}^*(z^*) = \hat{p}^*(z^*) - \hat{P}^* - \hat{C}^*.$$ (9.163)

Equations (9.157)–(9.163) form a system of six equations in the six unknowns $(\hat{C}, \hat{C}^*, \hat{y}(z), \hat{y}^*(z^*), (\hat{p}(z) - \hat{P}), (\hat{p}^*(z^*) - \hat{P}^*)$, which can be solved to give[13]

$$\hat{C} = -\frac{\beta(1+\theta)}{2\theta}\hat{b}, \tag{9.164}$$

$$\hat{C}^* = \frac{\beta(1+\theta)}{2\theta}\left(\frac{n}{1-n}\right)\hat{b}, \tag{9.165}$$

$$\hat{y}(z) = \frac{\beta}{2}\hat{b}, \tag{9.166}$$

$$\hat{y}^*(z^*) = \frac{-\beta}{2}\left(\frac{n}{1-n}\right)\hat{b}, \tag{9.167}$$

$$\hat{p}(z) - \hat{P} = -\frac{\beta}{2\theta}\hat{b}, \tag{9.168}$$

$$\hat{p}^*(z^*) - \hat{P}^* = \frac{\beta}{2\theta}\left(\frac{n}{1-n}\right)\hat{b}. \tag{9.169}$$

By (9.164) and (9.165), average world consumption is not affected ($\hat{C}^w = 0$), but the steady state change in *relative* consumption is

$$\hat{C} - \hat{C}^* = -\frac{\beta(1+\theta)}{2\theta(1-n)}\hat{b}. \tag{9.170}$$

From the money demand functions, it follows that the steady state change in the nominal exchange rate is

$$\hat{S} = \hat{M} - \hat{M}^* - \frac{1}{\epsilon}\left[\hat{C} - \hat{C}^*\right]. \tag{9.171}$$

Adjustment to Monetary Shocks under Sticky Prices

Consider an unanticipated and permanent monetary shock at time t, where $\hat{M}_t = \hat{M}$ and $\hat{M}_t^* = \hat{M}^*$. As in Redux, the new steady state is attained at $t+1$, so that $\hat{S}_{t+1} = \hat{S}$, $\hat{P}_{t+1} = \hat{P}$, and $\hat{P}_{t+1}^* = \hat{P}^*$.

Date-t nominal goods prices are set and fixed one period in advance. By (9.10) and (9.11), it follows that the general price levels are also predetermined: $\hat{P}_t = \hat{P}_t^* = 0$. The short-run versions of (9.141) and (9.142) are

$$\hat{M} = \frac{1}{\epsilon}\hat{C}_t + \frac{\beta}{\epsilon(1-\beta)}\hat{\delta}_t, \tag{9.172}$$

$$\hat{M}^* = \frac{1}{\epsilon}\hat{C}_t^* + \frac{\beta}{\epsilon(1-\beta)}[\hat{\delta}_t + \hat{S} - \hat{S}_t]. \tag{9.173}$$

---

[13] The solution looks slightly different from the Redux solution, because the internationally tradable asset is a nominal bond, whereas in the Redux model it is a real bond.

Subtracting (9.173) from (9.172) gives

$$\hat{M}_t - \hat{M}_t^* = \frac{1}{\epsilon}(\hat{C}_t - \hat{C}_t^*) - \frac{\beta}{\epsilon(1-\beta)}(\hat{S} - \hat{S}_t). \tag{9.174}$$

From (9.153) and (9.154), you have

$$\hat{C}_t = \hat{\delta}_t + \hat{C} + \hat{P}, \tag{9.175}$$

$$\hat{C}_t^* = \hat{\delta}_t + \hat{C}^* + \hat{P}^* + \hat{S} - \hat{S}_t. \tag{9.176}$$

At $t+1$, PPP is restored: $\hat{P} = \hat{P}^* + \hat{S}$. Subtract (9.176) from (9.175), to give

$$\hat{C} - \hat{C}^* = \hat{C}_t - \hat{C}_t^* - \hat{S}_t. \tag{9.177}$$

The monetary shock generates a short-run violation of purchasing-power parity and therefore a short-run international divergence of real interest rates. The incompleteness in the international asset market results in imperfect international risk-sharing. Domestic and foreign consumption movements are therefore not perfectly correlated.

To solve for the exchange rate, take $\hat{S}$ from (9.171) and plug into (9.174), to give

$$\left[1 + \frac{\beta}{\epsilon(1-\beta)}\right]\left(\hat{M}_t - \hat{M}_t^*\right) = \frac{1}{\epsilon}\left(\hat{C}_t - \hat{C}_t^*\right)$$

$$+ \frac{\beta}{\epsilon^2(1-\beta)}\left(\hat{C} - \hat{C}^*\right) + \frac{\beta}{\epsilon(1-\beta)}\hat{S}_t.$$

Using (9.177) to eliminate $\hat{C} - \hat{C}^*$, you get

$$\hat{S}_t = \frac{\beta + \epsilon(1-\beta)}{\beta(\epsilon-1)}\left[\epsilon(\hat{M}_t - \hat{M}_t^*) - (\hat{C}_t - \hat{C}_t^*)\right]. \tag{9.178}$$

This is not the solution, because $\hat{C}_t - \hat{C}_t^*$ is endogenous. To obtain the solution, you have, from the consolidated budget constraints (9.143) and (9.144),

$$\hat{C}_t = n\hat{x}_t(z) + (1-n)[\hat{S}_t + \hat{v}_t(z)] - \beta\hat{b}_t, \tag{9.179}$$

$$\hat{C}_t^* = (1-n)\hat{x}_t^*(z^*) + n[\hat{v}_t^*(z^*) - \hat{S}_t] + \beta\frac{n}{1-n}\hat{b}_t, \tag{9.180}$$

and you have, from (9.147)–(9.150),

$$\hat{x}_t(z) = \hat{C}_t; \quad \hat{x}_t^*(z^*) = \hat{C}_t^*; \quad \hat{v}_t(z) = \hat{C}_t^*; \quad \hat{v}_t^*(z^*) = \hat{C}_t. \tag{9.181}$$

Subtract (9.180) from (9.179) and, using the relations in (9.181), you have

$$\hat{S}_t = (\hat{C}_t - \hat{C}_t^*) + \frac{\beta}{2(1-n)^2}\hat{b}_t. \tag{9.182}$$

Substitute the steady state change in relative consumption (9.170) into (9.177), to give

$$\hat{b} = -\frac{2\theta(1-n)}{\beta(1+\theta)}[\hat{C}_t - \hat{C}_t^* - \hat{S}_t], \qquad (9.183)$$

and plug (9.183) into (9.182), to give

$$\hat{C}_t - \hat{C}_t^* - \hat{S}_t = -\frac{\theta}{(1+\theta)}[\hat{C}_t - \hat{C}_t^* - \hat{S}_t].$$

It follows that $\hat{C}_t - \hat{C}_t^* - \hat{S}_t = 0$. Looking back at (9.183), it must be the case that $\hat{b} = 0$, so there are no current account effects from monetary shocks. By (9.164) and (9.165), you see that $\hat{C} = \hat{C}^* = 0$, and by (9.155) and (9.156) it follows that $\hat{P} = \hat{M}$ and $\hat{P}^* = \hat{M}^*$. Money is therefore *neutral* in the long run.

Now substitute $\hat{S}_t = \hat{C}_t - \hat{C}_t^*$ back into (9.178) to obtain the *solution* for the exchange rate:

$$\hat{S}_t = [\epsilon(1-\beta) + \beta](\hat{M}_t - \hat{M}_t^*). \qquad (9.184)$$

The exchange rate overshoots its long-run value and exhibits more volatility than the monetary fundamentals if the *consumption elasticity* of money demand $1/\epsilon < 1$.[14] Relative prices are unaffected by the change in the exchange rate: $\hat{p}_t(z) - \hat{q}_t(z^*) = 0$. A domestic monetary shock raises domestic spending, part of which is spent on foreign goods. The home currency depreciates $\hat{S}_t > 0$ as foreign firms repatriate their increased export earnings. Because goods prices are fixed, there is no expenditure-switching effect. However, the exchange rate adjustment does have an effect on relative income. The depreciation raises current-period dollar (and real) earnings of US firms and reduces current-period euro (and real) earnings of European firms. This redistribution of income causes home consumption to increase relative to foreign consumption.

Real and nominal exchange rates. The short-run change in the real exchange rate is

$$\hat{P}_t - \hat{P}_t^* - \hat{S}_t = -\hat{S}_t,$$

which is perfectly correlated with the short-run adjustment in the nominal exchange rate.

Liquidity effect. If r_t is the real interest rate at home, then $(1 + r_t) = (P_t)/(P_{t+1}\delta_t)$. Since $\hat{P}_t = 0$, it follows that $\hat{r}_t = -(\hat{P} + \hat{\delta}_t) = -(\hat{\delta}_t + \hat{M})$ and (9.175)–(9.172) can be solved, to give

$$\hat{\delta}_t = (1-\beta)(\epsilon - 1)\hat{M}, \qquad (9.185)$$

---

[14] Obstfeld and Rogoff [108] show that a sectoral version of the Redux model with tradable and nontradable goods produces many of the same predictions as the pricing-to-market model.

which is positive under the presumption that $\epsilon > 1$. It follows that

$$\hat{r}_t = [\epsilon(\beta - 1) - \beta]\hat{M} \tag{9.186}$$

is negative if $\epsilon > 0$. Now let r_t^* be the real interest rate in the foreign country. Then, $(1 + r_t^*) = (P_t^* S_t)/(P_{t+1}^* S_{t+1} \delta_t)$ and $\hat{r}_t^* = \hat{S}_t - [\hat{P}^* + \hat{S} + \hat{\delta}_t]$. But you know that $\hat{P}^* = \hat{M}^* = 0$, $\hat{S} = \hat{M}$, so $\hat{r}_t^* = \hat{r}_t + \hat{S}_t$. It follows from (9.184) and (9.186) that $\hat{r}_t^* = 0$. The expansion of the domestic money supply has no effect on the foreign real interest rate.

International transmission and co-movements. Since $\hat{\delta}_t + \hat{S} - \hat{S}_t = 0$, it follows from (9.172) that $\hat{C}_t = [\epsilon(1 - \beta) + \beta]\hat{M} > 0$ and from (9.173) that $\hat{C}_t^* = 0$. Under pricing-to-market, there is no international transmission of money shocks to consumption. Consumption exhibits a low degree of co-movement. From (9.181), output exhibits a high degree of co-movement: $\hat{y}_t = \hat{x}_t = \hat{C}_t = \hat{y}_t^* = \hat{v}_t^*$. The monetary shock raises consumption and output at home. The foreign country experiences higher output, less leisure, but no change in consumption. As a result, foreign welfare must decline. Monetary shocks are positively transmitted internationally with respect to output, but are negatively transmitted with respect to welfare. Expansionary monetary policy under pricing-to-market retains the "beggar-thy-neighbor" property of depreciation from the Mundell–Fleming model.

The terms of trade. Let P_{xt} be the home-country export price index and let P_{xt}^* be the foreign-country export price index:

$$P_{xt} = \left(\int_0^n [S_t q_t^*(z)]^{1-\theta}\, dz\right)^{1/(1-\theta)} = n^{1/(1-\theta)} S_t q_t^*,$$

$$P_{xt}^* = \left(\int_n^1 [q_t(z^*)/S_t]^{1-\theta}\, dz^*\right)^{1/(1-\theta)} = [(1-n)^{1/(1-\theta)} q_t]/S_t.$$

The home terms of trade are

$$\tau_t = \frac{P_{xt}}{S_t P_{xt}^*} = \left(\frac{n}{1-n}\right)^{1/(1-\theta)} \frac{S_t q_t^*}{q_t},$$

and in the short run are determined by changes in the nominal exchange rate, $\hat{\tau}_t = \hat{S}_t$. Since money is neutral in the long run, there are no steady state effects on τ. Recall that in the Redux model, the monetary shock caused a nominal depreciation and a deterioration of the terms of trade. Under pricing-to-market, the monetary shock results in a short-run improvement in the terms of trade.

Summary of pricing-to-market and comparison with Redux. Many of the Mundell–Fleming results are restored under pricing-to-market. Money is neutral in the long run, exchange rate overshooting is restored, real and nominal exchange rates are perfectly correlated in the short run, and – under reasonable parameter values – expansionary monetary policy is a "beggar-thy-neighbor" policy that raises domestic welfare and lowers foreign welfare.

Short-run PPP is violated, which means that real interest rates can differ across countries. Deviations from real interest parity allow imperfect correlation between home and foreign consumption. While consumption co-movements are low, output co-movements are high and that is consistent with the empirical evidence found in chapter 5. There is no exchange rate pass-through and there is no expenditure-switching effect. Exchange rate fluctuations do not affect relative prices but do affect relative income. For a given level of output, the depreciation generates a redistribution of income by raising the dollar earnings of domestic firms and reducing the "euro" earnings of foreign firms.

In the Redux model, the exchange rate response to a monetary shock is inversely related to the elasticity of demand, θ. The substitutability between domestic and foreign goods is increasing in θ. Higher values of θ require a smaller depreciation to generate an expenditure switch of a given magnitude. Substitutability is irrelevant under full pricing-to-market. Part of a monetary transfer to domestic residents is spent on foreign goods, which causes the home currency to depreciate. The depreciation raises domestic firm income, which reinforces the increased home consumption. What is relevant here is the consumption elasticity of money demand $1/\epsilon$.

In both Redux and pricing-to-market, one-period nominal rigidities are introduced as an exogenous feature of the environment. This is mathematically convenient, because the economy goes to a new steady state in just one period. The nominal rigidities can perhaps be motivated by fixed menu costs, and the analysis is relevant for reasonably small shocks. If the monetary shock is sufficiently large, however, the benefits to immediate adjustment will outweigh the menu costs that generate the stickiness.

▶ **Chapter Summary**

1. Like Mundell–Fleming models, the new international macroeconomics features nominal rigidities and demand-determined output. Unlike Mundell–Fleming, however, these are dynamic general equilibrium models with optimizing agents, where tastes and technology are clearly spelled out. These are macroeconomic models with solid microfoundations.

2. Combining market imperfections and nominal price stickiness allows the new international macroeconomics to address features of the data, such as international correlations of consumption and output, and real and nominal exchange rate dynamics, that cannot be explained by pure real business cycle models in the Arrow–Debreu framework. It makes sense to analyze the welfare effects of policy choices here, but not in real business cycle models, since all real business cycle dynamics are Pareto efficient.

3. The monopoly distortion in the new international macroeconomics means that equilibrium welfare lies below the social optimum which potentially can be eliminated by macroeconomic policy interventions.
4. Predictions regarding the international transmission of monetary shocks are sensitive to the specification of financial structure and price-setting behavior.

Problems

1. Solve for the effect on the money component of foreign welfare following a permanent home money shock in the Redux model.
    (a) Begin by showing that

    $$\Delta U_t^{*3} = -\gamma \left(\frac{M^*}{P_0^*}\right)^{1-\epsilon} \left[\hat{P}_t^* + \frac{\beta}{1-\beta}\hat{P}^*\right].$$

    (b) Next, show that $\hat{P}_t^* = -n\hat{S}_t$ and

    $$\hat{P}^* = \frac{rn(\theta^2 - 1)}{\epsilon[r(1+\theta) + 2\theta]}\hat{S}_t.$$

    (c) Finally, show that

    $$\Delta U_t^{*3} = \left[\frac{-(\theta^2 - 1)}{\epsilon[r(1+\theta) + 2\theta]} - 1\right]\left(\frac{M^*}{P_0^*}\right)^{1-\epsilon} n\gamma\hat{S}_t.$$

    This component of foreign welfare evidently declines following the permanent M_t shock. Is it reasonable to think that it will offset the increase in foreign utility from the consumption and leisure components?
2. Consider the Redux model. Fix $M_t = M_t^* = M_0$ for all t. Begin in the "0" equilibrium.
    (a) Consider a permanent increase in home-government spending, $G_t = G > G_0 = 0$, at time t. Show that the shock leads to a home depreciation of

    $$\hat{S}_t = \frac{(1+\theta)(1+r)}{r(\theta^2 - 1) + \epsilon[r(1+\theta) + 2\theta]}\hat{g},$$

and an effect on the current account of

$$\hat{b} = \frac{(1-n)[\epsilon(1-\theta)+\theta^2-1]}{\epsilon[r(1+\theta)+2\theta+r(\theta^2-1)]}\hat{g}.$$

What is the likely effect on $\hat{b}$?

(b) Consider a temporary home-government spending shock in which $G_s = G_0 = 0$ for $s \geq t+1$, and $G_t > 0$. Show that the effects on the depreciation and current account are

$$\hat{S}_t = \frac{(1+\theta)r}{\epsilon[r(1+\theta)+2\theta+r(\theta^2-1)]}\hat{g}_t,$$

$$\hat{b} = \frac{-\epsilon(1-n)2\theta(1+r)}{r\epsilon[r(1+\theta)+2\theta+r(\theta^2-1)]}\hat{g}_t.$$

3. Consider the pricing-to-market model. Show that a permanent increase in home-government spending leads to a short-run depreciation of the home currency and a balance-of-trade deficit for the home country.

10

Target-Zone Models

This chapter covers a class of exchange rate models where the central bank of a small open economy is, to varying degrees, committed to keeping the nominal exchange rate within specified limits, commonly referred to as the target zone. The target-zone framework is sometimes viewed in a different light from a regime of rigidly fixed exchange rates, in the sense that many target-zone commitments allow for a wider range of exchange rate variation around a central parity than is the case in explicit pegging arrangements. In principle, target-zone arrangements also require less frequent central bank intervention for their maintenance. Our analysis focuses on the behavior of the exchange rate while it is inside the zone.

Target-zone analysis has been used extensively to understand exchange rate behavior for European countries that participated in the Exchange Rate Mechanism of the European Monetary System during the 1980s, where fluctuation margins ranged anywhere from 2.25 percent to 15 percent about a central parity. The adoption of a common currency makes target-zone analysis less applicable for European issues. However, there remain many developing and newly industrialized countries in Latin America and Asia that occasionally fix their exchange rates to the dollar, for which the analysis is still relevant. Moreover, there may come a time when the Fed and the European Central Bank will establish an informal target zone for the dollar–euro exchange rate.

Target-zone analysis typically works with the monetary model set in a continuous-time stochastic environment. Unless noted otherwise, all variables except interest rates are in logarithms. The time derivative of a function $x(t)$ is denoted with the "dot" notation, $\dot{x}(t) = dx(t)/dt$. In order to work with these models, you need some background in stochastic calculus.

10.1 FUNDAMENTALS OF STOCHASTIC CALCULUS

Let $x(t)$ be a continuous-time deterministic process that grows at the constant rate, η, such that $dx(t) = \eta dt$. Let $G(x(t), t)$ be some possibly time-dependent continuous and differentiable function of $x(t)$. From calculus, you know that the total differential of G is

$$dG = \frac{\partial G}{\partial x} dx(t) + \frac{\partial G}{\partial t} dt. \qquad (10.1)$$

If $x(t)$ is a continuous-time stochastic process, however, the formula for the total differential (10.1) does not work and needs to be modified. In particular, we will be working with a continuous-time stochastic process $x(t)$ called a *diffusion process*, where the growth rate of $x(t)$ randomly deviates from η:

$$dx(t) = \eta dt + \sigma dz(t). \qquad (10.2)$$

ηdt is the expected change in x conditional on information available at t, $\sigma dz(t)$ is an error term, and σ is a scale factor. $z(t)$ is called a *Wiener process* or *Brownian motion* and it evolves according to

$$z(t) = u\sqrt{t}, \qquad (10.3)$$

where $u \overset{iid}{\sim} N(0,1)$. At each instant, $z(t)$ is hit by an independent draw u from the standard normal distribution. Infinitesimal changes in $z(t)$ can be thought of as

$$dz(t) = z(t+dt) - z(t) = u_{t+dt}\sqrt{t+dt} - u_t\sqrt{t} = \tilde{u}\sqrt{dt}, \qquad (10.4)$$

where $u_{t+dt}\sqrt{t+dt} \sim N(0, t+dt)$ and $u_t\sqrt{t} \sim N(0, t)$ define the new random variable $\tilde{u} \sim N(0,1)$.[1] The diffusion process is the continuous-time analog of the random walk with drift η. Sampling the diffusion $x(t)$ at discrete points in time yields

$$x(t+1) - x(t) = \int_t^{t+1} dx(s)$$

$$= \eta \int_t^{t+1} ds + \sigma \underbrace{\int_t^{t+1} dz(s)}_{z(t+1)-z(t)}$$

$$= \eta + \sigma\tilde{u}. \qquad (10.5)$$

If $x(t)$ follows the diffusion process (10.2), it turns out that the total differential of $G(x(t), t)$ is

$$dG = \frac{\partial G}{\partial x} dx(t) + \frac{\partial G}{\partial t} dt + \frac{\sigma^2}{2} \frac{\partial^2 G}{\partial x^2} dt. \qquad (10.6)$$

This result is known as *Ito's lemma*. The next section gives a nonrigorous derivation of Ito's lemma and can be skipped by uninterested readers.

---

[1] Since $E[u_{t+dt}\sqrt{t+dt} - u_t\sqrt{t}] = 0$, and $\text{Var}[u_{t+dt}\sqrt{t+dt} - u_t\sqrt{t}] = t+dt-t = dt$, $u_{t+dt}\sqrt{t+dt} - u_t\sqrt{t}$ defines a new random variable, $\tilde{u}\sqrt{dt}$, where $\tilde{u} \overset{iid}{\sim} N(0,1)$.

ITO'S LEMMA

Consider a random variable X with finite mean and variance, and a positive number $\theta > 0$. *Chebyshev's inequality* says that the probability that X deviates from its mean by more than θ is bounded by its variance divided by θ^2:

$$P\{|X - E(X)| \geq \theta\} \leq \frac{\text{Var}(X)}{\theta^2}. \tag{10.7}$$

If $z(t)$ follows the Wiener process (10.3), then $E[dz(t)] = 0$ and $\text{Var}[dz(t)^2] = E[dz(t)^2] - [Edz(t)]^2 = dt$. Apply Chebyshev's inequality to $dz(t)^2$, to give

$$P\{|[dz(t)]^2 - E[dz(t)]^2| > \theta\} \leq \frac{(dt)^2}{\theta^2}.$$

Since dt is a fraction, as $dt \to 0$, $(dt)^2$ goes to zero even faster than dt does. Thus the probability that $dz(t)^2$ deviates from its mean dt becomes negligible over infinitesimal increments of time. This suggests that you can treat the deviation of $dz(t)^2$ from its mean dt as an error term of order $O(dt^2)$.[2] Write it as

$$dz(t)^2 = dt + O(dt^2).$$

Taking a second-order Taylor expansion of $G(x(t), t)$ gives

$$\Delta G = \frac{\partial G}{\partial x} \Delta x(t) + \frac{\partial G}{\partial t} \Delta t$$
$$+ \frac{1}{2} \left[\frac{\partial^2 G}{\partial x^2} \Delta x(t)^2 + \frac{\partial^2 G}{\partial t^2} \Delta t^2 + 2 \frac{\partial^2 G}{\partial x \partial t} [\Delta x(t) \Delta t] \right] + O(\Delta t^2), \tag{10.8}$$

where $O(\Delta t^2)$ are the "higher-ordered" terms involving $(\Delta t)^k$, with $k > 2$. You can ignore those terms when you send $\Delta t \to 0$.

If $x(t)$ evolves according to the diffusion process, you know that $\Delta x(t) = \eta \Delta t + \sigma \Delta z(t)$, with $\Delta z(t) = u\sqrt{\Delta t}$, and $(\Delta x)^2 = \eta^2 (\Delta t)^2 + \sigma^2 (\Delta z)^2 + 2\eta\sigma (\Delta t)(\Delta z) = \sigma^2 \Delta t + O(\Delta t^{3/2})$. Substitute these expressions into the square-bracketed term in (10.8), to get

$$\Delta G = \frac{\partial G}{\partial x} (\Delta x(t)) + \frac{\partial G}{\partial t} (\Delta t) + \frac{\sigma^2}{2} \frac{\partial^2 G}{\partial x^2} (\Delta t) + O(\Delta t^{3/2}). \tag{10.9}$$

As $\Delta t \to 0$, (10.9) goes to (10.6), because the $O(\Delta t^{3/2})$ terms can be ignored. The result is Ito's lemma.

---

2   An $O(dt^2)$ term divided by dt^2 is constant.

10.2 THE CONTINUOUS-TIME MONETARY MODEL

A deterministic setting. To see how the monetary model works in continuous time, we will start in a deterministic setting. As in chapter 3, all variables except interest rates are in logarithms. The money market equilibrium conditions at home and abroad are

$$m(t) - p(t) = \phi y(t) - \alpha i(t), \tag{10.10}$$

$$m^*(t) - p^*(t) = \phi y^*(t) - \alpha i^*(t). \tag{10.11}$$

International asset-market equilibrium is given by uncovered interest parity:

$$i(t) - i^*(t) = \dot{s}(t). \tag{10.12}$$

The model is completed by invoking PPP:

$$s(t) + p^*(t) = p(t). \tag{10.13}$$

Combining (10.10)–(10.13), you get

$$s(t) = f(t) + \alpha \dot{s}(t), \tag{10.14}$$

where $f(t) \equiv m(t) - m^*(t) - \phi[y(t) - y^*(t)]$ are the monetary-model "fundamentals." Rewrite (10.14) as the first-order differential equation

$$\dot{s}(t) - \frac{s(t)}{\alpha} = \frac{-f(t)}{\alpha}. \tag{10.15}$$

The solution to (10.15) is[3]

$$s(t) = \frac{1}{\alpha} \int_t^\infty e^{(t-x)/\alpha} f(x)\, dx$$

$$= \frac{1}{\alpha} e^{t/\alpha} \int_t^\infty e^{-x/\alpha} f(x)\, dx. \tag{10.16}$$

---

[3] To verify that (10.16) is a solution, take its time derivative:

$$\dot{s}(t) = \frac{1}{\alpha} e^{t/\alpha} \left[\frac{d}{dt} \int_t^\infty e^{-x/\alpha} f(x)dx \right] + \left[\int_t^\infty e^{-x/\alpha} f(x)dx \right] \alpha^{-2} e^{t/\alpha}$$

$$= -\frac{1}{\alpha} f(t) + \frac{1}{\alpha^2} e^{t/\alpha} \int_t^\infty e^{-x/\alpha} f(x)dx$$

$$= -\frac{1}{\alpha} f(t) + \frac{1}{\alpha} s(t).$$

Therefore, (10.16) solves (10.15).

A stochastic setting. The stochastic continuous-time monetary model is

$$m(t) - p(t) = \phi y(t) - \alpha i(t), \tag{10.17}$$

$$m^*(t) - p^*(t) = \phi y^*(t) - \alpha i^*(t), \tag{10.18}$$

$$i(t) - i^*(t) = E_t[\dot{s}(t)], \tag{10.19}$$

$$s(t) + p^*(t) = p(t). \tag{10.20}$$

Combine (10.17)–(10.20), to give

$$E_t[\dot{s}(t)] - \frac{s(t)}{\alpha} = \frac{-f(t)}{\alpha}, \tag{10.21}$$

which is a first-order stochastic differential equation. To solve (10.21), mimic the steps used to solve the deterministic model to get the continuous-time version of the present-value formula:

$$s(t) = \frac{1}{\alpha} \int_t^\infty e^{(t-x)/\alpha} E_t[f(x)] \, dx. \tag{10.22}$$

To evaluate the expectations in (10.22) you must specify the stochastic process governing the fundamentals. For this purpose, we assume that the fundamentals process follows the diffusion process

$$df(t) = \eta dt + \sigma dz(t), \tag{10.23}$$

where η and σ are constants, and $dz(t) = u\sqrt{dt}$ is the standard Wiener process. It follows that

$$
\begin{aligned}
f(x) - f(t) &= \int_t^x df(r) \, dr \\
&= \int_t^x \eta \, dr + \int_t^x \sigma \, dz(r) \\
&= \eta(x - t) + \sigma u\sqrt{(x - t)}.
\end{aligned}
\tag{10.24}
$$

Take expectations of (10.24) conditional on time-t information, to obtain the prediction rule

$$E_t[f(x)] = f(t) + \eta(x - t), \tag{10.25}$$

and substitute (10.25) into (10.22) to obtain

$$
\begin{aligned}
s(t) &= \frac{1}{\alpha} \int_t^\infty e^{(t-x)/\alpha} [f(t) + \eta(x - t)] dx \\
&= \frac{1}{\alpha} \left[\underbrace{e^{t/\alpha}(f - \eta t) \int_t^\infty e^{-x/\alpha} \, dx}_{(a)} + \underbrace{\eta e^{t/\alpha} \int_t^\infty x e^{-x/\alpha} \, dx}_{(b)} \right] \\
&= \alpha \eta + f(t),
\end{aligned}
\tag{10.26}
$$

which follows because the integral in term (a) is $\int_t^\infty e^{-x/\alpha} dx = \alpha e^{-t/\alpha}$ and the integral in term (b) is $\int_t^\infty x e^{-x/\alpha} dx = \alpha^2 e^{-t/\alpha}(t/\alpha + 1)$. Equation (10.26) is the no-bubbles solution for the exchange rate under a permanent free-float regime where the fundamentals follow the (η, σ)-diffusion process (10.23) and are expected to do so forever on. This is the continuous-time analog to the solution obtained in chapter 3, when the fundamentals followed a random walk.

10.3 INFINITESIMAL MARGINAL INTERVENTION

Now consider a small open economy whose central bank is committed to keeping the nominal exchange rate s within the target zone, $\underline{s} < s < \bar{s}$. The credibility of the fix is not in question. Krugman [87] assumes that the monetary authorities intervene whenever the exchange rate touches one of the bands in a way to prevent the exchange rate from ever moving out of the bands. In order to be effective, the authorities must engage in *unsterilized* intervention, by adjusting the fundamentals $f(t)$. As long as the exchange rate lies within the target zone, the authorities do nothing and allow the fundamentals to follow the diffusion process, $df(t) = \eta\, dt + \sigma\, dz(t)$. But at those instants when the exchange rate touches one of the bands, the authorities intervene to an extent necessary to prevent the exchange rate from moving out of the band.

During times of intervention, the fundamentals do not obey the diffusion process but are following some other process. Since the forecasting rule (10.25) was derived by assuming that the fundamentals always follow the diffusion process, it cannot be used here. To solve the model using the same technique, you need to modify the forecasting rule to account for the fact that the process governing the fundamentals *switches* from the diffusion to the alternative process during intervention periods.

Instead, we will obtain the solution by the method of undetermined coefficients. Begin by conjecturing a solution in which the exchange rate is a time-invariant function $G(\cdot)$ of the current fundamentals:

$$s(t) = G[f(t)]. \tag{10.27}$$

Now, to figure out what the function G looks like, you know, by Ito's lemma, that

$$\begin{aligned} ds(t) &= dG[f(t)] \\ &= G'[f(t)]\, df(t) + \frac{\sigma^2}{2} G''[f(t)]\, dt \\ &= G'[f(t)][\eta\, dt + \sigma\, dz(t)] + \frac{\sigma^2}{2} G''[f(t)]\, dt. \end{aligned} \tag{10.28}$$

Taking expectations conditioned on time-t information, you have $E_t[ds(t)] = G'[f(t)]\eta\, dt + (\sigma^2/2)G''[f(t)]\, dt$. Dividing this result through by dt, you get

$$E_t[\dot{s}(t)] = \eta G'[f(t)] + \frac{\sigma^2}{2}G''[f(t)]. \tag{10.29}$$

Now substitute (10.27) and (10.29) into the monetary model (10.21) and rearrange to give the second-order differential equation in G:

$$G''[f(t)] + \frac{2\eta}{\sigma^2}G'[f(t)] - \frac{2}{\alpha\sigma^2}G[f(t)] = -\frac{2}{\alpha\sigma^2}f(t). \tag{10.30}$$

A digression on second-order differential equations.   Consider the second-order differential equation

$$y'' + a_1 y' + a_2 y = bt. \tag{10.31}$$

A trial solution to the homogeneous part ($y'' + a_1 y' + a_2 y = 0$) is $y = Ae^{\lambda t}$, which implies $y' = \lambda Ae^{\lambda t}$ and $y'' = \lambda^2 Ae^{\lambda t}$, and $Ae^{\lambda t}(\lambda^2 + a_1\lambda + a_2) = 0$, for which there are obviously two solutions,

$$\lambda_1 = \frac{-a_1 + \sqrt{a_1^2 - 4a_2}}{2} \quad \text{and} \quad \lambda_2 = \frac{-a_1 - \sqrt{a_1^2 - 4a_2}}{2}.$$

If you let $y_1 = Ae^{\lambda_1 t}$ and $y_2 = Be^{\lambda_2 t}$, then clearly, $y^* = y_1 + y_2$ also is a solution, because $(y^*)'' + a_1(y^*)' + a_2(y^*) = 0$.

Next, you need to find the particular integral, y_p, which can be obtained by undetermined coefficients. Let $y_p = \beta_0 + \beta_1 t$. Then $y_p'' = 0$, $y_p' = \beta_1$, and $y_p'' + a_1 y_p' + a_2 y_p = a_1\beta_1 + a_2\beta_0 + a_2\beta_1 t = bt$. It follows that $\beta_1 = b/a_2$ and $\beta_0 = -a_1 b/a_2^2$.

Since each of these pieces are solutions to (10.31), the sum of the solutions is also a solution. Thus the general solution is

$$y(t) = Ae^{\lambda_1 t} + Be^{\lambda_2 t} - \frac{a_1 b}{a_2^2} + \frac{b}{a_2}t. \tag{10.32}$$

Solution under Krugman intervention.   To solve (10.30), replace $y(t)$ in (10.32) with $G(f)$, and set $a_1 = 2\eta/\sigma^2$, $a_2 = -2/\alpha\sigma^2$, and $b = a_2$. The result is

$$G[f(t)] = \eta\alpha + f(t) + Ae^{\lambda_1 f(t)} + Be^{\lambda_2 f(t)}, \tag{10.33}$$

where

$$\lambda_1 = \frac{-\eta}{\sigma^2} + \sqrt{\frac{\eta^2}{\sigma^4} + \frac{2}{\alpha\sigma^2}} > 0, \tag{10.34}$$

$$\lambda_2 = \frac{-\eta}{\sigma^2} - \sqrt{\frac{\eta^2}{\sigma^4} + \frac{2}{\alpha\sigma^2}} < 0. \tag{10.35}$$

To solve for the constants A and B, you need two additional pieces of information. These are provided by the intervention rules.[4] From (10.33), you can see that the function mapping $f(t)$ into $s(t)$ is one-to-one. This means that there are lower and upper bands on the fundamentals, $[\underline{f}, \bar{f}]$, that correspond to the lower and upper bands for the exchange rate $[\underline{s}, \bar{s}]$. When $s(t)$ hits the upper band $\bar{s}$, the authorities intervene to prevent $s(t)$ from moving out of the band. Only infinitesimally small interventions are required. During instants of intervention, $ds = 0$, from which it follows that

$$G'(\bar{f}) = 1 + \lambda_1 A e^{\lambda_1 \bar{f}} + \lambda_2 B e^{\lambda_2 \bar{f}} = 0. \tag{10.36}$$

Similarly, at the instant when s touches the lower band $\underline{s}$, $ds = 0$ and

$$G'(\underline{f}) = 1 + \lambda_1 A e^{\lambda_1 \underline{f}} + \lambda_2 B e^{\lambda_2 \underline{f}} = 0. \tag{10.37}$$

Equations (10.36) and (10.37) are two equations in the two unknowns A and B, which you can solve to give

$$A = \frac{e^{\lambda_2 \bar{f}} - e^{\lambda_2 \underline{f}}}{\lambda_1 [e^{(\lambda_1 \bar{f} + \lambda_2 \underline{f})} - e^{(\lambda_1 \underline{f} + \lambda_2 \bar{f})}]} < 0, \tag{10.38}$$

$$B = \frac{e^{\lambda_1 \underline{f}} - e^{\lambda_1 \bar{f}}}{\lambda_2 [e^{(\lambda_1 \bar{f} + \lambda_2 \underline{f})} - e^{(\lambda_1 \underline{f} + \lambda_2 \bar{f})}]} > 0. \tag{10.39}$$

The signs of A and B follow from noting that λ_1 is positive and λ_2 is negative, so that $e^{\lambda_1(\bar{f}-\underline{f})} > e^{\lambda_2(\bar{f}-\underline{f})}$. It follows that the square-bracketed term in the denominator is positive.

The solution becomes simpler if you make two symmetry assumptions. First, assume that there is no drift in the fundamentals $\eta = 0$. Setting the drift to zero implies that $\lambda_1 = -\lambda_2 = \lambda > 0$. Second, center the admissible region for the fundamentals around zero with $\bar{f} = -\underline{f}$ so that $B = -A > 0$. The solution becomes

$$G[f(t)] = f(t) + B[e^{-\lambda f(t)} - e^{\lambda f(t)}], \tag{10.40}$$

with

$$\lambda = \sqrt{\frac{2}{\alpha \sigma^2}},$$

$$B = \frac{e^{\lambda \bar{f}} - e^{-\lambda \bar{f}}}{\lambda [e^{2\lambda \bar{f}} - e^{-2\lambda \bar{f}}]}.$$

Figure 10.1 shows the relation between the exchange rate and the fundamentals under Krugman-style intervention. The free float solution $s(t) = f(t)$ serves as a reference point and is given by the dotted 45-degree line. First, notice that $G[f(t)]$ has the shape of an "S." The S-curve lies below the $s(t) = f(t)$ line for

---

[4] In the case of a pure float and in the absence of bubbles, you know that $A = B = 0$.

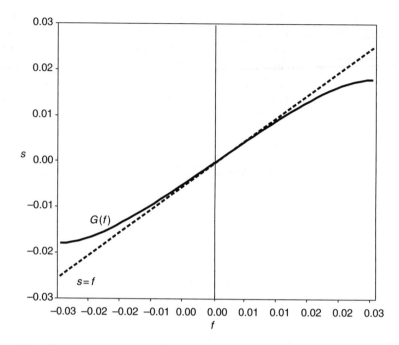

Figure 10.1   The relation between the exchange rate and the fundamentals under pure float and Krugman interventions.

positive values of $f(t)$ and vice versa for negative values of $f(t)$. This means that under the target-zone arrangement, the exchange rate varies by a smaller amount in response to a given change in $f(t)$ within $[\underline{f}, \bar{f}]$ than it would under a free float.

Second, note that by (10.21), we know that $E(\dot{s}) < 0$ when $f > 0$, and vice versa. This means that market participants expect the exchange rate to decline when it lies above its central parity, and they expect the exchange rate to rise when it lies below the central parity. The exchange rate displays *mean reversion*. This is potentially the explanation for why exchange rates are less volatile under a managed float than they are under a free float. Since market participants expect the authorities to intervene when the exchange rate heads toward the bands, the expectation of the future intervention dampens *current* exchange rate movements. This dampening result is called the *honeymoon effect*.

ESTIMATING AND TESTING THE KRUGMAN MODEL

De Jong [35] estimates the Krugman model by maximum likelihood and by the simulated method of moments (SMM), using weekly data from January 1987 to September 1990. He ends his sample in 1990, so that exchange rates affected by news or expectations about German reunification, which culminated in the European Monetary System crisis of September 1992, are not included.

We will follow De Jong's SMM estimation strategy to estimate the basic Krugman model:

$$\Delta f_t = \eta + \sigma u_t,$$

$$G_t = \alpha \eta + f_t + A e^{\lambda_1 f_t} + B e^{\lambda_2 f_t},$$

where $f = -\bar{f}$, the time unit is one day ($\Delta t = 1$), and $u_t \overset{iid}{\sim} N(0,1)$. λ_1 and λ_2 are given in (10.34)–(10.35), and A and B are given in (10.38) and (10.39). The observations are daily DM prices of the Belgian franc, French franc, and Dutch guilder from February 1, 1987 to October 31, 1990. Log exchange rates are normalized by their central parities and multiplied by 100. The parameters to be estimated are $(\eta, \alpha, \sigma, \bar{f})$. SMM is covered in section 2.3.

Denote the simulated observations with a "tilde." You need to simulate sequences of the fundamentals that are guaranteed to stay within the bands $[\underline{f}, \bar{f}]$. You can do this by letting $\hat{f}_{j+1} = \tilde{f}_j + \eta + \sigma u_j$ and setting

$$\tilde{f}_{j+1} = \begin{cases} \bar{f} & \text{if } \hat{f}_{j+1} \geq \bar{f}, \\ \hat{f}_{j+1} & \text{if } \underline{f} \leq \hat{f}_{j+1} \leq \bar{f}, \\ \underline{f} & \text{if } \hat{f}_{j+1} \leq \underline{f}, \end{cases} \tag{10.41}$$

for $j = 1, \ldots, M$. The simulated exchange rates are given by

$$\tilde{s}_j(\eta, \alpha, \sigma, \bar{f}) = \tilde{f}_j + \alpha \eta + A e^{\lambda_1 \tilde{f}_j} + B e^{\lambda_2 \tilde{f}_j}, \tag{10.42}$$

and the simulated moments by

$$H_M[\tilde{s}(\eta, \alpha, \sigma, \bar{f})] = \begin{bmatrix} \frac{1}{M} \sum_{j=3}^{M} \Delta \tilde{s}_j \\ \frac{1}{M} \sum_{j=3}^{M} \Delta \tilde{s}_j^2 \\ \frac{1}{M} \sum_{j=3}^{M} \Delta \tilde{s}_j^3 \\ \frac{1}{M} \sum_{j=3}^{M} \Delta \tilde{s}_j \Delta \tilde{s}_{j-1} \\ \frac{1}{M} \sum_{j=3}^{M} \Delta \tilde{s}_j \Delta \tilde{s}_{j-2} \end{bmatrix}.$$

The sample moments are based on the first three moments and the first two autocovariances:

$$H_t(s) = \begin{bmatrix} \frac{1}{T} \sum_{t=3}^{T} \Delta s_t \\ \frac{1}{T} \sum_{t=3}^{T} \Delta s_t^2 \\ \frac{1}{T} \sum_{t=3}^{T} \Delta s_t^3 \\ \frac{1}{T} \sum_{t=3}^{T} \Delta s_t \Delta s_{t-1} \\ \frac{1}{T} \sum_{t=3}^{T} \Delta s_t \Delta s_{t-2} \end{bmatrix},$$

with $M = 20T$, where $T = 978$.[5]

---

[5] No adjustments were made for weekends or holidays.

Table 10.1   SMM estimates of the Krugman target-zone model (units in percent) with the deutschemark as base currency

Currency	η (s.e.)	σ (s.e.)	α (s.e.)	$\bar{f}$ (s.e.)	χ_1^2 (p-value)
Belgian franc	1.493 (104.4)	2.213 (46.295)	0.987 (65.787)	2.073 (7.237)	9.584 (0.002)
French franc	−0.000 (0.114)	0.099 (1.232)	0.686 (2287)	3.558 (73.527)	12.388 (0.000)
Dutch guilder	2.972 (1.078)	2.804 (0.361)	3.007 (7.997)	5.021 (1.937)	7.811 (0.005)

The results are given in Table 10.1. As you can see, the estimates are reasonable in magnitude and have the predicted signs, but they are not very precise. The χ^2 test of the (one) overidentifying restriction is rejected at very small significance levels, which indicates that the data are inconsistent with the model.

10.4 DISCRETE INTERVENTION

Flood and Garber [54] study a target-zone model where the authorities intervene by placing the fundamentals back in the middle of the band after one of the bands is hit. If the bandwidth is $\beta = \bar{f} - \underline{f}$ and either $\bar{f}$ or $\underline{f}$ is hit, the central bank intervenes in the foreign exchange market by resetting $f = \bar{f} - \beta/2$. Because the intervention produces a discrete jump in f, the central bank loses foreign exchange reserves when $\bar{f}$ is hit and gains reserves when $\underline{f}$ is hit.

Letting $\tilde{A} \equiv Ae^{\lambda_1 \bar{f}}$ and $\tilde{B} \equiv Be^{\lambda_2 \underline{f}}$, rewrite the solution (10.33) explicitly as a function of the bands $\underline{f}$ and $\bar{f}$:

$$G(f|\bar{f},\underline{f}) = f + \alpha\eta + \tilde{A}e^{\lambda_1(f-\bar{f})} + \tilde{B}e^{\lambda_2(f-\underline{f})}. \tag{10.43}$$

Impose the symmetry conditions, $\eta = 0$ and $\underline{f} = \bar{f}$. It follows that $\lambda_1 = -\lambda_2 = \lambda = \sqrt{2/(\alpha\sigma^2)} > 0$, and $\tilde{B} = -\tilde{A} > 0$. Equation (10.43) can be written as

$$G(f|\underline{f},\bar{f}) = f + \tilde{B}\left[e^{-\lambda(f-\underline{f})} - e^{-\lambda(\bar{f}-f)}\right]. \tag{10.44}$$

Under the symmetry assumptions, you need only one extra side-condition to determine $\tilde{B}$. We get it by looking at the exchange rate at the instant t_0 at which $f(t)$ hits the upper band $\bar{f}$:

$$s(t_0) = G[\bar{f}|\underline{f},\bar{f}] = \bar{f} + \tilde{B}[e^{-\lambda\beta} - 1]. \tag{10.45}$$

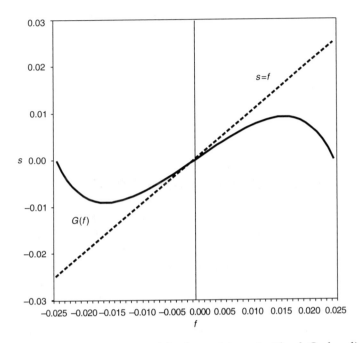

Figure 10.2   The exchange rate and fundamentals under Flood–Garber discrete interventions.

Market participants know that at the next instant the authorities will reset $f = 0$. It follows that

$$E_{t_0} s(t_0 + dt) = s(t_0 + dt) = G[0|\underline{f},\bar{f}] = 0. \tag{10.46}$$

To maintain international capital market equilibrium, uncovered interest parity must hold at t_0.[6] The expected depreciation at t_0 must be finite, which means that there can be no jumps in the time-path of the exchange rate. It follows that

$$\lim_{\Delta t \to 0} s(t_0 + \Delta t) = s(t_0),$$

which implies that $s(t_0) = s(t_0 + dt) = 0$. Adopt a normalization by setting $s(t_0) = 0$ in (10.45). It follows that

$$\tilde{B} = \frac{-\beta}{2[e^{-\lambda\beta} - 1]}.$$

But if $s(t_0 + dt) = G(0|\underline{f},\bar{f}) = 0$ and $s(t_0) = G(\bar{f}|\underline{f},\bar{f}) = 0$, then there are at least two values of f that give the same value of s, so the G-function is not one-to-one. In fact, the G-function attains its extrema before f reaches $\underline{f}$ or $\bar{f}$ and behaves like a parabola near the bands, as shown in figure 10.2.

---

[6] If it does not, there will be an unexploited and unbounded expected profit opportunity that is inconsistent with international capital market equilibrium.

As $f(t)$ approaches $\bar{f}$, it becomes increasingly likely that the central bank will reset the exchange rate to its central parity. This information is incorporated into market participants' expectations. When f is sufficiently close to $\bar{f}$, this expectational effect dominates and further movements of f toward $\bar{f}$ results in a decline in the exchange rate. For given variation in the fundamentals within $[f, \bar{f}]$, the exchange rate under Flood–Garber intervention exhibits even less volatility than it does under Krugman intervention.

10.5 EVENTUAL COLLAPSE

The target zone can be maintained indefinitely under Krugman-style interventions, because reserve loss or gain is infinitesimal. On the other hand, any fixed exchange rate regime operating under a discrete intervention rule must eventually collapse. The central bank begins the regime with a finite amount of reserves, which is eventually exhausted. This is a variant of the *gambler's ruin problem*.[7]

The problem that confronts the central bank goes like this. Suppose that the authorities begin with foreign exchange reserves of R dollars. The bank loses one dollar each time $\bar{f}$ is hit and gains one dollar each time f is hit. After the intervention, f is placed back in the middle of the $[f, \bar{f}]$ band, where it evolves according to the driftless diffusion $df(t) = \sigma dz(t)$ until another intervention is required.

Let L be the event that the central bank *eventually* runs out of reserves, let G be the event that it gains one dollar on a particular intervention, and let G^c be the event that it loses a dollar on a particular intervention.[8] In the first round, the probability that f hits $\bar{f}$ is $\frac{1}{2}$. That is, $P(G^c) = \frac{1}{2}$. By implication, $P(G) = 1 - P(G^c) = \frac{1}{2}$. It follows that, before the first round starts, the probability that reserves eventually get driven to zero is

$$\Pr(L) = \tfrac{1}{2}\Pr(L|G) + \tfrac{1}{2}\Pr(L|G^c). \qquad (10.47)$$

Equation (10.47) is true before the first round and is true for *any* round as long as the authorities still have at least one dollar in the reserves.

Let p_j be the *conditional probability* that the reserves eventually become zero, given that the current level of reserves is j dollars. For any $j \geq 1$, (10.47) can be expressed as the difference equation

$$p_j = \tfrac{1}{2}p_{j+1} + \tfrac{1}{2}p_{j-1}, \qquad (10.48)$$

---

[7] See Degroot [36].
[8] G is the event that f hits f, and G^c is the event that f hits $\bar{f}$.

with $p_0 = 1.$[9] Backward substitution gives $p_2 = 2p_1 - 1$, $p_3 = 3p_1 - 2$, $p_k = kp_1 - (k - 1), \ldots$ or, equivalently, for $k \geq 2$,

$$p_k = 1 - k(1 - p_1). \tag{10.49}$$

Since p_k is a probability, it cannot exceed 1. Upon rearrangement, you have

$$p_1 = 1 + \frac{p_k}{k} - \frac{1}{k} \to 1, \quad \text{as } k \to \infty; \tag{10.50}$$

but if $p_1 = 1$, the recursion in (10.49) says that for any $j \geq 1$, $p_j = 1$. Translation? It is a sure thing that any finite amount of reserves will eventually be exhausted.

10.6 IMPERFECT TARGET-ZONE CREDIBILITY

The discrete intervention rule is more realistic than the infinitesimal marginal intervention rule. But if the reserves run out with probability 1, there will come a time in any target-zone arrangement when it is no longer worthwhile for the authorities to continue to defend the zone. This means that the target-zone bands cannot always be completely credible. In fact, during the 12 years or so that the Exchange Rate Mechanism of the European Monetary System operated reasonably well (1979–92), there were 11 realignments of the bands. It would be strange to think that a zone would be completely credible given that there is already a history of realignments.

We now modify target-zone analysis to allow for imperfect credibility, along the lines of Bertola and Caballero [9]. Let the bands for the fundamentals be $[\underline{f}, \bar{f}]$ and let $\beta = \bar{f} - \underline{f}$ be the width of the band. If the fundamentals reach the lower band, there is a probability p that the authorities realign and a probability $1 - p$ that the authorities defend the zone.

If realignment occurs, what used to be the lower band of the old zone, $\underline{f}$, becomes the upper band of the new zone, $[\underline{f} - \beta, \underline{f}]$. The realignment is a discrete intervention that sets $f = \underline{f} - \beta/2$ at the midpoint of the new band. If a defense is mounted, the fundamentals are returned to the midpoint, $f = \underline{f} + \beta/2$. An analogous set of possibilities describes the intervention choices if the fundamentals reach the upper band. Figure 10.3 illustrates the intervention possibilities.

We begin with the symmetric exchange rate solution (10.44) with $\eta = 0$ and an initial symmetric target zone about zero, where $\underline{f} = -\bar{f}$, $\lambda_1 = -\lambda_2 = \lambda = \sqrt{2/(\alpha\sigma^2)} > 0$, and $\tilde{B} = -\tilde{A} > 0$.

---

[9] Clearly, $p_0 = 1$, since if $j = 0$, the reserves have been exhausted. If $j = 1$, there is a probability of $\frac{1}{2}$ that the reserves are exhausted on the next intervention and a probability of $\frac{1}{2}$ that the central bank gains a dollar and survives to play again, at which time there will be a probability of p_2 that the reserves will eventually be exhausted. That is, for $j = 1$, $p_1 = \frac{1}{2}p_0 + \frac{1}{2}p_2$. Continuing in this way, you obtain (10.48).

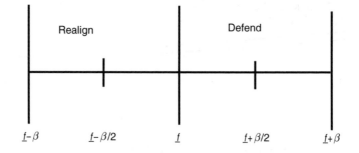

Figure 10.3   Bertola–Caballero realignment and defense possibilities.

To determine $\tilde{B}$, suppose that f hits the upper band $\bar{f}$ at time t_0. Then

$$s(t_0) = G(\bar{f}|\underline{f}, \bar{f}) = \bar{f} + \tilde{B}(e^{-\lambda\beta} - 1). \qquad (10.51)$$

At the next instant, $t_0 + dt$, the authorities either realign or defend:

$$s(t_0 + dt) = \begin{cases} G(\bar{f} + \beta/2|\bar{f}, \bar{f} + \beta) = \bar{f} + \beta/2 & \text{w.p.} \quad p \\ G(\bar{f} - \beta/2|\underline{f}, \bar{f}) = \bar{f} - \beta/2 & \text{w.p.} \quad 1 - p. \end{cases} \qquad (10.52)$$

To maintain uncovered interest parity at the point of intervention, market participants must not expect jumps in the exchange rate. It follows that $\lim_{\Delta t \to 0} E_{t_0} s(t_0 + \Delta t) = s_{t_0}$. Using (10.52) to evaluate $E_{t_0} s(t_0 + dt)$ and equating to $s(t_0)$ gives

$$p\left[\bar{f} + \frac{\beta}{2}\right] + (1 - p)\left[\bar{f} - \frac{\beta}{2}\right] = \bar{f} + \tilde{B}(e^{-\lambda\beta} - 1),$$

and solving for $\tilde{B}$ gives

$$\tilde{B} = \frac{(2p - 1)\beta/2}{(e^{-\lambda\beta} - 1)}. \qquad (10.53)$$

This solution is a striking contrast to the solution under Krugman interventions. $\tilde{B}$ is negative if the target zone lacks sufficient credibility ($p > \frac{1}{2}$). This means that the exchange rate solution is an inverted "S-curve." The exchange rate under the discrete intervention rule combined with low defense credibility is even *more* volatile than it would be under a free float.

▶ Chapter Summary

1. The theory covered in this chapter is based on the monetary model, where today's exchange rate depends in part on market participants' expectations of the future exchange rate. Under a target zone, these expectations depend on the position of the exchange rate within the zone. As the exchange rate moves farther away from the central parity, intervention that manipulates the exchange rate becomes increasingly likely and the expectation of this intervention feeds back into the current value of $s(t)$.

2. When the fundamentals follows a diffusion process for $\underline{f} < f < \bar{f}$ and the target zone is perfectly credible, the exchange rate exhibits mean reversion within the zone. The exchange rate is less responsive to a given change in the fundamentals under a target zone than under a free float. The target zone can be said to have a volatility reducing effect on the exchange rate.

3. Any target zone – and therefore any fixed exchange rate regime – operating under a discrete intervention rule will eventually break down, because the central bank will ultimately exhaust its foreign exchange reserves. But if the target zone must ultimately collapse, it cannot always be fully credible.

4. When the target zone lacks sufficient credibility, the zone itself can be a source of exchange rate volatility, in the sense that the exchange rate is even more sensitive to a given change in the fundamentals than it would be under a free float.

11

Balance-of-Payments Crises

In chapter 10, we argued that there is a presumption that any fixed exchange rate regime must eventually collapse – a presumption that the data supports. Britain and the US were forced off of the gold standard during the First World War and the Great Depression. More recent collapses have occurred in the face of crushing speculative attacks on central bank reserves. Some well-known foreign exchange crises include the breakdown of the 1946–71 IMF system of fixed but adjustable exchange rates, Mexico and Argentina during the 1970s and early 1980s, the European Monetary System in 1992, Mexico in 1994, and the Asian crisis of 1997. Evidently, no fixed exchange rate regime has ever truly been fixed.

This chapter covers models of the causes and the timing of currency crises. We begin with what Flood and Marion [55] call *first-generation* models. This class of models was developed to explain balance-of-payments crises experienced by developing countries during the 1970s and 1980s. These crises were often preceded by unsustainably large government fiscal deficits, financed by excessive domestic credit creation that eventually exhausted the central bank's foreign exchange reserves. Consequently, first-generation models emphasize macroeconomic mismanagement as the primary cause of the crisis. They suggest that the size of a country's financial liabilities (the government's fiscal deficit, short-term debt, and the current account deficit) relative to its short-run ability to pay (foreign exchange reserves) and/or a sustained real appreciation from domestic price-level inflation should signal an increasing likelihood of a crisis.

In more recent experience, such as the European Monetary System crisis of 1992 or the Asian crisis of 1997, few of the affected countries appeared to be victims of macroeconomic mismanagement. These crises seemed to occur independently of the macroeconomic fundamentals, and do not fit into the mold of the first-generation models. *Second-generation* models were developed to understand these phenomena. In these models, the government explicitly balances the costs of defending the exchange rate against the benefits of realignment. The government's decision rule gives rise to multiple equilibria, in which the costs of exchange rate defense depend on the public's expectations. A shift in the public's expectations can alter the government's cost–benefit calculation, resulting in a shift from an equilibrium with a low probability of devaluation to one with a high probability of devaluation. Because an ensuing crisis is made more likely by changing public opinion, these models are also referred to as models of self-fulfilling crises.

11.1 A FIRST-GENERATION MODEL

In first-generation models, the government exogeneously pursues fiscal and monetary policies that are inconsistent with the long-run maintenance of a fixed exchange rate. One way to motivate government behavior of this sort is to argue that the government faces short-term domestic financing constraints that it feels are more important to satisfy than long-run maintenance of external balance. While this is not a completely satisfactory way to model the actions of the authorities, it allows us to focus on the behavior of speculators and their role in generating a crisis.

Speculators observe the decline of the central bank's international reserves and time a speculative attack in which they acquire the remaining reserves in an instant. Faced with the loss of all of its foreign exchange reserves, the central bank is forced to abandon the peg and to move to a free float. The speculative attack on the central bank during the final moments of the peg is called a balance-of-payments, or a foreign exchange, crisis. The original contribution is due to Krugman [86]. We'll study the linear version of that model, developed by Flood and Garber [53].

FLOOD–GARBER DETERMINISTIC CRISES

The model is based on the deterministic, continuous-time monetary model of a small open economy of section 10.2. All variables except for the interest rate are expressed as logarithms: $m(t)$ is the domestic money supply, $p(t)$ is the price level, $i(t)$ is the nominal interest rate, $d(t)$ is domestic credit, and $r(t)$ is the home-currency value of foreign exchange reserves. From the log-linearization of the central bank's balance sheet identity, the log money supply can be decomposed as

$$m(t) = \gamma d(t) + (1 - \gamma) r(t). \tag{11.1}$$

Domestic income is assumed to be fixed. We normalize units such that $y(t) = y = 0$. The money market equilibrium condition is

$$m(t) - p(t) = -\alpha i(t). \tag{11.2}$$

The model is completed by invoking purchasing-power parity and uncovered interest parity:

$$s(t) = p(t),$$ (11.3)

$$i(t) = E_t[\dot{s}(t)] = \dot{s}(t),$$ (11.4)

where we have set the exogenous log foreign price level and the exogenous foreign interest rate both to zero: $p^* = i^* = 0$. Combine (11.2)–(11.4) to obtain the differential equation

$$m(t) - s(t) = -\alpha \dot{s}(t).$$ (11.5)

The authorities establish a fixed exchange rate regime at $t = 0$ by pegging the exchange rate at its $t = 0$ equilibrium value, $\bar{s} = m(0)$. During the time that the fix is in effect, $\dot{s}(t) = 0$. By (11.5), the authorities must maintain a fixed money supply at $m(t) = \bar{s}$ to defend the exchange rate.

Suppose that the domestic credit component grows at the rate $\dot{d}(t) = \mu$. The government may do this because it lacks an adequate tax base and money creation is the only way to pay for government spending. But keeping the money supply fixed in the face of expanding domestic credit means that reserves must decline at the rate

$$\dot{r}(t) = \frac{-\gamma}{1-\gamma}\dot{d}(t) = \frac{-\mu\gamma}{1-\gamma}.$$ (11.6)

Clearly, this policy is inconsistent with the long-run maintenance of the fixed exchange rate, since the government will eventually run out of foreign exchange reserves.

Nonattack exhaustion of reserves.   If reserves are permitted to decline at the rate in (11.6) without interruption, it is straightforward to determine the time t_N at which they will be exhausted. Reserves at any time $0 < t < t_N$ are the initial level of reserves minus reserves lost between 0 and t:

$$r(t) = r(0) + \int_0^t \dot{r}(u)\, du$$

$$= r(0) - \int_0^t (\gamma\mu/(1-\gamma))\, du$$

$$= r(0) - \gamma\mu/(1-\gamma)t.$$

Since reserves are exhausted at t_N, set $r(t_N) = 0 = r(0) - \gamma\mu/(1-\gamma)t_N$. Solving for t_N gives

$$t_N = \frac{r(0)(1-\gamma)}{\gamma\mu}.$$ (11.7)

Time of attack.   The time-path for reserves described above is not your typical balance-of-payments crises. Central banks usually do not have the luxury of watching their reserves smoothly decline to zero. Instead, fixed exchange rates usually end with a balance-of-payments crisis in which speculators mount an attack and instantaneously acquire the remaining reserves of the central bank.

Economic agents know that the exchange rate must float at t_N. They anticipate that the exchange rate will make a discrete jump at the time of abandonment. To avoid realizing losses on domestic currency assets, agents attempt to convert the soon-to-be-overvalued domestic currency into foreign currency at $t_A < t_N$. This sudden rush into long positions in the foreign currency will cause an immediate exhaustion of available reserves. Call t_A the time of attack.

To solve for t_A, let $\tilde{s}(t)$ be the shadow-value of the exchange rate. This is the hypothetical value of the exchange rate given that the central bank has run out of reserves.[1] Market participants will attack if $\bar{s} < \tilde{s}(t)$. They will not attack if $\bar{s} > \tilde{s}(t)$. But if $\bar{s} < \tilde{s}(t)$, the attack will result in a discrete jump in the exchange rate of $\tilde{s}(t) - \bar{s}$. The jump presents an opportunity to profits of unlimited size, which is a violation of uncovered interest parity. We rule out such profits in equilibrium.

Thus, the time of attack can be determined by finding $t = t_A$ such that $\tilde{s}(t_A) = \bar{s}$. First, obtain $\tilde{s}(t)$ by the method of undetermined coefficients. Since the "fundamentals" are comprised only of $m(t)$, conjecture the solution $\tilde{s}(t) = a_0 + a_1 m(t)$. Taking time-derivatives of the guess solution yields $\dot{s}(t) = a_1 \dot{m}(t) = a_1 \gamma \mu$, where the second equality follows from $\dot{m}(t) = \gamma \dot{d}(t) = \gamma \mu$. Substitute the guess solution into the basic differential equation (11.5), and equate coefficients on the constant and on $m(t)$, to give $a_0 = \alpha \gamma \mu$ and $a_1 = 1$. You now have

$$\tilde{s}(t) = \alpha \gamma \mu + m(t). \tag{11.8}$$

When the reserves are exhausted, $r(t) = 0$, and the money supply becomes

$$m(t) = \gamma d(t) = \gamma \left[d(0) + \int_0^t \dot{d}(u)\, du \right] = \gamma [d(0) + \mu t].$$

Substitute $m(t)$ into (11.8), to give

$$\tilde{s}(t) = \gamma [d(0) + \mu t] + \alpha \gamma \mu. \tag{11.9}$$

Setting $\tilde{s}(t_A) = \bar{s} = m(0) = \gamma d(0) + (1 - \gamma) r(0)$ and solving for the time of attack gives

$$t_A = \frac{(1 - \gamma) r(0)}{\gamma \mu} - \alpha = t_N - \alpha. \tag{11.10}$$

The level of the reserves at the point of attack is

$$r(t_A) = r(0) - \frac{\mu \gamma}{1 - \gamma} t_A = \frac{\mu \alpha \gamma}{1 - \gamma} > 0. \tag{11.11}$$

Figure 11.1 illustrates the time-path of money and its components when there is an attack. One of the key features of the model is that an episode of large

[1] The home currency is "overvalued" if $\bar{s} < \tilde{s}(t)$. A profitable speculative strategy would be to borrow the home currency at an interest rate $i(t)$ and use the borrowed funds to buy the foreign currency from the central bank at $\bar{s}$. After the fix collapses, sell the foreign currency at $\tilde{s}(t)$, repay the loans, and pocket a nice profit.

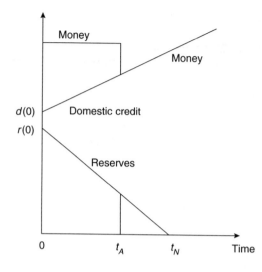

Figure 11.1 The time-path of monetary aggregates under the fix and its collapse.

asset market volatility, namely the attack, does not coincide with big news or corresponding large events. The attack comes suddenly, but is the rational response of speculators to the accumulated effects of domestic credit creation that is inconsistent with the fixed exchange rate in the long run.

One dissatisfying feature of the deterministic model is that the attack is perfectly predictable. Another feature is that there is no transfer of wealth. In actual crises, the attacks are largely unpredictable and typically result in sizable transfers of wealth from the central bank (with costs ultimately borne by taxpayers) to speculators.

A STOCHASTIC FIRST-GENERATION MODEL

Let's now extend the Flood and Garber model to a stochastic environment. We will not be able to solve for the date of attack, but we can model the conditional probability of an attack. In discrete time, let the economic environment be given by

$$m_t = \gamma d_t + (1 - \gamma) r_t, \tag{11.12}$$

$$m_t - p_t = -\alpha i_t, \tag{11.13}$$

$$p_t = s_t, \tag{11.14}$$

$$i_t = E_t(\Delta s_{t+1}). \tag{11.15}$$

Let domestic credit be governed by the random walk

$$d_t = \left(\mu - \frac{1}{\lambda}\right) + d_{t-1} + v_t, \tag{11.16}$$

where v_t is drawn from the *exponential* distribution.[2] Also, assume that the domestic credit process has an upward drift, $\mu > 1/\lambda$. At time t, agents attack the central bank if $\tilde{s}_t \geq \bar{s}$, where $\tilde{s}$ is the shadow exchange rate.

Let the publicly available information set be I_t and let p_t be the probability of an attack at $t+1$ conditional on I_t. Then,

$$p_t = \Pr[\tilde{s}_{t+1} > \bar{s}|I_t]$$
$$= \Pr[\alpha\gamma\mu + m_{t+1} - \bar{s} > 0|I_t]$$
$$= \Pr[\alpha\gamma\mu + \gamma d_{t+1} - \bar{s} > 0|I_t]$$
$$= \Pr\left[\alpha\gamma\mu + \gamma\left(d_t + \left[\mu - \frac{1}{\lambda}\right] + v_{t+1}\right) - \bar{s} > 0|I_t\right]$$
$$= \Pr\left[v_{t+1} > \frac{1}{\gamma}\bar{s} - (1+\alpha)\mu - d_t + \frac{1}{\lambda}|I_t\right]$$
$$= \Pr(v_{t+1} > \theta_t|I_t)$$
$$= \int_{\theta_t}^{\infty} \lambda e^{-\lambda u} du = \begin{cases} e^{-\lambda\theta_t}, & \theta_t \geq 0, \\ 1, & \theta_t < 0, \end{cases} \tag{11.17}$$

where $\theta_t \equiv (1/\gamma)\bar{s} - (1-\alpha)\mu - d_t + (1/\lambda)$. The rational exchange rate forecast error is

$$E_t s_{t+1} - \bar{s} = p_t[E_t(\tilde{s}_{t+1}) - \bar{s}], \tag{11.18}$$

and is systematic if $p_t > 0$.

Thus there will be a peso problem as long as the fix is in effect. By (11.17), we know how p_t behaves. Now let's characterize $E_t(\tilde{s}_{t+1})$ and the forecast errors. First note that

$$E_t(\tilde{s}_{t+1}) = \alpha\gamma\mu + \gamma E_t(d_{t+1})$$
$$= \alpha\gamma\mu E_t\left[\mu - \frac{1}{\lambda} + d_t + v_{t+1}\right]$$
$$= \alpha\gamma\mu + \mu - \frac{1}{\lambda} + d_t + E_t(v_{t+1}). \tag{11.19}$$

$E_t(v_{t+1})$ is computed conditional on a collapse next period, which will occur if $v_{t+1} > \theta_t$. To find the probability density function of v conditional on a collapse, normalize the density of v such that the probability that $v_{t+1} > \theta_t$ is 1 by solving

---

[2] A random variable X has the exponential distribution if for $x \geq 0$, $f(x) = \lambda e^{-\lambda x}$. The mean of the distribution is $E(X) = 1/\lambda$.

for the normalizing constant ϕ in $1 = \phi \int_{\theta_t}^{\infty} \lambda e^{-\lambda u} \, du$. This yields $\phi = e^{\lambda \theta_t}$. It follows that the probability density conditional on a collapse next period is

$$f(u|\text{collapse}) = \begin{cases} \lambda e^{\lambda(\theta_t - u)}, & u \geq \theta_t \geq 0, \\ \lambda e^{-\lambda u}, & \theta_t < 0. \end{cases}$$

and

$$E_t(v_{t+1}) = \begin{cases} \int_{\theta_t}^{\infty} u \lambda e^{\lambda(\theta_t - u)} \, du = \theta_t + 1/\lambda, & \theta_t \geq 0, \\ \int_0^{\infty} u \lambda e^{-\lambda u} \, du = 1/\lambda, & \theta_t < 0. \end{cases} \quad (11.20)$$

Now substitute (11.20) into (11.19) and simplify to obtain

$$E_t(\tilde{s}_{t+1}) = \begin{cases} \bar{s} + \gamma/\lambda, & \theta_t \geq 0, \\ (1 + \alpha)\gamma \mu + \gamma d_t, & \theta_t < 0. \end{cases} \quad (11.21)$$

Substituting (11.21) into (11.18), you obtain the systematic but rational forecast errors predicted by the model:

$$E_t(s_{t+1}) - \bar{s} = \begin{cases} p_t \gamma/\lambda, & \theta_t \geq 0, \\ (1 + \alpha)\gamma \mu + \gamma d_t - \bar{s}, & \theta_t < 0. \end{cases} \quad (11.22)$$

11.2   A SECOND-GENERATION MODEL

In first-generation models, exogenous domestic credit expansion causes international reserves to decline in order to maintain a constant money supply that is consistent with the fixed exchange rate. A key feature of second-generation models is that they explicitly account for the policy options available to the authorities. To defend the exchange rate, the government may have to borrow foreign exchange reserves, raise domestic interest rates, reduce the budget deficit, and/or impose exchange controls. Exchange rate defense is therefore costly. The government's willingness to bear these costs depends in part on the state of the economy. Whether the economy is in a good state or in a bad state in turn depends on the public's expectations. The government engages in a cost–benefit calculation to decide whether to defend the exchange rate or to realign.

We will study the canonical second-generation model due to Obstfeld [107]. In this model, the government's decision rule is nonlinear and leads to multiple (two) equilibria. One equilibrium has a low probability of devaluation whereas the other has a high probability. The costs to the authorities of maintaining the fixed exchange rate depend on the public's expectations of future policy. An exogenous event that changes the public's expectations can therefore raise the government's assessment of the cost of exchange rate maintenance, leading to a switch from the low probability of devaluation equilibrium to the high probability of devaluation equilibrium.

What sorts of market sentiment shifting events are we talking about? Obstfeld offers several examples that may have altered public expectations prior to the 1992 EMS crisis: the rejection by the Danish public of the Maastricht Treaty in June 1992, a sharp rise in Swedish unemployment, and various public announcements by authorities that suggested a weakening resolve to defend the exchange rate. In regard to the Asian crisis, expectations may have shifted as information about over-expansion in Thai real-estate investment and poor investment allocation of Korean Chaebol came to light.

● OBSTFELD'S MULTIPLE DEVALUATION THRESHOLD MODEL

All variables are in logarithms. Let p_t be the domestic price level and let s_t be the nominal exchange rate. Set the (log of the) exogenous foreign price level to zero and assume PPP: $p_t = s_t$. Output is given by a quasi-labor demand schedule which varies inversely with the real wage $w_t - s_t$, and with a shock $u_t \overset{iid}{\sim} (0, \sigma_u^2)$:

$$y_t = -\alpha(w_t - s_t) - u_t. \tag{11.23}$$

Firms and workers agree to a rule whereby today's wage was negotiated and set one period in advance, so as to keep the *ex ante* real wage constant:

$$w_t = E_{t-1}(s_t). \tag{11.24}$$

Optimal Exchange Rate Management

We first study the model where the government actively manages, but does not actually fix, the exchange rate. The authorities are assumed to have direct control over the current-period exchange rate.

The policy-maker seeks to minimize costs that arise from two sources. The first cost is incurred when an output target is missed. Notice that (11.23) says that the *natural output level* is $E_{t-1}(y_t) = 0$. We assume that there exists an entrenched but unspecified labor market distortion that prevents the natural level of output from reaching the *socially efficient* level. These distortions create an incentive for the government to try to raise output toward the efficient level. The government sets a target level of output, $\bar{y} > 0$. When it misses the output target, it bears a cost of $(\bar{y} - y_t)^2/2 > 0$.

The second cost is incurred when there is inflation. Under PPP with the foreign price level fixed, the domestic inflation rate is the depreciation rate of the home currency, $\delta_t \equiv s_t - s_{t-1}$. Together, policy errors generate current costs, ℓ_t, for the policy-maker, according to the quadratic loss function

$$\ell_t = \frac{\theta}{2}(\delta_t)^2 + \frac{1}{2}[\bar{y} - y_t]^2. \tag{11.25}$$

Presumably, it is the public's desire to minimize (11.25), which it achieves by electing officials to fulfill its wishes.

The static problem is the only feasible problem. In an ideal world, the government would like to choose current and future values of the exchange rate to minimize the expected present value of future costs:

$$E_t \sum_{j=0}^{\infty} \beta^j \ell_{t+j},$$

where $\beta < 1$ is a discount factor. The problem is that this opportunity is not available to the government, because there is no way that the authorities can credibly commit themselves to pre-announced future actions. Future values of s_t are therefore not part of the government's current choice set. The problem that *is* within the government's ability to solve is to choose s_t each period to minimize (11.25), subject to (11.24) and (11.23). This boils down to a sequence of static problems, so we omit the time subscript from this point on.

Let s_0 be yesterday's exchange rate and let $E_0(s)$ be the public's expectation of today's exchange rate, formed yesterday. The government first observes today's wage $w = E_0(s)$, and today's shock u, and then chooses today's exchange rate s to minimize ℓ in (11.25). The optimal exchange rate management rule is obtained by substituting y from (11.23) into (11.25), differentiating with respect to s, and setting the result to zero. Upon rearrangement, you obtain the government's *reaction function*:

$$s = s_0 + \frac{\alpha}{\theta} \left[\alpha(w - s) + \bar{y} + u \right]. \tag{11.26}$$

Notice that the government's choice of s depends on yesterday's prediction of s by the public, since $w = E_0(s)$. Since the public knows that the government follows (11.26), it also knows that their own forecasts of the future exchange rate partly determine the future exchange rate. To solve for the equilibrium wage rate, $w = E_0(s)$, take expectations of (11.26), to give

$$w = s_0 + \frac{\alpha \bar{y}}{\theta}. \tag{11.27}$$

To cut down on the notation, let

$$\lambda = \frac{\alpha^2}{\theta + \alpha^2}.$$

Now, you can obtain the rational expectations equilibrium depreciation rate by substituting (11.27) into (11.26):

$$\delta = \frac{\alpha \bar{y}}{\theta} + \frac{\lambda u}{\alpha}. \tag{11.28}$$

The equilibrium depreciation rate exhibits a systematic bias as a result of the output distortion.[3] The government has an incentive to set $y = \bar{y}$. Seeing that

---

[3] This is the inflationary bias that arises in Barro and Gordon's [7] model of monetary policy.

today's nominal wage is predetermined, it attempts to exploit this temporary rigidity to move output closer to its target value. The problem is that the public knows that the government will do this, and it takes this behavior into account in setting the wage. The result is that the government's behavior causes the public to set a wage that is higher than it would set otherwise.

Fixed Exchange Rates

The foregoing is an analysis of a managed float. Now, we introduce a reason for the government to fix the exchange rate. Assume that in addition to the costs associated with policy errors given in (11.25), the government pays a penalty for adjusting the exchange rate. Where does this cost come from? Perhaps there are distributional effects associated with exchange rate changes, where the losers seek retribution on the policy-maker. The groups harmed in a revaluation may differ from those harmed in a devaluation, so we want to allow for differential costs associated with devaluation and revaluation.[4] So let c_d be the cost associated with a devaluation and let c_r be the cost associated with a revaluation. The modified current-period loss function is

$$\ell = \tfrac{\theta}{2}(\delta)^2 + \tfrac{1}{2}(\bar{y} - y)^2 + c_d z_d + c_r z_r, \tag{11.29}$$

where $z_d = 1$ if $\delta > 0$ and is zero otherwise, and $z_r = 1$ if $\delta < 0$ and is zero otherwise. We also assume that the central bank either has sufficient reserves to mount a successful defense or has access to sufficient lines of credit for that purpose.

The government now faces a binary choice problem. After observing the output shock u and the wage w, it can either maintain the fix or realign. To decide the appropriate course of action, compute the costs associated with each choice and take the low-cost route.

Maintenance costs. Suppose that the exchange rate is fixed at s_0. The expected rate of depreciation is $\delta^e = E_0(s) - s_0$. If the government maintains the fix, adjustment costs are $c_d = c_r = 0$, and the depreciation rate is $\delta = 0$. Substituting the real wage $w - s_0 = \delta^e$ and output $y = -\alpha \delta^e - u$ into (11.29) gives the cost to the policy-maker of maintaining the fix:

$$\ell^M = \tfrac{1}{2}\left[\alpha \delta^e + \bar{y} + u\right]^2. \tag{11.30}$$

Realignment costs. If the government realigns, it does so according to the optimal realignment rule (11.26), with a devaluation given by

$$\delta = \frac{\alpha}{\theta}[\alpha(w - s) + \bar{y} + u]. \tag{11.31}$$

---

[4] Devaluation is an increase in s, which results in a lower foreign exchange value of the domestic currency. Revaluation is a decrease in s, which raises the foreign exchange value of the domestic currency.

Add and subtract $(\alpha^2/\theta)s_0$ from the right-hand side of (11.31). Noting that $\delta^e = w - s_0$ and collecting terms gives

$$\delta = \frac{\lambda}{\alpha}\left[\alpha\delta^e + \bar{y} + u\right]. \tag{11.32}$$

Equating (11.31) and (11.32), you have the real wage:

$$w - s = \frac{\theta\delta^e - \alpha(\bar{y} + u)}{\alpha^2 + \theta}. \tag{11.33}$$

Substitute (11.33) into (11.23), to obtain the deviation of output from the target:

$$\bar{y} - y = \frac{\theta}{\theta + \alpha^2}\left[\alpha\delta^e + \bar{y} + u\right]. \tag{11.34}$$

Substitute (11.32) and (11.34) into (11.29), to get the cost of realignment:

$$\ell^R = \begin{cases} \dfrac{\theta}{2(\theta + \alpha^2)}\left[\alpha\delta^e + \bar{y} + u\right]^2 + c_d, & \text{if devalue} \\[4mm] \dfrac{\theta}{2(\theta + \alpha^2)}\left[\alpha\delta^e + \bar{y} + u\right]^2 + c_r, & \text{if revalue.} \end{cases} \tag{11.35}$$

Realignment rule. A realignment will be triggered if $\ell^R < \ell^M$. The central bank *devalues* if $u > 0$ and $2c_d < \lambda[\alpha\delta^e + \bar{y} + u]^2$. It will *revalue* if $u < 0$ and $2c_r < \lambda[\alpha\delta^e + \bar{y} + u]^2$. The rule can be written more compactly as

$$\lambda[\alpha\delta^e + \bar{y} + u]^2 > 2c_k, \tag{11.36}$$

where $k = d$ if devalue and $k = r$ if revalue. The realignment rule is sometimes called an *escape-clause* arrangement. There are certain extreme conditions under which everyone agrees that the authorities should escape the fixed exchange rate arrangement. The realignment costs c_d, c_r are imposed to ensure that during normal times the authorities have the proper incentive to maintain the exchange rate and therefore price stability.

Central bank decision-making given δ^e. Let's characterize the realignment rule for a given value of the public's devaluation expectations δ^e. By (11.36), large positive realizations of u are big negative hits to output and trigger a devaluation. Large negative values of u are big positive output shocks and trigger a revaluation.

Equation (11.36) is a piece-wise quadratic equation. For positive realizations of u, you want to find the critical value $\bar{u}$ such that $u > \bar{u}$ triggers a devaluation. Write (11.36) as an equality, set $c_k = c_d$, and solve for the roots of the equation. You are looking for the positive devaluation trigger point, so ignore the negative root because it is irrelevant. The positive root is

$$\bar{u} = -\alpha\delta^e - \bar{y} + \sqrt{\frac{2c_d}{\lambda}}. \tag{11.37}$$

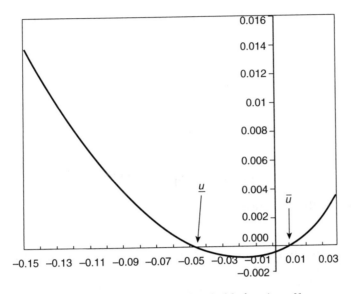

Figure 11.2 Realignment thresholds for given δ^e.

Now do the same for negative realizations of u, and throw away the positive root. The lower trigger point is

$$\underline{u} = -\alpha\delta^e - \bar{y} - \sqrt{\frac{2c_d}{\lambda}}. \tag{11.38}$$

The points $[\underline{u}, \bar{u}]$ are those that trigger the escape option. Realizations of u in the band $[\underline{u}, \bar{u}]$ result in maintenance of the fixed exchange rate. Figure 11.2 shows the attack points for $\delta^e = 0.03$, with $\bar{y} = 0.01$, $\alpha = 1$, $\theta = 0.15$, and $c_r = c_d = 0.0004$.

Multiple Trigger Points for Devaluation

$\underline{u}$ and $\bar{u}$ depend on δ^e. But the public also forms its expectations conditional on the devaluation trigger points. This means that $\underline{u}$, $\bar{u}$, and δ^e must be solved simultaneously.

To simplify matters, we restrict attention to the case where the government may either *defend* the fix or *devalue* the currency. Revaluation is not an option. We therefore focus on the devaluation threshold $\bar{u}$. We will set c_r to be a very large number, to rule out the possibility of a revaluation. The central bank's devaluation rule is

$$\delta = \begin{cases} \delta_0 = 0, & \text{if } u < \bar{u}, \\ \delta_1 = (\lambda/\alpha)\left[\alpha\delta^e + \bar{y} + u\right], & \text{if } u > \bar{u}. \end{cases} \tag{11.39}$$

Let $\Pr[X = x]$ be the probability of the event $X = x$. The expected depreciation is

$$\delta^e = E_0(\delta)$$
$$= \Pr[\delta = \delta_0]\delta_0 + \Pr[\delta = \delta_1]E[(\lambda/\alpha)(\alpha\delta^e + \bar{y} + E(u|u > \bar{u}))]$$
$$= \Pr[u > \bar{u}](\lambda/\alpha)[\alpha\delta^e + \bar{y} + E(u|u > \bar{u})].$$

Solving for δ^e as a function of $\bar{u}$ yields

$$\delta^e = \frac{\lambda\Pr(u > \bar{u})}{1 - \lambda\Pr(u > \bar{u})}\frac{1}{\alpha}\left[\bar{y} + E(u|u > \bar{u})\right]. \tag{11.40}$$

To proceed further, you need to assume a probability law governing the output shocks, u.

Uniformly distributed output shocks.   Let u be uniformly distributed on the interval $[-a, a]$. The probability density function of u is $f(u) = 1/(2a)$ for $-a < u < a$, and the conditional density given $u > \bar{u}$ is $g(u|u > \bar{u}) = 1/(a - \bar{u})$. It follows that

$$\Pr(u > \bar{u}) = \int_{\bar{u}}^{a} (1/(2a))\,dx = \frac{(a - \bar{u})}{2a}, \tag{11.41}$$

$$E(u|u > \bar{u}) = \int_{\bar{u}}^{a} x/(a - \bar{u})\,dx = \frac{(a + \bar{u})}{2}. \tag{11.42}$$

Substituting (11.41) and (11.42) into (11.40) gives

$$\delta^e = f_\delta(\bar{u}) = \frac{\lambda(a - \bar{u})}{2\alpha a}\left[\left(\bar{y} + \frac{a + \bar{u}}{2}\right)\bigg/\left(1 - \frac{(\lambda a - \bar{u})}{a}\right)\right]. \tag{11.43}$$

Notice that δ^e involves the square terms $\bar{u}^2$. Quadratic equations usually have two solutions. Substituting δ^e into (11.37) gives

$$\bar{u} = -\alpha f_\delta(\bar{u}) - \bar{y} + \sqrt{\frac{2c_d}{\lambda}}, \tag{11.44}$$

where $f_\delta(\bar{u})$ is defined in (11.43). Equation (11.44) has two solutions for $\bar{u}$, each of which trigger a devaluation. For parameter values $a = 0.03, \theta = 0.15, c = 0.0004, \alpha = 1$, and $\bar{y} = 0.01$, solving (11.44) yields the two solutions, $\bar{u}_1 = -0.0209$ and $\bar{u}_2 = 0.0030$. Equation (11.44) is displayed in figure 11.3 for these parameter values.

Using (11.43), the public's expected depreciation associated with $\bar{u}_1$ is 2.7 percent, whereas δ^e associated with $\bar{u}_2$ is 45 percent. The high expected inflation (high δ^e) gets set into wages and the resulting wage inflation increases the pain from unemployment and makes devaluation more likely. Devaluation is therefore more likely under the equilibrium threshold $\bar{u}_2$ than under $\bar{u}_1$. When perceptions switch the economy to $\bar{u}_2$, the authorities require a very favorable output shock in order to maintain the exchange rate.

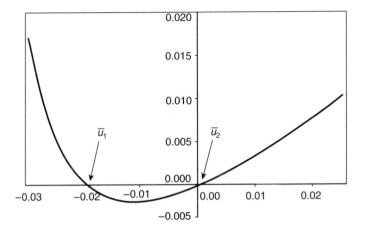

Figure 11.3   Multiple equilibria devaluation thresholds.

There is not enough information in the model for us to say which of the equilibrium thresholds the economy settles on. The model only suggests that random events can shift us from one equilibrium to another, moving from one where devaluation is viewed as unlikely to one in which it is more certain. Then, a relatively small output shock can suddenly trigger a speculative attack and subsequent devaluation.

> ▶ **Chapter Summary**
>
> 1. A fixed exchange rate regime will eventually collapse. The result is typically a balance-of-payments or currency crisis characterized by substantial financial market volatility and large losses of foreign exchange reserves by the central bank.
> 2. Prior to the 1990s, crises were seen mainly to be the result of bad macroeconomic management – policy choices that were inconsistent with the long-run maintenance of the exchange rate. First-generation models focused on predicting when a crisis might occur. These models suggest that macroeconomic fundamentals such as the budget deficit, the current account deficit, and external debt relative to the stock of international reserves should have predictive content for future crises.
> 3. Second-generation models are models of self-fulfilling crises, which endogenize government policy-making and emphasize the interaction between the authorities's decisions and the public's expectations. Sudden shifts in market sentiment can weaken the government's willingness to maintain the exchange rate, which thereby triggers a crisis.

Bibliography

[1] Hirotugu Akaike 1974. "A new look at the statistical model identification." *IEEE Transactions on Automatic Control* AC-19: pp. 716–23.

[2] Donald Andrews 1991. "Heteroskedasticity and autocorrelation consistent covariance matrix estimation." *Econometrica* 59: pp. 817–58.

[3] Kenneth J. Arrow 1964. "The role of securities in the optimal allocation of risk-bearing." *Review of Economic Studies* 31: pp. 91–6.

[4] David Backus, Alan Gregory, and Chris I. Telmer 1993. "Accounting for forward rates in markets for foreign currency." *Journal of Finance* 48: pp. 1887–908.

[5] David Backus, Patrick J. Kehoe, and Finn E. Kydland 1992. "International real business cycles." *Journal of Political Economy* 100: pp. 745–75.

[6] Bela Balassa 1964. "The purchasing power parity doctrine: a reappraisal." *Journal of Political Economy* 72: pp. 584–96.

[7] Robert J. Barro and David B. Gordon 1983. "A positive theory of monetary policy in a natural rate model." *Journal of Political Economy* 91: pp. 589–610.

[8] Geert Bekaert 1996. "The time variation of risk and return in foreign exchange markets: a general equilibrium perspective." *Review of Financial Studies* 9: pp. 427–70.

[9] Guiseppe Bertola and Ricardo J. Caballero 1992. "Target zones and realignments." *American Economic Review* 82: pp. 520–36.

[10] Caroline Betts and Michael B. Devereux 2000. "Exchange rate dynamics in a model of pricing-to-market." *Journal of International Economics* 50: pp. 215–44.

[11] Steven Beveridge and Charles R. Nelson 1981. "A new approach to decomposition of economic time series into permanent and transitory components with particular attention to measurement of the 'business cycle'." *Journal of Monetary Economics* 7: pp. 151–74.

[12] Alok Bhargava 1986. "On the theory of testing for unit roots in observed time series." *Review of Economic Studies* 53: pp. 369–84.

[13] Fisher Black 1986. "Noise." *Journal of Finance* 41: pp. 529–43.

[14] Oliver Blanchard and Danny Quah 1989. "The dynamic effects of aggregate demand and supply disturbances." *American Economic Review* 79: pp. 655–73.

[15] Stephen R. Blough 1992. "The relationship between power and level for generic unit root tests in finite samples." *Journal of Applied Econometrics* 7: pp. 295–308.

[16] David Bowman 1998. "Efficient tests for autoregressive unit roots in panel data." Unpublished manuscript. Board of Governors of the Federal Reserve System.

[17] Craig Burnside 1994. "Hansen–Jagannathan bounds as classical tests of asset-pricing models." *Journal of Business and Economic Statistics* 12: pp. 57–79.

[18] John Campbell and Pierre Perron 1991. "Pitfalls and opportunities: what macroeconomists should know about unit roots." In Olivier Jean Blanchard and Stanley Fischer, eds. *NBER Macroeconomics Annual 1991*. Cambridge and London: MIT Press, pp. 141–201.

[19] John Campbell and Robert Shiller 1987. "Cointegration and tests of present value models." *Journal of Political Economy* 95: pp. 1062–88.

[20] Matthew B. Canzoneri, Robert E. Cumby, and Behzad Diba 1999. "Relative labor productivity and the real exchange rate in the long run: evidence for a panel of OECD countries." *Journal of International Economics* 47: pp. 245–66.

[21] Gustav Cassel 1921. *The World's Monetary Problems*. London: Constable.

[22] S. Cavaglia, W. Verschoor, and C. Wolff 1994. "On the biasedness of forward foreign exchange rates: irrationality or risk premia?" *Journal of Business* 67: pp. 321–43.

[23] Stephen G. Cecchetti, Pok-sang Lam, and Nelson C. Mark 1993. "The equity premium and the risk free rate: matching the moments." *Journal of Monetary Economics* 31: pp. 21–46.

[24] Stephen G. Cecchetti, Pok-sang Lam, and Nelson C. Mark 1994. "Testing volatility restrictions on intertemporal marginal rates of substitution implied by Euler equations and asset returns." *Journal of Finance* 49: pp. 123–52.

[25] Chi-Young Choi 2000. *Panel Unit-Root Tests under the Null Hypothesis of Stationarity and Confirmatory Analysis*. Unpublished Ph.D. Dissertation. The Ohio State University.

[26] Lawrence J. Christiano and Martin Eichenbaum 1990. "Unit roots in real GNP: Do we know, and do we care?" *Carnegie–Rochester Conference Series on Public Policy* 32: pp. 7–61.

[27] Richard Clarida and Jordi Gali 1994. "Sources of real exchange-rate fluctuations: How important are nominal shocks?" *Carnegie–Rochester Conference Series on Public Policy* 41: pp. 1–56.

[28] John H. Cochrane 1988. "How big is the random walk in GNP?" *Journal of Political Economy* 96: pp. 893–920.

[29] John H. Cochrane 1991. "A critique of the application of unit root tests." *Journal of Economic Dynamics and Control* 15: pp. 275–84.

[30] Harold L. Cole and Maurice Obstfeld 1991. "Commodity trade and international risk sharing: How much do financial markets matter?" *Journal of Monetary Economics* 28: pp. 3–24.

[31] Thomas Cooley and Steve LeRoy 1985. "A theoretical macroeconometrics: a critique." *Journal of Monetary Economics* 16: pp. 283–308.

[32] Thomas F. Cooley and Edward C. Prescott 1995. "Economic growth and business cycles." In Thomas F. Cooley, ed. *Frontiers of Business Cycle Research*. Princeton: Princeton University Press, pp. 1–38.

[33] Gerard Debreu 1959. *Theory of Value*. New Haven, CT: Yale University Press.

[34] Russel Davidson and James G. MacKinnon 1993. *Estimation and Inference in Econometrics*. New York: Oxford University Press.

[35] Frank de Jong 1994. "A univariate analysis of EMS exchange rates using a target zone model." *Journal of Applied Econometrics* 9: pp. 31–45.

[36] Morris H. Degroot 1975. *Probability and Statistics*. Reading, MA: Addison-Wesley.

[37] J. Bradford De Long, Andrei Shleifer, Lawrence H. Summers, and Robert J. Waldman 1990. "Noise trader risk in financial markets." *Journal of Political Economy* 98: pp. 703–38.

[38] Rudiger Dornbusch 1976. "Expectations and exchange rate dynamics." *Journal of Political Economy* 84: pp. 1161–76.

[39] Darrell Duffie and Kenneth J. Singleton 1993. "Simulated moments estimation of Markov models of asset prices." *Econometrica* 61: pp. 929–52.

[40] Martin Eichenbaum and Charles Evans 1995. "Some empirical evidence on the effects of shocks to monetary policy on exchange rates." *Quarterly Journal of Economics* 110: pp. 975–1009.

[41] Charles Engel 1984. "Testing for the absence of expected real profits from forward market speculation." *Journal of International Economics* 17: pp. 299–308.

[42] Charles Engel 1992. "On the foreign exchange risk premium in a general equilibrium model." *Journal of International Economics* 32: pp. 305–19.

[43] Charles Engel 2000. "PPP may not hold after all." *Journal of International Economics* 51: pp. 243–73.

[44] Charles Engel and John H. Rogers 1996. "How wide is the border?" *American Economic Review* 86: pp. 1112–25.

[45] Martin D. D. Evans 1996. "Peso problems: their theoretical and empirical implications." In G.S. Maddala and C.R. Rao, eds. *Statistical Methods of Finance*, Handbook of Statistics Series, vol. 14. Amsterdam: Elsevier, North Holland, pp. 613–46.

[46] Eugene F. Fama 1984. "Spot and forward exchange rates." *Journal of Monetary Economics* 14: pp. 319–38.

[47] Eugene F. Fama 1991. "Efficient capital markets: II." *Journal of Finance* 46: pp. 1575–617.

[48] Jon Faust 1996. "Near observational equivalence and theoretical size problems with unit root tests." *Econometric Theory* 12: pp. 724–31.

[49] Federal Reserve Bank of New York 1998. "Foreign exchange and interest rate derivatives market survey turnover in the United States." Unpublished manuscript.

[50] Robert C. Feenstra, Joseph E. Gagnon, and Michael M. Knetter 1996. "Market share and exchange rate pass-through in world automobile trade." *Journal of International Economics* 40: pp. 189–207.

[51] R. A. Fisher 1932. *Statistical Methods for Research Workers*, 4th edn. Edinburgh: Oliver and Boyd.

[52] Marcus J. Fleming 1962. "Domestic financial policies under fixed and under floating exchange rates." *International Monetary Fund Staff Papers* 9: pp. 369–79.

[53] Robert P. Flood and Peter M. Garber 1984. "Collapsing exchange-rate regimes: some linear examples." *Journal of International Economics* 17: pp. 1–13.

[54] Robert P. Flood and Peter M. Garber 1991. "The linkage between speculative attack and target zone models of exchange rates." *Quarterly Journal of Economics* 106: pp. 1367–72.

[55] Robert P. Flood and Nancy Marion 1999. "Perspectives on the recent currency crisis literature." *International Journal of Finance and Economics* 4: pp. 1–26.

[56] Jeffrey A. Frankel and Menzie Chinn 1993. "Exchange rate expectations and the risk premium: tests for a cross section of 17 currencies." *Review of International Economics* 1: pp. 136–44.

[57] Jeffrey Frankel and Andrew K. Rose 1996. "A panel project on purchasing power parity: mean reversion within and between countries." *Journal of International Economics* 40: pp. 209–24.

[58] Jacob A. Frenkel 1978. "Purchasing power parity: doctrinal perspective and evidence from the 1920s." *Journal of International Economics* 8: pp. 169–91.

[59] Jacob A. Frenkel and Harry G. Johnson, eds. 1976. *The Monetary Approach to the Balance of Payments*. Toronto: University of Toronto Press.

[60] Jacob A. Frenkel and Richard M. Levich 1977. "Transaction costs and interest arbitrage: tranquil versus turbulent periods." *Journal of Political Economy* 85: pp. 1209–26.

[61] Milton Friedman 1953. "Methodology of positive economics." In *Essays in Positive Economics*. Chicago: University of Chicago Press.

[62] Kenneth Froot and Jeffrey A. Frankel 1989. "Forward discount bias: Is it an exchange risk premium?" *Quarterly Journal of Economics* 104: pp. 139–61.

[63] James D. Hamilton 1994. *Time Series Analysis*. Princeton: Princeton University Press.

[64] Alan W. Gregory and Gregor W. Smith 1991. "Calibration as testing: inference in simulated macroeconomic models." *Journal of Business and Economic Statistics* 9: pp. 297–303.

[65] Vittorio Grilli and Graciela Kaminsky 1991. "Nominal exchange rate regimes and the real exchange rate." *Journal of Monetary Economics* 27: pp. 191–212.

[66] Alastair R. Hall 1994. "Testing for a unit root in time series with pretest data-based model selection." *Journal of Business and Economic Statistics* 12: pp. 461–70.

[67] Lars P. Hansen 1982. "Large sample properties of generalized method of moment estimators." *Econometrica* 50: pp. 1029–54.

[68] Lars P. Hansen and Robert J. Hodrick 1980. "Forward rates as unbiased predictors of future spot rates." *Journal of Political Economy* 88: pp. 829–53.

[69] Lars P. Hansen and Ravi Jagannathan 1991. "Implications of security market data for models of dynamic economies." *Journal of Political Economy* 99: pp. 225–62.

[70] Lars P. Hansen and Kenneth J. Singleton 1982. "Generalized instrumental variables estimation of nonlinear rational expectations models." *Econometrica* 50: pp. 1269–86.

[71] Michio Hatanaka 1996. *Time-Series-Based Econometrics: Unit Roots and Cointegration*. New York: Oxford University Press.

[72] Lawrence E. Hinkle and Peter J. Montiel 1999. *Exchange Rate Misalignment: Concepts and Measurement for Developing Countries*. Oxford: Oxford University Press.

[73] Robert J. Hodrick 1987. *The Empirical Evidence on the Efficiency of Forward and Futures Foreign Exchange Markets*. Chur, Switzerland: Harwood Academic Publishers.

[74] Robert J. Hodrick and Edward C. Prescott 1997. "Postwar U.S. business cycles: an empirical investigation." *Journal of Money, Credit, and Banking* 29: pp. 1–16.

[75] John Huizinga 1982. "An empirical investigation of the long-run behavior of real exchange rates." *Carnegie–Rochester Conference Series on Public Policy* 27: pp. 149–214.

[76] Kyung So Im, M. Hashem Pesaran, and Yongcheol Shin 1997. "Testing for unit roots in heterogeneous panels." Unpublished manuscript. Trinity College, University of Cambridge.

[77] Peter Isard 1977. "How far can we push the 'law of one price'?" *American Economic Review* 67: pp. 942–8.

[78] Søren Johansen 1991. "Estimation and hypothesis testing of cointegration vectors in Gaussian vector autoregressive models." *Econometrica* 59: pp. 1551–80.

[79] Søren Johansen 1995. *Likelihood-Based Inference in Cointegrated Vector Autoregressive Models*. New York: Oxford University Press.

[80] Graciella Kaminsky and Rodrigo Peruga 1990. "Can a time-varying risk premium explain excess returns in the forward Market for foreign exchange?" *Journal of International Economics* 28: pp. 47–70.

[81] Robert G. King, Charles I. Plosser, and Sergio Rebelo 1988. "Production, growth and business cycles: I. The basic neoclassical model." *Journal of Monetary Economics* 21: pp. 195–232.

[82] Robert G. King and Sergio T. Rebelo 1993. "Low frequency filtering and real business cycles." *Journal of Economic Dynamics and Control* 17: pp. 207–31.

[83] M. G. Kendall 1954. "Note on bias in the estimation of autocorrelation." *Biometrika* 41: pp. 403–4.

[84] Michael M. Knetter 1993. "International comparisons of price-to-market behavior." *American Economic Review* 83: pp. 473–86.

[85] William Krasker 1980. "The 'peso problem' in testing the efficiency of forward exchange markets." *Journal of Monetary Economics* 6: pp. 269–76.

[86] Paul R. Krugman 1979. "A model of balance-of-payments crises." *Journal of Money, Credit, and Banking* 11: pp. 311–25.

[87] Paul R. Krugman 1991. "Target zones and exchange rate dynamics." *Quarterly Journal of Economics* 106: pp. 669–82.

[88] Stephen Leroy and Richard D. Porter 1981. "The present-value relation: tests based on implied variance bounds." *Econometrica* 49: pp. 555–74.

[89] Andrew Levin and Chien Fu Lin 1993. "Unit root tests in panel data: new results." University of California, San Diego, Department of Economics Working Paper, pp. 93–56.

[90] Bong Soo Lee and Beth Fisher Ingram 1991. "Simulation estimation of time-series models." *Journal of Econometrics* 47: pp. 197–205.

[91] Karen K. Lewis 1989. "Changing beliefs and systematic rational forecast errors with evidence from foreign exchange." *American Economic Review* 79: pp. 621–36.

[92] James R. Lothian and Mark P. Taylor 1996. "Real exchange rate behavior: the recent float from the perspective of the past two centuries." *Journal of Political Economy* 104: pp. 488–509.

[93] Robert E. Lucas Jr. 1982. "Interest rates and currency prices in a two-country world." *Journal of Monetary Economics* 10: pp. 335–59.

[94] Ronald MacDonald 1996. "Panel unit root tests and real exchange rates." *Economics Letters* 50: pp. 7–11.

[95] Ronald MacDonald and Jerome Stein, eds. 1999. *Equilibrium Exchange Rates.* Boston: Kluwer.

[96] Ronald MacDonald and Mark P. Taylor 1993. "The monetary approach to the exchange rate: rational expectations, long-run equilibrium, and forecasting." *International Monetary Fund Staff Papers* 40: pp. 89–107.

[97] G. S. Maddala and Shaowen Wu 1999. "A comparative study of unit root tests with panel data and a new simple test." *Oxford Bulletin of Economics and Statistics* 61: pp. 631–52.

[98] Nelson C. Mark 1985. "On time varying risk premia in the foreign exchange market: an econometric analysis." *Journal of Monetary Economics* 16: pp. 3–18.

[99] Nelson C. Mark and Donggyu Sul 2001. "Nominal exchange rates and monetary fundamentals: evidence from a small post-Bretton Woods panel." *Journal of International Economics* 53: pp. 29–52.

[100] Nelson C. Mark and Yangru Wu 1998. "Rethinking deviations from uncovered interest parity: the role of covariance risk and noise." *Economic Journal* 108: pp. 1686–706.

[101] Bennett T. McCallum 1994. "A reconsideration of the uncovered interest parity relationship." *Journal of Monetary Economics* 33: pp. 105–32.

[102] Richard Meese and Kenneth Rogoff 1983. "Empirical exchange rate models of the 1970's: Do they fit out of sample?" *Journal of International Economics* 14: pp. 3–24.

[103] Rajnish Mehra and Edward Prescott 1985. "The equity premium: a puzzle." *Journal of Monetary Economics* 15: pp. 145–62.

[104] B. Modjtahedi 1991. "Multiple maturities and time-varying risk premia in forward exchange markets." *Journal of International Economics* 30: pp. 69–86.

[105] Robert A. Mundell 1963. "Capital mobility and stabilization policy under fixed and flexible exchange rates." *Canadian Journal of Economics and Political Science* 29: pp. 475–85.

[106] Maurice Obstfeld 1985. "Floating exchange rates: experience and prospects." *Brookings Papers on Economic Activity* 2: pp. 369–450.

[107] Maurice Obstfeld 1994. "The logic of currency crises." *Cahiers Economiques et Monetaires*, Bank of France: pp. 189–213.

[108] Maurice Obstfeld and Kenneth Rogoff 1995. "Exchange rate dynamics Redux." *Journal of Political Economy* 103: pp. 624–60.

[109] Whitney Newey and Kenneth D. West 1987. "A simple, positive semi-definite heteroskedasticity and autocorrelation consistent covariance matrix." *Econometrica* 55: pp. 703–8.

[110] Whitney Newey and Kenneth D. West 1994. "Automatic lag selection in covariance matrix estimation." *Review of Economic Studies* 61: pp. 631–53.

[111] Stephen J. Nickell 1981. "Biases in dynamic models with fixed effects." *Econometrica* 49: pp. 1417–26.

[112] David Papell 1986. "Exchange rate and current account dynamics under rational expectations: an econometric analysis." *International Economic Review* 27: pp. 583–600.

[113] David Papell 1997. "Searching for stationarity: purchasing power parity under the current float." *Journal of International Economics* 43: pp. 313–32.

[114] David Papell and Hristos Theodoridis 2001. "The choice of numeraire currency in panel tests of purchasing power parity." *Journal of Money, Credit, and Banking* forthcoming.

[115] Torben Mark Pederson 1999. "Spectral analysis, business cycles, and filtering of economic time series: a survey." Unpublished manuscript. Institute of Economics, University of Copenhagen, Denmark.

[116] Peter C. B. Phillips and Pierre Perron 1988. "Testing for a unit root in time series regression." *Biometrika* 75: pp. 335–46.

[117] Paul A. Samuelson 1964. "Theoretical notes on trade problems." *Review of Economics and Statistics* 46: pp. 145–54.

[118] Gideon Schwarz 1978. "Estimating the dimension of a model." *The Annals of Statistics* 6: pp. 461–4.

[119] G. William Schwert 1989. "Tests for unit roots: a Monte Carlo investigation." *Journal of Business and Economics Statistics* 7: pp. 147–59.

[120] Robert J. Shiller 1981. "Do stock prices move too much to be justified by subsequent changes in dividends?" *American Economic Review* 71: pp. 421–35.

[121] Jeremy J. Siegel 1972. "Risk, interest rates and the forward exchange." *Quarterly Journal of Economics* 86: pp. 303–9.

[122] Christopher A. Sims 1980. "Macroeconomics and reality." *Econometrica* 48: pp. 1–48.

[123] Mark P. Taylor 1989. "Covered interest arbitrage and market turbulence." *Economic Journal* 99: pp. 376–91.

[124] Mark P. Taylor and Lucio Sarno 1998. "The behavior of real exchange rates during the post-Bretton Woods period." *Journal of International Economics* 46: pp. 281–312.

[125] Henri Theil 1966. *Applied Economic Forecasting*. Amsterdam: North Holland.

[126] John Williamson 1994. *Estimating Equilibrium Exchange Rates*. Washington, D.C.: Institute for International Economics.

[127] Yangru Wu 1996. "Are real exchange rates non-stationary? Evidence from a panel-data test." *Journal of Money, Credit, and Banking* 28: pp. 54–63.

Author Index

Subject Index

sticky-price adjustment rule
   Dornbusch model, 186
   stochastic Mundell–Fleming model, 189
sticky-price models, 179–238
stochastic calculus, 240–2
stochastic process
   continuous time, 241
   diffusion, 241
stochastic trend process, 50
stochastic-difference equation
   first-order in the monetary model, 67
   nonlinear in real business cycle model, 112
   second-order in real business cycle model, 113, 123
strict exogeneity, 25
Studentized coefficient, 34
survey expectations, 144–6
swap transactions, 3

target zone, eventual collapse, 252
technical change, deterministic, 108
technological growth
   biased, 170
   unbiased, 170
technology shock, 110
terms of trade, 217, 220, 236
tranquil peg, 6
transversality condition, 68
trend-cycle components decomposition, 108
triangular arbitrage, 2
triangular structure of exogenous shocks, 192
trigonometric relations, 54
turbulent peg, 6

uncovered interest parity, 7–9
   deviations from, 128–34
   Fama decomposition regressions, 132–3
   Hansen–Hodrick tests, 129–30
   monetary model, 67
uniform distribution from a to b, 17

unit root
   univariate test procedures, 34–9
      analyses of time series with, 31–52
      augmented Dickey–Fuller test, 35
      Bhargava framework, 34–5
      Dickey–Fuller test, 35
      testing for PPP, 171–4
   panel data, 39–49
      cross-sectional dependence, 40, 41, 45
      Im–Pesaran–Shin test, 46–7
      Maddala–Wu test for PPP, 47, 48, 176
      Levin–Lin, 40–4
      potential pitfalls, 48
      size distortion, Levin–Lin test, 43
      size distortion, tests of PPP, 177
      testing for PPP, 175

variance ratio statistic, 38
vector autoregression
   structural
      Clarida–Gali SVAR, 196–8
   unrestricted, 18–26
      asymptotic distribution of coefficient vector, 18
      Cooley–Leroy critique, 24–6
      decomposition of forecast-error variance, 22
      Eichenbaum–Evans five-variable VAR, 194–6
      impulse–response analysis, 20
      impulse–response standard errors by parametric bootstrap, 22
      orthogonalizing the innovations, 21
vector error correction model, 50–2
   monetary model, 73
vehicle currency, 2
volatility bounds, 141–3
volatility of exchange rates, stock prices, 71

welfare analysis, Redux model, 221–3
Wiener process (Brownian motion), 241
Wold vector moving-average representation, 20, 21